SEIZE THE DAY

MEDITATIONS FOR THE YEAR

by Lawson Murray

Soli Deo Gloria

To Ann,

Thank you so much for your ministry at O.C.C. Tons of blessings as you continue to seize the day.

SEIZE THE DAY - Meditations for the Year
Lawson Murray

International Standard Book Number:
1-894928-01-6

His Way Books
Canada

Printed in the United States of America

DEDICATION

Soli Deo Gloria.
To the glory of God alone.
No one else has any right to the glory
but Jesus - take it Lord.

He touches my tongue, His word to spread.
He guides my hands, His work to pursue.
He moves my feet, His way to tread.
He stirs my heart, His will to do.

ACKNOWLEDGEMENTS

Special thanks are extended to those who gave permission for their material or story to be quoted in this book. Every effort has been taken to trace original copyright holders where required but in some cases this was impossible. Any oversights will be happily corrected in future editions.

My heartfelt gratitude goes out to everyone who made the writing of this book possible:

To Karen for being a wonderfully supportive wife, friend and counsellor. Thank you for asking the tough questions against the backdrop of the things I say and do. Thank you for loving me unconditionally, for always being there as we've faced the daily trials and triumphs of the ministry.

To Christie, Matthew and Jonathan. You're a triple blessing in my life. I thank the Lord daily for your vibrant faith, obvious joy, fruitful lives, and down to earth walk with Jesus. A dad couldn't ask for more. Your encouragement as I've written this book has been very much appreciated.

To Gwen Miller for writing the foreword and to Gwen Miller and Jennifer Silvester for countless hours of proof-reading.

To Brenda Scriver for the exceptional work and "above the call of duty" effort in the typesetting and formatting of this book.

To the congregation of Orillia Community Church for your prayers, encouragement, and fellowship in Christ.

FOREWORD

At a time when publications seem so often to be directed to special groups in society (i.e. youth, seniors, women, singles, etc.) It is refreshing to find one where the emphasis (except for a few special occasions) lies simultaneously on no-one and on everyone.

While this book of meditations does have readings for the year, it differs from the usual book of devotions in a number of ways. Instead of the usual Scripture quotation at the head, there is a title as there might be a chapter heading in any other book. This title capsules the substance of the message. Some of the messages are stories, some are poems, some are memories, some are expositions, and if variety is the spice of life, this variety is truly the spice which leads to a deeper understanding of the spiritual life.

In all there is one objective - to direct the reader to a greater awareness of his/her place within the family of God - or outside that family because another unique feature of this volume is the fact that it does not assume that every reader is a believer in Jesus Christ and so it often carries a message of evangelism. The vision behind this book is very comprehensive as it leads the reader into a deeper awareness of what Christianity is all about, and most especially how growth in that life can be effected. In short, it is enlightening, it is encouraging, it is challenging, and always rewarding.

Gwenville Miller

WEEK FIFTEEN
God's plus sign for a needy world
Colouring outside the lines
The Lord's Prayer
Incomparable
Peace

WEEK SIXTEEN
Recharge your batteries
Around the dinner table
Weeping into rejoicing
Warriors or witnesses
The Second Law of Thermodynamics

WEEK SEVENTEEN
In the heat of the battle
Food for thought
Watch yourself!
Undivided attention
Accept the Son - you get it all

WEEK EIGHTEEN
Shalom
Baleka!
Voice mail
Because my mother always did it!
A heart on fire

WEEK NINETEEN
When it's stormy
In circulation
Back to ground zero
Happy are the nobodies
The cracked pot

WEEK TWENTY
Bull's-eye
The key to leadership
The strange one
Faith in prayer
On the brink of disaster

WEEK TWENTY-ONE
The empty bird cage
He's alive
For the lost
Money or your life!
Shampoo in your eyes

WEEK TWENTY-TWO
You are not alone
Discerning God's will
Hard to believe
Ouch!
Sound waves

WEEK TWENTY-THREE
Lessons from a father
Man overboard!
When trees come down
To perk you up
Worship

WEEK TWENTY-FOUR
Locusts
Example is better than precept
Taming the tongue
In a fast paced world
Thirsty for more

WEEK TWENTY-FIVE
"This is the day . . . "
How to have a quiet time
Stay close
Bless us all . . .
Vision

WEEK TWENTY-SIX
Persevering prayer
"Mistooks"
Gospel "Elvis-isms"
Who made the watermelon?
Kids in church

WEEK TWENTY-SEVEN
Together
BOND
No other gods
"When you fast . . . "
Mighty men

WEEK TWENTY-EIGHT
Making the world a better place
Bundles of prejudice
Winning the lottery can ruin your life
Grandma's cake
Assumptions

WEEK FORTY-THREE
Is your god too safe?
Wonderfully made
Is your church healthy?
We are what we eat
Give it all you've got!

WEEK FORTY-FOUR
Is something missing?
More . . .
Saved through faith
Dead or dynamic
Has your love waned?

WEEK FORTY-FIVE
Slave or free?
Persistence
A clear conscience
The power of prayer
The will of God

WEEK FORTY-SIX
Minimize your fears
AWOL
WDJD
Beware of hypothermia!
Tell them before it's too late

WEEK FORTY-SEVEN
Angels
Devote yourselves . . .
Totally Jesus
Pray for your church
With freedom and confidence

WEEK FORTY-EIGHT
Codfish and catfish
Holiness
Steps to intimacy with Christ
Hypocrisy
Cleansed by the blood

WEEK FORTY-NINE
Friendship
Demolishing walls
The mystery of Christmas
Slow down
Reach out

WEEK FIFTY
Two babes in a manger
Is there room?
Three trees
Invite Him to stay
The skeptic who believed

WEEK FIFTY-ONE
He became flesh
In the fulness of time
"Good news of great joy"
The Christmas Nail
Son shine sketches of a little town

WEEK FIFTY-TWO
Thank God for His priceless gift
Wise men still seek Him
Reflecting
Just the beginning
How to keep Christmas

DISAPPOINTMENTS ARE NOT DEAD ENDS

Perhaps you've given up. Your hopes have been crushed. You're tired of trying, weary with effort, wondering whether it's worth pressing on, feeling dejected, limping along. Maybe not on the surface, but in your heart.

There's probably a good reason too - persistent pain, gut-wrenching grief, a sense of betrayal, unrealistic expectations, money matters, the loss of a loved one, feelings of uselessness, a terminal illness, or any one of the countless setbacks we encounter in life. Whatever it is it's too much to endure. In fact it may be so bad you've even thought the unthinkable - about riding off into the sunset, writing the final chapter, calling it quits. After all, you've argued, what's the point. Nothing seems to help and no one seems to care. The bottom line is you're too tired, too sick, or too dejected to press on. In short you feel you're at the end of the road.

Life can be like that. Hard. Unyielding. A Gordian knot. But we need to be reminded that there are no hopeless situations, serious, even tough, but never hopeless. There are only people who have become hopeless about their situation. People who have stopped believing that depression can be defeated, that anxiety can be attacked, and that concerns can be conquered.

So keep trying. Be patient. Don't give up. Change your perspective. For opportunity often knocks twice. There is no insurmountable barrier until you stop trying.

Disappointments are not dead ends. There is always something around the corner. And even though you may be discouraged, remember God never gets discouraged. For man's extremity is God's opportunity. Your defeat can become God's victory. "Do you not know? Have you not heard? The Lord is the everlasting God, the Creator of the ends of the earth. He will not grow tired or weary . . . He gives strength to the weary and increases the power of the weak" Isaiah 40:28-29.

Yes, setbacks are stepping stones to success. If you're not offended by learning a lesson from an animal, you may be interested in hearing about the mule who fell into an old dry well. The efforts to rescue him were fruitless. Finally, the owner of the mule, assuming the mule was injured and dying from the fall, decided it would be more merciful to kill him. Unable to think of a better way of dispatching him he had a truckload of dirt thrown into the well. However, as the dirt was thrown in, instead of allowing himself to be buried alive, the mule quickly shook off the dirt, pressed it down with his hooves, and raised himself above his original position. This continued until the mule, as complacently as if nothing strange had happened, was finally able to step out onto firm, safe ground.

That's an excellent illustration. A reminder of how a setback can become the thing that brings you out on top. That an experience is not a failure if it prods us to keep on trying, and that the hard places of life, although painful, will later produce "a harvest of righteousness and peace for those who have been trained by it" Hebrews 12:11.

BEAUTIFUL ATTITUDES

Matthew 5:1-12 is no doubt Jesus' greatest sermon. For the Beatitudes contain the essence of Jesus' instruction, "the Compendium of Christ's Doctrine" and "the Magna Charta of the Kingdom." It reveals the kind of people we should be in our inward habits and our outward walk. And, as such, it should be pondered and practiced if we're to be effective and intelligent disciples.

It therefore seems applicable to interpret the eight macarisms with the hope that these beautiful attitudes will enable you to know genuine happiness and real blessedness in life.

THE BEAUTIFUL ATTITUDES.

■ I'm approved when I acknowledge my dependence on God and confess that I can achieve nothing by myself; for then God's sovereign rule is mine.

■ I'm approved when I have a deep inner agony for personal and corporate sin; for then I'll be comforted by the Comforter.

■ I'm approved when my instincts, impulses, passions and power are under the Spirit's control; for then I'll receive my allotted portion of all that God has promised.

■ I'm approved when I have a continual, sharp, intense and unconditional desire to be totally right with God; for then I'll be absolutely satisfied.

■ I'm approved when I have forgiveness and compassion for the needy and help lessen their suffering; for when I'm merciful, God will care for me.

■ I'm approved when I have unadulterated, single-minded and holy motives in my inner being; for then I'll continually see God for myself.

■ I'm approved when I act to resolve conflict by ministering love and reconciliation, in Christ, to those estranged from one another or from God; for then I have the dignity and honour of doing God's work.

■ I'm doubly approved when I'm willing to accept people's opposition, mocking, harassment, insults, false accusations, scorn and abuse because of my loyalty to Christ; for then God's sovereign rule is mine and I can rejoice with Jesus' guarantee of a great, joyful and eternal reward being kept for me in heaven.

ONE THING

Does life seem to be passing you by? Somehow divided - about many things but about nothing? Are you torn between competing obligations? Are you feeling scattered, confused, and lacking integration? Are your loyalties divided? Do you feel "like a wave of the sea, blown and tossed by the wind" James 1:6.

If so then one thing is needed. You need a singleness of purpose. You need a focus that brings meaning and consistency to your life. You need to pursue one thing; not anything; not something; just one thing.

So what is this one thing? What brings clarity to life? How does one achieve simplicity? And what's needed for an integrated, meaningful, holistic existence?

The story of two women provides the answer. Mary and Martha were sisters who had invited Jesus to visit their home. While Mary sat and listened to what Jesus was saying Martha was distracted by all the preparations that had to be made in the kitchen - torn between competing obligations. Finally Martha cracked. Coming to Jesus and Mary she interrupted saying, "Lord, don't you care that my sister has abandoned me and left me to do all the work? Tell her to help me!" Jesus answered saying, "Martha, Martha, you are worried and upset about many things, but *only one thing is needed*. Mary has chosen what is better . . ." Luke 10:38-42.

In other words, Martha needed Jesus. Jesus is the one thing that's needed when we're worried and upset about many things. He's the One thing that brings meaning and focus to our lives. And He's the One who integrates our existence and makes us whole. So "seek first his kingdom and his righteousness, and all these things will be given to you as well" Matthew 6:33.

FOR GOD . . .

My Father-in-law, the late Ken Terhoven, had been teaching a Sunday School attended by a number of Indian children. His custom was to teach the boys and girls a memory verse each week and then test them on their ability to recall the verse the next week.

On the Sunday in question he faced the expectant throng of eager children and asked them to raise their hand if they knew how to say John 3:16. As usual a score of hands darted into the air and some children eagerly called out; "Me Sah! Me Sah! Me Sah!" One little fellow was especially persistent and it was obvious that he would burst if he wasn't given the singular honour of saying John 3:16. Dad was never one to disappoint a child so he succumbed to the boy's persistence and asked him to stand up and say John 3:16 in a loud clear voice so that all the others would hear. With a noticeable sense of importance and dignity the boy got to his feet, waited for absolute silence, and then said seriously; "John 3:16." That was it! Just those three words, and then he sat down with a sense of pride at his achievement.

Of course we all laugh at this story for we recognise how easy it is for children to misunderstand instructions. But it's a far greater plight when both adults and children fail to act on what they do understand.

Check your understanding of John 3:16 by answering the following three questions: Do you know "God so loved (you)?" Do you know that "God so loved (you) that he gave his one and only Son (for you)?" And do you know "that (if you) believe in him (you) shall not perish but have eternal life?"

If you have answered yes to all three questions then rejoice in your salvation. If you have answered no then act right now by responding to what you now know. Confess your sin, accept His love for you, and believe in Him for eternal life.

BCRE8TVE

I believe it's important to be creative; vital to find ways and means to express the originality of thought and imagination God has given us. And I guess, in part, that's why I've taken the time to write these meditations.

Poetry is one way in which I try to be creative. Mind you; I'm not very good at it. My first attempt was in my early twenties when I thought I'd try and be romantic and write a limerick for my wife. It went like this:

> I'm not very good at prose.
> It's probably because of my nose.
> But it needs to be said,
> That I'm happily wed.
> To a wife who looks like a rose.

You can't say I didn't warn you!

In fact, while I'm confessing, I should probably tell you that whenever I write poetry I use a little book entitled, *The Vocabulary of Rhymes*. I'd be lost without it. My creativity just doesn't stretch that far.

But the degree of expertise in the things we do are not that important. What is important is that we exercise our creative potential as an act of worship. For in so doing we identify with God as Sovereign over all things and the source of all that there is. As D. K. McKim says, "Since God as Creator is the explanation for the existence of the world and for human existence, it is the activity of creation that establishes our deepest and most essential relation to God: as Creator and thus Lord."

So why not pull out that palette, crank up the potting wheel, get those knitting needles clicking, hang some wallpaper, finish that cross stitch, or shape a piece of wood in the lathe . . .

After you finish your devotions.

Consider the following poem as your prayer for the day.

> Three things my Father asks of me,
> If I'm to serve Him faithfully.
> The first I give - the open hand,
> Then next my mind - to understand,
> And last, not least - a praying heart,
> A threefold cord that shall not part.

SMILE AWHILE

Holiness and happiness go hand in glove. God is the "Father of Laughter." And "joy is the serious business of heaven" C. S. Lewis.

So smile awhile. Consider a good guffaw, or at least a snicker, a twitter, a chortle, a hiss, a blast, or a wheeze. For "a cheerful heart is good medicine" Proverbs 17:22. And "the joy of the Lord is your strength" Nehemiah 8:10.

Here are a few actual church bulletin bloopers to get you going:

■ Bertha Belch, a missionary from Africa will be speaking tonight at Calvary Memorial Church. Come and hear Bertha Belch all the way from Africa.

■ Why not sign up for the Prayer and Fasting Conference. The cost of the conference includes meals.

■ Morning service: Jesus walks on water. Evening service: Searching for Jesus.

■ Ushers will eat latecomers.

■ For those of you who have children and don't know it, we have a nursery downstairs.

■ Due to the Pastor's illness, Wednesday's healing services will be discontinued until further notice.

■ Miss Charlene Mason sang, "I will not pass this way again," giving obvious pleasure to the congregation.

■ Weight watchers will meet at 7:00 p.m. Please use the large double door at the side entrance.

■ Ladies, don't forget the rummage sale. It's a chance to get rid of those things not worth keeping around the house. Don't forget your husbands.

■ The church will host an evening of fine dining, superb entertainment, and gracious hostility.

■ Potluck supper next Tuesday. Prayer and medication to follow.

■ Due to a conflict the peacemaking meeting scheduled for today has been cancelled.

■ The ladies of the church have cast off clothing of every kind. They may be seen in the basement on Friday afternoon.

■ Today's Sermon: HOW MUCH CAN A MAN DRINK? With hymns from a full choir.

■ Remember in prayer the many who are sick of our church and community.

■ A bean supper will be held Tuesday evening in the Church Hall. Music will follow.

■ The choir invites any members of the congregation who enjoy sinning to join us at the Saturday practice.

■ The Associate Minister unveiled the church's new tithing campaign slogan last Sunday: "I upped my pledge - up yours."

■ Next Sunday is the family hay-ride and bonfire at the Fowlers. Bring your own hot dogs and guns. Friends are welcome! Everyone come for a fun time.

■ This being Easter Sunday, Mrs. Lewis will be coming forward to lay an egg on the altar.

■ Don't let worry kill you off - let the church help.

Seriously, God has a sense of humour. Just take a look at the church - there's no doubt about it!

LIVING LIFE TO THE FULL

When I attended Ontario Theological Seminary, Kevin Quast, the professor of New Testament Studies began a class by writing on the board:

ISAWABUNDANCEONTHETABLE

I was somewhat perplexed. I thought Kevin was losing it. The stress of marking our assignments had no doubt brought on some kind of anaphylactic shock. On the other hand, maybe it was a case of excessive academia resulting in a rare outbreak of theological dementia. It's not every day that a professor sees a bun dance on the table!

But I was wrong. Kevin was illustrating how the ancient Greek manuscripts were written without spacing of the letters, capitalization or punctuation, and how, as a result, one could miss the point.

Which makes one wonder. If we miss the point with little things, do we miss the point with bigger things? For example, when it comes to our relationship with Jesus is it possible that some of us fail to see what it's all about? Do we get part of the picture but not the whole picture? Can we read the script yet be blind to the intended meaning? Do we see buns dancing on the table or do we see abundance on the table? Jesus said, "I have come that they may have life, and have it to the full."

In other words, God hasn't come to give you a life that's 90% full or even 99.9% full. He's come to give you a life that's 100% full. An abundant life, a plentiful life, a great life, a life heaped with oodles and oodles of good things. As it says in Luke 6:38 He's come to give you "a good measure, pressed down, shaken together . . . running over . . . poured into your lap."

I think we sometimes miss this reality. Caught in the modicum of mediocrity we often fail to see the abundant table God has laid before us. We miss the largess that we have in Christ. We miss the flood of blessings God sends our way. We miss the liberal provisions waiting for those who are prepared to "taste and see that the Lord is good" Psalm 34:8. And in so doing we settle for the good and miss out on God's best.

But it needn't be that way. You can live life to the full. Christ has laid a table fit for a king. Consider the abundance you have in Christ:

■ You've been switched on. When you were born again you received light - the light of the world. You have Jesus, "the true light that gives light to every man" John 1:9.

■ You're alive. "God made you alive with Christ. He forgave us all our sins, having cancelled the written code, with its regulations, that was against us and that stood opposed to us; he took it away, nailing it to the cross" Colossians 2:13-14.

■ You've had your tanks filled with a high octane blend of joy, peace and hope. The God of hope fills you "with all joy and peace as you trust in him, so that you may overflow with hope by the power of the Holy Spirit" Romans 15:13.

■ You have rights. You have the rights of a son. "God sent his Son . . . to redeem those under law, that we might receive the full rights of sons . . . and since you are a son, God has made you also an heir" Galatians 4:4,7.

■ You have an inheritance. You're a citizen of heaven. Eternally secure. "When you heard the word of truth, the gospel of your salvation. Having believed, you were marked in him with a seal, the promised Holy Spirit, who is a deposit guaranteeing our inheritance until the redemption of those who are God's possession - to the praise of his glory" Ephesians 1:13-14.

■ You have freedom in Christ. "It is for freedom that Christ has set us free . . . but do not use your freedom to indulge the sinful nature; rather, serve one another in love" Galatians 5:1,13.

■ You can do all things through Christ. Philippians 4:13 says you "can do everything through him who gives" you "strength."

■ You are filled with God's power, which works mightily in you. "For God did not give us a spirit of timidity, but a spirit of power, of love and of self discipline" 2 Timothy 1:7.

■ You don't have to be anxious about anything (Philippians 4:6). You can "cast all your anxiety on him because he cares for you" 1 Peter 5:7.

■ You are complete in Christ. "You do not lack any spiritual gift" 1 Corinthians 1:7. "God lives in us and his love is made complete in us" 1 John 4:12.

It doesn't stop there. If you scour the Scriptures, you'll discover a whole lot more. So why not open the Word and find the texts that reveal how you're protected by the name of Jesus; have peace with God; share in the righteousness of God; set free by the truth; kept from the evil one; free from condemnation; cleansed by Christ's blood; healed by His stripes; being conformed to the image of Christ; inseparable from the love of Christ; more than a conqueror through Him who loved us; have eternal life in Christ; have the image and glory of God; a new creation in Christ; have wisdom and insight to know His will; can come boldly into Christ's presence; can receive way more than all you ask or think; guarded by God's peace; able to walk worthy of the Lord; presented to God as holy, blameless, and beyond reproach; can come boldly before God's throne of grace and find mercy every time; and blessed with every spiritual blessing in Christ Jesus.

TROUBLE ENOUGH

Most folk would agree that "each day has enough trouble of its own" Matthew 6:34. My friend John Reid will agree that there was one day with more than enough trouble.

It started out as a tranquil day. John and I were preparing materials for a grade nine metalwork project. As we were cutting a sheet of brass on the guillotine, we heard what sounded like popping balloons. The sporadic pop-popping continued and we barely gave it a second thought until the school came alive to the sound of police sirens and screeching tyres. Being real rubbernecks we immediately ran outside to see what was happening. We had a grandstand view. A desperate criminal was racing across a sports field and the police were in hot pursuit. It was like being in the middle of an action movie. Guns were blazing away and the police were converging on the criminal from all sides. I even had to leap out of the way as a police car went into a skid and nearly ran me over. Then as quickly as it had started it stopped. The criminal had run out of ammunition and the police were disarming him and clapping on handcuffs.

By the time the police had placed the criminal in the back of a truck John and I were walking back to the workshop. On the way we passed his car and noticed that a stray bullet had torn through the rear fender. It was only when we made this discovery that the reality of what we had just witnessed began to dawn on us. It was then, when we were back in the workshop, that we realised how fortunate we were that neither of us had been shot!

You may not have been in life threatening situations but you'll certainly have times when you fret and worry. Remember the words of Jesus. He tells you not to "worry about tomorrow, for tomorrow will worry about itself . . . but seek first his kingdom and his righteousness . . . for your heavenly Father knows what you need" Matthew 6:32-34.

"BIG O"

A "once upon a time" story is told of a circus strongman who displayed remarkable feats of physical strength. He became renowned in towns and cities across the land for his ability to bend bars of iron and smash huge blocks of ice, but above all else he was famous for his ability to squeeze an orange completely dry. For this reason he became known as "Big O." Everyone had heard of "Big O" and at the end of his show he always challenged the people in the audience to see if someone could come and squeeze another drop of juice out of the crushed fruit. Over the years many strong men had given it a try but no one had ever been successful in getting one more drop out of the orange that "Big O" had squeezed.

One day, a diminutive little man volunteered to give it a try. The spectators roared with laughter as the puny man made his way to the centre of the ring in order to take up the challenge. Undaunted by the cat calls and jibes from the people the little man took what appeared to be nothing more than a shrivelled piece of rind and slowly and firmly compressed his right hand. Every eye was rivetted on him as he squeezed. A couple of seconds elapsed and then to everyone's amazement a drop of orange juice formed and dropped to the floor. There was a stunned silence and "Big O's" jaw dropped open in amazement. But the little man wasn't finished, before anyone could recover from the shock of it all a second drop of juice plopped onto the floor. Cheers erupted around the tent and willing spectators rushed into the ring and hoisted the little man up onto their shoulders. When the applause subsided, the ring master beckoned the little man over to the microphone and asked him to tell the people how he had developed such power. "Nothing to it," replied the man. Then with a wry grin he added, "It just so happens that I'm the treasurer at the local Baptist Church!"

It's a good joke. We identify with it if we've endured arm twisting and browbeating appeals for money. But the church should never have to get to the point where it's having to squeeze money out of us. The money should be brought into "the storehouse" (cf. Malachi 3:10) as an act of loving obedience. If each of us excelled at "the grace of giving" (2 Corinthians 8:7) there would be more than enough to support the Lord's work. So don't hold back. Outshine, outstrip and surpass yourself in your giving. Give in proportion to how the Lord has blessed you. And as you do; give systematically, sacrificially, proportionately, voluntarily, privately, personally and ungrudgingly.

Use your money while you're living;
Do not hoard it to be proud.
For you cannot take it with you;
There's no pocket in a shroud.
Gold can carry you no further;
Than the graveyard where you lie.
You may be rich while you are living;
But you're a pauper when you die!

CAN YOU GUESS WHO I AM?

Can you guess who I am? I have no respect for justice and no mercy for defenceless humanity. I ruin without killing; I tear down homes; I break hearts and wreck lives. You will find me in the pews of the pious as well as in the haunts of the unholy. I'm wily, cunning, malicious, and I gather strength with age. I have made my way where many fear to tread. My victims are as numerous as the sands of the sea, and often as innocent! I feed on good and bad alike. I never forgive and seldom forget. I travel from mouth to mouth. My name? My name is gossip!

Can you guess who I am? Yes, sadly, I admit that I can. For I've seen the havoc wrought by a gabby mouth, I've watched an unruly tongue separate close friends, and I've been around long enough to realise that gossip is more deadly than a cruise missile.

We sometimes forget these realities. We use words without restraint. We tell stories without considering the consequences. We parade our thoughts with little to no regard for truth, no respect for justice and no concern for the innocent. We look at the speck of sawdust in someone else's eye and pay no attention to the plank in our own eye (cf. Matthew 7:3). And we casually, even flippantly, engage in spiteful chatter without a twinge of concern for the people we malign.

No wonder the Bible refers to the tongue as "a fire, a world of evil among the parts of the body . . . a restless evil, full of deadly poison . . . it corrupts the whole person, sets the whole course of his life on fire, and is itself set on fire by hell" James 3:6,8.

But it needn't be that way. The tongue can be tamed. You can overcome a tendency to gossip. You can learn to be discreet. You can make a choice that will positively influence your future. You can discover the enduring quality of words used wisely.

The secret to success is discovering how victory over gossip has nothing to do with self control but everything to do with Christ control. That's right. You can change for the better. You can stop spewing out mud. You can swim against the current. You can use your tongue like honey, rather than vinegar. You can use your words to caress, rather than cut. You can keep your tongue from evil and deceit. You can make it your life's resolution to abstain from slander. And you can build people up, instead of breaking them down. It starts when you identify gossip as sin, when you stop trying to deal with the problem in your own strength, when you admit you're helpless and powerless to change, when you turn to the only One who can make you different, and when you ask for forgiveness and hand over the reins of your tongue to Christ.

So ask Christ to tame your tongue. Tell Him you want the necessary understanding to hold your tongue (cf. Proverbs 11:12). Pray for a tongue that brings healing and commendation (cf. Proverbs 12:18). And appeal to Him to keep your tongue from sin (cf. Psalm 39:1). There is no other way. "No man can tame the tongue" James 3:8. Without Christ you will fail. Without His forgiveness and cleansing you'll stay in the grip of gossip. Without the inner power that comes from knowing the fullness of His Spirit you will not be able to live, think, act, and speak with discernment. And without His intervention you will continue to succumb to the vulgar and shoddy attire of an indiscreet tongue.

FOR MATTHEW

Hi Matt.

I've been thinking about the things a dad should be teaching his son. If it's okay with you, here are a few thoughts buzzing around in my head. God willing, they'll be something to establish your life on in the years ahead.

Be a risk taker. There's an old Danish proverb that says that we shouldn't sail out farther than we can row back, but this proverb is superfluous when most people aren't even prepared to go sailing. So get into the boat. Trim the jib and catch the wind. Of course I'm referring to the wind of the Spirit. God is looking for men who'll be risk takers for Him. I pray you'll be that man, that you will "be strong and very courageous" Joshua 1:6. And I hope that when God looks for a man to stand before Him "in the gap on behalf of the land" (Ezekiel 22:30) you'll be prepared to heed the call.

Watch your words. You have a sharp mind, a ready wit, and you're certainly not tongue tied. These are wonderful gifts, but in using what God has given you never forget that to whom much is given much will be expected. So pay careful attention to God's Word and allow Him to teach you how to be a man of His Word (cf. Proverbs 4:5). As I often tell myself, blunt words have sharp edges, and good words are worth much and cost little.

Money matters. To be a man of God you must know how to manage money. It's not complicated. I do everything on the 10 - 10 - 80 principle. After taxes have been deducted, I make sure that for every dollar I receive I start by giving 10% or more to the Lord's work The tithe is just a guide. We should excel at the grace of giving as it teaches in 2 Corinthians 8:7. If you can give more than 10%, do it gladly and generously. The next priority is saving 10%. Put this money away in RRSP's or endowment policies. The 80% (or less) that remains should be budgeted for daily expenses as well as offerings for missions and the poor. As Mum and I have practised the 10 - 10 - 80 principle we've had the joy of seeing God supply all of our needs. I believe God will do the same for you if you handle His money this way. Note: Concerning the borrowing of money. Personally, I believe if the Lord hasn't given me the money for something then I'm either meant to wait and save up for it or I'm not meant to have it. Thus, although I know many people won't agree, I don't believe we honour God by borrowing money. Of course there's an exception to every rule and for the sake of a roof over our heads Mum and I had to take out a mortgage. When it comes to housing it seems prudent to pay a mortgage instead of paying rent.

Be merciful and just. According to the morality of the world it's okay to step on others in climbing to the top. It's survival of the fittest, so they say. But that's the law of the jungle, not the law of liberty in Christ. So be a man unlike most other men. Be man enough to feel another's pain and overlook the faults you see. Deny yourself the sharp impatient response. Never react when you're all steamed up. Cool off before addressing an issue. Try to put yourself in the other person's shoes. When it comes to mercy, "with the measure you use, it will be measured to you" Matthew 7:2.

"Get wisdom, get understanding" Proverbs 4:5. A man is truly wise when he makes the pursuit of wisdom his lifelong goal. Don't chase after the wisdom of the world, that's selfish ambition. Biblical wisdom is that which comes from heaven and "is first of all pure; then peace loving, considerate, submissive, full of mercy and good fruit, impartial and sincere" James 3:17. In other words, a wise man is known for his good deeds. Aim to be such a man. And remember, the only way to get wisdom is to continually lay hold of God's words and to make sure that you never swerve away from them.

Well enough for now. I know we'll have many more chats about being a man of God. In the meantime, put these things into practice.

I love you "Middle Mannetjie."

- Dad.

DON'T . . .

Most people don't like being told what they can or can't do and sixteen-year-old youths are no exception. In fact it seems like some teenagers are convinced they've got all the experience they need when deciding what they should or shouldn't be doing. Brian Joffe was one such fellow. He was a cocksure chap who always seemed to know better. Nobody could tell him anything and least of all his teachers. Thus it came as no surprise, one day, to discover Brian at the wood-turning lathe and disregarding a safety regulation. So I switched the machine off and said; "Please don't sand your lamp-stand while the tool-rest is still in place. This is the umpteenth time I've had to tell you to take the tool-rest off when you're sanding!" Reluctantly, he removed the tool-rest.

The following day Brian's class was again in the Woodwork Centre and working diligently on their lamps when the din of tools and machines was pierced by a sharp cry of pain. Running towards the sound I quickly assessed the situation and noticed a youth at one of the lathes with his hand jammed between the tool-rest and the wood that was still being spun around at high speed. I dived for the switching mechanism and thumped the red button. The machine quickly stopped and as it did I was immediately loosening the tool-rest and extracting a mess of sandpaper and finger. It was terrible. Brian's index finger had most of the skin and flesh stripped down to the bone and blood was splattered everywhere. Brian was rushed to a hospital and it was several months of infections and skin grafts before his finger healed.

Brian was never very cocky after that escapade. He learnt the hard way that there are a number of "don'ts" for our benefit and protection. The Ten Commandments (cf. Deuteronomy 5:6-21) are one such set of "don'ts." "Honour your father and mother . . ." is written as a positive injunction but the other laws are written as prohibitions, i.e. "You shall not." These great laws provide a valuable moral framework for our well-being. So "learn them and be sure to follow them" and "walk in the way that the Lord your God has commanded you, so that you may live and prosper and prolong your days" Deuteronomy 5:1, 33.

IT'S TIME . . .

It's time for revival, time for a renaissance of religion, time for the church to get 'back to the future.'

Yes, it's time for us to see that God is "doing a new thing" Isaiah 43:19.

Time for this generation to be reached with the Gospel of Jesus Christ.

Time for Christians to be real - not religious.

Time for confession and contrition.

Time for brokenness and humility.

Time for God's people to be led by their dreams instead of being pushed by their problems.

Time to change and take risks.

Time for churches to break out of the mold, move on, retool, and adopt entirely new packages of language and creativity while maintaining the timeless truth of God's Word.

Time for the understanding and expression of Christianity to be what God wants it to be.

Time to stop franchising ourselves with past patterns and practices.

Time for churches to be adaptive, entrepreneurial, sensory and participatory.

Time to "pour new wine into new wineskins" Matthew 9:17.

Time for eyes to be opened, ears unplugged and tongues loosened.

Time for the softening of hearts and the sharpening of spirits.

Time for minds to be renewed and holiness pursued.

Time for the church to be a place that's thick with God's presence.

Time for Christians to understand the times and know what to do.

Time to act on the spiritual and strategic opportunities before us.

Time to get hot wired to Jesus.

Time to react, respond and reach contemporary society for His glory and His fame.

Time to encourage Spirit filled spontaneity and synergy.

Time to process what God is doing in faith and openness.

Time to "not dwell on the past" Isaiah 43:18.

Time for grace and compassion to be practical realities.

Time to be spiritually natural and naturally spiritual.

Time to appreciate we can't copy what others have done and can't continue with yesterday's success.

Time to see that past glory is no guarantee for tomorrow's survival.

Time to forge into new territory as the Holy Spirit leads.

Time to embrace the unique context and community in which God has placed us.

Time to balance the Spirit and the Word.

Time to be willing to fail in order to succeed.

Time for the church to be organic in nature and open in practice.

Time to go beyond our comfort zones.

Time to take time.

Time to listen to God for today's agenda.

Time to catch the fire and fan the flame.

Time to be "built together to become a dwelling in which God lives by his Spirit" Ephesians 2:22.

Time for God's power to be unleashed in the schools, shops, streets, and suburbs of our city.

Time for the church to be a powerhouse of prayer, throbbing with passionate worship, filled with joyful loving people, awestruck at miraculous signs and wonders, inspired by anointed Bible preaching and teaching, marked by generosity and sincerity, and buzzing with stories of the difference Christ has made in people's lives.

Time to please God and see Jesus lifted up.

Time to recognize it's not about you and me but about surrendering to Christ's ways and following Him to the end of our days.

It's time.

Pray it will happen soon. Pray that God will start with you.

PICK-UP LINES

Our family was on a camping holiday in Prince Edward Island and one evening as we were rolling out our sleeping bags, Christie said to Matt, "You can't believe the pick-up lines some people use. A few weeks ago I was serving this guy coffee (Christie worked at Tim Horton's) and asked him, as I ask all the customers, 'Can I get you anything else?' and he said, 'No thanks, I couldn't afford you!' I was so embarrassed." "No way! What did he look like?" asked Matt. "He was old. It was like disgusting!" replied Christie. As our laughter abated, I said, "As pick-up lines go you've got to give the guy some credit. If you used a pick-up line what would you say?"

An animated discussion ensued. One of Matthew's corny lines was, "Are those astronaut pants? Because you're out of this world!" Christie's pick-up lines weren't much better, "Do your feet hurt? You've been running around in my mind all day." And, "You are the reason women fall in love."

Pick-up lines have been around for a long time. According to *Mikey's Funnies*, Adam used these pick-up lines on Eve:

"You know you're the only one for me!"

"Do you come here often?"

"Trust me, this was meant to be!"

"Look around. All the other guys around here are animals!"

"I already feel like you're a part of me!"

"Honey, you were made for me!"

"Why don't you come over to my place and we can name some animals?"

"You're the girl of my dreams!" (cf Genesis 2:21).

"I like a girl who doesn't mind being ribbed!"

"You're the apple of my eye!"

With a full disclaimer against anyone who's foolish enough to use them, here are some contemporary efforts:

Are you accepting applications for your fan club?

Excuse me, I've lost my phone number and was wondering if I could borrow yours?

You should be someone's husband.

Were you in the Boy Scouts? You sure tied my heart in a knot.

I hope you know CPR because you took my breath away.

Did the sun come out or did you just smile at me?

You're so sweet. You put Hershey's out of business.

What does it feel like to be the most beautiful woman in this room?

Okay, I know. That's more than enough! Pick-up lines are trite and pathetic at best. When you make yourself all honey the flies will soon devour you.

Which brings us to the Lord. He never uses hackneyed speech, flattery, twaddle, or twittering claptrap. He cuts through the superfluous, pierces the heart. When God says, "I love you," it's altogether different - without compare. Consider some of His lines:

"I am my lover's and my lover is mine" Song of Songs 6:3.

"I have loved you with an everlasting love; I have drawn you with loving-kindness" Jeremiah 31:3.

"'I have loved you,' says the Lord" Malachi 1:2.

"As the Father has loved me, so have I loved you" John 15:9.

WHY CREEPY-CRAWLIES?

Some years ago I was teaching a course entitled "Tough Questions Christians Ask". The students studied a variety of topics that included: Should miracles be expected today? How can a loving God allow evil and pain? Can Christians know God's will for their lives? What is the role of women in the church today? But one topic we never addressed was, why did God make a variety of nasty little bugs? That's a good question. You've probably thought about it. If so, you may appreciate the liberties I've taken with the well-known children's hymn, *All Things Bright and Beautiful*. Feel free to sing along:

Some things not so beautiful. Those creatures wild and fell.
Pests that nip and worry you.
The Lord made them as well.
Each little leech that suctions. Each little flea that springs.
He made their hungry habits. He made their tiny stings.

Some things not so beautiful, etc.
The scaly-headed rattlesnake. The spider running by.
The ever hungry locust. Brings darkness to the sky.

Some things not so beautiful, etc.
The blackfly in the summer. These insects swarm and bite.
The midges near the water. Torment us every night.

Some things not so beautiful, etc.
He gave us nerves to feel them. And skin to itch and swell.
Now did God have a reason, for making them as well?
Some things not so beautiful, etc.

As with many tough issues in Christianity there are sometimes more questions than answers. As we ask the questions, we begin to realize we're limited in our perspectives. We recognize that "now (we) know in part (and) then (we) shall know fully" 1 Corinthians 13:12. But the part we do know is that when God made all these creatures He "saw that it was good" Genesis 1:25. Yes the leech, the flea, the snake, the spider, the locust, the blackfly, the midges, and countless other insects and reptiles were made by God and rated by Him as "very good" Genesis 1:31. So even if you're nursing a painful bee sting, as I was doing when I wrote this devotion, remember that Mrs. C. F. Alexander is quite correct when she penned the words; "All things bright and beautiful. All creatures great and small . . . How great is God Almighty. Who has done all things well."

WATCH YOUR EYE

I've long since forgotten the youth's first name (his surname was Bard) but I'll never forget that he was the boy with the glass eye. When he first arrived at the school, many of his peers teased him about the eye. He was sometimes called "glassy" or "socket" and probably a host of other nicknames. But their teasing quickly dissipated for he wasn't easily offended and his ready smile and winsome ways soon gathered a good circle of friends around him. He was also much sought after to participate in pranks. His friends would persuade him to take his eye out and leave it on the teacher's table or they'd get him to walk up to one of the girls and give her the vacant socket stare!

But the event I will never forget was when his rugby team was competing in a tense and even game against another school and he lost his eye in a maul. I was the referee, so I stopped the game, explained the situation to the other team, and within seconds the rivalry was forgotten as thirty young men scoured the pitch on their hands and knees. It was a comical sight but eventually the eye was found, washed, and replaced in the socket. But the incident had left the opposition a little reticent to tackle him for fear of knocking his eye out again. Thus it came as no surprise when Bard dived over the goal line for the winning try!

Now you probably don't have a glass eye that needs your attention but you do need to watch your eye. For your "eye is the lamp of your body" and "when your eyes are good, your whole body also is full of light. But when they are bad, your body also is full of darkness" Luke 11:34. So "if your eye causes you to sin, pluck it out" for "it is better for you to enter the kingdom of God with one eye than to have two eyes and be thrown into hell" Mark 9:47.

WHO CAN LIVE WITHOUT HOPE?

Unbelievable as it may seem, it is possible for a person to live up to seventy days without food. It is also possible to exist for nearly ten days without water. And one can live for up to six minutes without air. But there is one thing it is impossible to live without - hope.

You can lose your business, your money, and maybe even your family, but hope is the one thing you cannot afford to lose. For hope keeps man alive. It climbs over obstacles when no one is helping. It arouses the mind to explore possibilities. It sweetens when bitterness bites. It makes us optimists for tomorrow. It hangs in when everything seems to be slipping away. It smiles when no one is laughing. It urges us on. And it gives radiance despite the darkness. As O. S. Marden says, "There is no medicine like hope, no incentive so great, and no tonic so powerful as expectation of something better tomorrow."

The trouble is, hope seems to be in short supply. The average person doesn't have it and doesn't know where to get it. He's simply enduring the present or waiting for the future. Going through the motions. Performing according to his fears. Wondering how to make it. Surviving on forgotten dreams.

But it needn't be that way. You can look forward to tomorrow. Have a new song in your heart. Overcome failure. Defeat depression. Endure all things. Climb every mountain. Live it like it could be.

All it takes is a change of heart. As it says in Matthew 22:37, You must "love the Lord . . . with all your heart."

It's that simple. When you love the Lord with all your heart, you'll discover certainty in an uncertain world. You'll anticipate each day with confident expectation. You won't be moved by the vagrancies of life. You'll be freed from condemnation. You'll have courage to endure. And you'll be strengthened with patience and love.

For when you love the Lord with all your heart He's promised to "to make your paths straight" (Proverbs 3:6), to deliver you from the hand of the wicked, to be the Comforter, to be the One who can be relied upon, to be your strong refuge, to be with you when you're old, to be "your salvation all day long" (Psalm 71:15), to be your friend, to give you fullness of life.

So why not trust in the God of hope? Why not give your heart to the One who can be your all in all? And why not discover how Jesus makes the difference between hope and hopelessness - between life and death?

"I'M NEVER DOWN,
I'M EITHER UP OR GETTING UP"

Someone once said, "I'm never down, I'm either up or getting up."

That's well said. It's telling it like it could be. Like cream, this type of attitude will lift one to the top. Optimism helps us to be all that God intends for us to be. Success comes to those who have the will to keep on keeping on.

History reveals how people are successful, not because of aptitude but because of attitude. Persistence and desire are needed if one wants to be an achiever. Success isn't an accident. It's an ongoing process of growth and development. It's achieving one thing and using that as a stepping stone to future accomplishments. For the true measure of success is not what position you've reached in life, but what challenges you've overcome as you've endeavoured to reach your goal.

Which reminds me of my daughter when she was learning to walk. Karen and I would sit on the floor across from each other and encourage Christie to take a few wobbly steps. When she successfully lunged from her mother to me we'd clap and cheer her effort. If she began to fall, we tried to catch her, and if she did fall we encouraged her to get back up and try again.

Life is very much like a baby learning to walk. There are moments of success and times of distress. Sometimes the going is smooth and sometimes it's a stumbling effort where you have to repeatedly pick yourself up and give it another go. For, like a baby, as we walk along the path of life we'll have occasional falls due to inexperience or overconfidence.

The difference between success and failure is how we react after the fall. Regardless of the reason for a setback, we need to learn that failure only comes when we allow the fall to keep us down and dictate the future course of our life, whereas success comes when we keep getting up and trying again. As someone said, "Success comes to those who have the character to continue when all seems lost."

The life of the Apostle Paul provides an excellent example of a successful person. In 2 Corinthians 11:23-27 Paul says, "I have . . . been in prison more frequently, been flogged more severely, and been exposed to death again and again. Five times I received from the Jews the forty lashes minus one. Three times I was beaten with rods, once I was stoned, three times I was shipwrecked, I spent a night and a day in the open sea, I have been constantly on the move. I have been in danger from rivers, in danger from bandits, in danger from my own countrymen, in danger from

Gentiles; in danger in the city, in danger in the country, in danger at sea; and in danger from false brothers. I have laboured and toiled and often gone without sleep; I have known hunger and thirst and have often gone without food; I have been cold and naked."

But despite all of this he got ahead. He didn't stay down. He pressed on. He knew that failure didn't come from the fall but from not getting up from the fall. As he says in Philippians 4:13, "I can do everything through him who gives me strength."

And in these words we have a recipe for success. For ultimately, a successful person is one who reaches up and lets God pick him up. Yes, you'll never stay down if you look to God for the strength to try again.

BURDENS
INTO BRIDGES

"Go to the ant . . . consider its ways and be wise" Proverbs 6:6.

It seems to me that God often takes the little things, the seemingly unimportant, when he wants to catch our attention. That reminds me of the ants. Some years ago I was watching an ant struggling to move a piece of straw about five times its size. It was a mammoth effort. The ant pulled, pushed, and at times it even lifted its burden as it attempted to deliver its load to the nest. Along the way the ant came to a crack in the ground which was just a little too wide for it to cross. Tottering on the edge, the ant tried desperately to reach the other side, but to no avail. It stood for a time, seemingly perplexed by the situation, and then, to my surprise, put the straw across the crack and walked over the bridge.

I'm sure there was a look of absolute incredulity on my face. I couldn't believe that something as insignificant as an ant could be so wise. After all, the ant is little more than tissue and folic acid. Yet this insect had the ability to convert its burden into a bridge.

If we only had the sense of the ant. We seem to carry our burdens and never think of laying them down and converting them into bridges, of having our burdens bear us up instead of allowing them to bear us down. For unlike the ant, many of us struggle from day to day as we try to make progress under heavy loads like guilt, anger, bitterness, pride, hatred, discord, jealousy, selfish ambition, feelings of insecurity, impurity, immorality, bad temper, gluttony, drug addiction, drunkenness, and more.

So how do we deal with these burdens? How do we learn the secret of converting our burdens into bridges? And how do we make the kind of progress whereby we're borne up by our burden instead of being borne down by it?

The Bible provides the answer.

Firstly, **let go** of your burden by **confessing** your sin. "If we confess our sins," God "is faithful and just and will forgive us our sins and purify us from all unrighteousness" I John 1:9.

Secondly, **lay down** your burden by **casting** it on God. "Cast your cares on the Lord and he will sustain you" Psalm 55:22.

Thirdly, **leave** your burden by **committing** your way to the Lord. The Apostle Paul exemplifies this principle. Throughout his life he had been afflicted with a physical ailment which he referred to as a thorn in his flesh (cf. 2 Corinthians 12:7).

But when he recognized the burden to be a part of God's will for him, he exclaimed, "Therefore I will boast all the more gladly about my weaknesses, so that Christ's power may rest on me" 2 Corinthians 12:9.

Finally, **look** beyond yourself and help **carry** someone else's burdens. So "carry each others burdens, and in this way you will fulfill the law of Christ" Galatians 6:2.

LIFTING POTATO SACKS

An unknown author tells how his grandfather worked in a blacksmith shop when he was a boy, and how he had toughened himself up so he could stand the rigors of black-smithing. He developed his arm and shoulder muscles by standing outside behind the house and, with a five-pound sack in each hand, extended his arms straight out from his sides and held them there as long as he could. After a while he tried ten-pound potato sacks, then fifty-pound sacks and finally he got to where he could lift a hundred-pound potato sack in each hand and hold his arms out for more than a full minute!

Next, he started putting potatoes in the sacks.

I suspect we're all like that at times. We know how rigorous life can be. We want to be strong. We go into training. We pick up the potato sacks of education, work, and family responsibilities. We try to toughen up for inevitable tests and temptations. We know that we'll only succeed by the sweat of our brow. And we're prepared to hold the potato sacks as long as God doesn't put any potatoes in them!

But empty potato sacks don't build muscles. They don't develop the strength of character that's needed to deal with the vagaries and vicissitudes of life. As my rugby coach used to say, "No pain, no gain." Our intellectual, emotional, and spiritual muscles are only strengthened when we "face trials of many kinds" (James 1:2); when we struggle to pick up the sacks of loneliness, heartache, sorrow or suffering; when we "endure hardship" (2 Timothy 2:3); and when we run "the race marked out for us" Hebrews 12:1.

So lift the sackful of potatoes. Don't throw in the towel. Trust in God. Be "strong in the grace that is in Christ Jesus" 2 Timothy 2:1. Persevere (cf. James 1:4). "Fight the good fight" 1 Timothy 6:12. And even though you'll sometimes feel like giving up, remember that "no test or temptation that comes your way is beyond the course of what others have had to face. All you need to remember is that God will never let you down; he'll never let you be pushed past your limit; he'll always be there to help you come through it" 1 Corinthians 10:13 (*The Message*).

FRUIT IN OLD AGE

In Job 5:26 we read, "You will come to the grave in full vigour, like sheaves gathered in season." That's a fascinating verse. It reminds me of the scores of people who have made a profound contribution to society in their senior years.

Miguel Cervantes wrote *Don Quixote* when he was almost seventy. John Milton wrote *Paradise Regained* when he was sixty-three. Noah Webster wrote his monumental dictionary at seventy. Socrates gave his wise philosophies at seventy. Ignace Paderewski still gave concerts before large audiences at seventy-nine. William Gladstone was still a powerful political figure at eighty. Clara Barton founded the American Red Cross at fifty-nine. Benjamin Disraeli became the prime minister of England for the second time at seventy. Johann von Goethe completed *Faust* at eighty-two. Thomas Edison worked busily in his lab at eighty-three. Alfred Tennyson published his memorable poem, *Crossing the Bar*, at eighty-three. Guiseppe Verdi composed *Othello* at seventy-three, *Falstaff* in his seventies, and *Te Deum* at eighty-five. Michelangelo was in his late eighties when he painted some of his masterpieces. Arturo Toscanini conducted an orchestra at eighty-seven. Grandma Moses did many of her paintings after ninety. The Earl of Halsburg was ninety when he began preparing a twenty-volume revision of English law. Galileo made his greatest discovery when he was seventy-three. And at sixty-nine, Hudson Taylor was still vigorously working on the mission field opening up new territories in Indochina.

But that's how it should be. God never puts us on the shelf. We should come to the grave in full vigour. We should be fruitful in our old age. For it's God's will that the righteous "will still bear fruit in old age, they will stay fresh and green . . ." Psalm 92:14.

This anonymous story illustrates the point:

The first day of school our professor introduced himself and challenged us to get to know someone we didn't already know. I stood up to look around when a gentle hand touched my shoulder. I turned around to find a wrinkled, little old lady beaming up at me with a smile that lit up her entire being.

She said, "Hi handsome. My name is Rose. I'm eighty-seven years old. Can I give you a hug?" I laughed and enthusiastically responded, "Of course you may!" and she gave me a giant squeeze.

"Why are you in college at such a young, innocent age?" I asked. She jokingly replied, "I'm here to meet a rich husband, get married, have a couple of children, and then retire and travel."

"No seriously," I asked. I was curious what may have motivated her to be taking on this challenge at her age. "I always dreamed of having a college education and now I'm getting one!" she told me.

After class we walked to the student union building and shared a chocolate milkshake. We became instant friends. Every day for the next three months we would leave class together and talk nonstop. I was always mesmerized listening to this "time machine" as she shared her wisdom and experience with me. Over the course of the year, Rose became a campus icon and she easily made friends wherever she went. She loved to dress up and she revelled in the attention bestowed upon her from the other students. She was living it up.

At the end of the semester we invited Rose to speak at our football banquet. I'll never forget what she taught us. She was introduced and stepped up to the podium. As she began to deliver her prepared speech, she dropped her three by five cards on the floor. Frustrated and a little embarrassed she leaned into the microphone and simply said, "I'm sorry I'm so jittery. I gave up beer for Lent and this whiskey is killing me! I'll never get my speech back in order so let me just tell you what I know."

As we laughed, she cleared her throat and began, "We do not stop playing because we are old; we grow old because we stop playing. There are only four secrets to staying young, being happy, and achieving success. You have to laugh and find humour every day. You've got to have a dream. When you lose your dreams, you die. We have so many people walking around who are dead and don't even know it! There is a huge difference between growing older and growing up. If you are nineteen years old and lie in bed for one full year and don't do one productive thing, you will turn twenty years old. If I am eighty-seven years old and stay in bed for a year and never do anything I will turn eighty-eight. Anybody can grow older. That doesn't take any talent or ability. The idea is to grow up by always finding the opportunity in change. Have no regrets. The elderly usually don't have regrets for what we did, but rather for things we did not do. The only people who fear death are those with regrets."

She concluded her speech by courageously singing "The Rose." She challenged each of us to study the lyrics and live them out in our daily lives.

Rose finished the college degree she had begun all those years ago. One week after graduation Rose died peacefully in her sleep. More than two thousand college students attended her funeral in tribute to the wonderful woman who taught by example that it's never too late to be all you can possibly be.

CONFINED BY FEAR -
FREED BY FAITH

As a youngster I was an avid spelunker. It was an exciting sport that never failed to get my adrenalin pumping and heighten awareness of my frailty. For every time I climbed into a damp cavern and started worming my way into the bowels of the earth I had to fight against my feelings of claustrophobia. My heart would speed up, I would begin to sweat profusely, and a battle would rage in my mind as I pitted my intellect against my emotions.

As strange as it may seem, I was attracted to spelunking because it brought me face to face with my fear. It was the closest thing that I'd ever had to a near death experience. For whenever I was wriggling through a narrow hole or inching along on my stomach in a restricted passageway, I was being challenged to deal with the possibility of a panic attack; to take a test and see if I could succeed beyond the limits of my capacity to endure; to realise that if I became wedged between the rocks, they could easily become my coffin!

Since my days as a youngster I've learnt that life is very much like spelunking. Every one of us has to face the constricting circumstances of sickness, grief, uncertain futures and difficult relationships. Sometimes these challenges become so tough and life so precarious, it's like being wedged between a rock and a hard place. It's akin to worming through a long tunnel. It's similar to the blinding darkness experienced in the depths of a cave. Yes, the confinement of pain and suffering often brings us face to face with our fears. It stirs up panic and calls on our capacity to endure.

So how can we deal with the challenges of life and succeed? How can we face our fears and not give up? And how can we keep moving forward when it feels like the walls are pressing in and squeezing us to death?

The only way through is to have a guide; to have someone who knows how to navigate the labyrinth of dark passageways that we encounter in life; and to have someone who can help us get through and reach the other side.

That someone is Jesus Christ. He is the only One who knows the way. He is the only One who sees everything despite the darkness. And He is the only One who can lead us through the tunnels of depression, dejection, and despair.

As the Bible says; He will "shine on those living in darkness and in the shadow of death." He will "guide our feet into the path of peace" Luke 1:79. For "He who has compassion on them will guide them" Isaiah 49:10. Yes, "the Lord will guide you always; he will satisfy your needs . . ." Isaiah 58:11. So trust in Him today. For when you're confined by fear you can only be freed by faith - a faith in the Guide who knows the way and will help you reach the light of day.

KEYS TO PERSONAL REVIVAL

In Psalm 85:6 the Sons of Korah cry out, "Will you not revive us again, that your people may rejoice in you?" Do you have the same cry in your heart? Why not take the time to prayerfully consider the following fifteen keys to personal revival:

1. Ask the Holy Spirit to reveal unconfessed sin in your life (cf. Psalm 139:23-24).

2. Seek forgiveness from anyone you may have offended (cf. Matthew 6:14-15; James 5:16).

3. Forgive the people who have offended you and make restitution where necessary (cf. 2 Corinthians 2:10; Colossians 3:13).

4. Examine your life on a daily basis by asking the Holy Spirit to reveal motives, words and deeds that are not of Him (cf. Psalm 139:23-24).

5. Guard yourself against compromise, complacency and mediocrity (cf. Proverbs 4:23-27; Acts 20:31; 1 Corinthians 16:13).

6. Cultivate an attitude, and the practice, of grateful praise and thanksgiving regardless of your circumstances (cf. Ephesians 5:19-20; Philippians 4:4; 1 Thessalonians 5:16-18).

7. Live by the Spirit and refuse to be ruled by your sinful nature (cf. Galatians 5:16-17).

8. Pray for the filling of the Holy Spirit on a daily basis (cf. Ephesians 5:18).

9. Develop an absolute dependance on Jesus Christ as your Lord and Saviour by constantly submitting and humbling yourself before Him (cf. Philippians 2:1-5).

10. Study the attributes of God and rejoice in who you are in Him (cf. Ephesians 1:3-14).

11. Hunger and thirst after righteousness (cf. Matthew 5:6).

12. Love the Lord with all your heart and soul and mind; and love your neighbour as yourself (cf. Matthew 22:37-39).

13. Read, study, meditate and memorize the Word of God (cf. Psalm 119:1-176; Colossians 3:16).

14. Determine to live a holy life of faith and obedience (cf. 1 Peter 1:13-16).

15. Reach out to others with the love of Christ (cf. Matthew 28:19-20).

IN THE SCHOOL OF AFFLICTION

An old Chinese proverb says that a "diamond cannot be polished without friction, nor the man perfected without trials."

Cripple a man and you have a Sir Walter Scott. Raise him in abject poverty and you have an Abraham Lincoln. Deafen a genius composer and you have a Ludwig van Beethoven. Lock him in a prison cell, subject him to racial discrimination, and you have a Nelson Mandela. Call him a slow learner, "retarded," and write him off as ineducable, and you have an Albert Einstein.

As William Shakespeare so aptly says, "sweet are the uses of adversity."

But recognising the positive side of adversity is not enough. It doesn't help when you're struggling in tanks of particular and inescapable circumstances. And it doesn't help you in life's crucible of pain and tension.

So what can you do when adversity strikes? What can you do when affliction lays you low? And what can you do when adventure turns to disaster? God's Word provides a number of practical suggestions.

Firstly, handle adversity with prayer. Never forget that prayer is "powerful and effective" James 5:16. It's your anchor in the heart of a storm and your stability in the midst of a squall. Thus when your burdens seem great, remember this: "Daily prayers lessen, daily cares."

Secondly, handle adversity by trusting in God's provision. In 1 Peter 5:7 we read; "Cast all your anxiety on him because he cares for you." Adversity will be overcome when you stop trusting in yourself and start trusting in God. Instead of being fretful and frustrated, turn to God in simple faith. For faith is your pipeline to the Great Provider - your conduit to the riches of God's resources.

Thirdly, handle adversity with God's promises. Adoniram Judson said that "the prospect is as bright as the promises of God." Why? Because of the character of God. He is always faithful and always trustworthy. He has never failed to honour His promises in the past, and will never fail to honour His promises in the future. So turn to the Bible and discover how God's Word meets your every need. For ". . . he has given us his very great and precious promises, so that through them you may participate in the divine nature and escape the corruption in the world . . ." 2 Peter 1:4.

Finally, handle adversity with patience. Someone once said that "storms make oaks take deeper root." The truth of the matter is that without adversity you would be insipid, weak-willed, and good for nothing. You would be spineless, pathetic and hopeless. So be patient through hardships and learn how "suffering produces perseverance; perseverance, character; and character hope. And hope does not disappoint us . . ." Romans 5:3-5.

AN AXE AND TWO .38's!

According to one of the stories passed along the internet an elderly woman had just returned home from a church service when she was startled by an intruder who was robbing her home. Without hesitation she yelled, "Stop! Acts 2:38!" (Which reads in *The Good News Bible*, "Each one of you must turn away from his sins."). The burglar stopped dead in his tracks. The woman calmly phoned the police and explained what she'd done. Later, as the officer was cuffing the man, he asked the burglar, "Why did you just stand there? All the old lady did was yell a Scripture at you." "Scripture?" replied the burglar. "I thought she said she had an axe and two .38's!"

I don't know whether the story is true but I do know that "The word of God is living and active. Sharper than any double edged sword, it penetrates even to dividing soul and spirit, joints and marrow; it judges the thoughts and attitudes of the heart" Hebrews 4:12.

Yes, the Bible is alive. It cuts through everything. We can't get away from it - no matter what. There is no book like it. It outlasts, outranks and outruns all other books. It's the Book of books, an impregnable rock, the noblest of all literature, a perennial spring of wisdom, a strong staff, a healing balm, an anchor in the storms of life, an infallible guide of conduct, a light on the pathway in the darkest night, the champion of human liberties, an unfailing source of comfort, the revelation of the only way out of this present world into a better one, a living power, a love letter, and the very Word of God in the inspired speech of humanity.

Which means the Bible has the ability to speak to us, run after us, get inside us, and lay hold of us. No wonder it punctures all pretense, solves every great problem of life, answers the questions of the soul, awakens men and women opiated by sin, and . . . helps little old ladies capture burglars.

PUTTING OUT FIRES

The *Fort Worth Star Telegram* reported that firefighters in Genoa, Texas, were accused of deliberately setting more than forty destructive fires. When caught, they stated, "We had nothing to do. We just wanted to get the red lights flashing and the bells clanging."

We can sometimes be like that. Wanting some action or attention we deliberately start a fire. Not the kind you start with a match. The kind that's started with the tongue (cf. James 3:5-6). The kind that's started with mockery, criticism, gossip, jealousy, provocation, and the like.

It shouldn't be that way. The job of Christians is to put out fires, not start more of them. In other words, Christians should be peacemakers and reconcilers. They must build bridges, elevate truth, and look to God to bring His righteousness to bear so that right relationships can be strengthened between people.

With that in mind, here are three practical ways to help you put out fires:

1. Drop the matter. Many fires can be put out if we are willing to overlook an offense and forgive the person who has wronged us. Consider these texts. "A fool shows his annoyance at once, but a prudent man overlooks an insult" Proverbs 12:16. "Starting a quarrel is like breaching a dam; so drop the matter before a dispute breaks out" Proverbs 17:14. "A man's wisdom gives him patience; it is to his glory to overlook an offense" Proverbs 19:11. "Above all, love each other deeply, because love covers over a multitude of sins" 1 Peter 4:8.

2. Discuss the conflict. Certain fires can't be overlooked. They need to be confronted. Serious conflict should be resolved through confession and loving confrontation. Consider these texts. "He who conceals his sins does not prosper, but whoever confesses and renounces them finds mercy" Proverbs 28:13. "If . . . your brother has something against you . . . go and be reconciled to your brother" Matthew 5:23-24. "If your brother sins against you, go and show him his fault, just between the two of you" Matthew 18:15. "If someone is caught in a sin, you who are spiritual should restore him gently. But watch yourself, or you also may be tempted" Galatians 6:1.

3. Negotiate the issue. Some fires can be put out when solutions are found to meet the interests of everyone involved. The following verses suggest the wisdom of this approach; "In everything, do to others what you would have them do to you" Matthew 7:12. "Do nothing out of selfish ambition or vain conceit, but in

humility consider others better than yourselves. Each of you should look not only to your own interests, but also to the interests of others" Philippians 2:3-4.

So watch out for fires. Set a guard over your mouth (cf. Psalm 141:3). And remember that "without wood a fire goes out; without gossip a quarrel dies down" Proverbs 26:20.

FROM THE MOUTHS OF FOUR-YEAR-OLDS'

Four-year-olds' have their own unique perspective on the Christian faith. Here are some authentic stories to cheer you through the day.

On the way home from church one day, my son Jonathan, who was four years old at the time, said to his older sister, "Is the Holy Spirit a person?" "Not exactly," said Christie. "He's kind of like a ghost." "Well what clothes does he wear?" said Jonathan. To which Christie replied, "He doesn't wear clothes." "What! He goes around naked?" exclaimed Jonathan. "Well not exactly," said Christie, "Think of Him as a good ghost." There was a moment's silence as Jonathan digested what he'd heard. Then, with decisiveness, he said, "Oh! So He wears a sheet."

A father was at the beach with his children when his four-year-old son ran up to him, grabbed his hand, and led him to the shore where a sea gull lay dead in the sand. "Daddy, what happened to him?" the son asked. "He died and went to Heaven," the dad replied. The boy thought for a moment and then said, "Did God throw him back down?"

A mother invited some people to dinner. At the table, she turned to her four-year-old daughter and said, "Would you like to say the blessing?" "I wouldn't know what to say," the girl replied. "Just say what you hear Mommy say." The daughter bowed her head and said, "Lord, why on earth did I invite all these people to dinner?"

Another four-year-old was at the pediatrician for a check up. As the doctor looked down her ears with an otoscope, he asked, "Do you think I'll find Big Bird in here?" The little girl stayed silent. Next, the doctor took a tongue depressor and looked down her throat. He asked, "Do you think I'll find the Cookie Monster down here?" Again, the little girl was silent. Then the doctor put a stethoscope to her chest. As he listened to her heart beat, he asked, "Do you think I'll hear Barney in there?" "Oh no!" the little girl replied. "Jesus is in my heart. Barney's on my underpants!"

A Sunday School teacher asked her class of four year olds, "Why is it necessary to be quiet in church?" One little girl replied, "Because people are sleeping."

In another Sunday School class the teacher began her lesson with the question, "Boys and girls, what do we know about God?" "He's an artist!" said the kindergarten boy. "Really? How do you know?" asked the teacher. "You know - Our Father, who does art in Heaven . . ."

Then there was the four-year-old boy listening to a bedtime story. His father was reading about Sodom and Gomorrah being destroyed. He read, "The man named Lot was warned to take his wife and flee out of the city, but his wife looked back and was turned to salt." His son asked, "What happened to the flea?"

Finally, there was the four-year-old girl who was learning to say the Lord's Prayer. She was reciting it all by herself without help from her mother. She said, ". . . And lead us not into temptation, but deliver us some e-mail. Amen."

What wonderful stories. No wonder Jesus took a little child, maybe a four-year-old, and used the child as an object lesson. You probably remember the occasion. The disciples "came to Jesus and asked, 'Who is the greatest in the kingdom of heaven?' He called a little child and had him stand among them. And he said: 'I tell you the truth, unless you change and become like little children, you will never enter the kingdom of heaven. Therefore, whoever humbles himself like this child is the greatest in the kingdom of heaven. And whoever welcomes a little child like this in my name welcomes me. But if anyone causes one of these little ones who believe in me to sin, it would be better for him to have a large millstone hung around his neck and to be drowned in the depths of the sea'" Matthew 18:1-6.

THE COMRADES MARATHON

Over the years I've had a number of friends who have run the South African Comrades Marathon from Durban to Pietermaritzburg (or vice-versa). It's a gruelling race with thousands of runners who are usually skinny, no doubt brave, generally motivated, and somewhat masochistic.

The race begins before the crack of dawn. As I've watched the contestants at the beginning of the race, it's obvious that running is fun. People are laughing, joking, and waving to the crowds along the way. Their bodies look loose, their lungs are sucking in air, their heads are clear, their muscles strong, and their motivation high. Everyone looks to be in the best of condition.

But it doesn't last long. For the majority of runners the initial rush of pleasure soon becomes an effort. The effort becomes labourious, and, as the sun, coupled with the Valley of a Thousand Hills, wears the runners down it becomes obvious that many are struggling to overcome the overwhelming temptation to stop.

Marathon running is like that. At some point your feet begin to protest, your calves begin to burn, and your lungs feel like they're on fire. That's when you've started to "hit the wall." Although I never ran a marathon, in my younger days I discovered I'd hit the wall before completing ten kilometres. Through this experience I discovered that to run when you're hitting the wall is the ultimate test of a runner. As runners will tell you, a race is won or lost, retired from or finished, at "the wall."

Which is why I admire marathon runners. They dig down deeper than most. They call on reserves they don't feel they have. They push their bodies despite the gruelling pain. And they motivate themselves to somehow make it over the finish line.

That's what it's all about. Some runners will virtually kill themselves just to say they made it. You'll see them struggling with cramps. You'll see their legs collapsing under them. You'll see them staggering or crawling on hands and knees as they try to make it to the end. And you'll see some of them crossing the line and passing out from dehydration and exhaustion.

Yes, the start of the race is enjoyable. The finishing is hard work. But it's the finishing that counts.

This capacity to finish is what the Bible refers to as endurance or perseverance. It's the ability to bear a hard thing and turn the hardship into glory. It's the ability to stick to something and not to waver. It's the tenacity to keep on going when everything within you is crying out for you to stop. And it's the discharge of effort when you feel like you've got nothing left to give. No wonder Chrysostom said, "Endurance is the queen of all virtues."

Which brings me to another Comrades Marathon. It's the Christian race. It usually starts well. Then somewhere along the way it starts to get tough. You begin to experience pain. Little stabs at first, and then before you realise what's happening you're "hitting the wall." That's when you've got to dig deep. And that's when you've got to be determined you're not going to quit. For your life is "worth nothing" unless you "finish the race and complete the task the Lord Jesus has given" to you, "the task of testifying to the gospel of God's grace" Acts 20:24.

There's no way around it. Believers are marathon runners. There's no retiring and no dropping out. We must "throw off everything that hinders and the sin that so easily entangles, and . . . run with perseverance the race marked out for us" Hebrews 12:1. For we do not run aimlessly. No, we run in such a way as to finish the race and "to get the prize . . . a crown that will last forever" 1 Corinthians 9:24- 25.

EMERGENCY NUMBERS

Here's a handy list of emergency numbers you won't want to be without. All you need is the Directory.

When you have sinned, call Psalm 51:1-17.
When your faith needs to be encouraged, call Hebrews 11:1-40.
When you feel timid, call 2 Timothy 1:7.
When people seem unkind, call John 15:12-27.
When you're depressed, call Psalm 27:1-14.
When you are in danger, call Psalm 91:1-16.
For rest or weariness, call Matthew 11:28-30.
When you're discouraged about your work, call Psalm 126:1-6.
When you want to know how to be saved, call John 3:1-21.
When you're dealing with fear, call Psalm 34:7.
When you've tried and failed, call 1 Peter 5:6-10.
When you're struggling with temptation, call 1 Corinthians 10:7-12.
When a believer sins against you, call Matthew 18:15-17.
When your prayers are growing narrow or selfish, call Psalm 67:1-7.
When you're mourning the loss of a loved one, call John 14:1-3,27.
When you need an injection of worship to lift your spirits, call Psalm 150:1-6.
When you feel weak, call Isaiah 40:29-31.
When self pride takes hold, call Psalm 19:1-14.
When you're bitter and critical, call 1 Corinthians 13:1-13.
When you want to live by the Spirit, call Galatians 5:13-26.
For how to get along with others, call Romans 12:9-21.
When God seems far away, call Psalm 139:1-24.
When you want courage for a task, call Joshua 1:1-9.
When you're afraid of ridicule, call Proverbs 29:25.
When you can't forgive someone, call Matthew 18:21-35.
When the world seems bigger than God, call Psalm 90:1-16.
When you worry, call Matthew 6:25-34.
When you're going on a journey, call Psalm 121:1-8.
And when you're lonely and fearful, call Psalm 23:1-6.

Use these numbers whenever you need to. You can dial direct. The lines to heaven are always open. As God says, "Call to me and I will answer you . . ." Jeremiah 33:3.

YOUR DECISION
DETERMINES YOUR DESTINY

Here's a ludicrous story. A man named Fred inherited $10,000,000. The will provided that he had to accept his inheritance in Chile or Brazil. He chose Brazil. Unhappily, it turned out that in Chile he would have received land on which uranium, gold, and silver had just been discovered. Once in Brazil he had to choose between receiving his inheritance in coffee or nuts. He chose the nuts. Too bad! The bottom fell out of the nut market, and coffee went up to $1.30 a pound wholesale, unroasted. Poor Fred lost everything he had to his name.

In order to fly back to the States he went out and sold his gold watch for the money he needed. He had enough for a ticket to either New York or Boston. He chose Boston. When the plane for New York taxied up, he noticed it was a brand-new 747 jet with red carpets and chic people and wine-popping hostesses. Then the plane for Boston arrived. It was a 1928 Ford tri-motor with a sway back and it took a full day to get off the ground. It was filled with crying children and tethered goats. Over the Andes one of the engines fell off.

Fred made his way to the captain and said, "I'm a jinx on this plane. Let me out if you want to save your lives. Give me a parachute." The pilot agreed, but added, "On this plane, anybody who bales out must wear two chutes." So Fred jumped out of the plane, and as he fell dizzily through the air he tried to make up his mind as to which ripcord he should pull. Finally, he chose the one on the left. It was rusty and the wire pulled loose. So he pulled the other ripcord. This chute opened, but its shroud lines snapped.

In desperation the poor fellow cried out, "St. Francis save me!" A great hand from heaven reached down and seized the poor fellow by the wrist and held him dangling in mid air. Then a gentle but inquisitive voice asked, "St. Francis Xavier or St. Francis of Assisi?"

What a farce. Yet we relate to Fred because we know what it's like to make a wrong choice, to have crucial decisions turn sour, to see our dreams go awry or our plans go belly up.

That's a fact of life. The choices we make either advance our cause or leave us stranded. Our decisions determine our destiny.

So how can we make wise decisions?

It starts by recognising that God isn't limited by circumstances. Which means we must make decisions by considering them in the light of whom we are in Him and not as a result of the circumstances we find ourselves in. In other words, remember to look to God, not your circumstances, when you make a decision.

Secondly, the counsel we receive influences our decisions. Which means we must watch out for negative advice and be on guard against ungodly pessimists or carnal counsel. Never listen to people with a narrow or minimal view of God. One unsurrendered believer can set you on the wrong path and just a few unspiritual people can obstruct the good things God wants to accomplish in your life.

Thirdly, you can't make a wise decision if you aren't prepared to count the cost. Life isn't safer when we retreat. There's a price to be paid in making a decision. Appreciate that to accomplish much you need to sacrifice much. For success runs uphill. There will be times when there's no reaping without weeping. As Dwight D. Eisenhower said, "There are no victories at bargain prices."

So look for your security inside the will of God. Turn to Him in humble dependance. Listen to the counsel of godly, optimistic people. And see the possibilities of God within your circumstances. For when you do these things God will help you overcome life's challenges and bless you with His very best.

THE UNSEEN PEOPLE

In 1992, while attending Ontario Theological Seminary, I was honoured to receive the Watkins Roberts Memorial Fellowship in Missions and Development. As a result I had the privilege of working under the auspices of the Christian Children's Fund of Canada and conducting a research thesis on *The Development of Education in the Eastern Caribbean*.

It was a once in a lifetime experience. I had the joy of meeting and working with a number of wonderful people in Antigua and Barbuda, St Kitts and Nevis, Dominica, St Vincent and the Grenadines, and Grenada.

My mission was to identify the islanders who were most in need of relief and development assistance. One such group was the Carib Indians. The Caribs inhabited the islands before the European explorers arrived. They were originally fierce warlike people who resisted colonization well into the eighteenth century. Today there are no true Caribs left as they have mixed with people who originally hailed from Africa, Europe, India and South America. Despite this interbreeding there is still a distinct group known as the Caribs due to the fact that they display unique facial features and skin colouring that clearly reveals their heritage.

One community of Caribs live in a rural village named Sandy Bay. It's located in the north eastern portion of St. Vincent and is bordered by the ocean on its eastern flank and by the slopes of La Soufriere volcano to the west. It's completely off the beaten track. The only way to get to it is along a treacherous coastal road that hugs the shoreline on the windward side of the island. Which means these people are basically unseen.

The statistical office in Kingstown estimated the population in Sandy Bay to be three-thousand-three-hundred people (1990). The community represents a minority group on the island who have suffered political isolation, economic neglect and social alienation. Their living conditions leave much to be desired. At the time of my visit the region had no electricity, no telephones, and no proper health facilities. There was no residential doctor but a permanent nurse and a rudimentary clinic existed. Some people lived in reasonable accommodation but many lived in shanties constructed from boards, plastic, and galvanised iron sheeting. Overcrowding was evident and the people appeared apathetic, frustrated and bored. Some sectors of Sandy Bay had no sewerage disposal system of any kind, not even pit latrines. The children played in the excrement and garbage which lay between the homes and along the beach.

It was pitiful. But that's not surprising. The average earnings were $37 US per month for a family with 5 to 7 children. On top of that 5 to 10% of the population were addicted to drugs that were smuggled in by boat from St. Lucia and an additional 15% had serious problems with alcoholism. As a result the people had such a low sense of self esteem they were virtually unable to help themselves.

That's how it is for people trapped in poverty. And that's why I'm bringing them to your attention. For the Word of God says "that we should continue to remember the poor" Galatians 2:10. So do that now. Take time to think and pray. Consider practical ways in which you can make a difference. There is so much you can do. You can volunteer at a soup kitchen; serve in a shelter for the homeless; collect food and clothing for distribution by the Salvation Army; go on a short term missions trip to assist those in need; financially support a child through Christian Children's Fund of Canada, World Vision, or some other Christian organisation; or maybe even go to Sandy Bay and help turn things around. The important thing is that you "continue to remember the poor."

In the words of a Caribbean poet:

> "Ilan' life ain' no fun less ya treat errybody
> Like ya brudder, ya sister, or ya frien'
> Love ya neighbour, play ya part,
>   jes remember das de art
> For when ocean fence ya in, all is kin."

DANGER IN GOOD TIMES

It seems that many of our problems have come about as a result of progress. As we've tried to build a better world we've ended up with all sorts of added burdens. Despite the advantages of dish washers, antibiotics and pest resistant crops we also have ozone depletion, nuclear weapons, shrinking natural habitats and carcinogens without number.

The late Bruno Bettelheim remarks: "Never before have so many had it so good; no longer do we tremble in fear of sickness or hunger, of hidden evils in the dark, of the spell of witches. The burden of killing toil has been lifted from us, and machines, not the labour of our hands, will soon provide us with nearly all we need. We have inherited freedoms man has striven after for centuries. Because of all this and much more we should be living in a dawn of great promise. But now that we are freer to enjoy life, we are deeply frustrated in our disappointment that the freedom and comfort, sought with such deep desire, do not give meaning and purpose to our lives."

Very true. We live in an era of unprecedented prosperity and social progress. Yet the most technologically advanced countries are also the ones most plagued by drug addiction, divorce, suicide, alcoholism, abortion, and increasing crime.

But I'm not surprised. Beyond short term pleasures and shallow thrills, this world has nothing to give. Materialism is a dead end and hedonism is no different. Beneath the surface you discover that no matter what life offers, there's a certain discontentment, just because it's ours for the taking.

What can be done? How can we deal with discontentment?

We must acknowledge our limits and subject ourselves to God's rule. For the meaning of life isn't in life, it's outside of it - it's in the worship of God.

There you have it. The stark solution to disillusionment and discontentment is when we put God first, when we worship the Creator instead of our creation, and when we make the invisible kingdom more important than the visible kingdom. This is the only thing that's ultimately worthwhile. God must be number One. "The chief end of man is to glorify God." Which means the facts and fabric of this world cannot be the end of the matter. We must "fear God and keep his commandments, for this is the whole duty of man. For God will bring every deed into judgment, including every hidden thing, whether it is good or evil" Ecclesiastes 12:13-14.

"THE CRY OF THE BLOOD"

I never read obituary notices in the newspaper. That may seem odd. Especially as pastors have the responsibility of caring for the bereaved and conducting funerals for the departed. But the truth of the matter is, I'm more concerned with reaching the living than despatching the dead. That's not to say I have no compassion for people who've lost a loved one. Far from it. It's just that my energies are directed to matters of life, not death.

That's how God's wired me. He's called me to the prophetic task of warning the wicked to turn from sin and save their lives. I can't do anything else. I'm conscripted, compelled, and constrained. For I know God will hold me accountable for the blood of the not yet believers if I haven't used my life to make every effort to dissuade sinners from their evil ways. Which is why I've got no time to read the obituaries. I've only got one life to live and I'm trying to use every minute of it to reach sinners before they die. But then, I've heard "the cry of the blood."

That's the reality of my life. I live in the shadow of Ezekiel 3:17-19 which says, "So hear the word I speak and give them warning from me. When I say to a wicked man, 'You will surely die,' and you do not warn him or speak out to dissuade him from his evil ways in order to save his life, that wicked man will die for his sin, and I will hold you accountable for his blood. But if you do warn the wicked man and he does not turn from his wickedness or from his evil ways, he will die for his sin; but you will have saved yourself."

I'm not alone. Others have heard "the cry of the blood." Consider Amy Carmichael's *Things As They Are:*

The tom-toms thumped on all night, and the darkness shuddered round me like a living, feeling thing. I could not go to sleep, so I lay awake and looked; and I saw, and it seemed like this:

That I stood on a grassy sward, and at my feet a precipice broke sheer down into infinite space. I looked but saw no bottom: only cloud shapes, black and furiously coiled, and great shadow-shrouded hollows and unfathomable depths. Back I drew, dizzy at the depth.

Then I saw forms of people moving single-file along the grass. They were making for the edge. There was a woman with a baby in her arms and another little child holding onto her dress. She was on the very verge. Then I saw that she was blind.

She lifted her foot for the next step . . . it trod air. She was over, and the children over with her. Oh, the cry as they went over!

Then I saw more streams of people flowing from all quarters. All were blind, stone blind; all made straight for the precipice edge. There were shrieks as they suddenly knew themselves falling, and a tossing up of helpless arms, catching, clutching at empty air. But some went over quietly and fell without a sound.

Then I wondered, with a wonder that was simply agony, why no one stopped them at the edge. I could not. I was glued to the ground, and I could not call. Though I strained and tried, only a whisper would escape my lips.

Then I saw that along the edge there were sentries set at intervals. But the intervals were far too great; there were wide, unguarded gaps between. And over these gaps the people fell in their blindness, quite unwarned; and the green grass seemed blood red to me, and the gulf yawned like the mouth of Hell.

Then I saw, like the picture of peace, a group of people under some trees, with their backs turned toward the gulf. They were making daisy chains. Sometimes when a piercing shriek cut the quiet air and reached them it disturbed them and they thought it a rather vulgar noise. And if one of their number started up and wanted to go and do something to help, then all the others would pull that one down. "Why should you get so excited about it? You must wait for a definite 'call' to go. You haven't finished your daisy chains. "It would be really selfish," they said, "to leave us to finish the work alone."

There was another group. It was made up of people whose great desire was to get some sentries out; but they found that very few wanted to go, and sometimes there were no sentries for miles and miles at the edge.

Once a girl stood alone in her place, waving the people back; but her mother and other relations called and reminded her that her furlough was due; she must not break the 'rules'. And, being tired and needing a change, she had to go and rest awhile; but no one was sent to guard her gap, and over and over the people fell, like a waterfall of souls.

Once a child caught at a tuft of grass that grew at the very brink of the gulf: the child clung convulsively, and it called but nobody seemed to hear. Then the roots of the grass gave way, and with a cry the child went over, its two little hands still holding tight to the torn off bunch of grass. And the girl who longed to be back in her gap thought she heard the little one cry, and she sprang up and wanted to go; at which her relatives reproved her, reminding her that no one is that necessary. Anyway the gap would be well taken care of, they knew. And they sang a hymn.

Then through the hymn came another sound like the pain of a million broken hearts wrung out in one full drop, one sob. And a horror of great darkness was upon me, for I knew what it was - the cry of the blood.

Then thundered a Voice, the voice of the Lord; and He said. "Whom shall I send, and who will go for us?" Then said I; "Send me." And He said, "Go and tell this people . . . Jesus said, "Go into all the world and preach the good news to all creation . . . and I will be with you always." (Isaiah 6:8; Mark 16:15; Matthew 28:20).

THE ULTIMATE CONNECTION

What's superior to the telephone, better than E-mail, outclasses radio, and surpasses even a direct satellite link? On top of that, what has a free sign up, doesn't need operator assistance, is cordless, has crystal clear connections, instant messaging, unlimited minutes, no age requirement, world wide accessibility, secure lines, never breaks down, is open 24 hours a day, and can be described as nothing short of the ultimate in wireless communication?

The answer - prayer. It's the ultimate connection. The *ne plus ultra*. The best universal network this world has ever known.

And yet it seems to be a well-kept secret. It's not listed on the stock exchange. It's not advertised on T.V. The newspapers don't say much about it. Many schools have banned it. The opposition has pooh-poohed it. And a whole lot of people have never even given it a try.

Which is somewhat surprising when you look at its track record. Down through the ages when people have prayed, amazing and supernatural things have happened. The poor have been fed, the sick have been healed, the anxious have discovered peace, broken relationships have been reconciled and restored, the foolish have been made wise, the sorrowful filled with joy, wars have been averted, the weary have been sustained, barren women have conceived, the troubled have been counseled, the lost have been found, the weak made strong, and in a few unique situations the dead have been brought back to life.

But that's not surprising. For unlike any other communication device, prayer is a direct line to God. It transcends every other form of networking. It draws together the human and the divine. It's a person to Person call. And, as a result, it moves the Hand which moves the world.

So why not use it today? It's not complicated. It's easier than a telephone. You don't need a special format or recipe. The posture of your body isn't important. You don't need any unique language or grammatical ability. You can talk out loud or say it in your mind. And you don't even have to close your eyes or go to a holy place. All you need is the faith to do it!

Did I say faith? Yes, all you need is the faith to do it. Which, as we well know, is where the rubber hits the road. For you will never be able to pray without faith. Faith and prayer go together. Without faith your prayers will be nothing more than an engaged signal. Not that God's engaged. He's always ready to talk and listen to you. The problem is that without faith you're engaged.

Which brings me to the free sign up. If you want the phenomenal advantages of prayer, you need the faith to hook up. And in order to have the faith to hook you up you need to be "sure of what we hope for and certain of what we do not see" Hebrews 11:1. That's not as difficult as it seems. Romans 10:17 tells us that "faith comes from hearing the message, and the message is heard through the word of Christ." And what is the word of Christ? The word of Christ is that God loves you, sent His Son to die for your sins, and that everyone who calls on the name of the Lord and trusts in Him, will be saved (cf. Romans 10:6-13).

There you have it. Once you have faith you have access to God through prayer. You're signed up, hooked in, connected day and night. Which means He will always hear when you call (cf. Psalm 4:3). And He will always listen when you cry out (cf. Psalm 55:17).

So enjoy prayer. Speak as long as you like. Use it every day. And make it a habit to keep the line open. For prayer is the ultimate connection - the summit of communication.

FROM MY HEART

Over the years I've kept a journal. The goal has been to use this discipline to expand my relationship with God. I'm pleased I've done it. Journaling has helped me fixate on paper the stream of thoughts that the Spirit drops into my heart and mind. It's also helped me view things with a measure of objectivity. I find that when I get my thoughts down on paper I'm no longer trapped within my own subjectivity. That's why I recommend it. For in the act of writing I've discovered how my attention is channelled, my reflection cultivated, and my understanding deepened.

But I wasn't intending to tell you about why I journal. What I had in mind was to share some discoveries from my personal reflections in the hope that they'll bless you. So with no particular theme in mind, here are some extracts from my journal:

Being an authentic Christian demands that I honour my heritage as a pilgrim. The moment I strive to live permanently I have delayed the sacred journey. For, like the Israelites in the Exodus from Egypt, I must pass through the desert before reaching the Promised Land; I must live in a tent before dwelling in a mansion; I must stay on the move before settling in the New Jerusalem.

Kingdom builders must also be Kingdom defenders. One hand for work and one hand for war (cf. Nehemiah 4:16-18).

No matter where I search, where I turn, and what I discover; I'm destitute without Christ.

Our worst enemies are within us.

God's will is revealed when I yield the right to be right.

The world says, "Improve yourself." The Bible essentially says, "Crucify self." (cf. Galatians 2:20; Ephesians 4:22-24).

God, the Supreme Artist, created a masterpiece of grace when He painted the cross as the central motif on the canvas of human history.

When you're up - don't lose your head, and, when you're down - don't lose your heart.

Faith is revealed in the depths, rather than the shallows of life. It is only when a drowning man recognises his predicament that he cries out to the Rescuer (consider the story of Jonah).

You'll never see Jesus if you're looking at yourself.

Our world has many performance heroes but desperately needs character heroes.

Reflecting on Genesis 19 - When we constantly glance over our shoulder, we run the risk of turning into pillars of longing and regret, but when we look ahead vistas of hope and freedom are revealed.

A prayer of consecration: Father God, give me I pray: feet that will follow You; hands that will help others; lips that will know limits; a tongue that teaches truth; and a heart that always hopes. Amen.

FEARFULLY AND WONDERFULLY MADE

When my wife Karen thinks back to her kindergarten class of 1996, she remembers one student in particular - Shannon. Karen will tell you that this little girl was "a source of real encouragement." She was one of the "brightest and chattiest in the class, a delight, a blessing, and a very precious girl." Yet before Shannon was born the doctors had wanted to abort her. This is her story:

Tracy was just a few months pregnant when she had her first scan and discovered her baby had a severe case of congenital hydrocephalus (water on the brain). The condition was so bad the doctors informed Tracy that unless they aborted the baby she would have a non functioning child that would be deaf, blind, and unable to talk and walk. However, Tracy refused to have her baby aborted and insisted on going to full term.

It was a brave decision. When Shannon was born by Caesarean section on the 27th of September 1989 there were a number of complications. Brain tissue was protruding from her skull which had to be surgically removed. The doctors also had to perform a ventricular peritoneal shunt to drain the fluid in the brain cavity. Miraculously Shannon pulled through these operations yet the doctors were still convinced that she would be abnormal. Tracy was told that she shouldn't expect the child to function as a human being. But Tracy refused to give up. She wouldn't accept the harsh prognosis and continued to call on God to heal her daughter.

God answered these prayers and the doctors were soon marveling as Shannon went from strength to strength despite a number of epileptic fits. Tracy kept on praying. By the time Shannon was seven her seizures had stopped and CT-scans displayed "no physical ailments!"

This is not to say that Shannon didn't have some hurdles ahead. She had delayed milestones and a squint that needed to be corrected. Nonetheless, Shannon will probably complete her schooling. Tests reveal that she has an above average language ability and an earnest desire to learn. Yes, the "Shannon's" of this world are "fearfully and wonderfully made."

Isn't that tremendous? It reminds us of Psalm 139:13-16 where we read; "For you created my inmost being; you knit me together in my mother's womb. I praise you because I am fearfully and wonderfully made; your works are wonderful, I know that full well. My frame was not hidden from you when I was made in the secret place. When I was woven together in the depths of the earth, your eyes saw my unformed body. All the days ordained for me were written in your book before one of them came to be."

THE 3 C'S OF MARRIAGE

Socrates once advised a young man, "By all means get married. If you get a good wife, you will be happy. If you get a bad one, you'll become a philosopher!" Which explains why I'll never be a philosopher . . .

Here are 3 C's for a successful Christian marriage:

Marriage begins and continues when there's **COMMITMENT**. Faithfulness to one partner is essential. You've got to hang in and hang out but never hang up. When Mr. and Mrs. Henry Ford celebrated their golden wedding anniversary, a reporter asked them, "To what do you attribute your fifty years of successful married life?" "The formula is the same one I've used in making cars," said Ford. "Just stick to one model!" That's sound advice. Marriage is for keeps - nothing less. Too many people go into marriage too lightly. You must be true to your spouse through thick and thin. You've got to be in it for the long haul. It isn't something you can contemplate getting out of at any minute. When the going gets tough the tough stay put. They stick to one model - for life. There are always going to be grounds for divorce, what you have to keep finding are grounds for marriage. God's Word is clear, "Therefore what God has joined together, let man not separate" Matthew 19:6.

COMMUNICTION. Most of us understand the importance of it but few of us are adept at it. Even though words are my stock in trade, they fail me when my wife says, "Do you think I look fat?" If you know nothing of fear then you've never had to answer this question. The moment I hear it I break out in a sweat. For I know that if I say "no," it means "yes." If I say "yes," it means "yes." If I try to be smart and say, "It all depends on a person's point of view," it means "yes." If I reply with a question and ask, "What do you mean by fat?" I've as good as cooked my goose. And if I have a facial tic, a slight shifting of the eyes, or even a little smile, Karen will say, "I know what you're thinking!"

It can get worse. A woman went to a marriage counsellor for help. She said, "I'm fed up with my husband and think I should sue for divorce." "Do you have grounds?" asked the counsellor. "I have two acres on the other side of town," replied the woman. "Do you have a grudge?" asked the counsellor. "I have a carport for my car," said the woman. "Does your husband beat you up?" asked the counsellor. "I'm up an hour and a half before he is every morning," replied the woman. The counsellor asked, "Why are you considering a divorce?" "Because I can't communicate with him," said the woman.

Which illustrates how men and women are different. We think differently, feel differently, and see things differently. These differences will only be overcome when we learn to hit the "mute" button and master the art of listening. For a successful marriage is directly influenced by our ability to listen. As an old Spanish proverb puts it, "Two great talkers will not travel far together." James agrees. If he was a marriage counselor today, I'm sure he'd say that "everyone should be quick to listen, slow to speak and slow to become angry" James 1:19.

But commitment and communication, in and of themselves will never be enough to hold a marriage together without **CHRIST**. For it is Christ, and Christ alone, who supplies everything we need to love one another with a love that will endure to the end. Paul spells it out saying: "Submit to one another out of reverence for Christ. Wives submit to your husbands as to the Lord. For the husband is the head of the wife as Christ is the head of the church, his body, of which he is the Saviour. Now as the church submits to Christ, so also wives should submit to their husbands in everything. Husbands, love your wives, just as Christ loved the church and gave himself up for her . . ." Ephesians 5:21-25.

GOD'S PROTECTION

The day started like most other days. I began with devotions and enjoyed reading Psalm 91. As I closed my Bible and proceeded with the work for the day I was unaware that what I had read would soon come true.

It was harvest time at our farm, Murray's Brae, in Kwazulu-Natal. Pulling on my work clothes I went out to the workshop, collected a ladder, and set off to pick avocados in a tree near the water tower. I soon had the 24-foot ladder in place and had just climbed to the top when the ladder snapped in half. Despite the speed with which these mishaps happen everything seemed to occur in slow motion. For as I fell my body was "caught" in the air and gently laid down in the dirt below. That's the only way I can describe it. I was deposited flat on my back and there was no pain at all. No broken bones, no scratches, and I wasn't even winded. Without a moments hesitation I stood up, brushed myself off, and said, "Thanks Lord." For I knew without any measure of a doubt that I had just been "caught" by the angels and carefully lowered to the ground.

Later that same day I was in a pasture checking on the cattle when a night adder crossed the path directly in front of me. Although a bite from a night adder doesn't usually cause death in an adult, the venom can nonetheless cause severe localized pain and swelling. I was in a dangerous situation. Apart from open sandals my feet and bare legs were unprotected. Yet I felt no fear. Without hesitation I crushed the viper's head beneath my heel.

On the way back to the farmhouse I was deep in thought about the incident when I nearly stepped on a second night adder. It was unbelievable! It seemed as if they were out to get me. For night adders, as indicated by their name, are usually nocturnal. But that's neither here nor there. The important thing is I once again managed to trample the snake to death before it could strike.

Some would say it was just my lucky day. I disagree. Luck had nothing to do with it. God protected me. Psalm 91:9-13 tells it like it is, "If you make the Most High your dwelling - even the Lord, who is my refuge - then no harm will befall you, no disaster will come near your tent. For he will command his angels concerning you to guard you in all your ways; they will lift you up in their hands, so that you will not strike your foot against a stone. You will tread upon the lion and the cobra, you will trample the great lion and the serpent."

MONEY . . .

Money . . .

It can buy you a house, but not a home. It can buy you a bed, but not sleep. It can buy you a clock, but not time. It can buy you an education, but not wisdom. It can buy you a book, but not brains. It can buy you finery, but not beauty. It can buy you food, but not an appetite. It can buy you luxuries, but not culture. It can buy you a position, but not honour. It can buy you a vacation, but not satisfaction. It can buy you entertainment, but not happiness. It can buy you medicine, but not health. It can buy you blood, but not life. It can buy you sex, but not love. It can buy you companions, but not friends. It can buy you flattery, but not respect. It can buy you power, but not character. It can buy you security, but not salvation.

For money isn't everything. Things that really matter can't be bought. "But godliness with contentment is great gain. For we brought nothing into the world, and we can take nothing out of it. But if we have food and clothing, we will be content with that. People who want to get rich fall into temptation and a trap and into many foolish and harmful desires that plunge men into ruin and destruction. For the love of money is a root of all kinds of evil" 1 Timothy 6:6-10.

So for your own sake, and His sake, "Keep your lives free from the love of money and be content with what you have" Hebrews 13:5.

HUNGRY
FOR MORE

I have to admit my hunger exceeds my intake. I'm always wanting more. I'm never fully satisfied. I'm discontent with my diet. I have an emptiness that's never satiated. And I'm tired of surviving on food that's sometimes tasteless and bland. Yes, I'm hungry for more. I want to feast at a banquet table. I want to eat the finest fare. And I want to enjoy the very best of gastronomic delights.

That's not to say that I don't appreciate my wife's cooking. She's an excellent cook. The problem isn't in the kitchen. . . . It's in the church! We seem to be content with crumbs. We're prepared to dine on yesteryear's diet. And we've chosen to pass around a tattered plastic menu with faded images describing stale food.

No wonder people are settling for TV dinners and other fast foods. In a desperate attempt to fill their stomachs people are flocking to seminars on inner peace and self actualization. They're spending millions of dollars on a diet of popular psychology, psychic channeling and astrology. Desperate for hope, in need of nourishment, people will eat anything. They convince themselves that the canned script of paid marketers is spiritual insight. They stuff themselves with the rations of fake soothsayers, and some folk even attempt to feed on the words of mediums and channelers who tap the dark world of the occult. Oh, the depth of spiritual hunger!

Which makes one wonder. How can this be? Why are so many people feeding on the counterfeit? Why will people swallow the junk food that's passed off as a staple diet? And why do we stop short of consuming a decent meal?

Maybe it's because we're not really hungry. Maybe we've come to believe that we're full and content. Maybe our churches don't lay out a banquet anymore. Maybe we're willing to simply share the crumbs of a past visitation from God. Maybe we've settled for political correctness and tradition rather than a fresh outpouring of God's Spirit. Maybe we've chosen to "eat the bread of idleness" (Proverbs 31:27) rather than the bread that sustains the heart (cf. Psalm 104:15). And maybe we've become so accustomed to surviving on a beggars lunch we no longer know the difference between a fresh loaf and a mouldy crust!

That's why I'm hungry for more. That's why I hunger and thirst for righteousness (cf. Matthew 5:6). That's why I want to feast on God and be filled. And that's why I believe it's time for Christians to call on God to open the floodgates of heaven so that manna may fall and feed the spiritually hungry of our land.

So join me in prayer. Pray for God to pour out the "bread of life" (John 6:35) so that everybody can eat at God's table. And make it your obsession to pursue a God induced hunger for the bread of His presence. For, when all is said and done, Jesus tells us that we should "not work for food that spoils, but for food that endures to eternal life" John 6:27.

"Free me from snack-time devotion
from earth-style portions too small
to satisfy a Saviour-saved soul.

Withdraw my plate, remove my silverware
until I sup at the table prepared
in my enemies' presence -
starve me until I hunger only for You."

Mark Phillips.

HOW TO FIND HAPPINESS

One of mankind's great quests, is for happiness. Some seek it by pursuing peace and security. Some search for it in the acquisition of wealth and material benefits. Others hope to find it by procuring power and prestige.

There are countless examples of how the quest for happiness has ended in failure. Jay Gould, the American millionaire, was on his death bed when he said, "I suppose I am the most miserable man on earth." The French revolutionary, Voltaire, came to the end of his life and declared, "I wish I had never been born." Lord Byron lived a life of pleasure and ended up saying, "The worm, the canker and the grief are mine alone."

Another man went to his psychiatrist and said, "Doctor, I am lonely, despondent, and miserable. Can you help me?" The doctor told the man that the best cure for his depression was to go to the circus and see a famous clown who was reputed to make even the most miserable laugh with merriment. The man replied, "I am that clown."

No wonder a retired President of Harvard University said, "The world is searching for a creed to believe and a song to sing." Yes, many people are searching for happiness and few are finding it. If this is your quest, read on and discover three essentials for happiness:

The first essential for happiness is to trust in Jesus Christ. Happiness will delude you if you don't trust in God, for happiness isn't found in possessions or practices, but found in a person - in the Lord Jesus Christ. Thus happiness comes when we let God have His way with us, when we stop fighting with God, when we embrace Jesus in simple faith. As it says in the Bible, "Blessed is he who trusts in the Lord" and "blessed is he whose . . . hope is in the Lord his God" Proverbs 16:20; Psalm 146:5.

The second essential for happiness is to endure for Jesus Christ. Some people start out with God but then they turn their back on Him and refuse to persevere. If you choose to reject God then you run the risk of happiness becoming an elusive dream. The Bible says, "We consider blessed those who have persevered" James 5:11. Thus happiness comes when we hang in with God, when we keep on trusting in God despite setbacks, when we don't give up, when we keep on keeping on.

The third essential for happiness is to work for Jesus Christ. Someone once said, "The secret of true happiness is to do a little kindness to someone every day." Thus to be happy, you need to be helping the needy. You need to be serving one another in love. You need to be "rich in good deeds" (1 Timothy 6:18) and bringing some sunshine into the lives of others. This is confirmed in Proverbs 14:21 when it states, "Blessed is he who is kind to the needy."

It's that simple! You'll find happiness when you trust in Jesus, endure for Jesus and work for Jesus. Why not put it to the test?

IN CONFLICT

When I started teaching in 1982, at Greenside High School, I could barely make ends meet but was hanging on because I'd been promised a salary increase and was looking forward to buying a car audio system. Then we had a staff meeting and the principal told us we wouldn't be getting the increments we'd expected. Boy, was I upset. For months I'd been contemplating a drive down the freeway to the beat of Keith Green or Petra. Now it was just a pipe-dream.

A week later I was still fuming about how my rotten salary wasn't even enough for a "basic necessity" like a sound system when one of my grade twelve students came up to chat with me. "Sir," he began. "I notice your car doesn't have a radio and tape deck." "Everyone knows that!" I said somewhat sarcastically. "Well I was wondering if you'd like me to get you one Sir?" "Listen Sean. It's good of you to offer but I don't have any spare cash." "Oh! But it wouldn't cost much Sir. I can get you one for 10 percent of the price of a new system!" "What! That's impossible! Where do you get them from?" "Well Sir, you probably don't want to know the answer to your question but the bottom line is I can get you a really great system for next to nothing. So how about it?"

Needless to say it was a tempting offer. Obviously Sean was fencing stolen goods but I desperately wanted the system and for a few days I fought a tremendous inner conflict. It was a case of "the sinful nature (desiring) what is contrary to the Spirit, and the Spirit what is contrary to the sinful nature. They (were) in conflict with each other" Galatians 5:17.

Now this was no small conflict. It raged on and on. It gave me restless nights and it was even worse when I drove past another car with music blaring out and the occupant singing along. But a few years previously I'd accepted Christ as my Saviour and now I was having to learn that "those who belong to Christ Jesus have crucified the sinful nature with its passions and desires" Galatians 5:24. So because I was living "by the Spirit" I kept "in step with the Spirit" Galatians 5:25 and turned Sean's offer down.

Similarly, when temptation comes your way "live by the Spirit, and you will not gratify the desires of the sinful nature" Galatians 5:16.

BASICS FOR FATHERS

"The Lord delights in the way of the man whose steps he has made firm;
though he stumble, he will not fall, for the Lord upholds him with his hand"
Psalm 37:23-24.

According to statistics we have more children growing up without a father than we've ever had before. Margaret Philp of the *Globe and Mail* reports that a quarter of Canadian children are not living with their natural fathers and as a result "a growing absence of fathers from the lives of Canadian children is spawning a generation at far greater risk of juvenile delinquency, broken marriages, dropping out of school and becoming teen-aged parents than ever before." This problem isn't restricted to Canada. Countries around the world have all manner of socioeconomic problems as a result of absentee fathers.

That's something we should be deeply concerned about. It's obvious that the presence or absence of a father in the life of a child plays a vital role. As John Nicholson says, "The quality of a child's relationship with his or her father seems to be the most important influence in deciding how that person will react to the world."

Did you get that? If you're a dad you can single handedly make or break your child. Your actions play a vital part in his or her future. And therefore, what you do or don't do is one of the most important factors in determining whom your child becomes.

With these thoughts in mind here are two basics for fathers:

Before anything else a father should teach his children to love God. Deuteronomy 6:4-7 says, "The Lord our God, the Lord is one. Love the Lord your God with all your heart and with all your soul and with all your strength. These commandments that I give you today are to be upon your hearts. Impress them on your children. Talk about them when you sit at home and when you walk along the road, when you lie down and when you get up." Thus, the most significant contribution a father can make to his children is to love God and to teach his children to do the same. This is where fathering begins. A father must use every opportunity every day to teach his children the priority of following hard after God. This teaching should be through a diligent use of words, by writing, and with a godly example that flows out of a father's personal commitment to the Lord. After all, it stands to reason that the more important something is to a child's development the more the father should be directly involved in the content.

A father must also teach his children to love people. Our children are in the midst of a world marred by social strife, sardonic sectarianism, racial hatred, religious feuding, revolutionary upheavals and interpersonal relationships that are tainted by fits of rage, ridicule, revenge seeking, and other forms of revolting behaviour. They see the pictures of death and violence that flash across our television screens. And they encounter all manner of relational conflict each and every day. That's why fathers are needed to make a difference. Fathers must be role models of love in an unloving world. Fathers must hold people in high esteem, be patient, kind, not proud, not rude, not self seeking, not easily angered, and keeping no record of wrongs (cf. 1 Corinthians 13:4-7). For more is caught than taught. When fathers start being men of love their children will emulate their example. When a father shows respect and appreciation for his fellow man, his children will follow suit. And when a father puts other peoples interests before his own, his children will do the same. For children learn to walk by watching the steps their fathers take.

An anonymous poet wrote:

> "There are little eyes upon you,
> and they're watching night and day;
> There are little ears that quickly take in
> every word you say;
> There are little hands all eager to do everything you do.
> And a little boy who's dreaming of the day
> he'll be like you.
> You're the little fellow's idol,
> you're the wisest of the wise,
> In his little mind about you,
> no suspicions ever rise;
> He believes in you devoutly, holds all that you say and do,
> He will say and do in your way
> when he's grown up to be like you.
> There's a wide-eyed little fellow
> who believes you're always right,
> And his ears are always open
> and he watches day and night;
> You are setting an example every day in all you do,
> For the little boy who's waiting to grow up to be like you."

ROLL OVER

When the word "commit" is used in God's Word it literally means "to roll over." Which reminds me of my first pet. Cromdale was a Rhodesian Ridgeback and one of the best dogs I have ever known. Although bigger and stronger than me, he would always allow me to win our wrestling bouts. I know I won because Cromdale would roll over on his back and expose his throat to indicate his submission.

That's what commitment is all about. It's about rolling over. It's about exposing our vulnerable side to God. It's about being 100% submissive to Him. By an act of our will we must "make our way His way, and make His way our way" Warren Wiersbe. We must "open up before God, keep nothing back" Eugene Peterson. It must be a case of; "Take my life and let it be, consecrated Lord to Thee . . . Take my hands and let them move at the impulse of your love . . . Take my silver and my gold. Not a mite would I withhold . . . Take my will and make it Thine. It shall be no longer mine . . ." Frances Ridley Havergal.

Alan Chapman knew how to "roll over." I met Alan after his wife Dodi had recommitted herself to the Lord. Alan and Dodi had separated due to Alan's demanding ways and Dodi eventually cracking under the strain.

Fortunately, when we're prepared to allow God to have His way, the impossible becomes possible. The Holy Spirit began softening Alan's heart and the two of us began to meet for coffee at Tim Horton's. We had a number of frank discussions about the struggles in his marriage, his love for Dodi, his desire to win Dodi back, and his need for a Saviour. As our relationship developed Alan took every opportunity to question me on what it meant to be committed to the Lord Jesus Christ. He was getting close. But, not wanting him to make a commitment for the wrong reasons I cautioned him against proclaiming his devotion to Christ if his reason for doing so was to try and win Dodi back as his wife.

My caution was heeded. Over the course of the next few months Alan attended church. True to his background as an engineer he was earnest in the pursuit of truth. By now we were good friends. When we'd shake hands after I'd preached he would often say, "I'm getting closer." Sometimes I'd say to him, "Are you ready yet?" And he'd respond, "Soon, very soon."

Then, one evening, after I'd finished preaching, Alan came up to me and said, "I'm ready to 'roll over.' Can I meet you in your office this week?" I knew exactly what Alan was referring to. I'd been preaching from Psalm 37 and while commenting on verse five I'd explained what it meant to "commit your way to the Lord," by using my dog Cromdale as an illustration. Thus when Alan came in to see me on Tuesday I wasn't surprised to see the sparkle in his eye, witness the spring in his step, and hear the excitement in his voice as he told me how he had rolled over and submitted his life to the Lord Jesus Christ.

Alan was a different man. With Christ in charge everything changed. Dodi and Alan were reunited and enjoyed the best year of their married life. On New Years Eve, 31st December, 1999, I had the privilege of conducting a wedding renewal service for the Chapman's on the occasion of their 25th wedding anniversary. It was an extra special time.

But unknown to us, Alan had little time left. Just several months later, Alan died on the 4th of May 2000.

I miss Alan - but every time I remember him the memories are good. For Alan's life wasn't one that was lost - it was one that was found. Because he "rolled over" he had the joy of earthly relationships restored and eternal relationships secured.

CHECK THOSE LABELS

I'm grateful for the funny things we encounter through life. Thankful for words or actions that make us smile, appreciative of the wit and banter that cause us to laugh. After all, laughter is a divine medication, a Biblical therapy, and a God sent balm to take part of the sting out of the heavy stuff that comes our way. Which is why I look out for humour to lighten my load and why I make it a point to indulge in at least one hearty laugh every day. So join me as we consider these comic examples from actual label instructions on consumer goods:

On a Sears hair dryer: *Do not use while sleeping.*

On a bag of Fritos: *You could be a winner! No purchase necessary. Details inside.*

On a bar of Dial soap: *Directions - Use like regular soap.*

On some Swann frozen dinners: *Serving suggestion - defrost.*

On a hotel shower cap: *Fits one head.*

On Tesco's Tiramisu dessert (printed on the box bottom): *Do not turn upside down.*

On Mark's & Spencer's Bread Pudding: *Product will be hot after heating.*

On packaging for a Rowenta iron: *Caution - do not iron clothes on body.*

On Boots cough medicine for children: *Do not drive car or operate machinery.*

On Nytol sleep aid: *Warning - may cause drowsiness.*

On a Korean kitchen knife: *Warning - keep out of children.*

On a string of Chinese made Christmas lights: *For indoor or outdoor use only.*

On Sainsbury's peanuts: *Warning - contains peanuts.*

On a child's Superman costume: *Wearing of this garment does not enable you to fly.*

On an American Airlines packet of nuts: *Instructions - open packet, eat nuts.*

On a bird feeder: *Opus warranties this Top Flight Lifetime Feeder for the life time of the product.*

Now in case you're still feeling serious let me assure you that I'm not advocating something superficial or shallow. I'm concerned about something more significant. I'm concerned about exercising a God-given gift; about developing a lighter heart; about seeing how God has filled the world with things worth a laugh (here's looking at you!); about our spiritual, emotional and physical well being; and about the fact that there's "a time for everything, and a season for every activity under heaven . . . a time to weep and a time to laugh" Ecclesiastes 3:1,4.

The Christian can laugh, not because he's blind to trials and tribulations, but because he's convinced that these, in the light of eternity, are never terminal.

IT TAKES SO LITTLE

A teacher asked her class what each student wanted to become when he or she grew up. One by one they answered. One was going to be the president, another a fireman, another a teacher, and so on. Then the teacher asked Billy, "What do you want to be when you grow up?" "Possible," replied Billy. "Possible?" queried the teacher. "Yes," Billy said, "My mom is always telling me I'm impossible. So when I grow up I want to become possible."

We laugh, but we know of parents who put their children down instead of lifting them up (sometimes we're those parents). That's why we should think about what we say. For if we use words recklessly, criticizing and carping about the failings or shortcomings of our children, we'll shrivel their spirit.

So watch your words. Encourage children so they won't become "hardened by sin's deceitfulness" Hebrews 3:13. Nourish them with what you say (cf. Proverbs 10:21). Stimulate them and give them approval and help. Give them "an apt reply . . . a timely word" Proverbs 15:23. Inspire them with confidence and courage. And use your words to bring healing, health and sweetness into their lives (cf. Proverbs 16:24).

It takes so little to make a child sad,
Just a scornful word, a heartless jeer,
Just a contemptuous look on a face held dear;
And footsteps lag, though the goal is near.

It takes so little to make a child sad,
Just a caustic tongue or a wearisome glance,
Just a shoulder shrug brings sufferance;
And the spirit retreats when it could advance.

But it takes so little to make a child glad,
Just a kindly word, some heartfelt cheer,
Just a friendly look drives away the fear;
And the chest puffs up, when you draw near.

Yes, it takes so little to make a child glad,
Just a cheering clasp of a friendly hand,
Just a simple hug shows you understand;
And the child's encouraged as God has planned.

FROM TRIALS TO TRIUMPH

One of the memorable moments in my life occurred in the Kruger National Park when I watched the birth of a giraffe. I remember it as if it happened yesterday. The front hooves and head emerged first and the baby giraffe got its initial view of the world while dangling ten feet up in the air. There wasn't much time to admire the view. A few minutes later the calf was pushed out and unceremoniously dumped on its back. How it survived the fall is beyond me. It smacked down in a tangled heap of legs with such force I thought it would break every bone in its body. Then, lying in the mess of the birthing fluid, it barely had time to recover before the mother turned on it. She swung her rear leg and gave it a solid kick, sending it head over heals through the dirt. This violent process was repeated over and over again. The mother was merciless. Even as the calf struggled to get up the mother swung her long pendulous leg and sent the calf sprawling yet again.

There was method in her madness. The mother's kicks stimulated the calf's efforts and finally the calf managed to gather its legs under it and stand for the first time. I cheered enthusiastically. After all the abuse the baby giraffe had endured it was phenomenal to see it wobbling and staggering around.

The mother giraffe didn't share my sentiments. Taking aim she once again lashed out and kicked the calf off its feet. I was incensed. The savagery and brutality of the mother giraffe was unbelievable.

But my anger was rooted in ignorance. I later learnt that it's vital for the mother giraffe to treat the calf this way. In the wild the only defence a baby giraffe has against predators is its ability to get up and stay on its feet. If the calf can't do this it soon becomes a tasty meal for the lions, leopards or hyenas. Thus the mother giraffe wastes no time in teaching her calf to get up quickly and get with it. This is the most important lesson the baby giraffe will ever learn.

It's also one of the important lessons you and I must learn. For in our journey through life we will get through one trial and often be knocked down again by the next. That's life - getting up, getting knocked down, getting up, getting knocked down, and in the process, hopefully learning to grow up.

That's how God intended it to be. He never promised that life would be easy. Faith is always tested. Jesus, for example, warned His disciples, "In this world you will have trouble" John 16:33. And Paul told his converts that "We must go through many hardships to enter the kingdom of God" Acts 14:22. Yes, God never promised to take our trials away. They're part and parcel of life. It's unrealistic to expect things to always go our own way. After all, Satan and his demons fight us, the world opposes us, and bad things happen simply because we're human.

Fortunately this is only one side of the coin. On the flip side we discover a good God who promises to be with us and deliver us regardless of the cause, type, or severity of the trial that comes our way. He will never leave us or forsake us (cf. Hebrews 13:5). He is faithful and "will not let you be tempted beyond what you can bear. But when you are tempted, he will also provide a way out so that you can stand up under it" 1 Corinthians 10:13.

That's the bottom line. God uses trials to help us up. Testing works for us, not against us. He uses our distress for His glory and our benefit. John MacArthur recognizes this truth when he says, "The more we rejoice in our testings, the more we realize that they are not liabilities but privileges, ultimately beneficial and not harmful, no matter how destructive and painful the immediate experience of them might appear."

Trials aren't our enemy. They're our friends. They help us mature. For it's through trials that we draw closer to the Lord and learn to live for the things that matter most.

The story of Joseph is a fitting illustration. His brothers despised him, sold him into slavery, and along the way he was incarcerated for a crime he didn't commit. If anyone had cause to be bitter and angry it was Joseph. Yet when given the opportunity for revenge, Joseph said to his brothers, "But as for you, you meant evil against me; but God meant it for good . . ." Genesis 50:20 NKJV.

There you have it. There is triumph through trials because "in all things God works for the good of those who love him" Romans 8:28.

CASTE DIFFERENCES

In his autobiography, Mahatma Gandhi says that as a student in South Africa he was interested in the Bible. Deeply touched by the reading of the Gospels, he seriously considered becoming a convert to Christianity. From what he'd read it seemed to him that the Christian faith offered real solutions to bigotry, prejudice and pride. Full of hope he went along to church one Sunday, intent on speaking with the minister and asking for instructions on how to be saved. But when he entered the sanctuary, the ushers refused him a seat and suggested he go and worship with his own people. He left and never went back. "If Christians have caste differences also," he said to himself, "I might as well remain a Hindu."

In contrast, in 1983 in another church in South Africa, a remarkable demonstration of impartial love occurred. A service was underway when a tramp, reeking of sweat, alcohol, vomit, and marijuana, staggered down the central aisle and slumped to the floor in front of the pulpit. People were shocked and disgusted by the intrusion. The service leader faltered in mid sentence, and one lady was so nauseated by the smell she immediately moved to a seat next to a window in order to get some fresh air. Others were whispering and urging the deacons to throw the man out. But before anything could be done a dignified grey-haired gentleman got up from his seat in the back pew, walked down the aisle, and sat down next to the tramp. The two remained on the floor for the duration of the service - the one immaculate in his suit and tie, the other dishevelled and drunk. After the service the older man invited the tramp for a cup of coffee. With mugs in hand they spoke about the Gospel, and before long the tramp was converted to Christ.

It's obvious that the way we behave toward people indicates what we really believe about God. One attribute of God is His impartiality. There is no preferential treatment when God deals with us. He never shows favouritism with people and He expects His people to reflect that same impartiality (cf. Deuteronomy 10:17; James 2:1-13). Thus Christianity is about treating others the way God has treated us - with fairness and equality of privilege.

The trouble is, our natural inclination is to put one another in pigeonholes, in predetermined, stratified categories, grading by race, social status, intelligence, sporting prowess, nationality, gender, beliefs, age, ethnicity, political ideology, power, personality, wealth, and looks. Yet the type of car we drive or the type of house and neighbourhood we live in should be a non-issue. For there's no caste system with God (cf. Galatians 3:28). In His presence all earthly distinctions are null and void (cf. Colossians 3:11). Yes, favouritism is anathema with the nature of God for He's wholly and incorruptibly impartial. So let's not forget; "Whoever loves God must also love his brother" 1 John 4:21.

Yes, we all have sins to overcome
You do and I do, too.
For we make mistakes quite often
With the things we say and do.

Not one of us is perfect.
But we can make progress,
With grace and mercy attempting
To make prejudice grow less.

So may we aid each other,
Impartial striving to be.
With love and understanding
From favouritism let's flee.

THE DARWIN AWARD

There seem to be awards for everything. An award that recently caught my attention was the Darwin Award. The Darwin awards are awarded posthumously. They go to people who have managed to kill themselves in an extraordinary and stupid way. One recipient received the award after being crushed to death by a coke machine from which he was attempting to obtain a free can of pop.

But the Darwin Award that topped all awards was the one given to the mystery owner of a jet-propelled Chevy Impala. The story goes that the Arizona Highway Patrol discovered smoldering metal embedded 41 metres up the side of a cliff above a curve in the road. The wreckage resembled an airplane crash, but after the concerted efforts of a lab they discovered that the wreckage actually came from a car.

The driver had somehow got hold of a JATO unit (Jet Assisted Take Off - actually a solid fuel rocket) usually used to give heavy military transport planes an extra "push" when taking off from short runway airfields. With the JATO unit attached to his car the man ignited the unit about 8 kilometres from the crash site. Within five seconds maximum thrust was reached, causing the Chevy to hit speeds well in excess of 560 kilometres per hour and continue like that for about 20 to 25 seconds. The driver, soon to be pilot, most likely experienced G-forces such as those endured by F-14 fly-boys under full afterburners.

Somehow he kept the car on the highway for about 4 kilometres before applying and completely melting the brakes. Then the tires blew out leaving thick rubber marks across the asphalt just before the car became airborne for an additional 4 kilometres. When the car hit the cliff, it left a black crater a metre deep in the rock. Most of the driver's remains were completely unrecoverable although small fragments of bone, teeth, and hair were extracted from the crater.

What a story! It's hard to believe anyone can be so foolish. But then again, maybe it isn't. For God's Word reminds us that "the way of a fool seems right to him" and that "a fool is hotheaded and reckless" Proverbs 12:15; 14:16.

Which brings us back to the Darwin Awards. I wonder how long it will be before the panel of selectors come to the conclusion that the ultimate Darwin Award should go to the fool who "says in his heart, 'There is no God.'" Psalm 14:1.

CONFESSION

Confession of sins to each other is absolutely vital. It's insufficient to only confess your sins privately. For it's in mutual confession that we release the power that heals; that pretense is brought to an end; that we discover that we're not alone; that we catch sight of the One who takes us back to the place we wanted to be all along; that the channels of our hearts are cleared; that we recover wholeness and wellness; that we embark on good works; that we find the exhilaration of knowing God's esteem for us; that our spiritual and emotional vitality is reawakened; that we begin again to experience answers to prayer; that change begins from which revival flows; that the fog and confusion are lifted; that the direction of our life seems more certain; and that the final break through to fellowship with God and with one another occurs.

So "confess your sins to each other and pray for each other so that you may be healed" James 5:16. For "if we confess our sins, he is faithful and just and will forgive us our sins and purify us from all unrighteousness" 1 John 1:9.

> Just as I am, without one plea,
> But that Thy blood was shed for me
> And that Thou bidd'st me come to Thee.
> O Lamb of God, I come! I come!
>
> Just as I am, and waiting not
> To rid my soul of one dark blot.
> To Thee whose blood can cleanse each spot,
> O lamb of God, I come! I come!
>
> Just as I am, tho' tossed about,
> With many a conflict, many a doubt.
> Fightings within, and fears without,
> O Lamb of God, I come! I come!

Charlotte Elliott.

WHEN THE ARMOUR DOESN'T FIT

There's always something new in the familiar. The story of David and Goliath is a case in point. Having read, heard, and told the story over and over again you'd think there was nothing new for me to learn. Yet when reading it again for the umpteenth time, a fresh insight unfolded. Good stories are like that, they don't stay static, they deepen and grow, like a fine wine they mature with time.

And so it was as I read 1 Samuel 17:38-39: "Then Saul dressed David in his own tunic. He put a coat of armour on him and a bronze helmet on his head. David fastened on his sword over the tunic and tried walking around, because he was not used to them. 'I cannot go in these,' he said to Saul, 'because I am not used to them.' So he took them off."

I've never paused at this point in the story before. I've always rushed to join David as he approached the Philistine. The boy against the giant - a sling against a sword, spear and javelin. But I realise now that in my haste to get to the showdown I overlooked something important. Life can be like that if we're not careful. When we're intent on reaching a goal, we can miss the lessons along the way.

But I'm digressing. The point of this meditation is to consider what happens when the armour doesn't fit . . .

It's obvious that Saul was concerned for David. He wanted to help, and the best he could do was offer the use of his armour. No doubt it seemed like a good idea at the time. After all, these were weapons with proven effectiveness - weapons that had served Saul well. So if there was anything that would equip David for the task ahead Saul was convinced of the suitability of his weapons.

It's like that when an amateur enters the arena of the professional. There's all sorts of advice, all manner of help, loads of good intentions. There's instruction, training, and plenty of equipment. But when we become encumbered with this knowledge and experience we discover that when we try to walk we can hardly move. The armour doesn't help; it hinders. The weapons weigh us down. And thus burdened we're reduced to a stiff, awkward waddle.

That's when we need to do what David did. Although he admired Saul, served Saul, and loved Saul, it was necessary for David to walk away from Saul. The offer of help was politely refused. For David knew that if he went into battle against Goliath wearing Saul's armour he would fail - it would be a disaster.

And herein lies the lesson: You can't wear someone else's armour. A borrowed tunic never fits. A sword, even a king's sword, is useless against a giant. For battles are won when you engage the enemy using the skills and weapons with which God has made you familiar. Nothing else will do. Hand me downs will let you down.

So be true blue. Like David, trust in God and what He teaches you. Refuse to defer to the wisdom of man. Say, "No," to encumbrances. Travel light. Fear God - not Goliath. And walk into the Valley of Elah in the knowledge that little is much when God is in it.

CANADA'S GOLGOTHA

In the Canadian War Museum there's a bronze sculpture by an obscure British artist named Derwent Wood. Entitled *Canada's Golgotha,* the small bas-relief, less than a metre square, depicts a Canadian soldier crucified to the door of a barn while on-looking German soldiers mock his plight.

The origin of Canada's Golgotha goes back to the Second Battle of the Ypres. The Paris correspondent of the Morning Post reported that Canadian soldiers knew of a sergeant who was nailed to a door with bayonets and then shot. The Toronto Star of May 11, 1915, told of a Canadian sergeant lashed to a tree by his arms and legs and bayoneted 60 times. As is often the case, the story came from a second-hand witness who died in the arms of the story teller. "C. J. C. Clayton, a New Zealander who is serving with the British Red Cross and is now wounded, brings a message from Capt. R. A. Allen of the 5th Canadian Battalion, who comes from Vancouver and who died of wounds in a hospital in Boulogne May 2, confirming the horrible story of the crucifixion of a Canadian sergeant by the Germans . . ."

In commenting on the story, Canadian historian, Desmond Morton, says "It was a remarkably useful story. In a Christian age, a Hunnish enemy had proved capable of mocking Christ's agony on the cross . . . providing a means of transforming casual colonials into ruthless fighters."

But there are problems with the story. The German and Canadian governments believe the atrocity is unproven. The Imperial War Graves Commission says that Capt. Allen of the 5th Battalion died on April 30, not May 2. Furthermore, the sergeant is not identified. (A British wartime nurse pinpointed the incident and named Sgt. Harry Band of the 48th Highlanders as the victim. However, although a certain Harry Band died on April 24, 1915, with no known grave, he was a private from the 16th Regiment and not a sergeant). Yet the legend was born and has grown in the telling.

In contrast, Israel's Golgotha is a historical reality (cf. *The Works of Flavius Josephus,* Dissertation 1, p. 665). There is no doubt that the crucifixion of Jesus Christ of Nazareth actually happened. It isn't a legend or myth. "We believe that Jesus died and rose again" 1 Thessalonians 4:14. And as a result millions have banked their lives on it. As it says in God's infallible Word, "They brought Jesus to the place called Golgotha (which means The Place of the Skull). Then they offered him wine mixed with myrrh, but he did not take it. And they crucified him. Dividing up his clothes, they cast lots to see what each would get. It was the third hour when they crucified him. The written notice of the charge against him read: THE KING OF THE JEWS. They crucified two robbers with him, one on his right and one on his left" Mark 15:22-27.

Two Golgothas'; one Canadian and one Israeli, one recent and one ancient, one unproven and one proven, one designed to alienate and one designed to reconcile, one cast against the backdrop of hatred and one etched in love, one representing war and one representing peace, one largely forgotten and one ardently remembered . . .

HOW TO GET TO HEAVEN

A wise man once said that if you expect to go to heaven then you should take the trouble to learn what route will get you there. That's a good point. The trouble is *Canadian Tire* don't seem to have any maps and the people who go to heaven never come back to tell us how they got there. No wonder Lon Woodrum said, "the map of that high world is oddly traced and dim."

So how do you get to heaven? How do you find the way from this world to the place beyond this world? How do you get from this life to the afterlife without making a wrong turn? How do you travel from the seen world to the unseen world? And how do you make a trip when there seem to be no road signs to show the way?

The Bible provides directions. It tells us that "small is the gate, and narrow the road that leads to life, and only a few find it" Matthew 7:14. In other words, there is only one route to heaven - it's the **narrow road** and you can't get to heaven without getting on it.

But this raises a dilemma. Where is this narrow road? How does one find it? And how does one get onto it? For I've checked the map of Orillia where I live, even asked a few people, and everyone agrees there's no street called the narrow road.

Fortunately the Bible tells us the way. It maps the narrow road for us. And it teaches us how to get on the narrow road and stay on it. It's this simple:

1. **Realise** you are **separated** from God by your **sin.** "For all have sinned and fall short of the glory of God" Romans 3:23.

2. **Recognise** there is a **Saviour** with a **solution**. Jesus said, "I am the **way** and the truth and the life. No one comes to the Father except through me" John 14:6.

3. **Respond** to Jesus by a simple **surrender** of **self**. Three actions are needed. Firstly, *repent* of your sin. "Repent, then, and turn to God, so that your sins may be wiped out, that times of refreshing may come from the Lord" Acts 3:19. Secondly, *receive* Jesus by faith. ". . . confess with your mouth, 'Jesus is Lord,' and believe in your heart that God raised him from the dead, (and) you will be saved" Romans 10:9. Thirdly, *rejoice* in your salvation. "Rejoice in the Lord always" Philippians 4:4.

4. **Reach** out to others by **sharing** the love of the **Saviour**. Jesus said, "Go into all the world and preach the good news to all creation" Mark 16:15. For "if we love each other, God lives in us and his love is made complete in us" 1 John 4:12.

And there you have it. The narrow road to heaven, and the only road to heaven, is the road less traveled, the road of commitment and consecration to Jesus Christ, the road of salvation and sanctification in Jesus Christ, the road that starts with a surrendered heart, the road that continues with a steadfast faith, and the road that culminates in eternal life. Any other road is the broad road that leads to destruction (cf. Matthew 7:13) and many enter through it. But now you know the difference. You know how to get to heaven. So if you're not on the road to heaven then stop, make a U-turn, and keep going till you get there.

A prayer to help you find your way to heaven:

> Jesus, thank you for loving me.
>
> Thank you for providing my way to heaven. I realize I can't save myself.
>
> I know that You are the only solution.
>
> Thank you for dying for me so that I could have the gift of eternal life.
>
> Thank you for Your promise to save me when I call on Your name.
>
> Please forgive me for my sin.
>
> I turn to you in simple faith and accept Your gift of forgiveness and new life.
>
> Thank you.
>
> Amen

LOVE

A tribute to teachers. A paraphrase of 1 Corinthians 13.

I may be able to teach with eloquence and angelic rhapsody, but if I don't love my students, I'm only a fascinating entertainer or an educated actor. If I have powerful and inspired lessons and have the answer to every question, and if I have faith to tackle every challenge in my profession, but don't love, I'm nothing. I may give everything I have to my students and even burn out for them, but if I don't love, my efforts are useless.

Teachers should love their charges with a love that never gives up; with a love that compliments the students, recognises their needs, and nurtures them; with a love that's not possessive, neither coveting one student, nor begrudging another; with a love that doesn't try to impress or create an image; and with a love that doesn't cherish inflated ideas of accomplishments.

Teachers should love their students with a love that never fails. They should be a paradigm of good manners with a love that doesn't pursue selfish advantage, nor become touchy and hypersensitive, and certainly doesn't hold past mistakes against a student.

Furthermore, the teacher should be unhappy when students are wicked but glad when truth prevails. When the teacher has such love, she or he is trusting God implicitly and will have unlimited endurance and confidence to bear all things and look for the best in every student and every situation.

This God-given love is eternal. But inspired presentations and lectures will become obsolete; teaching methodologies will end; the pursuit of knowledge will be abandoned. For we only know a part of the truth and our instruction is always incomplete, but when the Teacher arrives, our shortcomings will pass away.

When I was a child, I had the behaviour and immaturity of a child. When I grew up, I turned my back on infantile ways. Now we seem to be peering through the fog at a silhouette; but the fog will eventually lift and we'll have clarity. Now I know partially; then I'll know completely - as totally as God's knowledge of me as a teacher. But for now I must have a steady faith, a consistent hope, and an extravagant love. But the greatest of these is love.

BOLDNESS

People say I'm bold. It wasn't always like that. When I had to deliver a speech at school I was terrified. I would mumble, forget my words, and sweat profusely. But it all changed when, just before my nineteenth birthday, I became a Christian. God removed the spirit of timidity and gave me a spirit of boldness.

Although I didn't know it at the time, that's exactly what happened with the early believers. When the day of Pentecost came, timid disciples were transformed by the filling of the Holy Spirit (cf. Acts 2:4). The change was profound. Peter, who had already proved that a girl by a campfire was all that was needed to get him to deny he'd ever heard of Jesus, became a spokesman who pleaded with the Jews to save themselves from their corrupt generation. As a result of his message about three thousand people were baptized and added to the church that day (cf. Acts 2:40-41).

That's what happens when a person is "filled with the Holy Spirit." God gives a competence beyond natural abilities. Paul speaks of this in 2 Corinthians 3:5-6 when he says that "our competence comes from God. He has made us competent as ministers of a new covenant."

Which means that the filling of the Spirit isn't something reserved for prophets and apostles. It's something for every believer. In fact, if you take the time to read through Acts, you'll discover that the phrase "filled with the Spirit" is often linked to a consequence: They spoke with boldness (cf. Acts 4:8-13; 5:29; 7:51; 9:27).

Yet tragic as it may sound, I've discovered that the filling of the Spirit, and the boldness that goes with it, is not a normative experience for many Christians today. Even a number of mature believers lack confidence and are afraid, hesitant, or unsure about sharing their faith with others.

In contrast, what strikes me about the early church is that the believers continually sought to be filled with the Holy Spirit and spoke boldly in His name (cf. Acts 4:23-31). It was quite straightforward. They prayed together, waited on God, and asked Him for His power (cf. Acts 2:42-47).

It hasn't changed. You can have the same boldness and effectiveness as the believers of the early church. The filling of the Spirit isn't something that's unique or restricted to a special group of people. It's for ordinary believers who want to do extraordinary things for God.

Make it a priority to have a fresh in-filling of God's power. Pray daily that you might "be filled with the Spirit" Ephesians 5:18. For when you're "filled to the measure of all the fullness of God" (Ephesians 3:19), impossible assignments are made possible. Yes, when you're filled with the Spirit you'll have the boldness to speak up and spread the Good News of salvation in Jesus Christ.

FATHER FORGIVE US . . .

. . . we do not fully obey You.

. . . we would rather play than pray.

. . . we are slow to listen.

. . . we judge without justice.

. . . we lean on our own understanding.

. . . we are quick to anger but slow to mercy.

. . . we please man instead of pleasing You.

. . . we live by sight, not by faith.

. . . we're unemotional, unbroken, and unwilling.

. . . we fight and quarrel.

. . . we make the past our hitching post instead of our guidepost.

. . . we lack contrition, conviction, and compassion.

. . . we know about You but don't really know You.

. . . we operate outside of your pleasure and anointing.

. . . we speak unity while living in disunity.

. . . we're not careful to do everything written in Your Word.

. . . we despise Your discipline.

. . . we want to become greater, not less.

. . . we submit grudgingly.

. . . we live with attitude instead of gratitude.

. . . we don't hold fast to You.

. . . we see ourselves as potent and forget You're omnipotent.

. . . we forget to say, "Thank you."

. . . we want to be happy but not holy.

. . . we serve out of duty instead of desire.

. . . we pursue our whims instead of Your Will.

. . . we're cold when we should be hot.

. . . we try to put You in a box.

. . . we show favouritism when we should be impartial.

. . . we give without generosity.

. . . we don't long for the fellowship of God's people.

. . . we use You as a resource and a means to an end.

. . . we value tolerance over passion for Your cause.

. . . we receive life but rarely reveal life.

. . . we make little effort to witness to the lost.

. . . we no longer tremble in Your presence.

. . . we complain, criticise and compare.

. . . we tolerate sin.

. . . we rarely weep for the persecuted.

. . . we don't give the poor a second thought.

. . . we're blind to the extent of our need for revival.

. . . we worship without wonder.

. . . we quit when we should persevere.

. . . we struggle to say, "I'm sorry."

. . . and we do not love You with all our heart and soul and strength.

GOD IS WATCHING

Do you worry about your life? Are you discouraged? Have songs given place to sighing? Has hope died within you? Do you feel lonely? Are you anxious about what you eat and drink? Are you concerned about the security of your job? Do you worry about whether your clothes are in fashion? Are you apprehensive about the performance of your investments on the stock market? Are you despondent due to illness? Are you struggling in a relationship? Do you feel bleak when you think about the future?

Well it's time to chill out. There is more to life than the food you eat or the finances you have in the bank. Look at the sparrow, unfettered and free. It's not restricted by a job description nor nervous about tomorrow. It's careless in the care of God. As we're reminded in Matthew 6:25-34 and 10:29-31, God's eye is on the sparrow but you're worth far more than many sparrows. So don't worry when shadows come; God is watching. You count more to Him than all the birds in the air . . .

I am ever in His thoughts,
My God is watching over me.
There's nothing hidden from His gaze,
He knows my heart and hears my plea.

He watches o'er the way I take,
He bears my burdens day by day.
He ever cares about my needs,
He rescues me if I should stray.

So I'll praise the One who sits above,
Who doesn't even blink an eye.
Who never falters in His love,
Nor catch His breath or pause to sigh.

For His eye is on the sparrow,
And He's watching over me.
Thus I know I need not worry,
Cause from fear He's set me free.

GALLOPING GRANNIES

They're affectionately called the Galloping Grannies. The term has never been used in a derogatory sense. In fact it's a term of endearment to describe a group of widows at Orillia Community Church who are young at heart.

I think that's great. Even though the average age is seventy something these widows are all go, a significant part of the church on the move. They pray earnestly, study and teach God's Word, encourage others, visit the sick, bake and cook meals for people in need, practice hospitality, reach out to their city with the Gospel of Jesus Christ, excel in generosity, and cheer the church along. As if that isn't enough, they even try to keep their pastor in line - a formidable task at the best of times!

But that's how it should be. In 1 Timothy 5:10 the widows are encouraged to be well known for their "good deeds, such as bringing up children, showing hospitality, washing the feet of the saints, helping those in trouble and devoting" themselves "to all kinds of good deeds."

Which raises a question. I wonder if the Galloping Grannies have washed the feet of their pastor?

But back to the topic in hand.

We can't leave this subject without mentioning some of the other things the Word of God says about widows. For even though the widows are called upon to be incomparable in good deeds, the church in turn, is called upon to be incomparable in looking after the widows. James 1:27 tells us that the "religion that God our Father accepts as pure and faultless is . . . to look after widows and orphans in their distress." In 1 Timothy 5:3 it says we must "give proper recognition to those widows who are really in need." And in Titus 2:3-4, the church is reminded to "teach the older women to be reverent in the way they live, not to be slanderers or addicted to much wine, but to teach what is good. Then they can train the younger women . . ."

Which brings us back to the pastor. I wonder if he's doing his bit in looking after the widows? I wonder if he's taken the time to wash the feet of the Galloping Grannies?

STRENGTH FROM THE STRUGGLE

A man found a cocoon of a butterfly which he brought indoors. A few days later a small opening appeared. He sat and watched the butterfly for several hours as it struggled to force its body through that little hole. Then it seemed to stop making any progress. It appeared as if it had got as far as it could go. So the man decided to help the butterfly. He took a pair of scissors and snipped off the remaining bit of the cocoon. The butterfly emerged with ease. But it had a swollen body and small, shriveled wings. As he continued to watch the butterfly the man expected that at any moment the wings would enlarge and expand to be able to support the body, which would contract with time. Neither happened! In fact, the butterfly spent the rest of its life crawling around with a swollen body and shriveled wings. It was never able to fly.

What the man, in his kindness and haste, did not understand was that the restricting cocoon and the struggle required for the butterfly to get through the tiny opening were God's way of forcing fluid from the body of the butterfly into its wings so that it would be ready for flight once it achieved its freedom from the cocoon.

It's the same for us. Sometimes struggles are exactly what we need in our lives. If God protected us from struggles and removed the obstacles we would end up spineless. We would never become strong. We would never emerge from the cocoon. We would never learn to fly!

So don't look for the easy way out. Don't ask God to snip open the restrictions imposed by life. And don't expect to overcome your present obstacles without a struggle. For God gives us difficulties to make us strong; problems to make us wise; dangers to make us courageous; and troubled people to make us love. In this sense the barriers of life are probably our greatest benedictions!

Countless people have learnt these lessons: Cripple him, and you have a Sir Walter Scott. Bury him in the snows of Valley Forge, and you have a George Washington. Lock him in a prison cell, and you have a John Bunyan. Deny her the ability to see, hear, and speak, and you have a Helen Keller. Make him play second fiddle in an obscure South American orchestra, and you have a Toscanini. Confine him to Robin Island, and you have a Nelson Mandela. Afflict him with asthma as a child, and you have a Theodore Roosevelt. Incarcerate her in a Nazi prison camp, and you have a Corrie Ten Boom. Have him lose a leg from cancer, and you have a Terry Fox.

Don't give up. If you're feeling pressurized by the challenges of life, keep on keeping on. Struggle against the cocoon. Stretch your wings. Aim to fly. And then, one day, you will.

Now that's not to say you can accomplish this in your own strength. Far from it. God forces the fluid from the body of the butterfly into its wings so that it will be ready for flight once it leaves the cocoon. It's the same for you. You need God to strengthen your wings. You need God to prepare you for flight. You need God to give you the emotional, intellectual, and spiritual resources to reach for the sky. For it's God who "gives strength to the weary and increases the power of the weak" Isaiah 40:29. It's God who lifts "you up in due time" 1 Peter 5:6. It's God's grace that's sufficient for you. And it's His power that's made perfect in your weakness (cf. 2 Corinthians 12:9).

"Those who hope in the Lord will renew their strength. They will soar on wings like eagles; they will run and not grow weary, they will walk and not be faint" Isaiah 40:31.

MY PRAYER FOR YOU

May *Christ* be your *Alpha and Omega* (Revelation 1:8)

May the *Arm of the Lord* embrace you (Isaiah 51:9)

May the *Bread of Life* sustain you (John 6:35)

May the *Counsellor* console you (Isaiah 9:6)

May the *Deliverer* rescue you (Romans 11:26)

May the *Ensign* be a banner over you (Isaiah 11:10 KJV)

May the *Forerunner* go in advance of you (Hebrews 6:20)

May the *Gift of God* be treasured by you (John 4:10)

May the *Holy One* purify you (Psalm 16:10)

May the *Image of God* attract you (2 Corinthians 4:4)

May the *Just One* be an example to you (Acts 7:52)

May the *King of Kings* have dominion over you (Revelation 19:16)

May the *Light of the World* shine for you (John 8:12)

May the *Mediator* reconcile you (Galatians 3:20)

May the *Nazarene* use you (Matthew 2:23)

May the *One and Only Son* save you (John 3:16)

May the *Physician* heal you (Luke 4:23)

May the *Rabbi* teach you (John 1:49)

May the *Sure Foundation* undergird you (Isaiah 28:16)

May the *Truth* set you free (John 8:32)

May the *Vine* bear fruit in you (John 15:1)

May the *Word* enrich you (John 1:1)

May the *Young Child* lead you (Matthew 2:8)

"OUT OF THE MOUTH OF BABES"

Psalm 8:2 says, "From the lips of children and infants you have ordained praise."

The following third grade homework assignment, on explaining God, was submitted to the teacher by eight-year-old, Danny Dutton of Chula Vista, California. It's a fabulous example of how God has sanctioned praise from the lips of children.

"One of God's main jobs is making people. He makes them to replace the ones that die, so there will be enough people to take care of things on earth. He doesn't make grownups, just babies. I think because they are smaller and easier to make. That way He doesn't have to take up His valuable time teaching them to talk and walk. He can just leave that to mothers and fathers.

God's second most important job is listening to prayers. An awful lot of this goes on, since some people, like preachers and things, pray at times beside bedtime. God doesn't have time to listen to the radio or TV because of this. Because He hears everything, there must be a terrible lot of noise in His ears, unless He has thought of a way to turn it off.

God sees everything and hears everything and is everywhere which keeps Him pretty busy. So you shouldn't go wasting His time by going over your Mom and Dad's head asking for something they said you couldn't have.

Atheists are people who don't believe in God. I don't think there are any in Chula Vista. At least there aren't any who come to our church.

Jesus is God's Son. He used to do all the hard work like walking on water and performing miracles and trying to teach the people who didn't want to learn about God. They finally got tired of Him teaching them and they crucified Him. But He was good and kind, like His Father, and He told His Father that they didn't know what they were doing and to forgive them and God said, 'O.K.'

His Dad (God) appreciated everything that He had done and all His hard work on earth so He told Him He didn't have to go out on the road anymore. He could stay in heaven.

So He did. And now He helps His Dad out by listening to prayers and seeing things which are important for God to take care of and which ones he can take care of Himself without having to bother God. Like a secretary, only more important. You can pray anytime you want and they are sure to help you because they got it worked out so one of them is on duty all the time.

You should always go to church on Sunday because it makes God happy, and if there's anybody you want to make happy, it's God. Don't skip church to do something you think will be more fun like going to the beach. This is wrong. And besides the sun doesn't come out at the beach until noon anyway.

If you don't believe in God, besides being an atheist, you will be very lonely, because your parents can't go everywhere with you, like to camp, but God can. It is good to know He's around you when you're scared in the dark or when you can't swim and you get thrown into the real deep water by big kids.

But . . . you shouldn't just always think of what God can do for you. I figure God put me here and He can take me back anytime He pleases.

And . . . that's why I believe in God."

"TO BE ALL EAR"

While working on Bible translation, a missionary in Africa had difficulty finding a word in the local dialect for "obedience." Then one day as the missionary was walking through a village his dog wandered off. The moment the missionary noticed the dog's absence he whistled for it to come to him. Hearing the whistle, the dog rushed to his side at top speed. An elderly native sitting by the roadside was deeply impressed by the instant obedience of the dog. He exclaimed, "Mui adem delegau ge!" which literally translated means, "Dog yours, ear is only." In other words, "Your dog is all ear." That gave the translator the word he needed for obedience - "to be all ear."

Which reminds me of some of the people who fill our church pews. They believe that if they hear a good sermon or attend a Bible study they'll grow in maturity and get God's blessing. Wrong! Nothing could be further from the truth. They're only kidding themselves if that's what they believe. For it's not enough to receive the Word, we must act on the Word. Any response to the Word other than faithful, unqualified obedience, is self-deceptive. For it's not the hearing of God's Word that brings blessing, it's the practice of the Word. As it says in James 1:22, "Do not merely listen to the word, and so deceive yourselves. Do what it says."

That's the bottom line. Hearing is not the same thing as doing. There can be no substitute for service. We have to act on the precepts of God's Word. It's no good marking our Bibles if our Bibles don't mark us. God didn't give us His Word to be simply learnt, but to be obeyed and applied. As Jesus said in John 8:31, "If you hold to my teaching, you really are my disciples." And, as it says in Psalm 119:1, "Blessed are they . . . who walk according to the law of the Lord."

In other words the distinctive trait of the true Christian is not a momentary feeling of compliance or short term commitment, but a long and consistent obedience to Scripture. On a moment by moment and day to day basis the real believer proves his faith by being a doer of the Word. He's a person whose life is characterised by what one commentator refers to as "holy energy." Which is another way of saying that a person who is truly saved manifests behaviour corresponding to the standards of God's Word.

Yes, if a profession of faith in Christ does not result in a hunger and thirst for God's Word, and a desire to obey that Word, then the profession is merely that - a mere profession. John puts it this way, "We know that we have come to know him if we obey his commands. The man who says, 'I know him,' but does not do what he commands is a liar, and the truth is not in him. But if anyone obeys his word, God's love is truly made complete in him. This is how we know we are in him: Whoever claims to live in him must walk as Jesus did" 1 John 2:3-6 (cf. 1 John 3:10).

Thus it's not a question of what one claims to have experienced but of whether or not we imitate Christ (cf. Philippians 2:1-7). It gets down to whether or not we're "all ear." As Jesus says, "Not everyone who says to me, 'Lord, Lord,' will enter the kingdom of heaven, but only he who does the will of my Father who is in heaven" Matthew 7:21.

GOD
AT WORK

In 1860 in Worcester, South Africa, a remarkable thing happened in the Moeder Kerk. The assistant minister, J. C. de Vries was leading a service, when shortly after it had begun, a servant girl began to cry out to the Lord in anguished prayer. Tears coursed down her cheeks as she confessed her sin and pleaded for forgiveness. Then, the sound of distant thunder was heard, like a train on the edge of the town, coming closer and closer, until it enveloped the hall and shook the building. At this point the whole congregation burst into prayer together, the majority audibly, a minority in whispering tones.

An unusual outpouring of the Holy Spirit seemed to be taking place. Andrew Murray, the senior minister, was immediately notified and hastened over to the church where he found everyone engaged in prayer. The people seemed to be distressed with soul anguish, mourning their sin, grieving from a deep inner agony, weeping tears of repentance, and, as they continued they cried to God for mercy, begged for deliverance, and prayed for friends and loved ones. Andrew Murray didn't know what to make of this unusual happening and thought it was confusion. He walked up and down among the distressed and praying people shouting: "Bly stil mense, bly stil . . . ek is jou dominee . . . bly stil." Which translated means, "Be quiet, be quiet, I'm your minister, be quiet."

But no one took the slightest notice of the minister. Each seemed more concerned with calling on God for forgiveness of an intolerable weight of sin and shame. Eventually, Andrew Murray shook his head and walked out.

In contrast, de Vries, convinced and overwhelmed by the movement of God's Spirit, remained in prayer with the people. The meetings continued day after day. Each meeting began with a profound silence, but as soon as the meeting was opened the people burst into simultaneous prayer and petition. Night after night the place was shaken and meetings often went on until 3:00 a.m. as the people were reluctant to disperse for sleep. It was during this time that an American in the congregation approached Andrew Murray and said, "Dominee be at peace, God is in control, this is not confusion, this is revival . . . this is God at work among His people."

O how I pray for a similar movement of God's Spirit. My hope is for rejoicing to spread across the land such as we've never seen before. Can it happen? Most definitely. The Lord forgives the iniquity of His people, covers all their sins, puts away His displeasure toward us, and grants us salvation (cf. Psalm 85:2,4,7). For when God is at work among His people He indeed gives "what is good" Psalm 85:12.

WHEN WILL THE WORLD END?

Predictions about the future capture our attention. Throughout history people have tried to predict when the world would end. The Church father, Hippolytus (170-236 A.D.) calculated Jesus' return for the year 500. He was wrong. William Miller, a self educated farmer from Vermont, predicted that Christ would return between March 21, 1843 and March 21, 1844. One hundred thousand people believed him, and as the time approached they quit their jobs, abandoned their fields, sold their possessions and waited. Nothing happened. The Millerites were wrong.

In recent times Hal Lindsey set himself up as an authority in these matters and suggested in his book, *The Late Great Planet Earth* that 1988 would be the end of the world. He was wrong. Mary Stewart Relfe, a wealthy Alabama real estate developer, in her 1981 book, *When Your Money Fails: The 666 System is Here*, said that Christ would return in 1990 to judge those who had not obeyed the gospel. She was wrong. And most recently Grant R. Jeffrey, author of *Armageddon: Appointment With Destiny*, suggested the year 2000 as "the probable termination date for the last days." He too was wrong.

I could go on. There's no shortage of people to tell you when they think the world is going to come to an end. Scores of prognosticators are tapping figures into their calculators and countless ignorant people are willing to believe their predictions.

But disclosing the future is not man's prerogative. It's God's! Just because the end may be near does not necessarily mean the end is here. Only God knows the exact time of the end of the age (cf. Matthew 24:35-36).

Nonetheless, we do know that the world will end after a time of deception by false prophets and men claiming to be Jesus (cf. Matthew 24:5, 11, 23-24); after subjection to all kinds of conflict and disaster (cf. Matthew 24:6-8); after rejection and oppression of Christians (cf. Matthew 24:9-10, 12-13); and after the proclamation of the gospel to all the world (cf. Matthew 24:14).

So keep a proper perspective. Instead of looking for something to happen, look for Someone to come. Live your life with the expectation of an imminent culmination, but plan your work as if you had a hundred years. In other words, keep your eye on the end but your feet on the earth. As someone once said, "The only way to live is to live as if Jesus died yesterday, lives today and is coming tomorrow."

Yes, the world will end when God is ready for it to end and not a moment before. Many will come in Christ's "name, claiming . . . 'The time is near.' Do not follow them" Luke 21:8. For "no one knows about that day or hour, not even the angels in heaven, nor the Son, but only the Father . . . Therefore keep watch . . . be ready, because the Son of Man will come at an hour when you do not expect him" Matthew 24:36,42,44.

WHAT A DAY!

What death did to Jesus is nothing compared to what Jesus did to death. For Christ did the unimaginable - He overcame death. It was a morning beyond belief. "Up from the grave He arose, with a mighty triumph o'er His foes. He arose a victor from the dark domain, and He lives forever with His saints to reign. He arose! He arose! Hallelujah! Christ arose!" Robert Lowry.

That's the Gospel truth. Christ conquered death. The impossible became possible. The grave couldn't hold Him. Darkness was vanquished. The graveclothes were empty - the body gone. O what a day! "When death stung Jesus Christ, it stung itself to death" Peter Joshua. For on the third day He was raised according to the Scriptures (cf. 1 Corinthians 15:4). As it says in Acts 2:24, "But God raised him from the dead, freeing him from the agony of death, because it was impossible for death to keep its hold on him." Hallelujah! After dying for our sins on the cross of Calvary Christ defeated death and hell through the power of His resurrection. This isn't an appendage to the Christian faith; this is the faith. The resurrection is the epicentre of our belief. It's indispensable. C. H. Dodd says, "It's not a belief that grew up within the church; it is the belief around which the church itself grew up, and the 'given' upon which its faith was based."

Yes, the stone was rolled to the mouth of the tomb in order to seal it, but God made sure it didn't stay there. It was rolled away and the angel sitting on it said to the women who came looking for Jesus, "Do not be afraid, for I know that you are looking for Jesus, who was crucified. He is not here; he has risen, just as he said . . . He has risen from the dead . . . Now I have told you" Matthew 28:5-7.

No other religion can match that. No other religion has a founder who's overcome death. Asoka, a past Emperor of India, distributed Buddha's ashes in minute portions to eighty-four thousand shrines all over India. Buddhism is therefore centred around the worship of ashes. It's focussed on a dead founder. But Christianity is different, radically different. It centres on none other than the living Lord Jesus Christ. For Christianity begins where all other faiths end - with an empty tomb, with its originator conquering death.

Yet cynics and critics have tried to explain the empty tomb away. They propose a number of theories: Skeptics argue that it was the wrong tomb. But if it were the wrong tomb, the Pharisees and Sadducees who put Jesus to death certainly would have found the right tomb, opened it up, and produced the dead and decaying body of Jesus Christ. Others say that Joseph of Arimathea took the body. But the problem with this theory is that Joseph had no motive or opportunity to take the body. Besides, Joseph was a devout Jew and he wouldn't have broken the Sabbath. Still others speculate that the disciples stole the body. This doesn't fit with what we know of the lives of these men. They weren't dishonest and they weren't very clever. On the night of Jesus' arrest they still didn't understand He was going to die, let alone be raised (cf. John 13:36). They also didn't know what to think when they saw the empty tomb (cf. John 20:9). Furthermore, if this hypothesis were true then we'd have to believe that the disciples persisted in a hoax and were prepared to die for a corpse, for something they knew to be false.

Thus there can be no other conclusion other than what the Bible teaches, i.e. the tomb was empty because Christ had risen from the dead. O what a day! Jesus had risen just as He said He would and in so doing proved once for all that He is the "resurrection and the life" John 11:25.

WHITE SHEETS
AND HOT SOUP

My friend Jill Roberts, an elementary school teacher, had endured enough impertinence for one day. Turning to the nine-year-old boy she said, "If you won't behave yourself, you must stand outside!" A while later she stepped out to talk to the boy, and, during the conversation realised there were obviously greater issues than cheekiness in this boy's life.

So Jill began making inquiries. She soon discovered that, unbeknownst to the school, the boy's mother had died and his father had moved to another city. When the father pushed off he had left his son with the twenty-one-year-old sister who had then abandoned him. He was now fending for himself in a desolate apartment and begging food from the neighbours. Jill was obviously distraught and immediately called Child Welfare (Social Services) and insisted that the boy be taken to a foster home.

The next day the boy arrived at school with clean clothes and a big smile. Jill gave him a hug and asked how he was. "Well Mrs Roberts," he said enthusiastically, "I slept in white sheets and had hot soup for supper!"

From a state of abandonment and despair the boy moved to a situation of security and happiness. The day he went to the foster home he wiped away his tears and hope was kindled in his heart.

Likewise the day we go to heaven "He will wipe every tear from (our) eyes. There will be no more death or mourning or crying or pain, for the old order of things has passed away" Revelation 21:4.

Sounds great - doesn't it? Despite the trials and tribulations in this life the day will come when we'll receive our eternal reward. And what a reward it will be. It will even surpass sleeping in white sheets and having hot soup for supper!

SILLY BILLY

Some years ago, I was sitting having tea with my good friend and fellow pastor, David Sparrow, as he reminisced about his time as a student at Treverton College. Here's one of his stories:

With lunch finished the grade twelve class had made their way to the math classroom. The teacher, William Temple, was late for class so they posted a sentry and entertained themselves with some horseplay. But the sentry was lax and didn't see Mr. Temple returning until the last moment. Only just nipping into the classroom ahead of the teacher he hissed; "Watch out! Here comes Billy!" By the time Bill walked into the class the students were seated in quiet expectancy. But Bill had heard the hurried warning and was not impressed. He was upset with their familiarity and proceeded to lambast them. He complained that he was not treated like a professional and reminded them that his name was not Billy but Mr. Temple.

Finally the lesson got under way, and, as it progressed, a student, Walter Hesterman, swung his chair back, hooked it under a bookcase, and fell asleep. Bill soon noticed this and called out; "Wake up Hesterman!" Walter came too with a start, and as he did he succeeded in knocking over his desk. Bill was furious and barked; "Hesterman you silly little fool! Get on your feet!" As Walter stood up Bill snarled; "Now tell me Hesterman what are you?" To which the dazed youth responded; "I'm a Silly Billy Sir!"

This is certainly a story that reminds us that we live cheek by jowl with foolishness. Yes, most teachers know that "a prudent man keeps his knowledge to himself, but the heart of fools blurts out folly" for they are "quick to quarrel" Proverbs 12:23; 20:3. We recognise that "fools despise wisdom and discipline" and they also "hate knowledge" Proverbs 1:7,22. And we are saddened when we note that "fools die for lack of judgment" and "fools mock at making amends for sin" Proverbs 10:21; 14:9. Yet the greatest tragedy is when the fool "trusts in himself" and "says in his heart, 'There is no God'" Proverbs 28:26; Psalm 53:1. This person must certainly be the prince of fools, a real Silly Billy!

Fools will be wise when sin they despise

MAKING THE MOST
OF THE SERMON

Someone once wrote, "Now I lay me down to sleep, the sermon long, the subject deep, if he gets through before I wake, will someone give me a little shake?" Though funny, this shouldn't happen. When we go to church it should be our aim to get as much as possible from the preaching of God's Word.

In Matthew 11:15 we read, "He who has ears, let him hear." That's a good reminder. Sometimes we're not always tuned in. Here are some practical guidelines to help you make the most of Sunday's sermon. Consider the following:

■ Come refreshed: Get enough sleep. How you spend Saturday night has a great deal to do with your concentration on Sunday morning. Luke 8:18 reminds us; "Consider carefully how you listen."

■ Prepare your heart: Sin is like wax in the ears - it blocks the intake of truth. Before coming to church examine your heart, look for things that would hamper your spiritual hearing, confess your sin, put away anything that is unholy, and ask God to help you overcome problems that might interfere with you listening to the message (cf. James 1:21).

■ Pray: Pray before, during and after every sermon. Pray that when the pastor opens his mouth he will speak with power and fearlessly declare God's Word (cf. Ephesians 6:19). Pray that God will grant you the will and ability to practice and apply what you learn.

■ Bring your Bible: Look up verses or passages that are mentioned. Underline or highlight key texts. Consider writing notes in the margin.

■ Sit at the front: This minimizes distractions and diversions such as people's idiosyncrasies, talking and moving, babies looking at you, or parents struggling to get their children to pay attention.

■ Take notes: This focuses your concentration and helps you remember a message more effectively. You can enhance your note taking by recording your own thoughts, questions, and applications.

■ Be discerning: It's your responsibility to check the Bible and make sure that what the pastor says is consistent with the Word of God (cf. Matthew 7:15; 1 Corinthians 10:15; 2 Peter 3:17).

■ Listen with humility: Remember you've come to hear the Word of God, not just a pastor's sermon. God is speaking to you. So listen attentively (cf. Nehemiah 8:3; Psalm 85:8) and ask God to make you receptive, to deepen your insight, to root His Word in your spirit, and to help you apply Biblical truth to your life.

■ Express gratitude: Show your appreciation for those who minister the Word of God (cf. 1 Thessalonians 5:12-13).

■ Respond obediently: "Do not merely listen to the word, and so deceive yourselves. Do what it says" James 1:22. Your responsibility after the sermon is to intentionally apply God's Word - to personalize the application and take the initiative in acting on what you've heard. For "the man who looks intently into the perfect law that gives freedom, and continues to do this, not forgetting what he has heard, but doing it - he will be blessed in what he does" James 1:25.

"BE ON YOUR GUARD"

It's amazing how quickly we can be caught off guard. Despite all our preparations and contingency plans we can be taken by surprise. No matter how careful we are disaster can strike.

A gang of criminals caught my mother off guard in 1984. My mother was the manageress of a shop that sold factory seconds from the clothing factory run by my father and brother. Both the factory and factory outlet store were in downtown Johannesburg. During a lull in business, seven drug intoxicated criminals burst into the shop. One grabbed Mum and pressed a knife smeared with poison to her throat. He dragged her to the back of the shop behind a wooden partition while his accomplices began to empty the till and ransack the stock.

Despite her shock Mum had the presence of mind to press a concealed alarm button. Unknown to the criminals it alerted my brother and father in the factory. My brother Frazer was the first to arrive as one of the criminals was desperately trying to close the shop door. Without breaking his stride Frazer kicked in the door while simultaneously levelling his revolver and demanding the surrender of the criminals.

He was immediately attacked. A man lunged forward wielding a machete. Frazer fired, but was barged to the ground as the man tried to escape through the door. A second man continued the attack slashing at Frazer with his knife but Frazer managed to squeeze off a second shot which smashed through the man's knee cap and stopped him in his tracks. In the melee a third man ducked through the door and slammed pell-mell into my father who was just arriving on the scene. As Dad rolled onto the sidewalk he shouted after the man to stop but the man kept on running. Dad fired two shots from his revolver and both hit the man who continued for several metres before dropping stone dead with a bullet through the heart.

Meanwhile, the fight continued in the shop. One bullet from Frazer's gun passed through the partition at the back of the shop and slammed into the wall alongside Mum who was still being held with the knife to her throat.

Another escaping criminal was purposefully run down by a motor mechanic from a garage up the road. When he heard the gunfire, he jumped into his truck and raced down the street to assist my brother and father. When he saw the man hightailing it down the road he swerved into him, knocked him off his feet, then jumped out and restrained him.

The remaining gang members gave up the fight and were held at gunpoint by my brother until the police arrived. Unknown to the criminals, Frazer had exhausted the bullets in his gun!

The outcome could have been very different. Mum could have had her throat slashed and Dad or Frazer could have been injured or killed. But all were preserved. Frazer's training on the gun range and Dad's experience as a retired British bobby and ex-Royal Military Policeman stood them in good stead. They had anticipated trouble and were ready for action.

Though most of you reading this account will probably never encounter a life and death gunfight you nonetheless need to be vigilant. You must "guard yourselves," "be on your guard" Acts 20:28,31. Keep watch for things seen and things unseen that could cost you dearly. Guard your words. Guard your emotions. Guard your mind. Guard your actions. And guard your life in Christ.

As the gospel artist Steve Green sings:

> "The human heart is easily swayed and often betrayed,
> at the hand of emotion.
> We dare not leave the outcome to chance.
> We must choose in advance,
> or live with the agony, such needless tragedy.
> Guard your heart.
> Guard your heart.
> Don't trade it for treasure.
> Don't give it away.
> Guard your heart.
> Guard your heart.
> As a payment for pleasure it's a high price to pay.
> For a soul that remains sincere with a conscience clear.
> Guard your heart."

"SOMEBODY HAS TO DO SOMETHING!"

John Paul Chan is the pastor of Gate Baptist Church in Hong Kong. The church is built next to the ancient city wall and on the other side of the wall are the drug dens of Kowloon. For days on end Pastor Chan had watched as corpses were hauled out of the lawless enclave alongside the church. It was a dreadful sight. Some of the corpses were permanently frozen in the squatted stance of the Asian drug addict. Finally he'd had enough. He decided to venture from his safe haven and see what was going on beyond the wall.

He wasn't prepared for what he encountered. It was as if he had literally gone from heaven to hell. In one small tin-roofed building he saw 100 people crammed together inhaling the fumes of heated heroin. Pastor Chan says, "I thought I had walked into a cemetery and was seeing ghosts and nobody was doing anything to help them." He remembers crying out, "Somebody has to do something!"

As it turned out, that somebody ended up being Pastor Chan. Within a short time he started an organization called Operation Dawn, a unique drug treatment programme that combines tough love with lots of Scripture. The tame middle-aged pastor was transformed into a tiger. For the past 25 years he's rescued ten times as many heroin and opium addicts as another programme in Hong Kong with 40 times his budget! [Source: Bennett Chuck. *Heroes on the Frontline.*]

Isn't that great? It's a testimony to the healing power of the Gospel of Jesus Christ. But what caught my attention was the fact that a gentle, easy-going pastor, when faced with the ravages of drug addiction, was transformed into a tiger. When the Spirit of God got hold of him, he could no longer accept the status quo, he could no longer be passive, he had to do something. With righteous indignation he became a powerhouse in the battle against sin.

Which suggests a question. Are you prepared to do something - to stick out your neck and make a difference? No excuses now. You don't have to be someone special. Pastor Chan was a tame middle-aged man. What transformed him was that he allowed the Spirit of God to have His way with him. So go for it. You can do it. Step out in faith, take up the challenge that's been on your heart and mind. And "be strong in the Lord and in his mighty power" Ephesians 6:10.

GOD'S PLUS SIGN
FOR A NEEDY WORLD

If you're like me, you're probably tired of hearing about violence, immorality, drugs, crime, corruption and other depressing topics. You're looking for something positive. You're searching for a message of hope. You're hunting for a word of encouragement. And you're wondering how to make sense of our daily struggles and burdens. This has not gone unnoticed by God. At the centre of world history He's placed a plus sign for a needy world. For everyone who has eyes to see God has raised a symbol of hope and an emblem of assurance.

This plus sign is an ancient witness to a modern world. It can be described as the benchmark "to which all previous history looked forward and to which all history since looks back" George Sweeting. It represents the most crucial event of all time. It's the pivot round which all the events of the ages revolve. It's the hinge to the door of salvation. It's the ladder that's high enough to touch heaven's threshold. It's the key event by which we reckon our relationship with God. It's the magnet that draws the heart of mankind to the One who suffered and died for sinners. It's the Cross of Calvary on which the Prince of Glory died.

Wow! In an instrument of death and torture we have a symbol which ultimately touches the lives and hopes of everyone. For God's Son, Jesus Christ, was crucified so that we might be brought to God. The purpose of the cross was to render sin powerless (cf. Romans 6:6). To draw you to the Saviour who hung there for your sin. To give you life to the full (cf. John 10:10). And to take away the wall of enmity that separates you from God.

So embrace God's plus sign for a needy world. Recognise the cross as "a symbol of God's heartbreak over a world that is gone astray" Sam Jones. Realise that we're not saved by theories but by fact, and what is the fact? Christ died on the cross to reconcile "the world to himself" 2 Corinthians 5:19. He died to set you free so "you will be free indeed" John 8:36. And He held Himself on the cross in order to take the penalty of sin on Himself by offering "for all time one sacrifice for sins" Hebrews 10:12. That's the good news! As Martin Luther says, "Alone upon the cross He hung that others He might save. Forsaken then by God and man, alone His life He gave!"

Isn't that a great plus sign? Even though Christ "committed no sin, and no deceit was found in his mouth . . . he himself bore our sins in his body on the tree, so that we might die to sins and live for righteousness . . ." 1 Peter 2:22, 24.

COLOURING OUTSIDE THE LINES

One of the things that attracted people to Jesus was His original and authentic approach. In a world of rigid rules, hackneyed phrases and empty religion, Jesus burst onto the scene with passion, integrity, and creativity. Unlike anyone before Him, or since, He modelled the importance of colouring outside the lines. He saw things in a new way, He used different entry points to tackle the challenges of life, and He was a master at bringing freshness to the familiar. No wonder it was said of Him, "No one ever spoke the way this man does" John 7:46.

Like Jesus, we need to colour outside the lines. No one's attracted to legalism, paternalism or hollow displays of piety. If we hope to draw people to Christ, then we need to create new and fresh styles with which to reach our world with the Gospel. We must be willing to shift and change, we must be adaptable. We must guard against being dated and institutionalised. If we hope to stay on the cutting edge then we must undergo drastic alterations. As the old Roman politician, Publius Syrus, said, "It is a bad plan that admits of no modification."

So flex your creative muscles. See things in a new way. Focus on your abilities - not your inabilities. Bypass obstacles with lateral thinking. Develop resources and habits which foster your creativity. Determine to work hard and learn as you go. Recognise that "if you don't feel awkward doing something new, you are not doing something new" Ken Blanchard. And remember, the aim of all creative endeavours must always be to point people toward the Saviour - not man.

After all, creativity is a means, not the end. As it says in Ephesians 2:10, "We are God's workmanship, created in Christ Jesus to do good works, which God prepared in advance for us to do." Thus, our creativity should never step beyond the parameters of God's Word. It should never be in conflict with orthodox belief (although it may find itself in conflict with traditional practice). For when all is said and done, the reason we colour outside the lines is to draw people inside the church.

THE LORD'S PRAYER

If you're more than forty years old you probably know the *King James Version* of the Lord's Prayer:

> Our Father who art in heaven,
> Hallowed be thy name.
> Thy kingdom come.
> Thy will be done in earth, as it is in heaven.
> Give us this day our daily bread.
> And forgive us our debts, as we forgive our debtors.
> And lead us not into temptation, but deliver us from evil:
> For thine is the kingdom,
> and the power, and the glory,
> forever. Amen.

More recently a number of contemporary English versions of the Lord's Prayer have been written. This one's from *The Message*:

> Our Father in heaven,
> Reveal who you are.
> Set the world right;
> Do what's best - as above, so below.
> Keep us alive with three square meals.
> Keep us forgiven with you and forgiving others.
> Keep us safe from ourselves and the Devil.
> You're in charge!
> You can do anything you want!
> You're ablaze in beauty!
> Yes. Yes. Yes.

And most recently:

dad@hvn, urspshl.we want wot u want&urth2b like hvn.giv us food&4giv r sins lyk we 4giv uvaz.don't test us! save us!bcos we kno ur boss, ur tuf&ur cool 4 eva!ok?

Now don't be shocked. This is the Lord's Prayer translated into text message format. It's part of a new scheme to send the Lord's Prayer to worshipers on their cell-phones. In an attempt to bring Christianity to a generation that seems too busy to go to church the satirical British Christian Web site *Ship-of-Fools.com*

designed an online competition to see who could cut the Lord's Prayer from 372 characters to 160 or fewer without losing anything important. The winner, and writer of the above version, was Matthew Campbell, a history student at York University in England.

No doubt there'll be a variety of opinions concerning these versions. You're welcome to your opinion. And if you want, u can tlk n txt. But at the end of the day what's important is that you're remembering to pray. So pray earnestly, constantly, and sincerely. And don't forget the Lord's Prayer. After all, Jesus had a reason for saying, "This is how you should pray: Our Father in heaven . . ." Matthew 6:9.

INCOMPARABLE

About thirty-three short years after His birth it was time for Jesus to face the cross. Though He was the only perfect man who'd ever lived, the most advanced religion of its time united with the most powerful empire of the day to bring Him down. It was a tragedy surpassing all others. Yet it was a drama of His own making. The Gospels hint that Christ was overseeing the whole process. He knew the fate that awaited Him. He knew He was born to die. From His birth His destination was Jerusalem and His destiny the cross. When death approached He called the shots. With the self restraint that only God could have, Jesus allowed every lash of the whip, endured every taunt and lie, and suffered the ignominy and agony of crucifixion.

The cross is probably the cruelest form of capital punishment known to man. If Jesus had come to die for our sins during the French Revolution, He would have faced the guillotine. If He had come to die for our sins during the Second World War in Nazi Germany, He would have faced the gas chamber. If He had come to die for our sins in present day USA, it would have been the lethal injection or the electric chair. If He had come to die for our sins when I was a teenager in South Africa, He would have been hung. The guillotine, the gas chamber, the injection, the chair, and hanging, are relatively humane compared to the cross. But then the cross was reserved for murderers, slave revolts, and other heinous crimes against Roman rule. When the Jews executed someone they usually stoned them. Roman citizens were beheaded, not crucified. In fact Cicero said, "The idea of the cross should never come near the bodies of Roman citizens, it should never pass through their thoughts, eyes or ears."

There's no doubt about it. The cross was an accursed way to die (cf. Deuteronomy 21:23). Jesus knew that full well. In choosing to die for our sins He never spared Himself. He literally went the whole stretch. Even to the point of "becoming a curse for us" Galatians 3:13. Yet herein lies the good news, the cross, rather than being the darkest spot in all history, is the searchlight that penetrates the surrounding gloom. For at Calvary Christ "disarmed the powers and authorities, he made a public spectacle of them, triumphing over them by the cross" Colossians 2:15. Praise the Lord! Rather than defeating Jesus, the cross became the instrument with which the opposition was defeated. The cross routed evil and darkness. And now the cross is a symbol of hope. It's the hinge to the door of salvation, the ladder that's high enough to touch the threshold of heaven, and the key event by which we reckon our relationship with God.

That's the great reversal. An instrument of death and torture is now a symbol of life and hope. Yes, the Son of God, Jesus Christ, was crucified so that we might be brought to God. That's why the cross is incomparable. For it's on the cross that Christ rendered sin powerless (cf. Romans 6:6). It's on the cross that Christ gave up His life so that you could have life to the full (cf. John 10:10). And it's on the cross that Christ took away the wall of enmity that separated you from God.

So embrace the cross. Realise that we're not saved by theories but by fact, and what is the fact? Christ died on the cross to reconcile "the world to himself" 2 Corinthians 5:19. He died to set you free so "you will be free indeed" John 8:36. And He held Himself on the cross in order to take the penalty of sin on Himself by offering "for all time one sacrifice for sins" Hebrews 10:12. That's the gospel! As Martin Luther says, "Alone upon the cross He hung that others He might save. Forsaken then by God and man, alone His life He gave!" It's incomparable! Even though Christ "committed no sin, and no deceit was found in his mouth . . . he himself bore our sins in his body on the tree, so that we might die to sins and live for righteousness . . ." 1 Peter 2:22, 24. Praise the Lord!

PEACE

Years ago, two artists competed with each other in an effort to produce a painting depicting peace. The one went up into the mountains, found an idyllic lake away from the clamour and clatter of life, and set about capturing the stillness and silence of the wilderness. The second artist also went up into the mountains, found a roaring waterfall with a gnarled tree partly obscured by the rising spray, and set about capturing the scene. Although beautiful, the turbulent waters certainly weren't peaceful. But as the painting developed it became evident that the focal point wasn't the roaring waterfall. In the cleft of a branch, surrounded by what seemed to be frightful danger, a tiny sparrow sat calmly and unperturbedly on her nest.

When it was time to judge their efforts, both artists agreed that the second picture came closest to depicting peace. For the first artist had depicted peace as a state of stillness or silence but the second artist had depicted a more profound peace - a state of serenity in the midst of turbulence.

In a world struggling with terrorism, the uncertainty of financial markets, natural disasters, refugees, AIDS, wars and rumours of wars, it's comforting to know that peace, like the sparrow on her nest, can be found in the turmoil of trials and trouble. That's a comforting thought. In the confusion, bewilderment, and perplexity of life you can still be at peace. What's needed is the right perspective. For even though this world is strewn with blasted lives, broken hearts, and blighted dreams there's peace if you know where to look. It's found on a tree, not any tree, just one tree, the tree of Calvary. More specifically, it's found in the One who hung on the tree at Calvary - God's Son, the Lord Jesus Christ.

Why not turn to Him today? Recognise that in Jesus Christ there is perfect peace (cf. John 14:27). And choose to receive that peace. "Do not be anxious about anything, but in everything, by prayer and petition, with thanksgiving, present your requests to God. And the peace of God, which transcends all understanding, will guard your hearts and minds in Christ Jesus" Philippians 4:6-7.

RECHARGE YOUR BATTERIES

If humans could be compared to batteries, I'm probably more like a Duracell. I can keep going and going and going. That's not much of an achievement though. When you get past the advertising hype there's a fundamental reality. The Duracell battery is an alkaline battery - which means it can only last so long. Once it's dead, it's good for nothing. A new one needs to be bought to replace it.

That's why I should aim to be a nickel cadmium battery. When they start running out of power they get placed in a charger until they're ready to be put back to work. Then they keep going until they're ready to be charged again, keep going until they're ready to be charged again, keep going until they're ready to be charged again, and so on. That makes them the best. The alternatives can't compare. Even a dimwit knows a nickel cadmium battery can outlast Duracell, Energizer, or Rayovac.

Which makes me wonder. Why do I keep behaving like an alkaline battery? (Which implies I'm a dimwit!) Why do I keep going and going and going? And why don't I allow myself to be placed in a charger until I'm ready to go back to work? After all, there's nothing worse than listening to a walkman running out of power. The music gets slower and slooower and sloooooower.

All of us need times to pause and be refreshed, to be renewed, to have our morale and vision reignited and our spiritual battery recharged. This is especially true when we're in the thick of the battle, when the pace is blistering, when our heart gets to be heavier than the load, or when the task is boring. For our ability to accomplish a task is directly linked to our morale and vision. When these two things are weakened, we begin to spiral into despondency. Life gets dreary. Challenges look larger. Days become tedious. The fuel pump of our inner drive gets clogged with pessimistic debris and then, before we know it, our battery is drained and we've lost our charge.

So take a regular time out. Make sure periods of activity are punctuated by rest periods when your imagination can get unclogged and your inner battery recharged. For optimism, bravery and faithfulness feed on high morale. The ability to push on, alone if necessary, requires clear vision. And in order for goals to be reached, there has to be the inner strength which comes from spending time with God.

That's the bottom line. God designed us to be rechargeable batteries. He wants us to return to Him again and again and again . . . We need to regularly pause and get plugged into His life-giving power. We need to frequently meet with Jesus for a transfusion of courage. We need to be renewed with the charge that comes from being in the tabernacle of His presence. We need to gain strength from going up into the hills to pray. We need to be revived by calling on His name. And we need to be refreshed by a daily filling with the Spirit. So don't delay. Recharge your batteries. In the words of Jesus, "Come with me by yourselves to a quiet place and get some rest" Mark 6:31.

AROUND THE DINNER TABLE

Families grow stronger around the dinner table. Now I'm not talking about physical strength as a result of a balanced diet. That's a given. I'm referring to more than the eating of a meal and the nurturing of our bodies. I'm a firm believer that families grow stronger when the veggie dip is surrounded with discussion, when the fork-fulls of lasagna are interspersed with laughter, and when dessert is topped off with devotions. As Proverbs 15:17 puts it, "Better a meal of vegetables where there is love than a fattened calf with hatred."

Of course the dinner table will never be a place for families to grow spiritually stronger unless we aim to make it special. We've done this in our home by establishing a few guidelines.

To begin, we've recognised that despite the fact we all lead busy and demanding lives we expect each other to be at the dinner table. Of course there will be exceptions and we certainly aren't legalistic about it. But as a family we treasure our dinner time together and try to avoid conflicting activities or appointments. We also don't allow the telephone to tyrannise our meal. Unless there's a really good reason for responding to the phone we leave the answering machine to deal with incoming calls.

We start each meal by sitting down, holding hands, and thanking God for His provision. Sometimes we sing a grace together. On other occasions we take turns praying. During the course of the meal we share the joys and challenges we've encountered through the day. It's a lively time. We joke, debate, address our concerns, reminisce, celebrate, sometimes cry, but mostly we just have fun.

Toward the end of the meal one of us leads devotions. It certainly isn't stiff or starchy. When Johnny leads, he likes to get up from the table and mime a Bible story. In recent months Matthew's been reading to us from a book about Christian martyrs. Christie usually shares an insight from her Teen Devotional Bible and tells us how a portion of Scripture has impacted her. Nana sometimes shares about something that happened when she and Dad were working in international evangelism. Karen often sings a chorus and gets us singing (which we all love to do), or takes God's Word and applies a spiritual truth. I usually read one of the articles I've recently written and use it as a basis for discussion. Our devotions are never dull. We're creative, varied, aware of each person's felt needs, and responsive to the movement of the Holy Spirit. When we're done, we close in prayer, praising God and interceding on behalf of one another.

Which is why dinner is often the highlight of my day. For it's at the dinner table that I'm reminded that God gives us our daily bread for both physical and spiritual nourishment. And it's around the dinner table that I can look into the faces of my family and be thankful for each one.

WEEPING INTO REJOICING

While working in research and development on the Caribbean island of St. Vincent and the Grenadines, I had the privilege of preaching for a number of weeks at a Pentecostal church pastored by Terry Gilbert. We enjoyed a wonderful time of fellowship and an extra special time of worship. One of the memorable choruses my family and I learnt was based on Psalm 30:5, "Weeping may endure for a night, but joy cometh in the morning" (KJV).

The message behind this text has been a wonderful inspiration in times of trial. It's a reminder of God's faithfulness, compassion, and restoration. A reminder that no matter how tough the going may be, God in His mercy sees us through and promises to turn our crying into laughter.

John Herwin knew the truth of Psalm 30:5. During the fierce occupation of Holland by the Spanish troops under the cruel and notorious Fernando Alvarez de Toledo, Duke of Alva, John Herwin was imprisoned for daring to fight back against the secular arm of the Papacy and the Spanish Inquisition. He had cut dykes and resisted the Spanish in order to have the right to worship God without the interference of priest, prelate or pope.

He was a man of passion and faith, filled with the Holy Spirit and dedicated to the Lord. "In prison," says the chronicler of the time, "he was wont to recreate himself by singing of psalms, and the people used to flock together to the prison door to hear him." That upset the Spanish Council of Blood immensely and in order to stop him singing they sentenced him to death.

At the place of execution he lifted up his head and began to sing his final song. An angry friar tried to stop him but John Herwin gestured to the gathered crowd and they too lifted their voices and joined him in the singing of his song.

And what did he sing? Psalm 30! "Hear Lord, have mercy, help me, Lord. Thou hast turned my sadness to dancing; yea, my sackcloth loos'd and girded me with gladness; that sing Thy praise my glory may and never silent be. O Lord my God, for evermore I will give thanks to Thee."

Then he said to the people, "I am now going to be sacrificed; follow you me when God of his goodness shall call you to it." With these final words he was strangled and burnt to ashes." His weeping had endured for a night, but in the context of eternity his joy came in the morning.

WARRIORS OR WITNESSES

It's probably true to say that all of us are either warriors or witnesses. In a world plagued by wars and rumours of wars no one is truly neutral. We're either supporting a war or watching it take place.

With this reality in mind it stands to reason that we should have an ethical framework from which we go into battle or watch others go.

Biblically speaking a good point of departure is Romans 14:19 which states, "Let us therefore make every effort to do what leads to peace and to mutual edification." In essence, we must wage peace. The dilemma is interpreting just how to go about doing so.

The principle interpretation has been the "just war" tradition. This tradition has provided a moral compass to those who would try to wage a justifiable war. It was originally articulated by St. Augustine (354-430 AD) when the Roman Empire adopted Christianity, a pacifist faith, as its official religion. With the Roman legions as the cornerstone of the empire the just war tradition was proposed as a basis for Christians to participate in war with a good conscience and in accordance with their faith.

The just war tradition is defined as the right to use military ends and ideals (with certain limitations) in order to arrive at a settlement of a dispute between two or more nations if other methods have failed. It suggests that the proper reason for going to war is to preserve, or recapture, the peace; i.e. one wars for peace.

In general, the eight tenets of the just war tradition are:

■ Just cause. Action must be defensive and not for purposes of aggression. The offense prompting war must be of a very serious nature.

■ Just intent. The restoration of peace and protection of the innocent. Revenge is never a justification for war.

■ Last resort. When all attempts at peaceful negotiation fail and every other means at resolving the conflict has been exhausted.

■ Formal declaration. War must be declared by the legitimate authority, not by an irate general.

■ Limited objectives. The conflict must have a specific limited purpose.

■ Proportional force. Only force sufficient to accomplish the objective should be used, i.e. the ends should be in proportion to the means.

■ Non-combatant immunity.

■ A reasonable hope for success.

A stark contrast to the just war tradition is the pacifist tradition. Pacifism is defined as the position opposing military ideals and advocates the settlement of disputes by arbitration. Although both traditions elicit considerable support from the Scriptures, pacifism has not been as popularly accepted as the just war tradition. The pacifist emphasises that Jesus didn't engage in war, that the Great Commandment majors on love, that the ideal should be to love one's enemies, that the Ten Commandments state that one should not kill, that nonviolence isn't cowardly, and that the early Christians were pacifists.

Which leaves the ball in your court. Here are some scriptures to consider:

Just war tradition - Romans 13:1-5; 14:19; Hebrews 11:33-34; Genesis 14:13-16; John 2:13-22; Revelation 19:11.

Pacifist tradition - Matthew 5:38-48; Luke 6:27; John 14:27; Ephesians 6:17; Romans 12:17,21, 13:10; 14:19; Hebrews 12:14-15; 1 Peter 2:21.

And some quotes to consider:

Constantine - ". . . (war) must be waged for the establishment of peace. Moreover, it has to be fought with inward love."

Athanasius - "To kill one's adversary in war is both lawful and praiseworthy."

Cherokee chieftain after reading the Bible - "Plenty good book. Strange thing; Christian man have it so long and be so warlike."

Mohandas Ghandi - "The only people on earth who do not see Christ and his teachings as nonviolent are Christians."

THE SECOND LAW OF THERMODYNAMICS

The Second Law of Thermodynamics informs us that there's a universal tendency for all natural systems to go from order to disorder, from complex to simple. According to this law our present universe is becoming less orderly, more random, and proceeding to an ultimate death. In essence - the earth is dying and will one day be dead.

The law is stated in broader terms in Psalm 102:25-26 where it says, "In the beginning you laid the foundations of the earth, and the heavens are the work of your hands. They will perish, but you remain; they will all wear out like a garment. Like clothing you will change them and they will be discarded."

Before the Second Law of Thermodynamics existed, many people had trouble believing Psalm 102:25-26. They reasoned that the universe had always been here and would always be here. But what the Bible says is true; the universe is running down, it's deteriorating. In God's time it will all come to an end, as indicated in Matthew 5:18 and Revelation 21:1, this earth, and the heavens around it, will pass away. This is not a remote possibility. Scientists can measure the decay. The day is coming when every star will have exhausted its supply of fuel. Each star will grow cold and dark, and life as we know it will cease to exist.

Which raises a conflict within the scientific world. If everything in this world is running down then how could the theory of evolution have any scientific validity? For the evolutionist believes the exact opposite to the Second Law of Thermodynamics. The evolutionist suggests that the universal tendency is for all natural systems to go from the simple to the complex. He suggests that life is gradually evolving into more and more sophisticated forms; that single celled organisms somehow diverged into multicellular organisms.

The mind boggles. Despite the fact that there's an ever growing list of fauna and flora that have become extinct, the evolutionist continues to hold on to his theory. Without a single scrap of fossil evidence to reveal the possibility of transitional forms, the evolutionist blindly and naively stands firm. As anyone knows who's taken the time to study the subject, the so called "missing links" of man's ancestry have been a litany of hoaxes or mistakes.

But then we shouldn't be surprised. Pride makes men do many foolish things. Evolutionists are attempting to be rationalistic and mechanistic, not so much for the sake of science, but primarily for the sake of secularism. Which leads to an obvious conclusion; evolution isn't about science, it's about a world view. The evolutionist

doesn't want to acknowledge that God is his creator because it would logically follow that God is his Lord and Master as well!

For further information consider networking with the *Institute for Creation Research* at www.icr.org

IN THE HEAT
OF THE BATTLE

In Ephesians 6:12 it says, "For our struggle is not against flesh and blood, but against the rulers, against the authorities, against the powers of this dark world and against the spiritual forces of evil in the heavenly realms."

Now you may be familiar with the above verse but are you familiar with the reality of the spiritual struggle about which this verse is speaking? Do you know where the battle lines have been drawn? Are you aware of where the fighting is the most fierce? Do you know how to identify the enemy? Do you know what weapons to use when you fight him? And are you engaged in the conflict? For like it or not, if you've accepted Jesus as your personal Saviour, then you need to be aware that at the moment of your conversion you were enlisted into the Lord's army and simultaneously singled out by Satan as the enemy.

That's quite a thought, isn't it? If you're a Christian, you're engaged in a conflict - in a war unlike any other war. For this isn't a war fought with guns and tanks. It doesn't involve jet fighters in the skies or nuclear submarines under the sea. Conventional warfare is irrelevant in the spiritual realm. In this battle the enemy is hard to pin down. Most of the time we can't even see him. He's a master of disguise, he skulks in the shadows, he attacks from within. His tactics are those of a terrorist. He infiltrates, ingratiates, then picks his moment and decapitates. Like the Islamic Fundamentalist, Osama bin Laden and his Al-Qaeda network, Satan and his demons are fanatical, they'll stop at nothing, use every conceivable weapon at their disposal, and attempt to wreak terror in every corner of the globe.

So don't be lulled into a false sense of security. "This is no afternoon athletic contest that we'll walk away from and forget about in a couple of hours. This is for keeps, a life-or-death fight to the finish against the Devil and all his angels" *The Message.*

Backing up . . . How does one fight this fight and how do we wage war against an enemy who's a terrorist?

It begins with the obvious. In the first place we can only fight the enemy when we're equipped by God (cf. Ephesians 6:13-18). We can never, and should never, fight in our own strength. We must concentrate on carrying out God's orders and have no objective other than pleasing our "commanding officer" 2 Timothy 2:4.

Secondly, we must know the enemy's tactics. This is a war about freedom. In Christ we've been set free (cf. Romans 6:7) and Satan aims to either limit or curtail that freedom.

And how does he go about doing that? Recognising that in many cases he can't keep Christians from going to church, reading their Bibles, and knowing the truth, his primary attack is on our time. He does everything in his power to keep us busy. The demons have been given their marching orders. Their job is to distract God's people from maintaining a meaningful relationship with Jesus Christ.

Yes, the powers of this dark world have been instructed to keep Christians busy with the nonessential of life and invent innumerable schemes to occupy our minds. We're tempted to spend, spend, spend, and borrow, borrow, borrow. We're persuaded to work long hours so we can afford empty lifestyles. Our minds are overstimulated by TVs, VCRs, CDs, PCs, radios and video games. There are few places left in which to hear the still small voice of God. Magazines, newspapers, billboards, catalogues, promotional offerings of free products, and the never-ending junk mail invade us on every front. Amusement parks, sporting events, plays, concerts, hobbies and movies keep us constantly on the go. In motoring terms, the devil's plan is to have us put the pedal to the metal.

Satan has devised hundreds of different ways to get us racing around the track. If the Christian isn't caught up by the things of the world then the spiritual forces of evil attempt to crowd the Christian's life with so many good causes, there's little to no time left to glorify God. Before believers know it, they're working in their own strength and sacrificing their health or their family for the good of the cause!

Don't be deceived. The battle for freedom is about time. Satan's plan is to cause Christians to get busier and more rushed than ever before. It's a simple yet sinister strategy. In tying up the believers time Satan knows that God, the family, the church, and the proclamation of the gospel can be marginalised or destroyed. No wonder BUSY has been referred to as an acrostic for **B**eing **U**nder **S**atan's **Y**oke.

Which is why I believe God is calling on believers to recognise the devil's tactics, go on the offensive by evaluating the use of their time, and make the adjustments that will enable them to seek first the kingdom of God (cf. Matthew 6:33).

You can do that now. You can walk away from the barrenness of a busy life. Make time and take time to draw up an inventory of how you use your time. With that done, cut out the things that cut you off from God. This won't be easy. This is where the battle is at its fiercest. You will need to "pray in the Spirit" (Ephesians 6:18), be scrupulously honest, and trust in God to help you evaluate what you do each day. Then with your new priorities in place make yourself accountable. Ask a mature believer to pray with you and lovingly encourage you as you seek to remain committed to having Christ as your number one priority. And finally, in the years ahead, never forget to always "stand firm" Ephesians 6:14. For in this battle - your life depends on it.

FOOD FOR THOUGHT

One of the great scandals in today's church is Christians without Christian minds. Every pew has a few - Christians who pray and worship as Christians, but don't think as Christians. You may know one or you may be one. The symptoms are obvious. The Christian without a Christian mind only eats once a week, is happy to be spoon-fed whatever the pastor is dishing up, and has little to no appetite for spiritual growth. In essence, they leave their minds unguarded, undisciplined and unthinking. It's a case of "anorexia religiosa" (Harry Blamires, *The Christian Mind*).

There are a number of reasons for this declining willingness to exercise the human brain. To begin, the Christian mind has developed a tendency to survive on fast food fads. Many Christians consider themselves too busy to study God's Word for themselves. They want everything predigested and conveniently packaged. Although they won't admit it they would rather be told what to think than be taught how to think. The result is a measure of shallowness and nervelessness unlike any prior period in the history of the church.

Another reason for the apathy between the ears is the choices that many Christians are making. If we are to have Christian minds there are things we must put out of our minds. As R. Kent Hughes says in his book, *Disciplines of a Godly Man*, "It is impossible for any Christian who spends the bulk of his evenings, month after month, week upon week, day in and day out watching the major TV networks or contemporary videos to have a Christian mind. This is always true of all Christians in every situation! A Biblical mental programme cannot coexist with worldly programming." Likewise, the renewing of the mind cannot coexist with some of the trivia and drivel we read, listen to, and laugh at. The psalmist would agree. Even though he never lived in the media age he said, "I will walk in my house with blameless heart. I will set before my eyes no vile thing" Psalm 101:2-3.

Now that's not to say that Christians should become legalistic and forbid many of the things available for our viewing and listening pleasure. I'm simply pointing out that input determines output. As it says in Proverbs 23:7, "For as he thinks within himself, so he is" (NASB).

That's food for thought. A reminder that the mind is like the stomach. It's what's put in that counts. That's why Philippians 4:8 provides a diet for the mind. It encourages us to feed on "whatever is true, whatever is noble, whatever is right, whatever is pure, whatever is lovely, whatever is admirable - if anything is excellent or praiseworthy - think about such things."

This can only happen when Christians are determined to stop conforming to the pattern of this world (cf. Romans 12:2) and immerse themselves continually in God's Word. There are no shortcuts. To renew the mind you must intentionally feast on the bread of life.

It shouldn't stop there. Along with reading the Bible we should read good Christian literature. My mind has been immeasurably enriched by classics such as Thomas a Kempis's *Of The Imitation of Christ*, Oswald Chambers's *My Utmost for His Highest*, Richard J. Foster's *Celebration of Discipline*, A. W. Tozer's *The Pursuit of God*, C. S. Lewis' *Mere Christianity*, St. Augustine's *Confessions*, Charles Colson's *Loving God*, and John Bunyan's *Pilgrim's Progress*.

But enough said. To think as a Christian you have to have the mind of Christ (cf. 1 Corinthians 2:16) and in order to have the mind of Christ you have to feed on the Word of God. So go to it. Make it your daily discipline to commit yourself to reading and studying God's Word. For as it says in 1 Timothy 4:7-8, the Christian should "have nothing to do with godless myths and old wives' tales; rather, train yourself to be godly. For . . . godliness has value for all things, holding promise for both the present life and the life to come."

WATCH YOURSELF!

In 1989, while coaching the Treverton College First Team Rugby Squad, I was injured. It happened because I failed to pay careful attention to what I was saying and doing. According to the players (to this day I still have no recollection of the incident due to memory loss) I gave an instruction for the pack of forwards to come up to me, rip the ball from my hands, and make it available to the back line players.

The forwards hurtled into the exercise with the abandonment of vigorous eighteen year olds in prime physical condition. In their enthusiasm they bulldozed me into the dirt, stomped all over me, and charged on. Dazed and bemused I struggled to my feet and proceeded with the training session. I repeated a "new" drill several times when it was only necessary to do it once. And I concluded by doing the warm down routine four times instead of once. By this stage the players were bewildered. That's not surprising. For none of us realised I had suffered a serious concussion, lost my short term memory and some long term memory, and would take some weeks to get it back. I still have no recollection of the incident apart from what others have told me.

As I look back on it all, I have to admit it was my own fault. I had intended to tell the players to walk through the drill but forgot a detail and ended up paying a penalty for my inattentiveness.

Don't make the same mistake. Pay attention to what you say and do. Be on your guard. "Watch your life . . . closely" 1 Timothy 4:16. "Set an example . . . in speech, in life, in love, in faith and in purity" 1 Timothy 4:12. "Be diligent in these matters; give yourself wholly to them, so that everyone may see your progress" and in this way "you will save both yourself and your hearers" 1 Timothy 4:15-16.

> Be the keeper of your vineyard,
> Watch your life and teaching closely.
> Give others an example,
> Of the Saviour who is holy.

UNDIVIDED ATTENTION

When my wife Karen thinks back to the first few years of her career as a kindergarten teacher she's reminded of little Richard Lockwood and the unique mannerism displayed by this boy. When he wanted to talk to Karen, he would climb onto her lap, cup her face in his hands, hold her cheeks steady, and force her to look at him while he spoke. Obviously when Richard needed Karen he wasn't prepared to share her with the other children. For Richard wanted to give Karen his full attention and he demanded 100 percent concentration in return.

In like manner, when we communicate with God we should give Him our undivided attention. We should make it our practice to "sit on His lap" and focus all our faculties on Him. Instead of sharing Him with the people and tasks that clamour for our attention we should be working to establish intimacy with God in much the same way as Richard did when he cupped Karen's face in his hands. Nothing should be allowed to distract us from the time we spend with God.

After all, our audience is with the "Lord of lords and King of kings" Revelation 17:14. We're speaking and listening to the One who will one day gather the nations for judgement (cf. Matthew 25:32ff). Thus you should ignore the telephone, turn off the television, and disconnect noisy mechanical devices and sound systems that could distract you from meeting with God. Furthermore, family and friends should be politely asked to avoid interrupting you unless there's an emergency. And those seemingly urgent tasks must simply wait till later. For Solomon reminds us to "pay attention" and "listen well" in order to "gain understanding" (Proverbs 4:1; 4:20; 5:1). And David informs us that God isn't interested in our sacrifices and offerings but He does want us to have an open ear (cf. Psalm 40:6).

So switch off the world and tune into God. Hear Him as He says; "Be still and know that I am God" Psalm 46:10. "Listen, listen to me . . . give ear and come to me; hear me, that your soul may live" Isaiah 55:2-3. For "the Lord is in his holy temple; let all the earth be silent before him" Habakkuk 2:20.

That's essential. If you want to hear from God you must engage every one of your senses to "listen," to "watch," and to "find" Him (cf. Proverbs 8:32-36). Refuse to be distracted. Rivet your concentration on the Lord. And recognise that He alone is worthy of your undivided attention.

Yes, you must "look with your eyes . . . and pay attention to everything" Ezekiel 40:4. Do this regularly and you'll discover that "whoever finds" God "finds life and receives favour from the Lord. But whoever fails to find" God "harms himself" Proverbs 8:35-36.

ACCEPT THE SON - YOU GET IT ALL

An art collector and his son owned paintings worth millions of dollars. The son went off to war and was killed in the act of carrying his wounded buddy to safety. The buddy was an artist and painted a portrait of the son which he brought to the father after he was discharged from the service. The portrait, although not great art, was placed over the fireplace, the most prominent location in the house.

The following spring the old man died and the art world waited with great anticipation for the auctioning of his fortune in paintings. The first painting on the block was the portrait of the son but there was no interest and the people derided it, urging the auctioneer to get on with the good stuff.

But the will stated that the portrait of the son must go first.

Finally, one of the family servants offered all he had - $10.00. "I loved the boy," he said. "And I would like to have the portrait if you're prepared to take what I have to offer for it."

When the portrait was purchased, the auctioneer announced that the auction was now concluded. This announcement brought loud protests from the crowd and demands for an explanation. So, under pressure from the people, the auctioneer responded saying, "The will states that whoever purchases the portrait of the son, gets everything."

What a fascinating story. But it's not an isolated case. There's a far greater inheritance available today, and, like the family servant who got everything, you could be the one who gets it all.

Let me tell you about it: It's an inheritance that's freely offered but can never be bought. Millions look for it but only a few find it. And although it's in this world it also goes beyond this world. And yet it's an inheritance that's easily within reach. For the conditions for attaining this inheritance are similar to the conditions in the art collector's will. All you have to do is love the Father's Son. For the Father will only give the full inheritance to the person who's prepared to love His Son with all they have. That's the bottom line. If you want the inheritance, you must love the Son.

So what's the inheritance, who is the Son, and how do you love Him? The inheritance is life in all of its fullness - both here on earth and in eternity to come.

The Son is none other than Jesus Christ. And you love Him by confessing your sin, turning from your wicked ways and unconditionally giving yourself to Him.

When you accept the Son, you get it all. For there are no half measures with the Heavenly Father. Everyone who loves the Son receives "an inheritance that can never perish, spoil or fade" 1 Peter 1:4. An inheritance for eternity (cf. Hebrews 9:15). For the Bible is very clear that "he who has the Son has life (but) he who does not have the Son of God does not have life" 1 John 5:12.

SHALOM

Jesus says, "Blessed are the peacemakers,
for they will be called sons of God" Matthew 5:9.

What a challenge! As we look around the world, it's obvious there's no peace. We don't have political peace, social peace, economic peace, or domestic peace. Families are experiencing breakups. Politicians are slinging mud. Children are encountering strife in the schools. Husbands and wives are arguing. Trade unions are organising strikes. Racial harmony is something of a misnomer. Teenagers are on the tear. And an increasing number of people are grappling with a myriad of psychological and emotional illnesses.

There seems to be no end to it. Man seems to have no peace in himself. Conflict is part and parcel of everyday life. We're fighting for our rights, fighting for recognition, and fighting for power and control. So much so it's probably fair to define the so-called peace of the world as an occasional moment in history when everybody stops to reload.

But it needn't be that way. God offers a peace that transcends all understanding (cf. Philippians 4:7), a peace that's deeper and enduring, a peace which brings the good things that God can give.

The Bible tells us how to find this peace:

- Personally make peace with God (cf. Ephesians 6:15).
- Help others make peace with God (cf. Romans 10:15).
- Encourage others to make peace with each other (cf. Matthew 5:23-24).
- Build bridges, not walls. Be at peace with one another (cf. Mark 9:50; Romans 12:18).
- Prove your love rather than proving your point (cf. Romans 15:2; 1 John 3:11ff).
- Be occupied with healing issues. Pray for your enemies (cf. Matthew 5:44).
- Spend your energy raising God up instead of putting someone down cf. Ephesians 4:22-32).
- Be committed to the message of reconciliation (cf. 2 Corinthians 5:18).
- Recognise that the things that divide are not as important as the things that bind us together. Live by the dictum, "In essentials unity, in non essentials liberty, and in all things love."
- Wherever you go; go in peace (cf. 1 Corinthians 7:15).

Which, when summarized, means you can live in peace if you "make every effort to do what leads to peace" Romans 14:19.

BALEKA!

It was a typical hot dusty day in the African bush veld and there I was inching along on my belly toward more than two thousand kilograms of black rhino. Blinking through beads of perspiration I could barely make out the two young women to my left as they slithered through the grass with the serpentine action of a boa constrictor after its prey.

The black rhinoceros, Diceros Bicornis, is the most dangerous of a highly dangerous family. They are up to 3 metres long, can run at 40 kilometres an hour, and can turn in 6 metres at that speed. They are armed with a sharp, vicious horn of matted hair, sometimes over two feet long, which can throw you 10 metres through the air. They have an acute sense of smell and hearing, but poor eyesight. They are highly irascible and given to murderous charges.

We were in the Umfolozi Game Reserve in Kwazulu-Natal and less than twenty metres from four aggressive beasts who were the product of a breeding programme to bring the black rhino back from the brink of extinction. I was teaching environmental and conservation studies and leading an expedition of twelve university students to study the unique ecosystem that supported the black rhino. We were working on foot with two Zulu game rangers.

But back to the action . . . The midday stillness was suddenly broken by two simultaneous sounds - the snorting of a charging rhino who had caught our scent and the command of our rangers as they shouted "Baleka! Baleka!" (Run away! Run away!). Suddenly the veld came alive as fifteen people sought safety. Everything happened at once. I found myself, with three women, at the base of a thorn tree. Ramming them up with a superhuman strength I didn't know I had, I glanced to my right to see the rhino, grunting with rage, red-eyed, a whirl of murder at full speed, only three metres away, and bearing right down on us. Everything seemed to be happening in slow motion. With the earth shaking I gave the last student a final heave while simultaneously praying that the rhino wouldn't see me huddled at the base of the tree.

My prayer was answered. The rhino swerved to its left and crashed off through the undergrowth in search of someone else to kill. Praise the Lord for giving them poor eyesight! We, of course, wasted no time departing in the opposite direction.

Most people know the sensible response in the face of danger is to flee. Paul gave this advice to Timothy. He told Timothy to flee from "false doctrines . . . envy, quarrelling, malicious talk, evil suspicions and constant friction between men of corrupt mind . . . foolish and harmful desires . . . and the love of money" 1 Timothy 6:3-5; 9-10.

So if you're facing temptation don't hang around - flee. Listen to the Guide. Respond to His shout of "Baleka!" "And pursue righteousness, godliness, faith, love, endurance and gentleness" 1 Timothy 6:11. Yes, when sin you see, it's time to flee!

VOICE MAIL

Imagine what it would be like if God installed voice mail. Upon praying you'd hear, "Thank you for calling the Throne Room. Please select one of the following options:

Press one for emergencies.

Press two for complaints.

Press three for information concerning the assigned destination of loved ones who have died, enter L-A-M-B-S-B-O-O-K, then press star. If you receive a negative response, disconnect and dial 6-6-6.

Press four for praise and thanksgiving.

Press five for reservations, then enter J-O-H-N, followed by 3-1-6.

Press six for the directory of angels.

Press seven for encouragement and assurance, then enter P-S-A-L-M, followed by 2-3.

Press eight for daily provisions or dial toll-free 1-800-M-A-T-T-H-E-W-6-25-34.

Press nine to be transferred to Gabriel's secretary.

Press ten for miscellaneous inquiries or operator assistance."

Of course, after you press the appropriate number, you'll probably hear the familiar excuse, "We're sorry, all our lines are busy. Your prayer is important to us so please don't disconnect. Your call will be answered in the order it was received." Then the familiar strains of *Sweet Hour of Prayer* will play softly in the background . . .

But as we know, we'll never encounter voice mail when we pray to God. Not even once. In fact it's an outright impossibility.

Which makes us "luckety blessed" as my wife would say. For we can "pray continually" (1 Thessalonians 5:17) and never be concerned about God putting us on hold. There's no delay. Simply call the Throne Room and you'll always get through. God's line will never be busy. He'll never have an angel fob you off, never ask you to select one of the following options, and will never be too occupied to listen. As He promises in Jeremiah 33:3, "Call to me and I will answer you . . ."

BECAUSE MY MOTHER ALWAYS DID IT!

The story is told of a young bride who was preparing a large piece of beef for lunch. The husband was shocked and mystified when she cut one end off the beef and threw it away. "Why did you do that?" he asked. "Because my mother always did," replied the wife.

A few weeks later the husband was visiting his mother-in-law and said, "Your daughter tells me you always cut one end off the beef before you roast it and I was wondering why you do that?" "Well," replied the mother, "I do it because my mother did it. Why not ask her?" So the husband phoned his wife's grandmother and asked her why she always cut one end off the beef before she cooked it. To which she replied, "I never owned a roasting pan large enough to hold a large cut of beef. Why do you ask?"

The influence of a mother over her child is profound. As the Bible says, "Like mother, like daughter" Ezekiel 16:44. That's a sobering thought. Mothers possess power and influence over their children. The example they provide influences their sons and daughters as children and adults. As Charles Dickens said, "The virtues of the mothers shall be visited on their children . . ."

It's therefore not surprising that the mother of Sir Walter Scott enjoyed poetry and music. George Washington formed his habits of orderliness and business from his mother. Charles Wesley developed his love for the Word of God from his mother Susannah. And Arthur Compton, the Nobel prize winner, had his love for astronomy cultivated when his parents gave him a telescope as a small boy.

This raises a simple question, "Mother, what kind of an example are you giving to your children?"

As you consider your answer why not contemplate the following. Proverbs 22:6 says, "Train a child in the way he should go, and when he is old he will not turn from it." Which is basically saying that children need a mother who will teach them right from wrong. Children need a mother who will inspire them toward high ideals. And society needs mothers who will model righteousness and truth so that these same values will become apparent in the lives of our children.

That's quite a challenge. But God gives mothers the ability to train up their children in the way they should go. When mothers turn to God through faith in His Son, Jesus Christ, they take the first step toward successful motherhood.

So, if you haven't done so already, begin with a personal relationship with God. Place your trust in Jesus and He will give you the strength and resources to nurture your children in His ways. As it says in Romans 10:9' ". . . if you confess with your mouth, 'Jesus is Lord,' and believe in your heart that God raised him from the dead, you will be saved." Do that today. For when you do, you will have taken the first step toward one day being able to say, "I have no greater joy than to hear that my children are walking in the truth" 3 John :4.

A HEART ON FIRE

Have you ever longed for more - hungered for a touch from the Holy Spirit? Have you felt that God has something special for you beyond your normal experience? When you read about Peter healing the crippled beggar (cf. Acts 3:1-10) or remember how Paul raised Eutychus from the dead (cf. Acts 20:7-12), have you ever wished that such divine workings were more common today? And as you've heard about men like Finney, Billy Graham, Wesley, Moody, and others, have you had an inner desire for God to touch your lips, strengthen your heart, and add an extra something to your life?

If you answered yes to any or all of the above questions then you're in good company. Spurgeon said, "We need red-hot, white-hot men, who glow with intense heat; whom you cannot approach without feeling that your heart is growing warmer; who burn their way in all positions straight onto the desired work; men like thunderbolts flung from Jehovah's hand, crashing through every opposing thing, till they have reached the target aimed at; men impelled by Omnipotence."

But even more important than Spurgeon's commendation is the will of God. It's His will for you to have that extra something in your life. He tells you directly and succinctly that He wants to "baptize you with the Holy Spirit and with fire" Matthew 3:11. He wants to give you the very things you long for. He wants you to have a heart that's on fire for Him. He wants you to be ablaze with His presence and on fire for His purpose. He wants you to be spiritually combustible. He wants your innermost nature refined by the fire and your outer nature made radiant by the fire. And He desires nothing less than your life aflame with His Shekinah glory. For the flaming hearted Saviour wants followers with flaming hearts. As He said, "I have come to bring fire on the earth, and how I wish it were already kindled!" Luke 12:49.

So how do you appropriate the fire? If you're a Christian, it happens when you "fan into flame the gift of God" (2 Timothy 1:6) which is already in you. In other words you need to tend the divine endowment. This isn't rocket science. If you want your life to take off, you've got to light it up. You've got to kindle the flame. You must recognise that God supplies the fire but you've got to keep it burning. And you must realise that as with all fires, if it's deprived of anything it will flicker and could eventually die out. General Booth put it in these words, "The tendency of fire is to go out; watch the fire on the altar of your heart."

There is no other way. If you want to be on fire for the Lord then you'll need to become an expert at using spiritual bellows. This takes effort and unreserved cooperation with the Holy Spirit. Yet it isn't something that's earned, worked up, scheduled, or simulated. Only God can meet your need. You cannot light the fire and you cannot produce it. You can only, by His grace, "fan it into flame." The fire is stoked when, in total integrity, you confess your sin, humble yourself before God, seek His face, and ask Him to reveal the things in your heart and life that prevent His infilling and empowering. For the fire only descends on prepared, faithful, and hungry hearts.

"Set us afire, Lord, stir us, we pray!
While the world perishes, we go our way!
Purposeless, passionless day after day!
Set us afire, Lord, stir us, we pray!"

Bishop Ralph Spaulding Cushman

WHEN IT'S STORMY

I've been in several really powerful storms.

One of the most memorable was the storm which devastated our farm in Claridge, Natal, South Africa. The hail stones were the size of tennis balls and punched holes' right through the corrugated iron roof of our house. They also smashed most of the windows and even stripped the paint off the walls that were exposed to the full brunt of the storm. It was phenomenal! The surrounding countryside looked like it had been passed through a shredder. We were fortunate to only receive property damage. Many of our neighbours didn't fare as well. More than a thousand people were left homeless. Scores of animals and several people were killed by the hail stones.

On another occasion I was on the sports field coaching the senior rugby team at Treverton College when a sudden gust of wind announced the arrival of a thunderstorm. In no time at all we were drenched and as we were already wet we decided to continue with the practice session. It was a foolish decision. Without warning there was a mighty clap of thunder and a simultaneous blinding flash of lightning that literally sucked the oxygen out of the air as it struck the field. The ground shook and several rugby players were knocked off their feet. The atmosphere, super charged with static electricity, caused our wet hair to stand on end! We were fortunate no one was killed.

Then there was the time Karen, Christie, Matthew, and my late father-in-law were travelling to Howick, Natal, when a storm hit with such force they were compelled, because of zero visibility, to pull over to what they thought was the side of the road. While stationary they were battered with hailstones that smashed the windscreen and reduced the car to a pitted wreck. Karen recalls how the din of the storm was so severe, she could see, but couldn't hear the children crying in terror as they clung to each other on the back seat.

I've also been caught, on two occasions, in swollen rivers after flash floods. God graciously spared my life. Others have been drowned due to flooding in the aftermath of violent storms. I've helped search for the bodies . . .

It's against the backdrop of these experiences that I read Psalm 29. Consider David's poetic description of God's strength and splendour as seen in a thunderstorm:

"Ascribe to the Lord, O mighty ones,
ascribe to the Lord glory and strength.
Ascribe to the Lord the glory due his name;
worship the Lord in the splendour of his holiness.

The voice of the Lord is over the waters;
the God of glory thunders,
the Lord thunders over the mighty waters.
The voice of the Lord is powerful;
the voice of the Lord is majestic.
The voice of the Lord breaks the cedars;
the Lord breaks in pieces the cedars of Lebanon.
He makes Lebanon skip like a calf,
Sirion like a young wild ox.
The voice of the Lord strikes with flashes of lightning.
The voice of the Lord shakes the Desert of Kadesh.
The voice of the Lord twists the oaks and strips the forest bare.
And in his temple all cry, 'Glory!'

The Lord sits enthroned over the flood;
the Lord is enthroned as King forever.
The Lord gives strength to his people;
the Lord blesses his people with peace."

There's a practical lesson in this psalm. A reminder that in much the same way as the earth endures thunderstorms, we have to face the storms of life. No one is exempt. There are times when the clouds gather and a storm sweeps in to hammer and shake us. But be encouraged. The One who "sits enthroned over the flood . . . gives strength to his people" and "blesses his people with peace" Psalm 29:10-11. So don't be afraid. God's with you when it's stormy.

IN CIRCULATION

During the reign of Oliver Cromwell and the Roundheads, the British government began to run low on silver coins. So Lord Cromwell sent a detachment of soldiers to a local cathedral to see if they could find any silver. After conducting a search the soldiers returned and reported that the statues of the saints standing in the corners of the church were made of silver. Cromwell was delighted, and exclaimed, "Good! We'll melt down the saints and put them in circulation!"

Now, although it wasn't Cromwell's intention to make a theological statement, what he said is excellent theology. His brief but direct order states the basic goal of authentic Christianity. It's practical theology at its best. For we were never meant to be silver saints adorning cathedrals and churches, but melted saints circulating through the mainstream of humanity. That's essential. One of the top priorities for a believer is to be in circulation - to be working out his or her faith in the world.

It isn't always like that. There are so-called Christians who substitute words for deeds. They have a profession of faith without practising the faith. They believe their words are as good as works. They use Christian jargon, but their walk doesn't measure up to their talk.

When this is the case, it's nothing more than dead faith. For a purely intellectual experience has never been, and will never be enough. There are no two ways about it. The genuineness of a person's salvation is evidenced by what a person does, and not by what a person says (cf. 1 John 3:17-18). Any declaration of faith that does not result in a changed life, and corresponding good works, is a false declaration. As John Calvin wrote, "It is faith alone that justifies, but faith that justifies can never be alone." Simply knowing theology or doctrine, and being able to quote Scripture or recite prayers, will never get you to heaven. Without good works you can have all the right spiritual words in the world and you'll have nothing more than a counterfeit faith. For if a person professes Christ as Lord and Saviour and yet lives a life that doesn't honour and obey Him, then such a person is a fraud.

James gets right to the point saying, "If you come upon an old friend dressed in rags and half-starved and say, 'Good morning, friend! Be clothed in Christ! Be filled with the Holy Spirit!' and walk off without providing so much as a coat or a cup of soup - where does that get you? Isn't it obvious that God-talk without God-acts is outrageous nonsense?" *The Message.*

That's straight talk. Separate faith and works and you get a corpse. For the Bible has consistently taught that a profession of faith without sanctification is dead faith. Yes, knowing without acting on God's Word, is simply proof of a false discipleship and nothing more. "The only thing that counts is faith expressing itself through love" Galatians 5:6. No wonder Jesus warned that "Not everyone who says to me, 'Lord, Lord,' will enter the kingdom of heaven, but only he who does the will of my Father who is in heaven" Matthew 7:21.

There you have it. Faith must be demonstrated. Words must be backed up by works. Faith is not a luxury; it's something which, at the cost of effort, toil, discipline and sacrifice, must be turned into the stuff of life. For there is nothing more dangerous than intellectual assent with no attempt to put it into action. As John MacArthur says, "The church today desperately needs to recognize and deal with the soul-damning idea that mere acknowledgement of the gospel facts as being true is sufficient for salvation. We must clearly and forcefully counter the deception and delusion that knowing and accepting the truth about Jesus Christ is equivalent to having saving faith in Him."

Now that's not to say that we're saved by works, far from it! We know that no one can be saved by works (cf. Ephesians 2:8-9); but equally, no one can be saved without producing works (cf. Ephesians 4:11-13). William Barclay puts it this way, "We are not saved by deeds; we are saved for deeds; these are the twin truths of the Christian life."

So let's make sure our thoughts are turned into deeds. As believers we must bear much fruit (cf. John 15:8). For in God's economy, we must be melted saints in circulation.

TO GROUND ZERO

In October 1809, Cape Town, South Africa awoke to a rumbling and shaking. For eight days the city was in the grip of a mighty earthquake that dislodged rocks from Table Mountain and destroyed homes. The people fled to the Cape Flats and watched with great fear as the "Paris of the South" (so named because of the wickedness and immorality) was shaken as if by the fury of a giant hand.

Kendrick, one of the few believers, wrote, "It was the greatest thing that could have happened to Cape Town as it brought a seriousness and fear of God upon the people to such an extent that many began to thirst after salvation. The spark of grace soon began to catch from soul to soul. Prayer meetings commenced and a most wonderful cry for God's mercy followed. The places of worship frequently became so crowded that many were unable to approach the door. Soldiers sought the Lord with cries and tears. Notorious sinners were pleading for pardon. Soon more than fifty men began to meet together and the number of Evangelicals in the Cape grew by hundreds."

Another shocking event occurred in Cape Town on July 25, 1993. While fourteen hundred Evangelicals met together for their morning service at St. James Kenilworth, their time with God was violated by a cowardly and vicious attack from the rear of the auditorium. Four gunmen threw hand grenades and sprayed the worshippers with gunfire from their AK47 automatic assault rifles. The sanctuary turned into a killing field. Eleven people died and more than fifty others were seriously injured.

Once again Cape Town was shaken, this time by the extent of mens wickedness. In much the same way as the 1809 earthquake alerted the people to their need for God, the killing spree at St. James drove the city back onto its knees. The City Hall was filled with people coming together to pray, and, rather than avoiding Sunday worship, people began to flock back to church.

It seems to me that it takes a shocking event in life before some folk are prepared to consider their need for God. That's borne out by a study of history. Most revivals of religion come at a time when people have reached a point of desperation, been startled out of their comfort zone, or been driven back to ground zero.

This is obvious in the life story of Jacob (cf. Genesis 25-35). From the day of his birth Jacob was striving and struggling to get ahead. He was always plotting and planning, devising and deceiving. Driven to be number one he would do anything to advance his lot in life and his tussle for power and control caused ongoing strife. Matters finally came to a head when Jacob's daughter, Dinah, was defiled by a local ruler's son. Jacob's sons retaliated by murdering a number of Canaanites and Perizzites and their action plunged Jacob into a crisis.

This was the beginning of Jacob's personal revival. When Jacob reached rock bottom, he turned to God. The events of the day shocked him to his spiritual senses and forced him to take drastic measures in order to save himself and his household. In Jacob's case he had to get back to ground zero. This involved getting rid of the foreign idols that had become the source of decay for his family.

It's the same for us. We need to get back to ground zero if we want to be revived. We must get rid of our idols. Nothing can have first place with the Lord - not our jobs, our hobbies, our goals, our business, our recreation, our marriage, our family, our theology, or even our church. Because if any of these things are placed first, or share first place with our commitment to God, then we've slipped into idolatry.

Now examine your heart. Identify sin. Purify yourself through confession. Deal with exterior and interior issues. And, under the pressure of the Holy Spirit's convicting power, remove the idols that have usurped your commitment to God. For you will only experience a force, freshness, and dynamic in your life when you confess your sin and return to your first love for God.

"And what does the Lord require of you?
To act justly and to love mercy
and to walk humbly with your God"

Micah 6:8.

HAPPY ARE THE NOBODIES

Most of us want to be happy. We want to grab all the gusto we can get. We want to pursue happiness wherever it can be found. We want to be able to do our own thing; live in pleasant houses, drive nice cars, wear beautiful clothes, go to a new restaurant, have a comfortable income, maybe have a facelift, amuse and please ourselves in all sorts of ways. In fact most of us believe happiness is our due, and some of us even think it's our inalienable right.

Which makes me wonder. Is it right for us to expect to be happy? Isn't it selfish to be wanting happiness when the world is plagued with poverty, anxiety and indifference? And, most important, what does Jesus have to say on the subject?

Well, believe it or not, Jesus has a lot to say about happiness. After all, Jesus is in the happiness business. That's right! He's not, as some would have us believe, a cosmic killjoy. He's not a God of do's and don'ts. Nor does He want to rain on your parade. Christianity is about being happy. Jesus wants you to be full of joy. For Jesus is the author of happiness, the way to happiness, the paradigm of happiness, and the One in whom happiness is fulfilled.

Now that's not to say that the happiness found in Jesus is the same as the happiness found in the world. Jesus doesn't say, "Happy are the somebodies." He doesn't measure happiness externally. Far from it. Jesus' happiness is revolutionary. It catches one short. It explodes in the mind. It calls for self examination. It shatters preconceived ideas. And it does away with easy believism. For, if I'm to paraphrase Jesus' words in Matthew 5:3, He essentially says, "Happy are the nobodies!"

THE CRACKED POT

Have you ever felt useless? Wondered why you exist? Desperate? Lacking in confidence? Believing you're inferior? Struggling to overcome low self esteem? Under the circumstances? Enduring contempt from others? Seeing your life leak away and your years fade out in sighs?

You're not alone. David, the psalmist king, on a number of occasions felt useless and weak with sorrow, grief or distress. For example, in Psalm 31:10,12 he says, "My life is consumed by anguish and my years by groaning; my strength fails because of my affliction, and my bones grow weak . . . as though I were dead; I have become like broken pottery."

The reference to broken pottery is a powerful metaphor. It denotes utter uselessness, forsakenness and disgracefulness. For broken pottery cannot be repaired and is only fit for the dump. Or is it? The story of the cracked pot reveals how brokenness isn't synonymous with uselessness:

A water bearer in India had two large pots hanging on the end of a pole which he carried around his neck. One pot was perfect and the other was cracked. The perfect pot always delivered a full quota of water at the end of the long walk from the stream to the Master's house. The cracked pot always arrived half full.

This went on for two years, with the water bearer delivering only one and a half pots of water every day. Of course the perfect pot was proud of its accomplishments and the cracked pot was ashamed of its imperfection and inability to perform.

Finally, distressed with its failure, the cracked pot spoke to the water bearer saying, "I'm ashamed of myself, and I want to apologise." "Why?" asked the bearer. "What are you ashamed of?" "Well," said the cracked pot, "For two years I have only been able to deliver half the quota of water because this crack in my side allows water to leak out on the way from the stream to the Master's house."

The water bearer smiled. "It's not as it seems," he said. "As we return to the Master's, house, I want you to see the beautiful flowers along the path." So, as they went up the hill, the cracked pot noticed the sun warming the beautiful flowers on the side of the path. But at the masters house, with half the quota of water leaked out, the pot still felt a failure.

Noticing the pot's sadness the water bearer said, "Did you observe how the flowers only grew on your side of the path and not on the other side? That's because I've always known about your flaw and taken advantage of it. I planted seeds on your side of the path, and every day as we journeyed from the stream to the Master's house, you've watered them. For two years I've been able to pick the flowers and decorate my

SEIZE THE DAY

Master's table with them. Without you being just the way you are the master wouldn't have had beautiful flowers adorning his house."

It's the same with people. We're all flawed. We're all cracked pots. But that's exactly what God uses. In His hands our imperfections become His perfection, our weakness becomes His strength, and our brokenness waters the flowers that adorn His house.

BULL'S-EYE

My friend and past colleague in the teaching profession, Colin Dykes, remembers an incident when he was a student at Maritzburg College. It had become popular for a number of young men to gather each morning for a game of darts. On one occasion they became so engrossed in their game they decided to skip the compulsory morning assembly. However, as the assembly ended a teacher discovered them playing and asked why they weren't in the school hall. The youth immediately tried to bluff their way out of the situation and said they'd run back from the school hall the moment the assembly concluded. They also said that the teacher could speak to Colin and verify the facts as they'd sat next to Colin throughout the assembly. They then rushed off to find Colin in order to persuade him to substantiate their story. But Colin refused to cooperate. Despite their pleading and cajoling he said he wouldn't lie.

Later that day Colin's resolve was tested when he was called to the principal's office to give an account of the events. He had the difficult task of telling the principal the truth, and, as he did, he knew full well that his testimony would result in his friends being severely punished.

What Colin's friends didn't realise was that he'd "resolved that (his) mouth (would) not sin" (Psalm 17:3). Colin knew that "the eyes of the Lord are on the righteous . . . and the face of the Lord is against those who do evil" Psalm 34:15-16. Thus Colin kept his "tongue from evil and (his) lips from speaking lies" Psalm 34:13.

We should live by the same standard. We shouldn't "fear the reproach of men or be terrified by their insults" Isaiah 51:7. Our lips should be harbingers of honesty and wary of lies. Our desire should be for God to "keep falsehood and lies far from (us)" so that "the words of (our) mouth . . . will be pleasing in (His) sight" Proverbs 30:8; Psalm 19:14.

Sir Henry Wotton says,

> "How happy is he born and taught,
> That serveth not another's will;
> Whose armour is his honest thought
> And simple truth his utmost skill."

THE KEY
TO LEADERSHIP

The key to effective leadership is the condition of the heart. For true leadership is more than character, more than ability, and more than desire. It's primarily about the state of the heart. There's nothing more essential. To be an effective leader you must know your own spiritual state well. Proverbs 4:23 says, "Above all else, guard your heart, for it is the wellspring of life."

Make no mistake, when it comes to leadership God is interested in your heart - not your performance, not your polish, not your position, not your power, and not your prowess. Man may look "at the outward appearance, but the Lord looks at the heart" 1 Samuel 16:7. And what is God looking for as He looks at the heart? He's looking for integrity, transparency, and purity. He's looking for a humble heart, a merciful heart, a malleable heart, and a servant's heart. For it's only when the leader has his heart wholeheartedly devoted to the Lord that he can be effectively used by the Lord.

Jack Hayford, pastor of the *Church on the Way* in Van Nuys, California, says, "The depth and height of success in the personal life of the leader . . . centers in a private venue: the heart. The true measure of a leader is in diametric opposition to his being controlled by techniques or methods, by slogans or statements, or by visible evidences of success, acceptance or recognition. Further, the criterion of a leader's ultimate measurement comes from a plane higher than human origin. The character of a true leader requires an answer to a call that sounds from the highest source and shapes him in the deepest, most personal corners of his soul. 'Success' at these levels - at the highest and deepest - will only be realized as a leader commits to an inner accountability to faithfully, constantly and honestly answer one question: Am I maintaining integrity of heart?"

Are you maintaining integrity of heart? Do you know what to watch out for? Are you aware of how your heart is prone to betray you? Here are some probing questions that leaders should regularly ask of themselves:

- Is it important for you to be right even when you're wrong?

- Are you nervous or worrisome when you're not in control?

- Does it bother you when no one notices you?

- Do you confuse significance with prominence?

- Are your plans more important than people?

- Do you consider yourself a cut above the rest?

- Are you in it for what you can get out of it?

- Are you a people pleaser rather than a God pleaser?

- Do you get angry when things don't go your way?

- Do you fear rejection?

- Are you proud of your academic credentials, your status, or your achievements?

- Do you get frustrated when you're taken for granted?

If you answered "yes" to any of the above questions then God's motives aren't fully present in your heart. Confession and a restoration of intimacy with God are needed. For it's only the pure of heart who possess the power of God. So consider Hebrews 10:22 as you endeavor to get your heart in sync with God's heart; "Let us draw near to God with a sincere heart in full assurance of faith, having our hearts sprinkled to cleanse us from a guilty conscience . . ."

THE STRANGE ONE

Here's a wonderful allegory I heard many years ago:

Once there was a colony of ants. These ants had only five legs. Whenever they walked, they went one-two-hitch, one-two-hitch all along the path.

These ants lived on decayed banana leaves and nothing else. I shouldn't say lived, for many of them died. Banana leaves, you know, especially in their rotten state, are very hard to find and so these ants had a very hard life. Many died young from over exertion and starvation.

Now it happened one day that a very strange ant was born among them. This ant had six legs. Everyone clicked their tongues in consternation. Many tried the best they could to console the parents on their child's deformity. Some suggested that for the good of the community they should kill him in infancy. But the mother begged hard, so they let him live.

Strangely enough, the little ant was soon rushing around much faster than his elders. This was ominous. And worse than that, he had a very awkward way of walking. "Look," they tried to tell him. "You don't know how to walk right. You have to go one-two-hitch, one-two-hitch. Now you try it right." So the little ant would try to put a little hitch in his step, but every time he tried that sixth foot would come down and he would leave his teachers behind. They gave up in disgust.

When he was half grown, the elders noticed another peculiarity. He was eating bread crumbs. "Stop," they cried, "they're poison, you mustn't eat that. If you eat even a mouthful, you'll die."

Now the job of moving the nest was very slow work. For in order to move an egg it had to be loaded onto the back of an ant and two others had to climb onto his back in order to hold the egg in place. They had to keep it from rolling off at every hitch, you see. So the egg was carried along, and the ant under the egg would be more dead than alive when they arrived.

They had just started moving their eggs in this way when they noticed the six legged monstrosity coming toward them at a rapid clip. "Hurry up you lazy thing!" they cried between puffs. "You have work to do." They had barely got the words out of their mouths when he passed them at the double and was carrying an egg on his two front feet, of all places. "You can't do that," they screamed. "You'll break it and you'll never get there." "I've already been there and back twice,' he replied. "Furthermore, I haven't broken one yet . . . here, let me show you how to do it."

That was the last straw. Rage came up in their throats and choked them. They dropped their eggs in a heap and rushed at him. "He has a devil," they cried. "He is beside himself," they shouted. "He is spoiling our nation," was the cry. "Kill him! Kill him! Away with him!"

"There," they growled in grim satisfied tones some time later. "He'll never try to teach us again. We'll solve our own problems, thank you very much."

Then they went back to work. One-two-hitch, one-two-hitch, one-two-hitch.

FAITH
IN PRAYER

The church father, Augustine, said, "When faith fails, prayer dies. In order to pray, then, we must have faith; and that our faith fail not, we must pray. Faith pours forth prayer; and the pouring forth of the heart in prayer gives steadfastness to faith."

The enemy of prayer is self-sufficiency. We struggle to pray because deep down we're convinced of our capacity to cope. Self-sufficiency opposes faith. Yet prayer begins when our human capacity ends - when we stop taking pride in our ability to order the world without help from God, and acknowledge that only He can supply all our needs.

The story is told of a young boy standing on the bank of the Ganges River in India. He was watching a Hindu holy man praying and decided that when the man completed his prayers he would go over and ask him to teach him how to pray.

When the holy man was finished, the boy walked over and asked to be taught how to pray. The holy man studied the boy intently for some minutes then suddenly gripped the boys head in his hands and thrust the boy under the water. The boy struggled frantically to free himself, but to no avail. The holy man's grip was steely firm.

Just as the boy thought he would die for lack of oxygen the holy man released his grip. The boy lay on the river bank spluttering and gasping for air. Finally he had enough strength to ask for an explanation. "Why did you do that?" he demanded. Looking at the boy steadily the holy man replied, "I just gave you your first lesson." "What, what do you mean?" asked the exasperated boy. "Well," said the holy man, "when you long to pray as much as you longed to breathe when your head was under the water - only then am I able to teach you to pray."

With this in mind let's examine our hearts. Do we long to pray as much as we long to breathe? Most of us probably don't. But we can take a meaningful step toward God today by admitting our self-sufficiency and calling on Him to increase our faith.

ON THE BRINK
OF DISASTER

On April 12, 1912, a steamship in England's White Star Line set out on its maiden voyage with 2227 enthusiastic passengers and crew members on board for the historic trip from Southampton, England, to New York City. It was a grand event. The ship was one of the largest movable objects ever built. It was 264.9 metres long, 27.6 metres wide, 31.2 metres high from keel to bridge, and had a displacement of 41,695 metric tons. It boasted electric elevators, a swimming pool, a squash court, a Turkish bath, and a gymnasium with a mechanical horse and a mechanical camel. No expense had been spared. An unprecedented seven and a half million dollars were poured into its design, construction, and fittings (equivalent to more than $400 million today). Its manufacturer, confident in their creation, referred to it as the "unsinkable" ocean liner. Little wonder that first class passengers were prepared to pay $4350 for a parlour suite (equivalent to $50,000 today). For it was a vessel second to none and anybody who was somebody wanted to be on board.

But then, most people considered the Titanic to be the flagship of all ships. It was an engineering marvel - the pinnacle of maritime achievement. The creme de la creme of ship building excellence. So when it slipped its mooring ropes the last thing on anyone's mind was the possibility of disaster. No one foresaw the tragedy that would soon unfold. Not even Nostradamus could have guessed what would soon happen when, a few days later, in the early hours of April 15, the ship had a fatal collision with an iceberg about 531 km southeast of Newfoundland, Canada.

Although it had taken three years to build, it took only two hours and forty minutes for the Titanic to sink and drop 3.75 km to the ocean floor. For unknown to the ship builders, there was a flaw in the steel plates of the bow. They had been incorrectly annealed. The steel was brittle, and instead of absorbing the impact of the ice they tore open and allowed the sea to rush in. In addition, although the ship was designed to hold 32 lifeboats, there were only 20 on board because the White Star management was concerned that too many boats would sully the aesthetic beauty of the ship. The end result - only 705 people survived.

No wonder it still captures our attention today, for among other things, Titanic reminds us that man's greatest achievements don't guarantee success. That perceived profits can quickly become astronomical loses. That life is fragile and death overtakes us when we least suspect it. That everything can appear safe yet disaster may be imminent. And that, "there is a way that seems right to a man but in the end it leads to death" Proverbs 16:25. Yes, Titanic reminds us that a man can sail in search of everything this world has to offer yet end up smashing into the iceberg of death and forfeiting his soul.

THE EMPTY
BIRD CAGE

One Sunday, George Thomas, pastor in a small New England town, came into church carrying a bent, rusty bird cage, and placed it on the pulpit. Eyebrows were raised and, as if in response, Pastor Thomas began to speak:

I was walking through town yesterday when I saw a young boy coming toward me swinging this old bird cage. On the bottom of the cage crouched three little wild birds, shivering with cold and fright. I stopped the lad and asked, "What you got there, son?" "Just some old birds," came the reply. "What are you gonna do with them?" I asked. "Take 'em home and have fun with 'em," he answered. "I'm gonna tease 'em and pull out their feathers to make 'em fight. I'm gonna have a good time." "But you'll get tired of those birds sooner or later. What will you do?" "Oh, I got some cats," said the boy. "They like birds. I'll take 'em to them."

The pastor was silent for a moment.

"How much do you want for those birds, son?" "Huh?! Why, you don't want them birds, mister. They're just plain old field birds. They don't sing. They ain't even pretty!" "How much?" I asked again. The boy sized me up as if I were crazy and said, "$10?" Reaching into my pocket I took out a ten-dollar bill and placed it in the boy's hand. In a flash he was gone. I picked up the cage and gently carried it to the end of the alley where there was a tree and a grassy spot. Setting the cage down, I opened the door, and by softly tapping the bars I coaxed the birds out, setting them free.

Well, that explained the empty bird cage. Then the pastor continued . . .

One day Satan and Jesus were having a conversation. Satan had just come from the Garden of Eden, and he was gloating and boasting. "Yes sir, I just caught those people down there. Set me a trap and used me some bait I knew they could never resist. Got 'em both!" "What are you going to do with them?" Jesus asked. Satan replied, "Oh, I'm gonna have some fun! When they get married, I'm gonna work on them to get divorced. If they try to love each other I'll teach them to hate and abuse each other. I'm gonna give 'em a good time drinking, smoking and partying. I'm gonna have 'em use weapons to kill each other. I'm really gonna have fun!" "And what will you do when you get done with them?" asked Jesus. "Oh, I'll dump 'em," Satan said proudly. "How much do you want for them?" Jesus asked. "Oh, you don't want those people. They ain't no good. You don't want those people!" "How much?" He asked again. Satan looked at Jesus and sneered, "All your blood, sweat and tears. I want your life." "DONE!" said Jesus. And the price was paid.

His message over, the pastor picked up the cage, left the pulpit, and walked out of the church.

HE'S ALIVE!

One of the profound memories from my childhood comes from the time when I was on holiday with my family at Cathedral Peak Hotel, in the Drakensberg Mountains of South Africa. It was an idyllic setting overshadowed by the sandstone and granite peaks that towered two thousand metres above the valley. We spent two weeks horseback riding (my father fell and broke his arm), swimming, hiking, lawn bowling, and eating lashings of good food.

One afternoon, toward the end of our holiday, the children at the hotel were having a whale of a time in the swimming pool playing dive bombers. Dive bombers is a very simple game. We ran across the lawns making Japanese zero fighter plane noises at the top of our lungs and then leapt into the pool with our legs folded up under us. The child who made the biggest splash and the largest waves was considered the best dive bomber. In the midst of a particularly fierce attack on an "American destroyer" one of the mums who was sitting off to one side leapt up and screamed, "Oh nooo . . . !"

We stopped dead in our tracks as a fully clothed man went hurtling toward the pool and dived in. Other adults came running from all sides as the woman kept screaming, "He's drowning! He's drowning! He's drowning!" I watched in horror, along with the other children, as the man who had dived in scooped the lifeless boy off the bottom of the pool and surfaced to the willing hands who hauled the limp body out of the pool and passed it to another man who then sprinted up toward the hotel.

It was a sickening sight. The boy's limbs swung lifelessly as the crowd of adults surged behind in consternation. What added to my shock was the realisation that the adults appeared helpless and afraid. For the first time in my life I felt fragile and vulnerable. About ten minutes later my mother arrived and said, "Don't worry lovey, everything is going to be all right." It didn't help much. I had seen the limp body and seen the fear in the adult's eyes. Furthermore, an uncanny hush had settled over the resort.

A few hours later it was time for supper. The normal hubbub of conversation had been replaced by hushed tones or vacant stares at the plates of food. Everyone seemed to be acting like they were guilty of something. It was awful. Then a most amazing thing happened. The hotel manager strode into the dining room and excitedly announced, "He's alive!"

It was unbelievable. Those two words electrified the room. People leapt to their feet and cheered. People laughed and rejoiced. Again and again, as if to confirm what they'd heard, people said to one another, "He's alive! He's alive! He's alive!"

Years later I heard an even greater story. The story "of first importance"
1 Corinthians 15:3. It was the account of the resurrection. The reality that Jesus
is not dead, He "has risen!" Luke 24:6. That "Christ died for our sins according to the
Scriptures, that he was buried, that he was raised on the third day according to the
Scriptures, and that he appeared to Peter, and then to the Twelve. After that, he
appeared to more than five hundred of the brothers at the same time . . . Then he
appeared to James, then to all the apostles, and last of all he appeared to
(Paul)" 1 Corinthians 15:3-8.

That's something worth rejoicing over. In the story of the resurrection we have the
deathless assurance that Christ is alive. He's no longer a memory, but a presence;
not a phantom, but a person; not a figure in time, but the timeless One who looks out
for us every millisecond of the day. As Gloria and William Gaither sing:

God sent His Son,
They called Him Jesus,
He came to love, heal, and forgive;
He lived and died to buy my pardon,
An empty grave is there to prove my Saviour lives.
Because He lives I can face tomorrow,
Because He lives all fear is gone;
Because I know He holds the future.
And life is worth the living just because He lives.

FOR
THE LOST

If you leave it to the pastor, the church will quickly die.
If you leave it to the seniors, the youth will pass it by.
For a church can never function with a few who do the work,
And the church will never grow if believers try to shirk.

Now each of us works hard, for all that we enjoy.
But let's be sure we don't forget, every unsaved girl and boy.
We need to pause, to stop and think, of life with no church here,
Of the children in our country, in a secular atmosphere.

When you see a church that's empty, when the people stay outside.
It's more than a vacant building - it's the vision that has died.
For it's not by one or two that the work of the church is done,
It's through a united witness that the lost to Christ are won.

For the church's work, its mission, is spelt out in the Word:
It's to worship, reach, and teach, until the world to God is turned.
So ignite your passion for the lost, humble yourself at His throne,
Then move forward in the Spirit, proclaiming Christ and Him alone.

MONEY OR YOUR LIFE!

The story is told of a knight out for adventure. Coming to a village, he heard of a terrible ogre in a pit. He decided to do battle with the ogre, despite the warning from the villagers that several courageous men had climbed into the pit and never returned.

When the knight arrived at the pit, he saw a narrow dark hole extending into the bowels of the earth. After trying to squeeze through the opening he was forced to strip himself of his armour and clothing before he was able to wriggle down the rope he had secured. All he had was a large dagger tied around his neck.

Hand over hand he lowered himself until he felt his feet touch the cool smooth floor of a chamber. Immobile, he waited several minutes until his eyes grew accustomed to the darkness. As his eyes adjusted, he focussed on a large mound which he realised were the bones of his predecessors.

Without warning he was surprised by the inhabitant of the pit. Surprised because the ogre was only as tall as a rabbit! Nonetheless he was a reasonably fierce, albeit little ogre, as he waved his arms and screeched, trying to appear as fierce as possible. The knight was undeterred. Drawing his dagger, he advanced on the ogre who quickly fled, disappearing down a small tunnel. The knight followed, and as he did he came across a second mound containing glittering balls of gold and diamonds as big as plums.

The ogre now forgotten, the knight wondered how he might get some of the treasure out of the pit. Without clothes he had no pockets. He needed his hands and feet to scale the rope. What was he to do? Then an idea came to him. He would take a diamond and carry it in his mouth. He reasoned that one large diamond would be more than enough to set him up for life and he could always come back for more.

Taking a suitable diamond in his mouth he began the arduous climb out of the pit. Higher and higher he climbed until the heavy exertion began to reduce him to breathlessness. Desperately needing air he opened his mouth to take a large gulp of air but as he did the diamond slipped and stuck in his throat. Choking on his treasure he soon lost consciousness and fell to his death on the mound of bones below. [Source: Anonymous].

You see the terrible ogre in the pit wasn't the little troll. The ogre in the pit was greed. It was the glitter of this world that choked him to death.

Jesus said, "Watch out! Be on your guard against all kinds of greed; a man's life does not consist in the abundance of his possessions" Luke 12:15.

SHAMPOO IN YOUR EYES

When Matthew was five and a half year's old, washing his hair was a major problem. He would sit in the bath while I put shampoo in his hair and then as soon as I tried to rinse the shampoo out he would tip his head forward and thereby cause the shampoo to run into his eyes. Tears would follow as he desperately tried to wipe away the shampoo.

It's not that I didn't give him the right instructions. I repeatedly appealed to him to tip his head back in order for his hair to be rinsed. But as soon as I started rinsing his hair, he would jerk his head out of the cradle of my hand, tip his head forward, and have the shampoo flowing down his forehead and into his eyes. The problem wasn't what I was doing. The problem was that his fear of water overcame his trust in me.

During one of these bathroom incidents I realised how Matt's struggle was similar to my relationship with God. Even though I know God loves me and is totally trustworthy, when I get in a bind I sometimes take my eyes off Him. That's when I get "shampoo" in my eyes. And that's when pain and tears are a result of my actions.

Which is why I tried so hard to explain to Matt that he could avoid the tears if he'd just keep his eyes on his dad. It was that straightforward, and it's been that basic, in a spiritual sense, for me. It's all a matter of trust. I need to keep my eyes fixed on the Lord so "shampoo" doesn't get in my eyes.

The psalmist must have learnt this lesson from his dad. He obviously knew about keeping the "shampoo" out of his eyes. In Psalm 121:1-2 he says, "I lift up my eyes to the hills - where does my help come from? My help comes from the Lord, the Maker of heaven and earth" Psalm 121:1-2.

YOU ARE
NOT ALONE

On 28 April, 1994, I attended the first ever *National Conference for Street Workers* held in Toronto, Canada. It was known as *Street Level,* and tremendous excitement and comradery was generated over the three days that we met. As I look back at the event, I'm reminded of two significant lessons:

The first lesson is from the conference slogan. The slogan was printed on the souvenir mug that everyone received. I have the mug sitting on a coaster alongside my computer. Clearly etched in black are the words, *You Are Not Alone.*

What a great reminder - I am not alone, God is with me. I'm encouraged by this reality every time I sip my coffee and I hope and pray that as you read these words the Holy Spirit will give you a little nudge and remind you that *You Are Not Alone.*

The second lesson came as a surprise. Until the participants came to the conference they were largely unaware of how many others were working as street ministry specialists. In a physical sense these workers had felt isolated. They thought that God had called them to a ministry niche where they would have to soldier on without fellowship. Yet when they came to the conference they discovered that there were more than a thousand people in Canada who, like them, worked to share the love of Christ with people living on the street.

Maybe you're experiencing something similar. You might not be a street worker, but you relate to the conference participants. You feel isolated. There's no one who seems to know what you're going through. You feel like you're the only one holding the fort. And if you could have one wish, you'd ask for some meaningful fellowship.

It was like that for Elijah. In 1 Kings 19 it reports on how Elijah was struggling with feelings of aloneness. He was running away from Jezebel, in fear for his life, and was dejected and depressed. In his lament to God he says, "I am the only one left, and now they are trying to kill me too" 1 Kings 19:14.

But Elijah was wrong. He wasn't the only one left. God revealed how He had seven thousand people in Israel whose knees hadn't bowed down to Baal or kissed him with their mouths (cf. 1 Kings 19:18).

So be encouraged. You are not alone. No matter where you are or what you're doing, God is with you. Furthermore, you are not "the only one left." God has thousands like you who are true blue and pressing through.

DISCERNING GOD'S WILL

People often ask me, "Pastor, how can I know God's will?" My response, "It's not as hard as it seems. Here are five principles to help you discern God's will."

1. Turn to God's Word. God speaks to us in and through His Word. As you go about your daily Bible reading ask God to illuminate His Word so that it speaks directly into your situation. Time and again God has given me direction with a verse or verses of Scripture. It's as if they jump off the page and in their own way say, "This is My will. Now walk in it."

2. Gather counsel and advice from mature believers. In Proverbs 10:13 we're told that "wisdom is found on the lips of the discerning" and in Proverbs 10:31 it reinforces the fact that "the mouth of the righteous brings forth wisdom." So seek out Christians who will lovingly and honestly be committed to your spiritual well-being. As it says in Proverbs 11:14, "For lack of guidance a nation falls, but many advisors make victory sure."

3. Ask God to open or close the door. When we trust God with our lives He will be the doorkeeper. Revelation 3:7 says, "What he opens, no one can shut; and what he shuts, no one can open." Thus we discern God's will through His control of our circumstances. Time and again I've simply prayed, "Lord if this is what you want me to do then open the door so that I can do it. But if it isn't, then shut the door so that I can move onto what you want me to do."

4. Seek the inner witness of the Holy Spirit. When God reveals His will He always gives us peace of mind. The Spirit within us confirms the decision. Romans 8:6 says, "The mind of sinful man is death, but the mind controlled by the Spirit is life and peace."

5. Act in faith. Don't vacillate. With the above four principles in place, make sure that once you've discerned God's will you act on what you know. Failure to do so is sin. As we're reminded in James 1:5-8, "If any of you lacks wisdom, he should ask God, who gives generously to all without finding fault, and it will be given to him. But when he asks, he must believe and not doubt, because he who doubts is like a wave of the sea, blown and tossed by the wind. That man should not think he will receive anything from the Lord; he is a double-minded man, unstable in all he does."

HARD TO BELIEVE

It's hard to believe anyone could deny the existence of God, yet one often encounters such people. They argue that there is no God and that positive evidence favours the assumption of nonexistence. They're also convinced that all religious belief, evidence and faith are false. As Friedrich Nietzsche, a renowned atheist said, "God is dead!"

But can the atheist be sure of this position? Is it rational to believe there is no God?

To begin, in order for an atheist to claim there is no God, he or she would have to possess unlimited and infinite knowledge of everything. To do this the atheist would have to have simultaneous access to every part of the created order. Which means that for an atheist to claim there is no God, the atheist would have to possess godlike characteristics. This is impossible, for as we well know, humans have limited abilities. Without omniscience and omnipresence the atheists' claim is clearly invalid and unjustifiable. For a claim is only valid when proved beyond reasonable doubt. Atheism is therefore nothing less than a logical fallacy.

Furthermore, the atheist has a deficient world view. Atheism makes little to no attempt to explain or make sense of the reality around us. It's unable to provide an adequate explanation for the existence of the universe and everything in it. Nor does atheism make an effort to explain the necessary preconditions which account for the laws of science, nature, logic, and morality. In short, atheism cannot account for the meaningful realities of life.

It's therefore hard to grasp how intelligent people can believe there is no God. In fact, it seems to me it takes more faith to believe in the nonexistence of God than it takes to believe in the existence of God. But maybe the atheist holds this position, not because the atheist is convinced of the nonexistence of God, but because the atheist wants to avoid being accountable to God. If so, then the words of H. G. Wells are appropriate when he said that "until a man has found God, he begins at no beginning, he works to no end."

That's a chilling thought with obvious implications. It indicates how ultimately, life is meaningless for the atheist. It's nothing more than "chasing after the wind" Ecclesiastes 2:11. Thus, as a theory atheism is bankrupt. For without a meaningful explanation for the existence of humanity, atheism robs mankind of any reason to live. No wonder *Time* magazine once concluded an article on Friedrich Nietzsche with these poignant lines: "God is dead. (Signed) Nietzsche. Nietzsche is dead. (Signed) God."

Fortunately, there's more to life than atheism's minimalistic and nihilistic view. Francis Schaeffer, the noted apologist, said, "God is there and He is not silent." That's a wonderful reality. Behind creation there is a Creator. God is very much alive. God is the originating cause, the continuing cause, and the conserving cause. As it says in His Word, "By him all things were created: things in heaven and on earth, visible and invisible . . . all things were created by him and for him. He is before all things, and in him all things hold together" Colossians 1:16-17. Yes, "In the beginning was . . . God . . . Through him all things were made; without him nothing was made that has been made. In him was life, and that life was the light of men. The light shines in the darkness, but the darkness has not understood it" John 1:1,3-5.

Now compared to atheism, that's not hard to believe, is it?

OUCH!

In the early eighties I was one of three teachers who accompanied a group of grade ten students for a week of leadership training in a remote wilderness area on the Botswana border. On the first night the students ignored the 10:00 p.m. curfew and by midnight the teachers were fed up.

It was time for action. Putting our heads together we came up with what we thought was a wonderful plan to restore law and order, and hopefully get some sleep. It was pitch black, but, armed with a stout stick and a thick pillow we groped our way over to the boys' tents. Then one of us said to an imaginary student, "Get out of your tent! . . . I've had enough of this nonsense! . . . You're going to get the lashing of your life!"

That got their attention. There was a deathly quiet. Meanwhile another teacher held up the pillow while the first teacher hissed for the imaginary boy to "Bend down!" Now it was my turn to enter into the drama. Swinging the stick through the air, I struck the pillow with a resounding thwack. A sharp yell of pain was enacted and then the first teacher commanded the imaginary boy to "Bend once more!"

Once again I swung the stick. But I lost sight of the pillow in the darkness and hit the second teacher across the top of his legs! This time there was a duller thwack and a sharp intake of breath followed by a painful moan.

The first teacher was oblivious to what had happened, although suitably impressed with the acting, and closed the drama with a final comment saying, "Well I hope you've learnt your lesson!"

It came as no surprise that the students were soon asleep. But the teachers lay awake all night. We couldn't sleep because of our colleague's groans!

Yes, things can go wrong when you're in the dark. Yet many people go through life walking "about in darkness" Psalm 82:5. They "do not know where (they are) going" John 12:35. They "walk in dark ways" and their path is often "dark and slippery" Proverbs 2:13; Psalm 35:6.

But God has a gracious invitation for such people. He says, "Let him who walks in the dark . . . trust in the name of the Lord and rely on his God" Isaiah 50:10. For "God is light; in him there is no darkness at all . . . and if we walk in the light, as he is in the light . . . the blood of Jesus his Son, purifies us from all sin" 1 John 1:5, 7.

SOUND WAVES

According to scientists, once a sound wave is set in motion, it continues on a never-ending journey, and that, with the right kind of equipment, each sound wave could be captured and reproduced at any time.

If that's true, then every word ever spoken, by any person who's ever lived, could be retrieved! The mind flip-flops. If someone invented an instrument to capture sound waves from the past, we'd have the potential to hear things we've only read about. Could you imagine it? History would come alive. We would hear the cry of the mob as they stormed the Bastille at the dawn of the French Revolution. We could listen in at the Berlin bunker as Hitler planned his suicide. We would hear the pleas for mercy as the Spanish Inquisition tortured some unfortunate soul. And we could listen to Cleopatra telling Antony of her undying love. We could also hear Jesus delivering His Sermon on the Mount or listen in as Elijah challenges the prophets of Baal on Mount Carmel.

Of course if this were possible then we would be able to hear every word we've ever spoken, or every word our friends and family have ever spoken. Which means that apart from the good things we've said, every bad thing we've said would also be heard. Every slip of the tongue, every angry word, the gossip, the lies, the sarcasm, the insults, the boasting, the complaining, the perversity, the cursing; everything would be heard. Nothing would be hidden. It's a scary thought. And it's even more scary when we realise that God doesn't need a sophisticated listening device to capture or record our words. Matthew 12:36-37 remind us "that men will have to give an account on the day of judgment for every careless word they have spoken. For by your words you will be acquitted, and by your words you will be condemned."

The anonymous poem entitled, *The Tongue,* is a fitting conclusion to today's meditation:

> "The boneless tongue so small and weak
> Can crush and kill," declared the Greek;
> "The tongue destroys a greater horde,"
> The Turk asserts, "than does the sword."
>
> The Persian proverb wisely says,
> "A lengthy tongue - an early death,"
> Or sometimes takes this form instead,
> "Don't let your tongue cut off your head."

"The tongue can speak a word, whose speed,"
Says the Chinese, "outstrips the steed,"
While Arab sages this impart:
"The tongue's great storehouse is the heart."

From Hebrew with the maxim sprung;
"Though feet may slip, don't let the tongue,"
The sacred writer crowns the whole;
"Who keeps his tongue, does keep his soul."

LESSONS FROM A FATHER

My father, George Murray, is a well known and prosperous business man in Johannesburg, South Africa. Here are some of the lessons I've learnt from him:

Firstly, success only comes to those who persevere. My father has weathered all sorts of challenges in business. He's been bankrupt, had innovations stolen, had his stock destroyed by fire and floods, been defrauded by an unscrupulous accountant, and even blazed it out in a gun battle with desperate criminals. On top of that he's survived the anti-apartheid sanctions, struggled through a stagnant economy, and been toe to toe with the opportunists who would gladly see him out of business in order to advance their own interests.

The business world is like that. It's a dog eat dog world. It's survival of the fittest.

It's no different in ministry. When the church is doing what it's supposed to do there will be people in opposition, people trying to run us out of town. After all, a healthy church is in opposition with the world, competing for territory, struggling "against the rulers, against the authorities, against the powers of this dark world" Ephesians 6:12. And, as in the business world, success will only come to the church that perseveres.

Secondly, you cannot sell a product that you're not wholeheartedly behind. My father is so committed to his product he works night and day, six days a week. He eats, sleeps, and dreams about his business. He's tireless in his efforts. He has a work ethic that few can match. He's charged with a single-minded purpose. And he'll give everything he's got to fulfill his objectives.

Ministry should be no different. You can't expect others to "buy in" to Jesus unless you're sold out to Jesus. There can be no half measures, no nine to five attitudes, no slipshod approach. God must be given our very best. Our love for Jesus must be characterized by a passion and fortitude that is unsurpassed. We must settle for nothing less than Jesus as Lord of all. Believers must be charged with a single-minded purpose, to promote Jesus Christ, and focus their lives on the attainment of this goal.

Thirdly, my father's business success has been built, in part, on his creative abilities. His business interests adapt to meet market expectations. He changes with the times. He pioneers new products and comes up with concepts and ideas with which to sell the same "old" product. He looks for ways to catch his customers' attention and capture their buying power. He works hard to keep current, to be one step ahead of his competitors. He establishes and maintains an environment, an atmosphere, in which his customers have confidence in him and his product. And he strives for what he calls a "win - win" situation in which both he and the customer come out on top.

If he didn't do these things, he would go out of business tomorrow.

Likewise, the church must be creative. Innovation must be encouraged. Adaptations must be made to engage shifting cultural trends. An environment must be created in which sinners will have confidence in Christ and His Church. Without compromising the gospel, the church must do what's needed to come out on top, to be in a "win - win" situation. We must catch the attention of the world and capture the souls of the lost. Which means we must tell the "old" story in a fresh and vital way.

Fourthly, it's all about profit. My father is constantly motivated to take new ground, planning on how to capture a bigger piece of the pie, strategising and pursuing practices that will open up the marketplace in a way that will increase his company's turnover and profits.

The church must have the same determination. Not for financial profit but for spiritual dividends. We must constantly plan to take new territory and attempt to advance the kingdom of God. We must never be content with the piece of the pie that we've got. Our aim must be to hot wire every person to God. To this end there must be strategies and practices that will result in noticeable advances every year.

Finally, never give up. After my father went bankrupt, he went right back into the fray. He refused to call it quits. He walked the streets until his only pair of shoes was worn out. He slept on the floor in his office after the bank took his assets and his home. And he struggled until he found a way to get back on top.

Thus when business started to improve I wasn't surprised when my father prepared calendars, catalogues, and T-shirts printed with the words, *Don't Ever Give Up.* Above these words was a caricature of a wattled crane trying to swallow a frog. It graphically portrayed the struggle my father had been through. The frog had its "hands" around the crane's throat and was squeezing with every gram of strength it could muster. Even though the crane was being strangled, and the frog was being swallowed, neither would give in.

So don't ever give up. Press on despite the opposition. For, as it says in James 1:4, "Perseverance must finish its work so that you may be mature and complete, not lacking anything."

MAN OVERBOARD!

"Some teachers have all the luck," shouted my colleagues good naturedly, as I drove away from the College with a busload of twenty year olds kitted out with their sun block and Ray Bans. The teachers were right. I was luckedy blessed. I'd been given the privilege of a week off from regular teaching duties in order to accompany the students on a five days, Ocean Sailing Academy, deck hand course.

A week of practical and theoretical instruction followed and each morning we had the thrill of sailing out of Durban harbour into the seemingly endless expanse of the Indian Ocean. Though there were many memorable moments I'll not forget the emphasis placed on the drill we were to follow if someone fell into the sea. Time and again we would practice the man overboard routine. Our instructor made it obvious that the Sailing Academy placed an emphasis on the preservation of human life and wanted to be sure that if someone was in jeopardy then the crew would know how to save him/her.

However, even with all the practice, I would look at the heavy swell of the sea, turn away from the blinding spray, and wonder just how successful we would be if someone really did fall overboard. I had a measure of doubt because I know that people are fallible, that equipment doesn't always perform as it should, and despite efforts people have been lost at sea and never found.

But there is one who never fails when we call on Him to save us. God "rescues and He saves" Daniel 6:27. "He rescues the life of the needy from the hands of the wicked" Jeremiah 20:13. And He rescues the poor, the oppressed, the distressed, and the weak, when they call out to Him (cf. Psalm 35:10; 72:14; 81:7; 82:4). For God's arm isn't too short and He doesn't lack strength (cf. Isaiah 50:2). So if you need Him today, call out and the infallible Rescuer "will sustain you and . . . rescue you" Isaiah 46:4. As William F. McDowell says, "We are saved by a Person, and only by a Person, and only by one Person."

WHEN TREES COME DOWN

In the Fall of 2000 the Muskoka's were battered by powerful winds. At Sparrow Lake dozens of trees fell under the onslaught of the winds. One large pine crushed the bunkie and smashed through the roof of Hugh and Marnie's cottage. Fortunately nobody was there at the time.

Later, as I stood with Hugh staring in disbelief at the damage, I was struck by the fact that no tree just suddenly breaks apart. When I examined where it had snapped off near the base of the trunk it was obvious that no one could have known ahead of time that the fall was inevitable. The pith and heartwood of the tree had died and although the sapwood, bark, and external appearance of the tree looked healthy, the internal decay had been present for years.

It can be like that with humans. Everything can look healthy on the outside but the core of an individual can be diseased or even dead. Sin is like that. It erodes from the inside out. Slowly and silently it eats away and destroys the very fibre of a person's being. In many cases no one notices. Life goes on as usual, even for decades, but then, when the winds of adversity blow, something snaps and everything comes crashing down.

Nobody was injured when the trees at Sparrow Lake fell but when people fall there are always injuries. Sin is no respecter of persons. Family, friends, fellow believers, and even distant acquaintances can be hurt.

At Hugh and Marnie's cottage the damage was quickly dealt with. The tree was reduced to firewood after a few hours of work with a chainsaw. Shingles and gutters on the roof were replaced, ceilings patched, the bunkie cleared away, and the other damage appropriately handled. But people aren't property. It's not as easy to clean away the debris and damage of a life that's come crashing down.

"So if you think you are standing firm, be careful that you don't fall!" 1 Corinthians 10:12. You may look good on the outside, may even be producing fruit, but never forget that strength comes from the core. You must look after the part that no one else can see. Look within. Don't close today's reading with a shrug. Spend a few minutes scrutinizing your life. Ask yourself, "How is it with the pith of my being? Is there any moral decay? Have I made any compromises? How is it with my soul?" And hide nothing. For if you fail to be healthy on the inside, the collapse that will ultimately come will cost immeasurably more than any damage caused by a fallen tree.

TO PERK
YOU UP

I was helping put out the garbage recently. It's not a job I do too often. Usually it's a "pink job" in our home. Nonetheless, here I was sorting out what needed to be recycled, composted, or designated for the dump, when it struck me how we regularly clear out the accumulated household trash yet often fail to get rid of the garbage in our hearts and minds. Every day we allow all kinds of negative stuff to enter our lives. We see and read the news on television and in the newspapers. We listen to colleagues, friends, and family who recycle their negative thoughts and issues our way. And week by week we store this clutter inside of us.

Little wonder we end up feeling depressed, uncertain, and lacking in vitality. The garbage clutters everything. As a result we're unable to achieve our full potential. Even worse, it becomes a case of garbage in and garbage out. The junk in our lives overflows into the things we say and do.

But it needn't be like this. God is in the business of cleaning out the garbage. He can help us dump the trash. It happens when we recognise that it needs to be dealt with regularly. So turn to God, in prayer, every day. Identify the garbage and hand it over to Him for disposal.

Furthermore, recognise that you can consume less junk. You can choose what to take in. "Do not conform any longer to the pattern of this world, but be transformed by the renewing of your mind" Romans 12:2. You can watch less television, read fewer newspapers, and politely tell negative people, "If it's okay with you, I'd rather not hear about that." It's all the housekeeping you'll need to do. By taking in less garbage every day you'll be rejuvenated because it will take less energy to get rid of it. In addition, you'll also have room in your life for things that are positive. You'll be better able to think about the things that are excellent and praiseworthy - to consider "whatever is true, whatever is noble, whatever is right, whatever is pure, whatever is lovely, whatever is admirable" Philippians 4:8. So go ahead and do it. You'll be surprised at how much better you'll feel.

WORSHIP

"Love the Lord your God with all your heart and
with all your soul and with all your mind" Matthew 22:37.

The chief end of man is to be occupied with God over everything else. Open the heart to the love of God, devote the will to the purpose of God, quicken the conscience by the holiness of God, feed the mind on the truth of God, and in so doing, recognise this isn't about us, it's all about Him.

Let's never forget; we're to be focussed on One. We should aim to worship Him actively, cheerfully, relevantly, creatively, sacrificially, reverentially and wholeheartedly. Don't hold back. Never be too comfortable to give your all to the Lord.

Of course this is only possible when we realise that worship is the recovery, then rejoicing in our first love for Him. It involves repentance and right attitude, brokenness and desire, and requesting His compassion. But it's also a lot more. Worship is forgetting our dignity and remembering His Deity. It's hunger pangs in our hearts. It's about a sacrifice of praise with a single intent - to attract God's attention. It's breaking down the walls of separation between us and God. It's acts of penitence which call on God to open the windows of Heaven. It's an invitation for God to come down and be among us. It's remembering how God loves to be with His children. It's intimacy with the Father. Like Bartimaeus, it's refusing to let God pass by. It's wanting an encounter with God that we won't be able to get over. And it's wanting nothing less than for God to reveal His face.

Furthermore, it must come from men and women who know what it means to have "a broken spirit; a broken and contrite heart" Psalm 51:17. That's essential. It's only when we worship the Lord with an outpouring of a burning heart that He will show up in a tangible and dynamic way. Worship should be the main course of everything we say or do. For it's only when our worship is more than a warm up act, more than an appetizer, and more than a curtain raiser that we'll truly get to meet Him.

So make sure your life is characterized by intimacy with the Father, by a vibrant relationship with the Son, and by a daily hosting of the Holy Spirit. For to stop short or settle for anything less isn't good enough. We must desire more than thrills and chills. More than holy goose-bumps. More than the smell of His fragrance. And more than a temporary visitation. Ultimately, we must want to know Jesus in all His vitality, glory and power - to pursue Him until we see Him face to face.

LOCUSTS

In the late sixties I was travelling with my parents through the Karoo, the semidesert in the South Western Cape of South Africa. As dusk crept in we were approaching a dorp (village) when regiments of locusts swarmed down. Darkness immediately enveloped us as the tiny insects blotted out the last of the sun's rays. Turning on the car's headlights, we made our way toward the hotel where we had planned to spend the night. By the time we'd parked the car the locusts had settled. There was a solid carpet of insects as far as we could see. It presented a dilemma. How were we to get from the car to the hotel? Mum immediately refused to budge, as far as she was concerned she would rather sleep in the car than get out and walk through the writhing brown sea.

Frazer and I were braver, or perhaps our hunger, and the thought of a comfortable bed seemed better than an indecisive night on the back seat. In a flash we were out of the car. As our feet touched the pavement there was a crunching sound accompanied by little clouds of locusts that rose up as we made our way to the lobby.

The following morning we were up at the crack of dawn. Full of bravado we ran outside as the locusts were lifting off and being borne away on a gentle breeze. Within 15 minutes most of them were gone. They had eaten everything. All that was left was dirt and stones. There wasn't a shred of vegetation anywhere. It reminded me of pictures that I'd seen of the lunar landscape and I remember thinking that taken singularly, the locusts weren't much of a force to be reckoned with, yet as a swarm they were amazingly powerful.

God's Word provides a similar insight. In Proverbs 30:27 it points out that locusts are extremely wise because they "have no king yet they advance together in ranks." That's a big lesson from a little thing. The locusts have the ability to accomplish something because they stick together. They don't have much power individually but they have strength in numbers.

In our individual capacity you and I are restricted in what we can accomplish for the cause of Christ. We have limited energy, a quotient of brainpower, and there are only so many things we can do with the skeleton and muscles that make up our body. However, when we get together in a group our corporate abilities are vastly superior to the sum of our individual abilities. As we're reminded in Ecclesiastes 4:12, "Though one may be overpowered, two can defend themselves. A cord of three strands is not quickly broken."

That's why we need to pull together. When God's people get united behind a common vision and task there's power to accomplish great things. So, like the locusts, stick with one another. Don't go it alone. It's united we stand or divided we fall.

EXAMPLE IS BETTER
THAN PRECEPT

Being a parent isn't always easy. Personally, I think the biggest challenge I have as a father is to be a good example for my children. I'm in good company. Abraham Lincoln said, "There is just one way to bring up a child in the way he should go and that is to travel that way yourself." That means my example is better than my precept. What I do is ultimately more important than what I say. And even though my children might not understand my advice they'll never misinterpret how I act and how I live. Allow me to elaborate:

Romans 2:21 says, ". . . you then, who teach others, do you not teach yourself?" This verse confirms the fact that what we say to our children must be in accordance with what we know and live by personally. It reminds us that "right example bolsters effectively the fruit of the lips" Anonymous. And it teaches us that "example is not the main thing in influencing others. It is the only thing!" Albert Schweitzer.

I'm therefore convinced that example schools our children. Actions speak louder than our words. As an old saying puts it, we must "be what we would make others."

Thus, if we want our children not to fight then we must control our tempers. If we want our children not to condemn then we mustn't criticise. If we want our children to be well mannered then we must be polite. If we want our children to be honest and fair then we must be true and just. If we want our children to share then we must be generous. If we want our children to be long suffering then we must be patient. And if we want our children to follow Jesus then we must follow the Lord.

In other words, it's in the daily life of the parents that children gain their most indelible impressions. We can therefore only appeal to our children on the basis of our own example. It's what we are that influences our children more than anything else.

The anonymous poem, *The Little Chap*, serves as a fitting postscript:

> A careful man I ought to be -
> A little fellow follows me.
> I do not dare to go astray,
> For fear he'll go the self same way.
>
> I cannot once escape his eyes.
> What'er he sees me do, he tries.
> Like me, he says he's going to be -
> The little chap who follows me.

He thinks that I am good and fine,
Believes in every word of mine.
Wrong steps by me he must not see -
The little fellow who follows me.

I must remember as I go,
Through summer's sun and winter's snow,
I'm building for the years to be,
The little chap who follows me.

TAMING
THE TONGUE

Someone once observed that the tongue is in a wet place and can easily slip. Someone else observed that the tongue is the world's smallest, but largest trouble maker. No wonder God put the tongue behind the bars of the teeth and walled it in with the mouth. For in so doing He reminds us that one of the greatest challenges we face in life is the taming of the tongue.

Which begs the question. How do we tame the tongue?

It begins, according to James 3:3-4, when we put the tongue under the control of a strong hand. Just as a jockey rides a powerful stallion using a bridle and bit, and a pilot steers a ship using a helm connected to a rudder, so too, the tongue must be controlled by someone beyond itself.

But who is that someone? Who can be trusted to tame the tongue? It can't be you or I. When left to our own devices there's no limit to what we can say. We have the old nature wanting to control us and make us sin. And there are circumstances around us that can lead us into saying things we know we shouldn't say. As James 3:2,8 tells us, "We all stumble in many ways . . . no man can tame the tongue. It is a restless evil full of deadly poison." Thus someone else is needed, someone greater, someone perfect, someone who is never at fault in what he says. And the only One who fits that criterion is God.

Yes, in order to tame the tongue you need to submit yourself to God. And in order to submit yourself to God, you need to yield your whole life to Him. For ultimately, the problem isn't the tongue; it's the heart. When something's wrong with the heart, there will be something wrong with the tongue. As we well know, what comes out of us is what's in us. As it says in Matthew 15:18, "The things that come out of the mouth come from the heart, and these make a man unclean."

There's the rub. There is no other way for the tongue to be tamed unless you ask God's Spirit to take control. The heart is the key to right speech. When God is Lord of the heart, then He's Lord of the lips too. "For out of the overflow of the heart the mouth speaks" Matthew 12:34.

IN A FAST PACED WORLD

Life seems to be racing along at top speed. The home and office are busier than ever. It's the world of two in one conditioner and shampoo. The world of pizza delivery in twenty minutes or less. A world in which we act as if everything comes to those who hustle while they wait. A world in which we buy time saving gadgets but don't have the time or patience to read the instructions and figure out how to use them. A world of the five minutes ab. exerciser. A world in which we've worked out 101 things to do at the traffic lights (My wife says she'll one day publish a book entitled *One Hundred and One Things to do at the Traffic Lights*). A world where we expect microwave maturity. And a world in which we arrive at the checkout lines of the grocery store, count how many people are in each line, assess the number of items per shopping cart, and work out which checkout will be the quickest. It's the world of the Queen of Hearts in Alice in Wonderland: "Now here, you see, it takes all the running you can do, to keep in the same place. If you want to get somewhere else, you must run at least as fast as that!"

Then Jesus comes on the scene. He reminds us that we can't go faster than the One who's leading. He says, "Come with me by yourselves to a quiet place and get some rest. So they went away by themselves in a boat to a solitary place" Mark 6:31-32.

Taking Him at His Word I often go on canoe trips. I highly recommend one. You'll be eaten alive by mosquitoes and black flies. You'll stagger across portages under intolerable burdens. You'll paddle until your muscles burn. You'll live cheek by jowl with people who spend most of their time talking about how to go to the washroom when there's no washroom to go to. You'll eat food flavoured with a potpourri of twigs and unknown entities that you don't want to know or ask about. Your clothes will smell of wood smoke, bug spray, sun-block, grease and sweat. And when you get to the end of a long tiring day on the open water you'll have a fitful night's sleep on a bed of rocks.

I'm not kidding. Everyone should go on a canoe trip. I try and do at least one or more a year. For a canoe trip brings life back into perspective. It reminds me that service must be followed by solitude. It reminds me of the many things I often take for granted. It helps me get rid of the stuff that props me up. It helps me sample the divine whisper. It reveals how we exchange depth for breadth. It enables me to travel down the waterway less travelled. It clears away the clutter of busyness. It removes the distractions of technology and material possessions. It addresses my problem with "hurry sickness." It enables me to practice the art of slowing down. And it helps me to stop skimming life and start living it.

Yes, I highly recommend that everyone go on a canoe trip. You'll see the stars like you've never seen them before. You'll thrill to the sound of the loon across the lake. You'll be captivated by the beauty of a water lily. You'll taste the smell of rain on parched earth. You'll marvel at the hues of a sunset. You'll wonder how cypress trees manage to grow in cracks in the rocks. You'll laugh at the mating dance of the dragonflies. You'll be enticed to swim in cool waters. You'll be silenced by the cry of a wolf. You'll be thankful for the warmth of the sun. You'll see people through softer eyes. You'll remember the One who gives you strength to press on. And you'll discover afresh how to give thanks to the God whose love endures forever.

THIRSTY FOR MORE

Every once in a while a teacher has the privilege of teaching a truly enthusiastic student. Peta Barnsley was one such student and I was the teacher. She attended the Howick School of the Bible and was enrolled in the Christian Ethics Course. Despite her responsibilities as a farmer's wife, a grandmother, and the session clerk at the Upper Umgeni Presbyterian Church, very little got her down.

Even after the conclusion of an intense three hour workshop on abortion she still had the energy to come and talk with me. As usual Peta was excited about what we had been learning and with irrepressible enthusiasm exclaimed; "I can't understand why all the Christians in town aren't taking this course . . . I just can't get enough of it!"

That comment; "I just can't get enough of it" has stuck with me. It's been a reminder of how I should thirst for more. How it should be my daily exercise to cry to God saying, "I just can't get enough of You!" That's the bottom line. My "soul" should "pant . . . for the living God . . . as the deer pants for streams of water" Psalm 42:1-2. And I should "earnestly . . . seek" Him just as I would seek water "in a dry and weary land" Psalm 63:1.

> "As the deer pants for the water, So my soul longs after You.
> You alone are my heart's desire, And I long to worship You.
> For You alone are my strength and shield;
> To You alone will my spirit yield.
> For You alone are my heart's desire, And I long to worship You."

Martin Nystrom

"THIS IS THE DAY . . ."

"This is the day the Lord has made; let us rejoice and be glad in it"
Psalm 118:24.

So stop waiting . . .
Until your car or home is paid off.
Until you get a new car or home.
Until you go back to school.
Until you finish school.
Until you get a job.
Until you lose your job.
Until you get a promotion.
Until you get married.
Until you have kids.
Until the kids leave the house.
Until your spouse gets his or her act together.
Until you're financially secure.
Until you lose 5 kg's.
Until you gain 5 kg's.
Until you can go on vacation.
Until you retire.
Until winter.
Until spring.
Until summer.
Until fall.
Until you die.

There is no better time than right now to live life to the full. Today is the first day of the rest of your life. It's pointless thinking of the lost hours of yesterday. Don't wait until tomorrow. Time waits for no one. Don't hold back. Forget about what might have been.

Act on the desire of your heart now.

Work like you don't need money. Sing like you've never sung before. Laugh as if the whole world laughs with you. Dance like no one's watching. Play with every ounce of your strength. Worship with all the passion you can muster. Love like you've never been hurt.

Seize the day!

HOW TO HAVE A QUIET TIME

Here's a guide to help you meet with God each day:

PREPARE. Begin by thanking God for the opportunity of meeting with Him. Remember, He is a holy God and you need to come into His presence by asking forgiveness for your sins.

PERIMETER. When you turn to God's Word look at the passage in context. Read what proceeds and follows the text under consideration. This will help you understand the entire message and hopefully not read anything into the passage that would distort the intended meaning.

PARAPHRASE. Once you have read a passage put it into simple words that help you to understand what God is saying to you. Maybe even write it out as if you were telling a little child what you have read.

PULVERISE. Now scrutinise each word, each phrase, and each sentence. Find the main point. Consider what's said in the opening and closing statements. Look for unique words. Try to find points of emphasis. Pay attention to the cultural, social, religious and political framework in which the passage was originally written.

PERSONALISE. Apply the passage to yourself. Beware of the paralysis of analysis. Sometimes we become critical analysts of God's Word rather than open-hearted recipients. "Knowledge puffs up . . . The man who thinks he knows something does not yet know as he ought to know" 1 Corinthians 8:1-2. So ask yourself, "What does God want me to learn today and how does He want me to respond?" Remember, "The word of God is living and active. Sharper than any double edged sword, it penetrates even to dividing soul and spirit, joints and marrow; it judges the thoughts and attitudes of the heart. Nothing in all creation is hidden from God's sight. Everything is uncovered and laid bare before the eyes of him to whom we must give account" Hebrews 4:12-13.

PRAISE. Give God the honour and glory that is His due.

PRAYER. Using the passage as the point of departure turn to God in prayer. Pray the Word back to Him. Thank Him for what you've learnt. Ask Him to help you to be obedient to His Word. And "be joyful always; pray continually; give thanks in all circumstances, for this is God's will for you in Christ Jesus" 1 Thessalonians 5:16-18.

PRACTICE. Spend the day putting into practice the things you've learnt from God today.

STAY CLOSE

Stay close:

If you love someone - tell them.
Never be afraid to express yourself.
Say what you mean and mean what you say.

Life is swift.
There's no time like the present.
Yesterday is history and tomorrow a mystery.

Show that you care.
Lend an ear.
Open your heart.

The clock is running.
Use it - don't abuse it.
Make a difference.

Treat your friends like family and your family like friends.

"This is the message you heard from the beginning:
We should love one another"
1 John 3:11.

BLESS US ALL . . .

Rick and Aime Brownbill are watch and clock specialists. At their shop *Perfect Timing* in downtown Orillia one can hear the familiar sound of the Westminster "Big Ben" chimes. Day in and day out this simple tune resonates through the shop as the many Grandfather and mantle clocks chime and strike out the hours. The lyrics to the Westminster chime are a prayer which says, "Oh Lord our God, Thy children call, Grant us Thy peace, And bless us all . . ."

The significance of the chime is not lost on Aime. She says, "I always hear the words in my mind as the clocks chime, and it has become our continual prayer for Orillia." Aime learnt the words to the chime when she was in Brownies. At the conclusion of the Brownies meeting they would sing the words. Looking back Aime realises that this was one of the ways in which God was establishing His truth in her life. Now, as a committed Christian, Aime wants everyone to know the truth that set her free. In a report in *The Local Web,* titled *Daily Chimes Bring "Big Ben" Prayer to Mind* it said, "The wish that Rick and Aime want to pass on is that we would come to God, that we know His peace and receive His blessings as we simply ask Him, just like children . . ."

What an excellent message. Rick and Aime aren't just running a business. They're Christians using their business as an opportunity to proclaim the hope they have in Christ Jesus. It reminds me of how we should all be blooming where we're planted. Like Rick and Aime we should be looking for the unique message in the situation where God has placed us so that Christ can use it to point people to Himself.

So why not do what Rick and Aime have done? Look around. Discover the message in your circumstances so that God can use it as a testimony to His honour and glory. Then, when you've identified the message find ways to tell others about it. Rick and Aime wrote an article for their local newspaper and sent it in for publication. As a result the message rang out beyond the confines of their shop. You can do the same. In the context of your life there's something special you can share with others that will proclaim the hope and blessings you have in Christ Jesus.

VISION

"Where there is no vision the people perish" Proverbs 29:18 KJV.

"A vision without a task is but a dream;
A task without a vision is drudgery;
A vision and a task is the hope of the world."
A church in Sussex, England.
1730.

"Eyes that look are common.
Eyes that see are rare."
J Oswald Sanders.

"The real danger in our situation lies in the fact that so many people see clearly
what they are revolting from and so few see at all what they are revolting to."
Harry Emerson Fosdick.

"In the last days, God says, I will pour out my Spirit on all people.
Your sons and daughters will prophesy,
your young men will see visions,
your old men will dream dreams" Acts 2:17

"Vision is of God. A vision comes in advance of any task well done."
Katherine Logan.

There's something to be admired in people who think laterally and use their
imagination. I was reminded of this when I heard about two Inuit in Northern
Canada who were out ice fishing. The one had his line down a hole about the size
of a small manhole and the other had cut a hole that was about the size and
shape of a whale! Now that's vision. This man who was thinking big. He was
ready for anything. He was expecting something more than small fry.

But I wonder what the other man must have been thinking. There he was at his
little hole and every now and again he probably looked over at the fellow with the
whale size hole. Did he ever think about making his hole bigger? I'm sure that's
what I would have done. For vision is contagious; even when it looks foolish it often
has a profound effect on others. Yes, there's nothing that excites and motivates
people like a vision to accomplish something special. And sadly, there's nothing

worse than a person with no vision. As Helen Keller, the blind and deaf poet wrote, "The greatest tragedy to befall a person is to have sight but lack vision."

To see
   . . . you must be focussed.

To be focussed
   . . . you must have an objective.

To have an objective
   . . . you must have vision.

To have vision
   . . . you must see what God wants you to see.

PERSEVERING PRAYER

In Luke 18:1-8 we encounter *The Parable of the Persistent Widow.* It's a fascinating contest of wits between a disenfranchised widow and a disinterested judge. The gratifying conclusion is that the widow, because she refused to give up, wins through. She moves from a position of powerlessness to power due to her persistence. The parable is a lesson in prayer. A reminder that God won't put us off if we faithfully persevere, crying out to Him day and night (cf. Luke 18:7).

Perseverance in prayer is obvious in the life of Martin Luther. In 1540, upon hearing of the imminent death of his friend and assistant Frederick Myconius, Luther wrote to him saying, "I command thee in the name of God to live because I still have need of thee in the work of reforming the church . . . the Lord will never let me hear that thou art dead, but will permit thee to survive me. For this I am praying, this is my will, and may my will be done, because I seek only to glorify the name of God."

Luther's words sound almost shocking because of the sensitive and cautious era in which we live. Yet they illustrate how his perseverance in prayer was rewarded. Myconius recovered completely, lived for six more years, and survived Luther by two months.

Both the widow in the parable and Luther, not to mention countless others, have persevered in prayer and seen God respond. So don't adopt the tourist mindset to prayer. Don't accept the notion of instant prayers because you live in an instant society. Acquire enthusiasm for a patient acquisition of this virtue. Sign up for a long apprenticeship in the school of prayer. And don't give up if you've been praying for a situation or a person for some time. For "prayer is the key that unlocks all the storehouses of God's infinite grace and power. All that God is, and all that God has, is at the disposal of prayer" R. A. Torrey.

"MISTOOKS"

During a severe drought in South Africa a school was utilizing a well in order to water the parched playing fields. The townsfolk didn't know the school had its own well and assumed the principal was using water from the local reservoir and disregarding the water restrictions imposed by the municipality. People were furious and a number of concerned citizens phoned the school and complained.

It was therefore necessary to inform the public that the school wasn't squandering the town's meagre water supply but was using underground water. The principal had a signboard prepared and instructed the school handyman to erect it in a prominent position alongside the main road leading in and out of the town. He assumed that the townsfolk would then read the signboard and everything would be hunky-dory. But things don't always work out as planned. When the townsfolk read the signboard they thought the principal was making fun of the situation. This is what the signboard said, "All the water in this establishment has been passed by the Principal."

Now it's humorous when people make these mistakes but it isn't funny when people make serious life threatening mistakes. Jeremiah addresses the person who makes a life threatening mistake when he speaks of the "one who trusts in man, who depends on flesh for his strength and whose heart turns away from the Lord. He will be . . . cursed . . . like a bush in the wastelands . . . in the parched places of the desert" Jeremiah 17:5-6.

If you're making this mistake, i.e., if you're trusting in your own strength and not the Lord, it's never too late to rectify the situation. Jeremiah tells us that if a person "trusts in the Lord . . . he will be like a tree planted by the water . . . it does not fear when heat comes . . . it has no worries in a year of drought" Jeremiah 17:7-8.

GOSPEL "ELVIS-ISMS"

Jim Anderson is "Gospel Elvis," a Christian by proclamation and a tribute artist by profession. Jim goes the whole nine yards. When you see him dressed in one of his Elvis costumes and hear him singing *I Believe, How Great Thou Art, Somebody Bigger,* or *Amazing Grace,* you're hard pressed to think of him as anything other than the real McCoy. But he's not Elvis. Jim is passionately in love with Jesus, committed to his wife and son, faithful in his home church, and a friend to all. He sings the gospel songs that Elvis sang for one reason and one reason alone, to proclaim salvation and fullness of life in Christ Jesus. As Jim unashamedly says, "I do not glorify Elvis Presley, I glorify Jesus Christ in an Elvis-like style."

I think of Jim as the Minstrel of Evangelism. You'll find him singing in shopping malls, downtown on the street, at secular and sacred music festivals, at weddings and banquets, in pubs and service clubs. Wherever Jim can find an audience, he'll sing. He knows God's calling on his life. Although Jim has never put it in these words, I'm sure he'll agree that his mission is to go into all the world and sing the good news to all creation.

Being "Gospel Elvis" is only part of what makes Jim special. Jim is nearly as smooth in his speech as he is in song. He's developed a unique genre of gospel "Elvis-isms." These are colourful sayings, proverbs and idioms that spice his conversation. I've come to enjoy them over the years and when I asked Jim if I could share a selection of them with you he graciously gave permission. I'll begin with some fun "Elvis-isms" then move onto the more serious ones.

I know I'm late but I'm worth waiting for.

It's better felt than tell't.

Rome wasn't built in a day but I didn't work on that job.

The theory of evolution made a monkey out of Darwin.

Some people will make it into heaven with the smell of smoke on their britches.

Necessity is the mother of invention. Frustration is the father!

Right or wrong I'm still the captain . . . but my wife is the admiral!

I'm the king of my castle and I have the Queen's permission to say so.

Before you stick your neck out for someone, remember they could slam the window on it.

> Would you like to swing on a star?
> Carry moonbeams home in a jar?
> Be better off than you are?
> Then you need more medication!

Children are gifts, as arrows, from God. Blessed is the man whose quiver is full. The fuller it is, the more he quivers.

Good deeds often evaporate but a mistake sticks like glue.

You can't choose whom your children will choose for friends but you can stock the pond.

Either lead - follow - or get out of the way.

I'm not the man I ought to be, but praise God! I'm not the man I used to be!

We get old too soon and smart too late.

What I can accomplish depends on what I overlook.

To everything there is a season - so plan ahead.

> Without a song the day would never end;
> Without a song a man ain't got a friend;
> Without a song the road would never bend;
> Without a song . . . so I'll keep singing the song.

What God has put in your hand is seed for your future.

If I'm the man God wants me to be, I'll do what God wants me to do.

If science disagrees with God's Word, it's not good science.

Sometimes I get so homesick - for heaven.

Come apart and rest awhile before you come apart.

I can't help how I feel but I can help how I act.

God has no grandchildren - only children.

Sharing Christ is one starving beggar giving a crust of bread to another.

WHO MADE THE WATERMELON?

I was eating a watermelon the other day when my son Matthew challenged me to a seed spitting competition. Since we were sitting outside, I agreed, and before long the whole family (Nana excluded) were eating and spitting, eating and spitting, eating and spitting in an effort to be the seed spitting champ of the year.

Now, before you condemn us for our deviant behaviour let me tell you that there's something to be said for this kind of activity. It's not too often that one has the opportunity to eat while simultaneously partaking in a sporting event. And it's even more rare to be able to eat, think, and play all at the same time.

But that's one of the advantages of a seed spitting competition, and, as I set a new distance record at the Murray Family Annual Seed Spitting Event, I realised the little black seeds that I was callously spitting all over the lawn deserved more respect than I was giving them. For the humble watermelon seed has the power of drawing from the ground, and through itself, two hundred thousand times its weight. Then, from the material that it draws out of the ground it forms an outside surface beyond the imagination of art, an inside white rind, and within that a succulent red heart thickly inlaid with black seeds which have the potential to reproduce more watermelons.

That bears some consideration. If something as common as the watermelon is amazing and mysterious it makes one wonder who made the watermelon? For surely the watermelon is caused by something beyond itself? And surely the design of the watermelon needed an intelligent designer? For intelligence is required to produce any design. And the more complex the design, the greater the intelligence required to produce it. After all, buildings imply architects, software implies programmers, aircraft imply aeronautical engineers, and books imply authors.

So where am I going with this argument? It's very simple. The only reasonable conclusion, when I ask myself who made the watermelon, is the realisation that there's a great designer behind the design. That stands to reason! To say that a watermelon came from a big bang just doesn't cut it. And, to say that the watermelon evolved by chance flies in the face of common sense. There had to be a designer. And I believe God is the Designer.

The Bible confirms it. In Colossians 1:16 it says, "By him all things were created: things in heaven and on earth, visible and invisible, whether thrones or powers or rulers or authorities; all things were created by him and for him." That's the reality. God made the watermelon and everything else. As it states succinctly in Genesis 1:1,31, "In the beginning God created the heavens and the earth . . . and God saw all that he had made, and it was very good." And to that I say a hearty, "Amen!"

KIDS IN CHURCH

Kids in church. We just can't do without them. Here are some stories to celebrate the joys, the embarrassments, and the challenges of kids in church.

A little boy was in a relative's wedding. As he was coming down the aisle he would take two steps, stop, and turn to the congregation. Then he would put his hands up like claws and roar. So it went, step, step, ROAR, step, step, ROAR, all the way down the aisle. The congregation was laughing so hard they had tears streaming down their faces. The little boy, however, was getting more and more distressed from all the laughing, and by the time he reached the pulpit he was in tears. When asked why he was crying he sniffed and said, "Why is everyone laughing at me? I was doing what I was told to do. I was being the Ring Bear."

On Christmas Day at Christ Church Hillbrow, my father-in-law, who was the minister, would call the children to the front of the church and ask them about their presents. The children always looked forward to being in the limelight and would take great delight in showing him their toys. When it was Mandy Hinton's turn, she stepped up onto the platform, pulled up her dress with a flourish, and said, "Look what I got - new panties!" It was a real show stopper.

One Sunday in a Midwest city a young child was "acting up" during the morning worship hour. The parents did their best to maintain some sense of order in the pew but were losing the battle. Finally the father picked the little fellow up and walked sternly up the aisle on his way out. Just before reaching the safety of the foyer, the little boy called loudly to the congregation, "Pray for me! Pray for me!"

During the minister's prayer there was a loud whistle from one of the back pews. Gary's mother was horrified. She pinched him into silence, and after church, asked: "Gary, whatever made you do such a thing?" Gary answered soberly: "I asked God to teach me to whistle . . . And He just then did!"

A little girl was sitting in church playing with her mother's Bible when an old leaf, that had been pressed between the pages, fell out. Looking at it with incredulity the little girl said, "Mommy, look what I found." "What have you got there, dear?" said her mother. With astonishment in her voice, she replied, "I think it's Adam's suit!"

Six-year-old Angie and her four-year-old brother Joel were sitting together in church. Joel giggled, sang, and talked out loud. Finally, his older sister had enough. "You're not supposed to talk out loud in church," she said. "Why? Who's going to stop me?" said Joel. Angie pointed to the back of the church and said, "You see those two men standing by the door? They're hushers."

Yes, church would never be church without our children. Let's never forget that they're a wonderful "heritage from the Lord . . . a reward" Psalm 127:3. And we're blessed because of them.

TOGETHER

I'm big on community. It's together we stand or divided we fall. No one is rich enough to do without another. "It's one for all and all for one." But then, that's how God intended it to be. He never planned for you to be in your small corner and I in mine. There's no call to self dependence in the Bible. For interdependence, not independence, is God's plan for you and me. In fact the word "together" is mentioned 484 times in the Scriptures and "gathered together" is mentioned 97 times. In terms of frequency that makes it an important word. In comparison, the word "prayer" is mentioned more than 100 times and the word "faith" appears 270 times. That's why I'm big on community. It's because God majors on community. He wants us to do everything - TOGETHER!

According to the Word we are called to:

Gather together. Dwell together. Assemble together. Eat and drink together. Fight together against evil. Worship together. Go to battle together. Sing together. Build together. Be purified together. Meet together in the house of God. Take counsel together. Mourn together. Rest together. Come together in judgment. Stick together. Be joined together. Exalt the name of God together. Have low and high, rich and poor together. Dwell together in unity. Meet together. Reason together. Consider and understand together. Plead together. Be silent together. Agree together. Commune together. Be glorified together. Endure pain together. Rejoice together. Believe together. Pray together. Hear the word of God together. Gather the church together. Break bread together. Be comforted together. Work together with Him. Be quickened together in Christ. Live together with Him. Be followers together of Him. Be heirs together of the gracious gift of life.

As if that's not enough we're to flow together, walk together, grow together, run together, talk together, strive together, stand together, labour together, be planted together, and be knit together in love.

Then when that's done we'll be raised together and made to sit together in heavenly places.

BOND

Bear Others Needs Daily.

BEAR

"Bear with each other and forgive whatever grievances you may have against one another. Forgive as the Lord forgave you" Colossians 3:13.

"We who are strong ought to bear with the failings of the weak and not to please ourselves" Romans 15:1.

"Be completely humble and gentle; be patient, bearing with one another in love" Ephesians 4:2

OTHERS

"Each of you should look not only to your own interest but also to the interests of others" Philippians 2:4.

NEEDS

"Do not let any unwholesome talk come out of your mouths, but only what is helpful for building others up according to their needs, that it may benefit those who listen" Ephesians 4:29.

"If it is contributing to the needs of others . . . give generously" Romans 12:8.

"If you do away with the yoke of oppression, with the pointing finger and malicious talk, and if you spend yourselves on behalf of the hungry and satisfy the needs of the oppressed, then your light will rise in the darkness, and your night will become like the noonday" Isaiah 58:9-10.

DAILY

"But encourage one another daily, as long as it is called Today, so that none of you may be hardened by sins deceitfulness" Hebrews 3:13.

"We can't go around measuring our goodness by what we don't do, by what we deny ourselves, by what we resist and by who we exclude. I think we get to measure goodness by what we embrace, what we create and who we include." The words of the priest in the film Chocolat.

NO OTHER GODS

A week before I turned sixteen, my father bought me my first motorbike. I was filled with excitement, trepidation and awe. In fact it was more than awe, I worshipped that bike. It was a gleaming god to carry me into manhood. I knew that once I was sitting on it, women would find me irresistible and men would know I'd arrived. I'd be the king of the mountain.

There was one little problem though. I didn't know how it worked. So at school the next day I asked some of my buddies to teach me the basics. The first lesson followed that afternoon in my back yard. My friends knew as little as I did about operating a motorbike but we figured some things out and I climbed on for my first ride.

After starting the bike, pulling in the clutch, and kicking it into first gear, I opened the throttle, released the clutch, and took off with a lurch down the lawn. It was magnificent. The wind was whistling through my hair, my friends were admiring my prowess, and . . . I didn't know what to do next! No one had told me how to change gears or how to operate the brakes.

There I was careering down the garden with nothing but the vegetable patch and a brick wall ahead of me. My friends were yelling and screaming instructions but it was too late; the front wheel connected with an enormous cabbage, I was bucked off, and the bike landed on me with the engine still running and the exhaust pipe burning into my bare leg.

My friends laughed fit to bust. I didn't think it was funny. My god had turned on me, bucked and burnt me, and worse of all, made me lose face. It didn't stop me though. By the end of the afternoon I was roaring up and down the street and by suppertime Suzuki had proven itself worthy of my adoration. It was everything I expected a god to be. In the months ahead I lovingly polished it, rode it, and introduced it to everyone who'd care to look at it.

Three years later I discovered Suzuki wasn't a god. That was when I met the living God, the One who said "You shall have no other gods before me" Exodus 20:3.

People are incurably religious. When the Lord isn't in first place, we find all manner of substitutes. For me it was Suzuki, followed by Yamaha, Honda and a number of high performance off-road motorbikes. When our loyalty isn't for God, we find other gods as objects of our affections. The following are some of those gods. If you recognise any of these gods as having stolen your loyalty, you should confess, repent, and ask the Holy Spirit to incline your heart to God and God alone.

There's the god of nature. When people should be in church worshipping the Lord, you sometimes find them on the golf course, out fishing, skiing down a mountain, or having a visit at someone's cottage. But the trees, the flowers, the water, the snow, and the grass, although given to us by God for our pleasure, can't comfort our hearts in sorrow or walk with us through the valley of the shadow of death - only God can do that.

There's the god of health and fitness. If for the sake of your health and fitness you can't make it out to a Bible study or fellowship meeting because you work out at the gym then you're worshipping the wrong god. Health and fitness are wonderful gifts from God but we're not to put them before the Lord.

There's the god of sports. Some people can tell you about nearly every player in a particular sport. They devour the sports page in the newspapers, watch sports games on television, travel to sport meetings with their children, yet neglect or have little time for God's Word. The heroes of the diamond, the basketball court, the ice rink, the soccer field, and the gridiron are more familiar to them than the heroes of the Bible.

There's the god of pleasure. The Bible speaks of people who are "lovers of pleasure rather than lovers of God" 2 Timothy 3:4. Every advertisement in the papers, on television, on the internet, and on the radio scream out that you can find happiness and pleasure in the things of the world. Now God's not against pleasure that's clean and uplifting but He won't share Himself with anything that takes you away from Him.

There's the god of popularity. Hollywood and the media thrive on creating celebrities. Singers, actors, business executives, politicians, and sportsmen and women are given preeminence in our society. People want their signatures, their clothes, and their values. What Bill Gates, Oprah Winfrey, Michael Jordan, George Bush, or one of the members of N'SYNC says is often more important than what Jesus Christ says. But God will not share His glory with any celebrity and all who worship images or boast to idols will be put to shame (cf. Psalm 97:7).

There are other forms of refined idolatry, but you get the point. The gods of nature, health and fitness, sports, pleasure, and popular celebrities are not the real thing. They may bring temporary happiness but it will be short lived. To have real and lasting fulfilment in life you must have no other gods before Him.

"WHEN YOU FAST . . ."

"When you fast, do not look somber as the hypocrites do, for they disfigure their faces to show men they are fasting. I tell you the truth, they have received their reward in full. But when you fast, put oil on your head and wash your face, so that it will not be obvious to men that you are fasting, but only to your Father, who is unseen; and your Father, who sees what is done in secret, will reward you" Matthew 6:16-18.

In a culture dominated by "McDonald's," "New York Fries," "Pizza Hut," "Second Cup," and countless other shrines to the stomach, fasting appears to be an anomaly. The popular conception in North America is that we need three large meals a day, with snacks thrown in between, and anything less is akin to starvation.

In analysing this love affair with food it's obvious many North Americans live for the flesh and are ruled by its appetites. Which is one of the reasons why fasting, in large part, although frequently mentioned in Scripture, is almost totally overlooked. But it's disregarded at our peril. In covering up what's inside us with good food and drink we hinder the Holy Spirit's work of transforming our lives. For if we don't practice the inward disciplines of our faith we're left with the outward form, and the outward form devoid of the inner disciplines, is a form bereft of spiritual power.

That's why today's meditation begins with Jesus' assumption, "When you fast . . ." It's a reminder that He wants us to have a faith that's more than skin deep, more than a carnal faith. For in fasting we discover a faith in which we're sustained, not by the food of the world, "but on every word that comes from the mouth of God" Matthew 4:4. This is the real benefit of fasting. It helps us to be nourished and strengthened by God. In fact fasting is feasting! In abstaining from food it enables us to feast on God's Word - and when we feast on God's Word light is thrown on our lives.

This is probably the single greatest lesson I've learnt in recent years. In the discipline of fasting the things that control me soon surface. If there's pride, bitterness, fear, anxiety, jealousy, timidity, anger - or any other sin, it will be revealed. During the writing of this book I undertook a forty-day liquid fast of fruit and vegetable juice along with water. As my family will tell you, I was difficult to live with toward the end of the fast. I complained about all sorts of things they did or didn't do - the fast exposed my sin, a critical spirit within me. In making this discovery I was able to turn to God for healing through the power of Jesus Christ. David obviously knew of this reality. In Psalm 69:10 he says, "When I wept and chastened my soul with fasting, that became my reproach." NKJV.

Yes, fasting enables us to grow up in Christ, keep balance, and identify sin or nonessentials that take precedence in our lives. It quickens us and brings breakthroughs in the spiritual realm that often can't happen any other way. So if fasting isn't a normal part of your Christian faith why not acquaint yourself more fully with the practical aspects of fasting and then begin to obey Christ's words, "When you fast . . ."

MIGHTY MEN

"This is the list of David's mighty men . . . Asahel the brother of Joab, Elhanan son of Dodo from Bethlehem, Shammoth the Harorite, Helez the Pelonite, Ira son of Ikkesh from Tekoa, Abiezer from Anathoth, Sibbecai the Hushathite, Ilai the Ahohite, Maharai the Netophathite, Heled son of Baanah the Netophathite, Ithai son of Ribai from Gibeah of Benjamin, Benaiah the Pirathonite, Hurai from the ravines of Gaash, Abiel the Arbathite, Azmaveth the Baharumite, Eliahba the Shaalbonite, the sons of Hashem the Gizonite, Jonathan son of Shagee the Hararite, Ahiam son of Sacar the Hararite, Eliphal son of Ur, Hepher the Mekerathite, Ahijah the Pelonite, Hezro the Carmelite, Naarai son of Ezbai, Joel the brother of Nathan, Mibhar son of Hagri, Zelek the Ammonite, Naharai the Berothite, the armor-bearer of Joab son of Zeruiah, Ira the Ithrite, Gareb the Ithrite, Uriah the Hittite, Zabad son of Ahlai, Adina son of Shiza the Reubenite, who was chief of the Reubenites, and the thirty with him, Hanan son of Maacah, Joshaphat the Mithnite, Uzzia the Ashterathite, Shama and Jeiel the sons of Hotham the Aroerite, Jediael son of Shimri, his brother Joha the Tizite, Elial the Mahavite, Jeribai and Joshaviah the sons of Elnaam, Ithmah the Moabite, Eliel, Obed and Jaasiel the Mezobaite" 1 Chronicles 11:11, 26-47.

I know, you're probably wondering why on earth I would quote such a passage. One needs a course in linguistics just to pronounce the names. In fact the first time I read through the Bible I glanced at the first name then skipped through to chapter twelve (maybe you didn't want to read it either?). But that meant I wasn't valuing this portion of Scripture like the rest. After all, "All Scripture is God-breathed and is useful for teaching, rebuking, correcting and training in righteousness, so that the man of God may be thoroughly equipped for every good work" 2 Timothy 3:16-17. Which presented a minor dilemma for me. How could a tongue twisting list of names teach, rebuke, correct, or train me in righteousness? Then the obvious hit me. David's mighty men are an example of the many mighty men God raises up to support those in leadership.

With this in mind I'm now grateful when I read this passage. For as I read about David's mighty men I'm reminded of the mighty men God has placed around me. Now I'm not for one moment comparing myself to David, far from it. But I am thankful for the mighty men who stand shoulder to shoulder with me on the Leadership Team of Orillia Community Church. And, like the writer of Chronicles I believe it's prudent to name them. Here are some modern day mighty men you probably don't know but may find a little easier to pronounce: John Audia from Italy, generous and merciful; Rick Aldom of Warminster, discipler and teacher of God's Word; Alan Jarvis from South Africa, a wise counsellor and man of praise;

John Annunziello of Orillia, true blue; Dean Langman and Ron Thompson, faithful doers of the Word; Ray Scriver from Peterborough, anointed worship leader; Paul Ego and Glen Gillespie, wise stalwarts in the faith. These are spiritual men, full of joy, united in purpose, steadfast in the Way.

You can probably think of a number of present day mighty men that you know. Why not take time to thank God for them and pray that He will continue to strengthen and protect them as they serve Him. In addition, write a note of encouragement or phone them up and tell them they're appreciated.

MAKING THE WORLD
A BETTER PLACE

The fundamental requirement in making this world a better place is captured in John 3:7, "You must be born again." That's the bottom line. It's the old story of the pig in the parlour. You have to change its nature before it is fit for such an environment.

We seem to have forgotten this truth. Billions of dollars are poured into social reform. Government and non government organizations strive to advance the well-being of society. Service clubs and charities endeavour to upgrade health care, improve the quality of the environment, and alleviate suffering.

But despite these efforts the world is not a better place. Crime is on the increase. Schools have become bloodbaths. Suicides are commonplace. Strike action is regularly reported in the newspapers. Child custody battles are fiercely contested. Struggles with depression are at an all time high. Families are left destitute because of gambling debts. Thousands of unwanted babies are aborted around the world every day. Alcoholics Anonymous has a steady stream of clients. And poverty is still evident on the streets of our cities.

The Band-Aid of secularism has obviously failed. But that's not surprising. For secularism begins with the effect and ignores the cause. It attempts external reform and negates the necessity for internal transformation. In short - the secular world view, with its attendant philosophies of moral relativism, multi-culturalism, pragmatism, and utopianism, is only skin deep.

In contrast, the Christian believes this world can be a better place when we become men and women of another type. When God's Kingdom is born within us - not created from without. When the root of all greed, selfishness, bitterness, anger, drunkenness, sexual immorality, envy, hatred, debauchery, discord, and the like, is confessed as sin and cleansed by the blood of Christ. If you want to make the community better, make the individual better. It's a matter of first principles - "You must be born again." Otherwise, you're putting the cart before the horse.

As D. L. Moody said, "The blood salvation has a wonderful effect upon men's characters. They rarely remain subjects of charity, but rise at once to comfort and respectability." History proves Moody right. Every time a clarion call is made for men and women to be "born again" the resultant transformation has resulted in a better world. For sin is a cancer and only the blood of Christ can cure it. Ignore this fact and this world will never improve.

Yes, when we have the courage to go deeper and further than social reform. When secularism is seen for what it is - an artificial, superficial and perfunctory salve. When we wake up to the fact that "the material order rests on the spiritual order," Kirk. When we get to the root of the trouble - SIN - and turn to Christ as the remedy. When we embrace a relationship - not religion. When we're "born again." Then hope for today's world will be renewed. Drunkards will be made sober, the rich generous, employers just, prostitutes pure, sad hearts glad, penitentiaries empty, trust restored, and peace will reign supreme.

BUNDLES OF PREJUDICE

In 1994 I had the privilege of teaching an adult Sunday School class at a church in Toronto. We were studying "Issues in Focus" and for an upcoming session I engaged the help of two of the students for an informal drama I had in mind. I gave Cathy and Nathan a simple directive. At the start of the following week's class they were to make some low key bigoted comments. Well the next Sunday, as we were gathering for our lesson, Cathy and Nathan started telling some Newfie jokes (jokes about, and directed at, people from Newfoundland). Much to my surprise others got in on the act and began to pass derogatory comments about Newfies, Red Necks, the Irish, and others. I was amazed. But the piece de resistance was yet to come. Nathan was playing to the group magnificently and fell back into his chair when it unexpectedly collapsed. Nathan took it in his stride. He leapt up, kicked the chair and exclaimed, "It was probably made by a Black!" There were nods of agreement around the room.

I was flabbergasted, decided it was time to interject, and called the class to order. Once I had their full attention, I said the following: "Today we will be discussing the issue of prejudice. Cathy and Nathan were asked to make some bigoted comments. They were acting under my instructions, taking dramatic licence. But the rest of you were not. You were simply expressing what was in your heart. For prejudice is not something unique to people living in Yugoslavia, Afghanistan or South Africa but something rooted deep within us all."

There was a stunned silence as it dawned on the group that prejudice isn't out there but inside. In that moment we realised how most of us are bundles of prejudice.

But Jesus wasn't prejudiced, He wasn't a bigot, and He wasn't a racist. He served and ministered to all groups (cf. Matthew 20:28). He excluded no one from his circle of ministry (cf. John 4:7-26). He was open to people who were rejected by others (cf. Matthew 9:10-13). He spoke out and acted against those who showed prejudice (cf. Matthew 19:13-15). And He responded gently to those who were prejudiced against Him (cf. Matthew 13:57).

Let's be like Him. Don't be "down on what you are not up on" Lloyd John Ogilvie.

WINNING THE LOTTERY CAN RUIN YOUR LIFE

When a tailor in New York won the million-dollar lottery he closed up his shop and went out on the town. For more than two years he lived the high life. He stayed in the very best of hotels, ate at the best restaurants, had a retinue of attendants attending to his every whim, and was extravagant with everything he did. Within a relatively short time he'd spent every last penny of the million dollars.

Exhausted and despondent he went back to the little tailor shop and opened up his business once again. As had been his custom in the past, he put aside two dollars a week for lottery tickets and would you believe it, only two years later two men arrived at his shop and announced that he had won the million-dollar lottery again!

It's reported that there was a stunned silence from the tailor and then with a deep groan he exclaimed, "Oh no! That means I have to go through all that again!"

Yes, winning the lottery can ruin your life. Surprisingly enough the *Wall Street Journal* recognised this reality. They said, "Money is an article which may be used as a universal passport to everywhere except heaven, and as a universal provider of everything except happiness."

Which raises a question. If money doesn't bring happiness then how can we use it so it doesn't ruin our lives?

John Wesley provides the answer: He said, "I fear, wherever riches have increased (exceeding few are the exceptions), the essence of religion, the mind that was in Christ has decreased in the same proportion. Therefore I do not see how it is possible, in the nature of things, for any revival of true religion to continue long. For religion must necessarily produce both industry and frugality; and these cannot but produce riches. But as riches increase, so will pride, anger, and love of the world in all its branches. What way then can we take that our money may not sink us to the nethermost hell? There is one way, and there is no other under heaven. If those who gain all they can, and save all they can, will likewise give all they can, then the more they gain, the more they will grow in grace, and the more treasure they will lay up in heaven."

Hebrews 13:5 has this concluding exhortation: "Keep your lives free from the love of money and be content with what you have."

GRANDMA'S CAKE

Do you ever feel like "everything" is going wrong? Are you struggling with relational problems, issues at home, fatigue, declining health, work related grievances, debt, prejudice, unemployment, or one of the hundreds of other challenges that are encountered through life. The story of Grandma's cake teaches a valuable lesson for times of difficulty:

After an especially trying time at school Tommy arrived home in tears. "I just can't take it anymore," he said to his grandmother who was visiting for the week. "I get picked on nearly every day." "Well why not have a snack and we'll talk about it," said Grandma as she continued mixing some batter in the bowl. "Sure," said Tommy. "What have you got?" Grandma picked up a bottle of oil sitting on the counter and offered it to Tommy. "Here, try some cooking oil," she said. "Gross!" replied Tommy with a look of incredulity on his face. "Well how about a couple of raw eggs?" "Grandma!" exclaimed Tommy. "Would you like some flour then? Or maybe some baking soda?" "Grandma, those are all yucky!" To which Grandma replied, "Yes, all those things seem bad all by themselves. But when they are put together in the right way, they make a wonderfully delicious cake! God works the same way. Many times we wonder why He would let us encounter the yucky things in life - why we have to go through difficult times. But God knows that when He puts everything in His order, they always work together for good! We just have to trust Him, and eventually He makes all things beautiful in His time."

ASSUMPTIONS

There's an old riddle which goes like this: "A blind beggar had a brother who died. What relation was the blind beggar to the brother who died?"

If you ask several people this question, they'll probably all say, "Brother." But they'd be wrong. The blind beggar was the sister of her brother who died. The reason we say "Brother" is because we jump to a false assumption. We assume the blind beggar must be a man.

Here's a conundrum. You have exactly $101 in your pocket. You have just two notes and no change. One of the notes is not a $1 bill. What are they?

Most people struggle with this poser. They're misled by the ambiguity in the wording. *One* of the notes is not a $1 bill. That is correct - it is a $100 bill. So the solution is the simple one of a $1 bill and a $100 bill.

Ambiguities occur not just in conundrums but in every sphere of life. As a preacher I'm amazed by the assumptions that people can make based on what they thought they heard me say. People take statements out of context and use it to fit their own preconceived ideas. I shouldn't be surprised. Making assumptions is a natural but lazy habit. But assumptions blind us. They screen us from other possibilities or options. Which is why when we jump to conclusions we often make the wrong decision.

The trouble is we make assumptions because we're conditioned to believe that a new situation is similar to a previous situation we've experienced. This was the mistake made by the British and French military high commands in the 1930's. Faced with German aggression they assumed any new war would be like the previous war but fought with better equipment. They therefore built the Maginot Line along the Franco-German border. It was completely inadequate. The German forces swept through Holland and Belgium in a blitzkrieg of fast moving armoured divisions and attacked an undefended section of France. All it took was some lateral thinking by the German generals and the Maginot Line was rendered useless.

Which is why we need to learn to test our assumptions. This is done by asking questions and by searching for inherent ambiguities. In part, I believe this is what Romans 12:2 calls us to do when it says, "Do not conform any longer to the pattern of this world, but be transformed by the renewing of your mind. Then you will be able to test and approve what God's will is - his good, pleasing and perfect will."

Since I was saved, I've sought to be transformed by the renewing of my mind. Of course transformation is the work of God's Spirit. I have no power to transform myself. But I must allow the Spirit to do His work and one of the ways He's been renewing my mind is by teaching me to ask questions. He won't allow me to take things at face value. I've learnt that God wants me to "test everything" 1 Thessalonians 5:21. Some folk resist doing this. Once they've got their theology in place, they suspend the process of critical analysis except to reject anything that doesn't fit in with what they believe. They prefer everything nicely packaged, everything making sense. But God can't be put in a box. The finite will never have the measure of the infinite. There'll always be an element of mystery when it comes to the things of God. So if we're earnest about following Him we need to be prepared for God to occasionally take our preconceived ideas and turn them inside out. But then, that's what transformation is - being turned about.

So don't jump to conclusions. Exercise judgement. Try to see things from God's perspective. And don't assume too much. For there's an old saying that to assume "makes an *ass* out of *u* and *me*."

DEAD!

It was Monday morning when Dania Read and Penny Fourie took the students across the road to the public swimming pool next to St Christopher's School. As they arrived, the previous class was coming out of the changerooms and chatting about the great swimming lesson they'd just enjoyed. Having heard how inviting the water was the students were quickly changed and itching to leap in. But the teachers insisted they sat on the tiered seats on the northern side of the pool so they could have the swimming drill explained before they were in the water.

They had barely sat down when one of the students asked, "What's that man doing in the pool?" "What man?" asked Dania in surprise. For the pool was closed to the public when the school was using the facility. "The one over there in the water," replied the boy. No one knew what the man was doing so one of the boys dived in to investigate. To their horror they discovered it was a submerged corpse! The police were called in, foul play was suspected, and a murder docket was opened!

Now no one expects to go to school and find a dead person. Yet there's a sense in which our schools are full of dead people and many of us haven't even noticed.

In nearly every classroom around the world there are scores of dead students and dead teachers. Not dead physically, but dead spiritually. They're dead in their "transgressions and sins" Ephesians 2:1. They're dead because they don't have a vital relationship with God. They follow "the ways of this world . . . gratifying the cravings of (their) sinful nature and following its desires and thoughts" Ephesians 2:2-3. And in so doing they become "objects of (God's) wrath" Ephesians 2:3.

Yet they needn't be left for dead. You can tell them the good news. You can tell them about God's "great love for us" and His "rich . . . mercy" Ephesians 2:4. And you can tell them how they can be "saved, through faith . . . the gift of God" to be "alive with Christ" Ephesians 2:8.

Don't delay. Jump right in and save a life today.

PASS OUT
THE TOWELS

It's time to clean up our act, time to become servants to the world, time to remember that the symbol of Christ's kingdom is a towel.

Jesus dramatically illustrated this for us in John 13 when he washed the disciples' feet. During the course of an evening meal Jesus noticed that no one's feet had been cleaned. Perhaps the stench came to His attention. With everyone crowded into the room Jesus probably sniffed out the problem.

Now it was the custom in those days to wash the dust and dung off the feet of guests before reclining for dinner. Remember, people wore open sandals and would quickly be caked with the grit, grime and glaur along the footpaths and roads. In the absence of a hired foot washer the disciples had conveniently ignored the need to clean their feet. It was another sad display of their pride. No one wanted such a lowly task. Nobody wanted to be a servant. But not Jesus. He "made himself nothing" Philippians 2:7. He took the servant's role. He actively chose to humble himself. He wasn't born a servant, but He accepted servitude without malevolence.

In so doing Jesus illustrated a kingdom principle. The way up is down. Whoever wants to be first must be a servant (cf. Matthew 20:26-27). Whoever wants to be great must take up the towel.

Don't be deceived. Like the disciples we're all soiled, all tainted by pride. We "stink" with sin. Let's not pretend we can't smell anything. Every church has the unpleasant aroma of self-righteousness. Every Christian has the body odor of unholy attitudes. But Jesus wants us to smell different. He wants us to be "a fragrant offering and sacrifice to God" Ephesians 5:2. He wants us to take the basin and humbly wash one another's feet. He wants us to pass out the towels.

So put your best foot forward and step into His world. "Each of you should look not only to your own interests, but also to the interests of others. Your attitude should be the same as that of Christ Jesus: Who, being in very nature God, did not consider equality with God something to be grasped, but made himself nothing, taking the very nature of a servant" Philippians 2:4-7.

COUNT YOUR BLESSINGS

G ratitude is an attitude that needs to be cultivated. It doesn't just happen. We need to learn how to be thankful. Here are some reminders from God's Word:

"Give thanks to the Lord, for he is good; his love endures forever" 1 Chronicles 16:34.

"Praise God's name in song and glorify him with thanksgiving" Psalm 69:30.

"Give thanks to him and praise his name" Psalm 100:4.

"Give thanks to the Lord for his unfailing love and his wonderful deeds for men" Psalm 107:15.

"Give thanks to the Lord, call on his name; make known among the nations what he has done, and proclaim that his name is exalted" Isaiah 12:4.

"But thanks be to God! He gives us the victory through our Lord Jesus Christ" 1 Corinthians 15:57.

"But thanks be to God, who always leads us in triumphal procession in Christ and through us spreads everywhere the fragrance of the knowledge of him" 2 Corinthians 2:14.

"Thanks be to God for his indescribable gift!" 2 Corinthians 9:15.

"Devote yourselves to prayer, being watchful and thankful" Colossians 4:2.

"Give thanks in all circumstances, for this is God's will for you in Christ Jesus" 1 Thessalonians 5:18.

"I urge, then, first of all, that requests, prayers, intercession and thanksgiving be made for everyone" 1 Timothy 2:1.

"Therefore, since we are receiving a kingdom that cannot be shaken, let us be thankful, and so worship God acceptably with reverence and awe" Hebrews 12:28.

So "Count your blessings. Name them one by one. Count your many blessings. See what God has done!"

NEW BEGINNINGS

Here's a great story: It's about a fellow who'd been raised in the back hills of West Virginia - I mean, so far out in the sticks he had never even seen a big city, to say nothing of modern conveniences such as electricity. Well he married a gal just like himself and they had one son whom they creatively named Junior. When Junior was about sixteen, his dad realized it wouldn't be long before his son became a man and went off to face the real world. So, feeling responsible for his son's education, the man started saving for a trip to the city. Three years later they were ready to go. They tossed their belongings into the back of an old truck and started the long journey over the rough winding roads.

It was a time of tremendous anticipation but their excitement soon turned to apprehension as they approached the outskirts of the city. The busy roads, the flashing neon lights, the tall buildings, all heightened their sense of anxiety and by the time they reached the hotel Papa was quite jumpy. Mama was therefore instructed to stay in the truck while the men went in to have a look around.

Papa and Junior walked wide eyed toward the lobby. They had never seen anything like it before! When they stepped on a mat, the doors opened automatically. As they walked inside, they were met by a shimmering chandelier that hung from a ceiling three stories high. Off to the right there was an enormous waterfall, pouring out of a wall and rippling over inlaid stones and rocks. And in the adjoining mall they could see an ice-skating rink, inside! They were awe struck.

Both stood captivated, watching one breathtaking sight after another, until their attention was arrested by a clicking sound behind them. Turning around they saw an amazing little room with doors that slid open and closed from the center. It was magical. People would walk up, push a button, and wait. Then lights would flicker above the doors, there would be a 'click,' and the doors would slide open. Some people would walk out of the little room, others would walk in and turn around, another 'click,' and the doors would slide shut. By now Papa and Junior were totally transfixed.

At that moment a wrinkled old lady shuffled up to the doors. She pushed the button and waited a few seconds. Then, 'click,' the doors opened with a swish and she hobbled into the little room. No one else stepped in with her, so 'click,' and the doors closed. No more than twenty seconds later the doors opened again - and there stood this fabulous attractive blonde, a young woman in her twenties - high heels, shapely body, beautiful face - a real knockout! As she stepped out, smiled, and turned to walk away, Papa nudged his boy and mumbled, "Hey, Junior . . . go git Mama!" (Source: *Stories for the Family's Heart*).

Now we laugh, but it seems to me that everybody's looking for a room like that. We would love to be able to push the right button, wait momentarily for the door of opportunity to slide open, then 'click', magic! In only a matter of seconds we're instantly transformed. Without any effort we've got a new beginning. But that's not the real world. When it comes to reality, nothing could be further from the truth.

This is especially true as we consider personal revival or the renewal of the local church. It doesn't just happen. It takes prayer, patience, hard work, and requires an ongoing struggle against the grip of mediocrity.

Which implies a "long obedience in the same direction" Eugene Peterson. Recognize that faithfulness and fortitude are essential ingredients for success. For true religion is far more than a visit to an attractive meeting when we have adequate leisure. True religion is something quite different from the world's passion for the immediate and the casual. And two thousand years of church history teach us that there will be no short cuts in the years ahead.

Yes, we're called to be life long apprentices to our master, Jesus Christ. We're called to put in a solid effort. And we're encouraged to perseverance and the pursuit of holiness.

"Therefore, since we are surrounded by such a great cloud of witnesses, let us throw off everything that hinders and the sin that so easily entangles, and let us run with perseverance the race marked out for us. Let us fix our eyes on Jesus, the author and perfecter of our faith, who for the joy set before him endured the cross, scorning its shame, and sat down at the right hand of the throne of God. Consider him who endured such opposition from sinful men, so that you will not grow weary and lose heart" Hebrews 12:1-3.

NOAH'S ARK

Jim Paterson is an exceptionally talented artist. We have two pictures of his hanging in our home. The one is an original watercolour described as *The Kingdom of Heaven is Like a Mustard Seed* and the other is a limited edition print titled, *Noah Building the Ark.*

This latter work is really two stories within one picture. First and most obviously is the story of Noah and his family building the ark as God had commanded. But it's no ordinary ark and the setting is a suburban backyard. Both traditional and modern tools are lying around the yard and the boat has traditional and modern elements to it. The reason Jim used this contrast is to illustrate that "just as Noah made a choice to obey God then we, like Noah, must now choose to obey God in building whatever 'ark' He has asked us to build."

That's a good point. It raises two questions. Are we prepared to build whatever "ark" God is asking us to build? And are we, despite the possible mocking of others, prepared to do whatever God wants us to do? After all, if Noah with a limited revelation of God could do "everything just as God commanded him," (Genesis 6:22) how much more shouldn't we be prepared to be ark builders despite the possible ridicule of neighbours and friends.

Ten additional things:

1. Learn to read the signs. The ark was the largest billboard of the time but people still never read it for what it was.

2. Remember, we're all in the same boat.

3. Plan ahead. It wasn't raining when Noah built the ark.

4. Beware. God's Spirit will not contend with man forever (cf. Genesis 6:3).

5. Stay fit. God uses seniors for big projects. Noah was 600 years old!

6. Don't miss the boat.

7. Do what needs to be done. If God has told you to do something, ignore the critics.

8. "Two are better than one" Ecclesiastes 4:9. It's better to travel in pairs.

9. It's okay to be an amateur. Noah never built a boat before building the ark. The Titanic was built by professionals.

10. With God you're always safe in a storm. He's set a rainbow in the clouds as a sign of His covenant with you.

THE TOKOLOSHE

When I was twelve years old, I remember the day my mother asked me to take a lunch tray of soup and crackers to our maid who was sick in bed with the flu. I had never been into our maid's room before and after knocking on the door I entered with the caution borne of unfamiliarity. What immediately caught my attention was the height of the bed. The legs were placed on four large paint cans so that it stood a good three and a half to four feet off the ground. Never one to be backward in coming forward I said, "Why is your bed stuck up on these paint cans?" The moment I'd asked I knew I'd crossed a line. Our maid's fear was as tangible as the tray I was still holding. Then with a whispered reply she said, "Utokoloshe." Before I could ask what Utokoloshe was she had whisked the tray away from me and turned her back in dismissal.

Mystified, I immediately asked my mother what Utokoloshe was. Her reply was that it was some kind of an evil spirit. In later years I discovered that the Tokoloshe was supposedly a small, hairy, and beast-like creature in African folklore that takes malicious pleasure in causing damage and distress. According to some accounts it can be called up by the sangoma (witch doctor) to persecute or punish a particular individual or household.

In later years I met a number of folk within the black community who had their beds raised so that the Tokoloshe couldn't reach them while they slept. The Tokoloshe is one of the unsolved mysteries of Southern Africa. Some evidence suggests that many years ago the sangomas would steal new born babies and rear them in small cages. On limited food and restricted by the bars of the cage the children would grow up deformed and dwarf like. The sangomas would then use these "Tokoloshe" for their own evil ends.

Whether the Tokoloshe were once living human beings or whether they are some kind of evil spirit like the poltergeist is not the point of this meditation. The purpose of telling you about the Tokoloshe is to remind you that Satan uses all manner of means to hold people in bondage. He will stop at nothing. Whatever device Satan can harness to deceive humanity he will use.

Which is why Ephesians 6:10-18 says, "Finally, be strong in the Lord and in his mighty power. Put on the full armour of God so that you can take your stand against the devil's schemes. For our struggle is not against flesh and blood, but against the rulers, against the authorities, against the powers of this dark world and against the spiritual forces of evil in the heavenly realms. Therefore put on the full armour of God, so that when the day of evil comes, you may be able to stand your ground, and after you have done everything, to stand. Stand firm then, with the belt of truth buckled around your waist, with the breastplate of righteousness in place, and with your feet fitted with the readiness that comes from the gospel of peace. In addition to all this, take up the shield of faith, with which you can extinguish all the flaming arrows of the evil one. Take the helmet of salvation and the sword of the Spirit, which is the word of God. And pray in the Spirit on all occasions with all kinds of prayers and requests. With this in mind, be alert and always keep on praying for all the saints."

In addition, remember to pray for the many folk in Africa who are gripped by fear, exploited by the sangomas, and desperately in need of Jesus Christ as their personal Lord and Saviour.

TEN ESSENTIALS
FOR MARRIAGE

Here are ten time tested Biblical essentials that can make all the difference for married couples:

1. Be truthful.

In Ephesians 4:25 we read that we must "put off falsehood and speak truthfully." Healthy marriages are based on truthful communication. When couples are direct and say what they mean they lay a foundation for growth and intimacy. But when couples are devious and shade the truth they'll find themselves on rocky ground. So speak the truth in love. For integrity and honesty are the glue that hold the marriage covenant together, whereas hypocrisy and phoniness lead to ruin.

2. Admit mistakes.

Proverbs 28:13 says, "The man who refuses to admit his mistakes can never be successful" *Living Bible*. When a husband or a wife refuse to admit they are wrong they immediately reveal that they love themselves more than they love truth. No wonder Samuel Butler said that "there is no mistake so great as that of always being right." So when you're wrong admit the mistake. Say, "I'm sorry." For success in marriage consists of saying sorry again and again. Ogden Nash says it well in this little poem; "To keep your marriage brimming with love in the loving cup. Whenever you're wrong, admit it. Whenever you're right, shut up!"

3. Be quick to reconcile.

Ephesians 4:26-27 says, "In your anger do not sin: Do not let the sun go down while you are still angry, and do not give the devil a foothold." This thought is custom-made for husbands and wives. After all, it stands to reason that when two people spend countless hours in each others company there are going to be situations and circumstances that breed anger. When difficulties and disagreements arise be quick to reconcile. Delays in dealing with a problem are both sinful and dangerous. Agree with your partner never to go to bed angry. Resolve an issue before you go to sleep and this discipline will enable you to avoid stumbling over the molehills of unresolved conflict. In essence, "Submit to one another out of reverence for Christ" Ephesians 5:21.

4. Be generous.

Robert Quillen said, "The one word above all others that makes marriage successful is 'ours'." In other words, what's hers is mine and what's mine is hers. It shouldn't be a case of; What's his is mine and what's mine is mine! For the spirit of generosity is at the core of love. So husbands, pay attention to Ephesians 5:33 and make sure each of you loves his wife as he loves himself.

5. Be positive and constructive.

Ephesians 4:29 says, "Do not let any unwholesome talk come out of your mouths, but only what is helpful for building others up according to their needs, that it may benefit those who listen." One of the great challenges in marriage is to use words that build, strengthen, and encourage one's spouse. When unwholesome, spiteful, harmful, hateful and hurtful words are used they tear at the fabric of marriage and can even strip a marriage leaving it naked and exposed to ruin. So use words positively and constructively. Remember, a timely word will lessen stress and a loving word will heal and bless.

6. Be kind and compassionate.

Ephesians 4:32 says, "Be kind and compassionate to one another, forgiving each other, just as in Christ God forgave you." A marriage is strengthened when we give kindness and compassion without hesitation. Grace and mercy must be extended to one another. For the building blocks of marriage are small kindnesses, small considerations, small acts of tenderness, and small acts of piety that are habitually practiced as we interact through the day.

7. Be longsuffering.

Someone once described marriage as being something like a cold. In the first year of marriage when the wife gets a cold the husband says, "Sugar Dumpling - I'm worried about my baby girl. You must have a few days in the hospital to get rid of that cold. I don't expect you to eat that terrible hospital food so I'm having your food sent up from your favourite restaurant." In the second year of marriage the husband says, "Listen darling, I don't like the sound of that cough, you be a good girl and go to bed. I'll see that everything is looked after." In the third year of marriage the husband says, "Come Sweetheart, maybe you had better lie down. I'll bring you something to eat." In the fourth year of marriage the husband says, "Look dear, after you feed the kids and get the dishes washed, you'd better hit the sack." In the fifth year of marriage the husband says, "Get yourself a couple of aspirins!" In the sixth year of marriage the husband says, "If you would just gargle or something and stop sitting around barking!" In the seventh year of marriage the husband says, "For Pete's sake, stop sneezing. Do you want to give me pneumonia?" Yes, let's remember that we need to be longsuffering in marriage. For "love is patient, love is kind. It does not envy, it does not boast, it is not proud. It is not rude, it is not self-seeking, it is not easily angered, it keeps no record of wrongs. Love does not delight in evil but rejoices with the truth. It always protects, always trusts, always hopes, always perseveres" 1 Corinthians 13:4-7.

8. Be prayerful.

Matthew 7:7 says, "Ask and it will be given to you; seek and you will find; knock and the door will be opened to you." That's good news for married couples. Christians don't have to face marriage without resources. God has promised His people that when they're in need they simply have to ask Him to supply their need and He will do just that. As believers we have an assurance from God that His limitless resources are at our disposal. Married couples have all the help they need in order to make their marriage work. That help is only a prayer away. So remember to turn to God in prayer and thereby build your marriage on His resources rather than in your own strength.

9. Be balanced.

We need to work hard at keeping our priorities straight. We can't place our love for our spouse before our love for our Saviour. We can't place our love for our parents before our love for our marriage partner. And we can't place our love for our children, work, or hobbies before our love for our spouse. But then success in marriage is more than finding the right person, it's being a balanced person.

10. Build with Christ.

Ecclesiastes 4:12 says, "A cord of three strands is not quickly broken." When all's been said and done I firmly believe that the most important factor in establishing a strong and successful marriage is to place Christ at the centre. He must be the raison d'etre of the marriage. Christ must be primary. He must be the cornerstone. This is the picture given to us in Ephesians 5:22-25, "Wives, submit to your husbands as to the Lord. For the husband is the head of the wife as Christ is the head of the church . . . Now as the church submits to Christ, so also wives should submit to their husbands in everything. Husbands, love your wives, just as Christ loved the church and gave himself up for her."

GO TO IT!

At a recent conference I was flabbergasted to hear that only 10% of Evangelicals can clearly and correctly verbalise the Great Commission. That's frightening, the Great Commission is the essence of the mission of the church. Every believer should know that we're called to "go and make disciples of all nations, baptizing them in the name of the Father and of the Son and of the Holy Spirit, and teaching them to obey everything I have commanded you" (Matthew 28:19-20).

This isn't an optional extra. The church must reach out and introduce people to Jesus; invite them to join the church, and involve them in acts of service in the church and in the world. On the personal level it means that every believer must be a soul winner, every believer must be in the disciple making business, and every believer must be 100% committed to reaching the world with the gospel of Jesus Christ.

But what is this gospel? What is the message of the church? It's captured in John 3:7, "You must be born again." This is the message of first principles. It's the message of a new life and a fresh start.

We can never be casual or cavalier about this message. We must go to it. We must proclaim and promote it with passion. Millions are going to a lost eternity every day and their blood cries out to us. We must therefore reach out and snatch them from the brink of disaster. We must "go for it" in the power of the Holy Spirit. We must pray for a crop yielding "thirty, sixty or even a hundred times what was sown" Mark 4:20. So let's not stop at false finish lines. It starts in our neighbourhood and goes out from there. We must want our neighbours, our neighbour's neighbours, and our neighbour's neighbour's neighbours hot wired to God. For that's what counts. That's what brings heavenly recognition. That's what gets the Sovereign's approval. That's what brings a smile to the face of God.

Anything short of telling people that they must be "born again" is inadequate. It's not enough for a church to have good services, good music and good preaching. The fundamental mission of the church is to call on boys and girls, on men and women, to be of another type, to be cleansed from sin, to have God's kingdom created within, to have lives transformed. If we ever stop preaching and living out this message we've stopped being the church and may as well pack up and ship out!

BREATH
OF HEAVEN

In the introduction to Ken Terhoven's book, *Breath of Heaven,* he tells how, in the early 1950's, he went to conduct an evangelistic campaign in a little Lincolnshire village in England. It was a watershed experience for him.

He arrived as a novice evangelist, fired up to set the place ablaze with his handful of sermons. His first disappointment was the chapel. It was a barn-like building in the middle of nowhere, capable of seating only about 50 people. To add to his consternation, only four farmers attended nightly for the first week.

As he preached to the same four people, he became more and more frustrated. Each evening, at the conclusion of the service, the four men invited my father-in-law to join them in prayer, and each evening he declined. On the fourth night he reluctantly went to pray with them. He was ushered into a farmhouse kitchen and watched as the farmers fell to their knees on the cold stone floor and began to pour out their hearts to God in prayer. How those old Methodists prayed! They reminded God of His covenant and His promises. They quoted the Word. They wept and pleaded. Dad felt completely out of his league.

But then his heart began to soften and by midnight he found himself confessing to God about his own pride and hardness of heart. As his coldness and indifference began to disappear the four men gathered around him in love and concern, praying for him and asking God to use him.

Through their prayers came the constant repetition of Malachi 3:10: "'Test me in this,' says the Lord Almighty, 'and see if I will not throw open the floodgates of heaven and pour out so much blessing that you will not have room enough for it.'"

So they prayed until the burden lifted and they found themselves praising God for having heard them.

Nothing unusual happened that week. Each night the gospel was preached to the four men.

And then it happened! For some inexplicable reason Dad arrived an hour early on the second Thursday night. He couldn't believe his eyes. The church was surrounded by cars, vans, tractors and bicycles and, coming from all directions, people walking to the church. He pushed his way in, to be met by more than 100 people, in a church that could only seat 50, with still more coming in. He was so excited he skipped the preliminaries and began to preach. At the invitation 36 remained behind, broken in repentance as they received Christ.

It continued night after night, until, at the end of the campaign, there were more converts than the church could contain. Something had happened which was quite beyond and in spite of Dad. God had done the extraordinary in answer to prayer. It was a breath of heaven.

Can it happen again? Most definitely. God's the same God today as He always has been. So call out to Him in prayer. Confess your pride. Plead for forgiveness. Claim His promises. And seek His face for a fresh outpouring of His Spirit.

PRE-FLIGHT CHECK

In 1982 a number of little things that were not attended to resulted in Air Florida flight 90 ending in a catastrophe. It was the 13th of January at National Airport, Washington, D.C. Swirling clouds had deposited a thick blanket of snow over the southern states of the USA. The Air Florida Boeing 737 twin-engine jet had taken on 71 passengers, three of them carrying babies, and had been delayed for an hour and forty-five minutes because snow plows were clearing the runway of snow. Airport workers de-iced the wings with glycol fluid and the plane taxied out for take off from runway 36.

As the pilots sent their jet down the slushy runway and still falling snow they decided to lift the nose wheel earlier than usual in order to help the take off. Inside thirty seconds of being airborne they knew that something was desperately wrong due to the shuddering and shaking of the plane. Just over a kilometre away from the airport on 14th Street Bridge, crossing over the Potomac River, drivers trapped in a traffic jam heard the plummeting jet before they saw it.

The plane hit the bridge with a massive bang. It ripped the tops off five cars and dragged others into the river with it. Bodies were left lying all over the bridge as some of the vehicles started burning.

A second later the plane hit the iced-over river like a rock smashing through a windscreen. It broke into three sections on impact. The nose plunged under and everyone in this part of the plane was killed instantly. The main fuselage flopped, settled long enough for bystanders to see the people strapped inside, and then slowly sank. Miraculously, the tail floated for 20 minutes and most of the survivors came from this part of the plane.

Even more people could have been saved if rescue workers could have got to them. People froze or drowned less than 15 metres from the shore due to the icy waters paralysing muscles and bringing on fatal hypothermia within 10 minutes. Seventy-eight people died.

When aviation experts tried to ascertain the cause of the accident, they concluded that there was nothing big that was responsible for the crash. A series of little things caused the disaster. Ice on the wings may have collected despite the de-icing procedure. Ice in the engine may have distorted air intake and reduced power. The take off speed may have been marginally slow and the nose may have been allowed to rise too soon.

Likewise, in the spiritual realm, failure to attend to little things can result in tragedy. That's why it's important to do a spiritual pre-flight check. Here are three essentials in order to avoid disaster:

"Be careful that you do not forget the Lord your God . . ." Deuteronomy 8:11.

"Give careful thought to your ways" Haggai 1:7.

"But each one should be careful how he builds" 1 Corinthians 3:10.

WISE TEACHER

Years ago the book of Ecclesiastes introduced me to the *wise teacher*. Having "met" this teacher, in chapter 12:9-12, I've taken every opportunity to introduce him to others in the hope that they will adopt the five secrets of his success:

Firstly, the wise teacher **persevered**. In verse 9a the KJV says, ". . . he still taught the people knowledge." In other words he never tired of teaching. He never gave it up. He pressed on despite challenges and obstacles coming his way. He gave his best no matter what happened.

Secondly, the wise teacher spent time in **preparation**. In verse 9b we're told that ". . . he pondered and searched out . . ." He knew that wisdom does not occur in a vacuum. To be wise one must study and keep studying. So he dug into books; he sat and cogitated; and he continually sought people from whom he could learn something new.

Thirdly, the wise teacher attended to **planning**. In verse 9b we read; "He . . . set in order." To "set in order" is to arrange a specified sequence and have every element in its rightful place. The wise teacher did this by ordering his time, arranging his materials, and planning his agenda.

Fourthly, the wise teacher used **pleasing words**. Verse 10 states that he ". . . searched to find just the right words, and what he wrote was upright and true." He wasn't casual with his choice of words. He thought about every word he used. For he knew that words should be like an instrument with overtones of honour and truth.

Fifthly, the wise teacher **produced** a harvest. Verse 11 says; "the words of the wise are like goads . . . like firmly embedded nails . . ." A goad is a sharp stick for prodding cattle. Thus the wise teacher produced words that urged people along. He drove his teachings into his students and embedded them into their thinking and actions. And he never forgot that ". . . much study wearies the body!"

Hopefully you'll learn from the wise teacher. If you have the responsibility of instructing others make sure you persevere in your work, prepare with diligence, plan efficiently, lace your lessons with pleasing words, and aim to produce a harvest to the glory of God.

PERHAPS TODAY

On the office desk of my late father-in-law there was a card which said, *Perhaps Today*. That little phrase says a lot. It's a reminder of the greatest thing that is yet to happen. Something far better than world peace. Something superior to the provision of shelter, clothing, and food for the millions who live in poverty. And something that surpasses the finding of a cure for AIDS, cancer and other diseases.

For the greatest thing that is yet to happen is the second coming of Jesus Christ. Yes, my father-in-law knew that the second coming is the one event that will make everything else pale into insignificance.

This is how it will be when Christ returns. People will be going about business as usual. They will be "eating and drinking, marrying and giving in marriage" Matthew 24:38. Then, at a time known only to the Father, when we least expect it, Christ is going to return personally and bodily (cf. Matthew 24:36, 44; Mark 13:26,32; Acts 1:11). His return will be spectacularly visible and unmistakable. He will be seen "coming on the clouds of the sky, with power and great glory" Matthew 24:30. And there will be "a loud command, with the voice of the archangel and with the trumpet call of God, and the dead in Christ will rise first. After that, we who are still alive and are left will be caught up with them in the clouds to meet the Lord in the air" 1 Thessalonians 4:16-17.

The Bible says a whole lot more about the second coming of Christ. Just read the New Testament and this great truth will leap out at you from nearly every page. For there are 318 references to Christ's return in the New Testament. That's one out of every thirty verses. And it's mentioned in 23 of the 27 books. Furthermore, for every prophecy in the Bible on the first coming of Christ, there are eight on Christ's second coming.

So be prepared for Christ to return at any time. Be on the lookout. "Be ready, because the Son of Man will come at an hour when you do not expect him" Matthew 24:44. Which, when boiled down, simply means you must "be on guard! Be alert!" For "you do not know when that time will come" Mark 13:33.

As Dad said, *Perhaps Today!*

TWO ARE BETTER THAN ONE

In the summer of 1985 I was teaching a variety of outdoor pursuits designed to challenge students both intellectually and physically. Group work was an integral part of the programme and at the commencement of the course students were randomly assigned to a group for the duration of the week. They then competed in obstacle courses, orienteering exercises, the lateria course, the stalking of the lantern, as well as other leadership and group building exercises. Some groups never "clicked," some had internal hostility, others lacked enthusiasm, and some worked effectively.

But the group I'll never forget was the one I felt was doomed to fail. This group probably had the nine smallest boys coupled with the largest. He was affectionately known as "Tubby" and weighed more than 130 kg/290 lbs.

The day arrived when they were going to compete on the obstacle course. The teachers wondered what would happen when Tubby came to negotiate vertical obstacles of more than six metres, a mud crawl, climbing nets, a horizontal wire walk, hanging tyres, and a zip line over a river. Well it was amazing. These nine little "terriers" snapped around Tubby as they shoved and heaved him around that course. They dragged him, prodded him, lifted him and stretched him over, under, and through each and every obstacle. Their tenacity soon had the hundred plus grade ten students cheering them on with shouts of encouragement and rounds of applause. It was a superhuman effort and when they had finished they were more dead than alive. Nonetheless it was no doubt worthwhile. One look at their mud splattered, yet grinning faces, confirmed their obvious sense of accomplishment and pride.

These students were an outstanding example of the fact that "two are better than one" Ecclesiastes 4:9. Every time Tubby stumbled and fell his friends helped him up. Success was achieved because they pulled together. In like manner you can overcome difficulties and "have a good return for (your) work" (Ecclesiastes 4:9), if you team up with a Christian friend and pull together. Yes, when you tackle the day's obstacles with a buddy in Christ you'll be assured of greater success.

So remember. When you're committed to God and a friend you are smart. For a threefold cord won't easily part!

HOLD ON

Someone once said that the bulldog's nose is slanted upward so that it can breathe while it holds on. That's a fascinating observation. A reminder that dogged persistence overcomes adversity and that the ability to endure brings success.

Which is the point made in James 1:4; "Perseverance must finish its work so that you may be mature and complete, not lacking anything."

So hold on. Don't retreat from the challenges or tests that God has allowed to come your way. Be determined, endure hardship, be tenacious, and don't quit. For a faith that fizzles before the finish is no faith at all.

Thomas Edison knew about gritty perseverance. In December 1914 his manufacturing facilities in West Orange, New Jersey, were heavily damaged by fire. Edison lost almost $1 million worth of equipment and the records of much of his work. The next morning, walking through the charred embers of his hopes and dreams, the sixty-seven-year-old inventor said, "There is value in disaster. All our mistakes are burned up. Now we can start anew."

That's the way to do it. If life hands you a lemon, make lemonade. Much is accomplished when we refuse to waver. So pay as little attention to discouragement as possible. Hold on and keep holding on. For it's "God's usual course not to give His children the taste of His delights till they begin to sweat in seeking after them" Richard Baxter.

An anonymous poet wrote:

> "When things go wrong, as they sometimes will,
> When the road you're trudging seems all uphill,
> When the funds are low and the debts are high,
> And when you want to smile, but you have to sigh,
> When care is pressing you down a bit -
> Rest if you must, but don't you quit.
>
> Life is queer with its twists and turns,
> As everyone of us sometimes learns,
> And many a failure turns about
> When you might have won had you stuck it out.
> Don't give up, though the pace seems slow -
> You may succeed with another blow.

Often the goal is nearer than
It seems to a faint and faltering man;
Often the struggler has given up
When he might have captured the victor's cup
And he learned too late, when the night's slipped down
How close he was to the golden crown.

Success is failure turned inside out -
The silver tint of the clouds of doubt,
And you never can tell how close you are,
It may be near when it seems afar;
So stick to the fight when you're hardest hit -
It's when things seems worst that you mustn't quit."

IN HARMONY

An old story tells of a father who had a family of quarrelsome sons. One day he called his sons to him and, picking out the strongest of them, handed him a stick. "Snap it," he said. The son did so with a gesture of contempt. The father handed him two sticks. "Snap them," he said. Again the son did. The father handed him ever increasing numbers of sticks. "Snap them," he said - a bundle of four, five, six. Soon the young man was straining to snap the sticks and finally had to admit defeat. "This is a lesson in unity," said the father. "Unity is strength. A house divided cannot stand. Anyone can overthrow you one by one. But stand together, in unity, and your united strength will give your enemies second thoughts."

Psalm 133:1 says, "How good and pleasant it is when brothers live together in unity!"

Just like the father of the quarrelsome sons wanted unity in his family, God wants unity for His sons and daughters - for the family of God. For unity is the one thing that will convince people that the church has something the world doesn't have. And unity is the one thing that makes the church virtually unstoppable as it goes into all the world and preaches the good news to all creation (cf. John 17:23).

That's why we can't afford to have some folk in the church pulling in one direction and others pulling in another. We've got to be all together, all pulling in the same direction. Not in the sense of uniformity. God wants unity, not uniformity. The Bible never teaches a uniformity brought about by political expediency, doctrinal compromise, ecumenical brotherhood, or organizational efficiency. The unity God desires is unity of spirit and purpose. The unity of being one with the Father and the Son (cf. John 17:21). For it's only when we're all together - one in Him, that the power of God is going to be unleashed in our midst.

A church worship team or choir provide an excellent example of church unity. When the members come together they don't all sing the same note. They don't sing in uniformity. They're not all clones singing exactly the same way. They don't have identical cadence or tone. They sing their own part and sound their own note. But as they sing their part; be it base, tenor, alto, or soprano, they do so in harmony - all singing the same song. That's unity. They stop and start at the same time. They sing the same words and they're governed by the same melody.

Likewise, we need to be on the same page of God's sheet music. I can't be singing one song while you're singing another. That's disunity. If I sing one song and you sing another we'll be out of tune with God. We'll be a discordant cacophony. We'll be like "a resounding gong or a clanging cymbal." 1 Corinthians 13:1. But when we sing the same song, each with our own part and note, each making sure we're in harmony with the spirit and purpose of the church, then we have unity.

In essence then, church unity exists when people come together with a common understanding of what God has called them to do. It's having a similar vision, being single-minded, cooperating with one another, having a shared mission, singing the same song.

Thus if you find you're the only one with a certain vision for the church, or there are only a few of you who think the church should be going in a particular direction, then it's unlikely that it's God's vision for the church. For God has never been, and will never be, the author of disunity. He doesn't sell pork chops in a synagogue.

We need to be clear on this. If you're clashing with others because your vision for the church is different from theirs, because you want to sing a different song, then one of two things may be needed: you may need to give up on your agenda, be submissive, and climb on board with everyone else. Or, you may need to find a church that sings the same song that you sing. Of course if there isn't a Bible believing Spirit filled church singing the song that you're singing then it begs the question, are you actually singing God's song?

Paul sums up saying, "I appeal to you brothers, in the name of our Lord Jesus Christ, that all of you agree with one another so that there may be no divisions among you and that you may be perfectly united in mind and thought" 1 Corinthians 1:10.

Now commit this to memory and commit it to life.

NEVER AGAIN

If you are a child of the King, a son or daughter of Jesus Christ, then here are a number of things that should "never again" happen in your life:

■ Never again will I be afraid to testify about the Lord Jesus Christ. "For God did not give us a spirit of timidity, but a spirit of power, of love and of self discipline" 2 Timothy 1:7.

■ Never again will I think of myself more highly than I ought. "For by the grace given me I say to every one of you: Do not think of yourself more highly than you ought, but rather think of yourself with sober judgment, in accordance with the measure of faith God has given you" Romans 12:3.

■ Never again will I say, "I can't." Philippians 4:13 says, "I can do everything through him who gives me strength."

■ Never again will I fear those who are not from God. "Because the one who is in me is greater than the one who is in the world" 1 John 4:4.

■ Never again will I complain that I'm short of money. For I know "my God will meet all (my) needs according to his glorious riches in Christ Jesus" Philippians 4:19.

■ Never again will I grumble about my circumstances. Like Paul "I have learned to be content whatever the circumstances" Philippians 4:11.

■ Never again will I lack wisdom to handle a situation. "If any of you lacks wisdom, he should ask God, who gives generously to all without finding fault, and it will be given to him" James 1:5.

■ Never again will I carry my burdens alone. I know I can "cast all (my) anxiety on him because he cares for" me. 1 Peter 5:7.

■ Never again will I feel guilty over past sins for which I have truly asked forgiveness. I am assured that "there is now no condemnation for those who are in Christ Jesus because through Christ Jesus the law of the Spirit of life set me free from the law of sin and death" Romans 8:1-2.

■ Never again will I be concerned about being separated from the love of Christ. For "in all these things we are more than conquerors through him who loved us" Romans 8:37.

BUILD THE
CHURCH

In 1 Corinthians 14:12 it says, "Excel in gifts that build up the church." That means the Lord wants you to concentrate on doing the things that will help the church develop and grow. None of us should be living carelessly or uselessly. The church should have our loyalty, our labour, and love. Let's not forget; we're to live for Him. And what does that mean? It means we're to join Christ in doing what He's doing. And what's He doing? He's building - He's building the church (cf. Matthew 16:18). He's the Contractor and we're the trades' people. We're what He uses to get the job done.

So according to your gift, get building. If you're an architect - design according to the Master's plan. If you're an engineer - help others handle the load and deal with stress. If you build foundations - build them on the Rock. If you're a carpenter - fit things together so that unity is brought to the whole structure. If you're an electrician - provide a spark to hot wire people to God. If you're a framer - erect each part straight and true. If you're a plumber - make sure things flow and help others tap into the Source. If you do renovations - make changes for the better. If you're a roofer - be responsible for keeping things out that shouldn't get in. If you're a dry-waller - make things smooth but don't fill cracks that haven't been fixed. If you're a painter or interior decorator - make the church a beautiful place. If you specialise in windows - help others see the light. If you're a locksmith - open doors and help people get in. If you lay carpets - bring warmth and comfort wherever it's needed. If you're a telephone technician - get people connected with the Operator and with one another. If you're a mason - work with block, brick and stone to strengthen the structure. If you do heating and air conditioning - make sure the church is never lukewarm. If you put in roads and driveways - hold to His path as you help others walk in the Way. And if you're a landscaper or gardener - make the church look good from the outside but don't forget to regularly come inside.

There's a job for everyone. All of us should be building. In season and out of season we should be hard at it. For God wants us to wear out - not rust out. We must build the church until the contract's complete.

THE LOVE OF GOD

The love of God is immeasurable, uninhibited, overshadowing, all pervading, and everlasting. It's swifter than the feet of repentance (cf. Luke 15:20). Broader than the measure of a man's mind. Can never be extinguished. Thinks nothing of trouble, feels no burdens, and is never soured by injustice. It's never blind, never deaf, and never silent. It's wider, longer, higher, and deeper than anything anyone can imagine. Even when we think we're beginning to understand it we discover it "surpasses knowledge" (cf. Ephesians 3:19).

Billy Graham says, "Orators whose words flow like a rippling brook have been unable to describe it. Artists whose brushes spread untold beauty have been unable to portray it on canvas. Writers whose words drip from their pens like dewdrops from a rose petal have been unable to write" effectively about it.

That's not surprising. Because we're right in the middle of it, because it's washing around us, over us, and under us - because it's enveloping us, we struggle to see it for what it really is. Even so, even with our limited perspective, the love of God is "like the Amazon River flowing down to water a single daisy" F. B. Meyer. It's like the wind. It comes from every direction. It's intimacy set on fire. A living thing. A wonder-worker. Never obsolete. It's what "makes the world go round" Lewis Carroll. In fact, it puts a new face on a weary world and as it does it enters everywhere - creeping where it isn't wanted. For the love of God, regardless of what it encounters, can never die.

But then the love of God is more than an accessory, more than an addendum, more than garnish, more than an increment.

There's no containing the love of God. It permeates creation. Seeps into every crack. Climbs the highest mountain. Reaches into the depths of the sea. Colonizes the atmosphere. Invades the cosmos. Makes life possible.

If you listen, you can't fail to hear it. It whispers and it shouts. No one can shut it out. Men may rail against it, try to explain it away, seek to distort it, drift away from it, turn their backs on it, be contemptuous of it, neglect it, even run from it, but every effort to silence it is futile. For God's love isn't a feeling to be forgotten. It isn't a memory that can be erased. And it isn't an experience you can explain away. It's a person. Not just any person. It's an exclusive Person - the Lord Jesus Christ.

Jesus Christ is the epitome, the essence, the full extent, the ad infinitum of God's love. Romans 5:8 says, "But God demonstrates his own love for us in this: While we were still sinners, Christ died for us." What an expression of love! Exemplified on the Cross of Calvary is the love of God for all mankind. Suspended from a wooden beam Christ gave His life so that we might know fullness of life. This is the love of God. "God made him who had no sin to be sin for us, so that in him we might become the righteousness of God" 2 Corinthians 5:21. This is love that doesn't hold back. This is unfathomable love. This is incalculable, unbounded, exhaustless love. For the condemnation that was rightly ours was taken by Him. The judgement of God for our sin, the shame, the suffering we deserved, the death penalty that hung over us, it was all taken by Him. No wonder John 15:13 exclaims, "Greater love has no one than this, that one lay down his life for his friends."

That's a love worth knowing. Isn't it? If you haven't done so before, believe in Him today. Turn to Him now. Repent of your sins. Say "Yes" to salvation in Jesus Christ. For when you do, when by faith you cast yourself on Him, then you'll know the love that surpasses all love, the love that never disappoints, the love that will never let you down . . . the love of God.

THE 'TATE' FAMILY

In the early 1980's Karen and I were introduced to children's ministry by the English evangelist David Iliffe. One of the talks that he did in the mission he ran at Christ Church Hillbrow was called the 'Tate' family. Using pictures of potatoes that he put up on a magnetic board we quickly learnt about the 'Tate's' we shouldn't be and the 'Tate's' we ought to be. You'll probably recognise a number of these 'Tate's' in the congregation you attend.

Grandpa Dictate wants to run everything his own way. It's his way or the highway. Nothing happens without his say.

Grandpa Dictate has a younger brother named Potentate. He's also a big shot who likes to call the shots.

Then there's Uncle Rotate. He's never happy with anything. He's always trying to turn things around. His sister, Aunt Agitate is no different. She takes every opportunity to stir up trouble and along with their half brother, Irritate, they make a deadly trio.

Cousin Hesitate, who never gets around to anything, and cousin Vegetate, who hates any kind of change, quickly pour cold water on whatever the family proposes. They get along well with Uncle Spectate. He's happy to sit on the sidelines and watch.

Aunt Agitate's brother-in-law, Mr. Imitate, thinks our church should copy what goes on in other churches and is convinced that what's successful in those churches will be successful in ours.

When it comes to preparing the annual budget, brother Devastate is inclined to be pessimistic. His doom and gloom prophecies surface whenever money matters are discussed.

Fortunately not all the members of the 'Tate' family are thorns in the flesh. Miss Facilitate will help out at the drop of a hat. You can always count on her support. When something needs to be done, she gets stuck right in.

The pastor, Rev. Commentate, is always telling others about the love of Jesus. He takes every opportunity to preach and teach the good news. It's obvious that something marvellous has happened to him and he can't keep his mouth shut.

Behind the scenes, and possibly one of the most important members of the family, is sister Meditate. She's quietly prayerful, regular in attendance, a keen student of God's Word, and encouraging in all she says and does.

READING THE HOLY WRIT

Statistics from *Pulpit Helps* indicate that 72 percent of people believe the Bible to be the Word of God, but only 12 percent read it on a daily basis. Eighteen percent of Protestants are daily Bible readers, 4 percent are Catholics. Forty-one percent of Protestants read the Bible less than once a month or never. Sixty-seven percent of Catholics never read the Bible.

These are disappointing statistics. The Bible should be bread for daily use, not cake for special occasions. Everyone should be reading it. "The young, to learn how to live. The old, to know how to die. The ignorant, for wisdom. The learned, for humility. The rich, for compassion. The poor, for comfort. The dreamer, for enchantment. The practical, for counsel. The weak, for strength. The strong, for direction. The haughty, for warning. The humble, for exaltation. The troubled, for peace. The weary, for rest. The sinner, for salvation. The doubting, for assurance. All Christians, for guidance." *Faith Baptist Church, Kokomo, Indiana.*

D. L. Moody said, "I never saw a useful Christian who was not a student of the Bible." With this in mind here are several more reasons why you should be reading God's Word:

1. To know God. John Stott said, "A man who loves his wife will love her letters and her photographs because they speak to him of her. So if we love the Lord Jesus we shall love the Bible because it speaks to us of him." The Word is the progressive revelation of the Father, the Son, and the Holy Spirit. We cannot hope to know the triune God unless we encounter Him through the scriptures that reveal Him.

2. To know yourself. God's Word is a mirror. In it we encounter who we truly are. It uncovers everything. As it says in Hebrews 4:12-13, "The word of God is living and active. Sharper than any double edged sword, it penetrates even to dividing soul and spirit, joints and marrow; it judges the thoughts and attitudes of the heart. Nothing in all creation is hidden from God's sight. Everything is uncovered and laid bare before the eyes of him to whom we must give account."

3. C. H. Spurgeon once said, "The appetite for the Word grows on that which it feeds on." The Bible was written for our transformation, not just for information. God's given us His Holy Writ for nourishment and growth. It's the blueprint for the Christian, God's instrument for growing mature believers. It's **B**asic **I**nstruction **B**efore **L**eaving **E**arth. As it says in 2 Timothy 3:16-17, "All Scripture is God-breathed and is useful for teaching, rebuking, correcting and training in righteousness, so that the man of God may be thoroughly equipped for every good work."

4. As Christians we're "the salt of the earth" and "the light of the world" Matthew 5:13-14. However, we can only be salt and light if we've rejected a temporal perspective and embraced the eternal values taught in the Word. Here's the reality. Dip into the Word every now and again and at best you'll be nothing more than salt without much flavour and a light that barely penetrates the darkness. But when the Bible's your constant companion it will enable you to be quality salt and a bright light.

5. We all need guidance. With the multiplicity of decisions that we have to make we need a working knowledge of the principles and prohibitions in God's Word. This takes disciplined study, memorization, and constant reinforcement from regular reading. It's only when we drink daily from the Biblical well that we'll be able to say, "Your word is a lamp to my feet and a light for my path" Psalm 119:105.

6. God's Word helps us to overcome temptation and endure in times of trial. Paul reminds us to "put on the full armour of God, so that when the day of evil comes, you may be able to stand your ground, and after you have done everything, to stand. Stand firm then, with the belt of truth buckled around your waist, with the breastplate of righteousness in place, and with your feet fitted with the readiness that comes from the gospel of peace. In addition to all this, take up the shield of faith, with which you can extinguish all the flaming arrows of the evil one. Take the helmet of salvation and the sword of the Spirit, which is the word of God" Ephesians 6:13-17.

IN CHRIST

Christians have so many wonderful blessings "in Christ." The phrase "in Christ" (or it's equivalent) appears 27 times in the epistle to the Ephesians, more than in any other New Testament book. Here are some of the "in Christ" statements from Ephesians. Meditate on them and use them to motivate you to "live a life worthy of the calling you have received" Ephesians 4:1.

We are "in Christ Jesus" Ephesians 1:1.

We are blessed "in the heavenly realms with every spiritual blessing in Christ" Ephesians 1:3.

"He chose us in him before the creation of the world" Ephesians 1:4.

"In love he predestined us to be adopted as his sons through Jesus Christ" Ephesians 1:4-5.

"He made us accepted in the Beloved" Ephesians 1:6 KJV.

"In him we have redemption through his blood" Ephesians 1:7.

"In him we have . . . forgiveness of sins, in accordance with the riches of God's grace" Ephesians 1:7.

"He made known to us the mystery of his will according to his good pleasure, which he purposed in Christ" Ephesians 1:9.

Everything is centred in Christ. He brings "all things in heaven and on earth together under one head, even Christ" Ephesians 1:10.

"In him we were also chosen, having been predestined according to the plan of him who works out everything in conformity with the purpose of his will" Ephesians 1:11.

We are "in Christ . . . for the praise of his glory" Ephesians 1:12.

"You also were included in Christ when you heard the word of truth, the gospel of your salvation" Ephesians 1:13.

We have "faith in the Lord Jesus" Ephesians 1:15.

In Christ we have "the Spirit of wisdom and revelation" Ephesians 1:17.

In Christ we have hope (cf. Ephesians 1:18).

In Christ we have "his incomparably great power" Ephesians 1:19.

"Because of his great love for us, God, who is rich in mercy, made us alive with Christ even when we were dead in transgressions" Ephesians 2:4-5.

"We are God's workmanship, created in Christ Jesus to do good works" Ephesians 2:10.

"In Christ Jesus you who once were far away have been brought near through the blood of Christ" Ephesians 2:13.

We grow together in Christ (cf. Ephesians 2:21).

"In him you too are being built together to become a dwelling in which God lives by his Spirit" Ephesians 2:22.

We are "sharers together in the promise in Christ Jesus" Ephesians 3:6.

The "manifold wisdom of God" (Ephesians 3:10-11) is manifested in Christ Jesus.

"In him and through faith in him we may approach God with freedom and confidence" Ephesians 3:12.

SIT DOWN AND SHUT UP!

It's reported that two young boys were discussing parent problems. Of course, they had lots of complaints. But the biggest issue became evident when one boy turned to the other and said, "First they teach you to talk, then they teach you to walk, and as soon as you do, it's 'Sit down and shut up!'"

To be truthful, most parents have done this at some time. Sometimes our preference is for children to be seen and not heard. The disciples may have had this attitude. According to the account in Mark 10 it would seem that the disciples preferred not having the children around. But, "when Jesus saw this, he was indignant. He said to them, 'Let the little children come to me, and do not hinder them'" Mark 10:14. In saying this Jesus teaches a vital principle - children shouldn't be ignored. They shouldn't be pushed aside. And they shouldn't be ostracised or marginalised.

In the era of latch key kids, day care facilities, and stay at home mums who are few and far between we need to remind ourselves of the importance of *paying attention to children*. Let's not forget that "sons are a heritage from the Lord," and "children a reward from him" Psalm 127:3. And let's not forget that one of the most important things parents can do for their children is to give of themselves with both quality and quantity time. So notice the children. Make time for them. Find creative ways to play games with them, to read with them, to worship God with them, to attend their school functions, to sit and talk with them, to listen to their daily exploits, to pray with them, to work with them, to take time to be their best friend, to share the Gospel with them, and to just hang out with them.

Which brings me to the woman who wrote to Gypsy Smith after an evangelistic campaign to tell him she'd been converted after hearing one of his messages. Her letter said, "I believe the Lord wants me to preach the Gospel, Brother Smith, but the trouble is that I have twelve children to raise! What shall I do?" She received this letter in reply: "My dear lady, I am happy to hear that you've been saved and feel called to preach, but I'm even more delighted to know that God has already provided you with a congregation of twelve." The new convert got the point!

SHAKE THE NATION

In the January 2002 edition of *Focus on the Family* there was an article entitled, *Shake the Nation*. It reported on a pro-life campaign in which baby rattles were sent by Americans to their senators in the hope that the sound of the rattles would be a constant reminder of the children whose lives are at stake because of the brutality of abortion. At the time of writing there had already been 20,000 rattles sent by pro-lifers across the country. As Folger said, "This campaign is a signal that Americans are not going to sit idly by or wait to react to the aggressive efforts of the abortion lobby. We will shake this nation back to life, and this historic campaign is only the beginning."

What a wonderful concept. Hopefully American pro-lifers will have great success as they seek to shake their nation back to life. But the campaign shouldn't be restricted to the U.S.A. It would be great if pro-lifers in every country sent rattles to local politicians in an effort to shake our world back to life.

It shouldn't stop with the pro-life campaign. It should also extend to the fight for the lives of those who are dead in trespasses and sin. Christians should be asking God to shake sinners back to life. We should be pleading for the miracle of the new birth and trusting God for a fresh harvest of baby Christians. It's time for every nation to be shaken back to life - to fullness of life, to the life that leads to eternal life.

So let's find Spirit led ways to be rattles that catch the attention of the not yet saved. Every Christian should be crying out to God to shake the nations of the world back to life. You can do that by praying for your nation today.

Consider the prophecy of Haggai 2:6-9 and ask God to make it a reality in our time: "This is what the Lord Almighty says: 'In a little while I will once more shake the heavens and the earth, the sea and the dry land. I will shake all nations, and the desired of all nations will come, and I will fill this house with glory,' says the Lord Almighty. 'The glory of this present house will be greater than the glory of the former house,' says the Lord Almighty. 'And in this place I will grant peace,' declares the Lord Almighty."

TRANSFUSION

Many lives have been saved by blood transfusions. Dr. James Blundell, an Englishman, was one of the first doctors to successfully use the technique to save the lives of women who were haemorrhaging after childbirth. Extant etchings poignantly capture Blundell looking on as a woman stands next to the bed of a dying woman and delivers her blood through a tube into the woman's vein.

The benefits of blood transfusion also impacted soldiers embroiled in the First World War. Battlefield medics carried a wooden box containing two large jars of the life-giving liquid and word quickly spread among the troops that "There's a bloke who pumps blood into you and brings you back to life even after you're dead" [Source: P. Brand. P. Yancey. *In His Image*].

These are wonderful stories but they don't begin to compare with the blood transfusion that took place when Christ went to the cross of Calvary and shed His blood as a ransom for our sins. Twenty centuries ago Christ voluntarily laid down His life so that we might live. He gave His blood freely, and for everyone. He gave incorruptible blood. And He gave blood that can be transfused into every "blood type" of every person who is prepared to receive it by faith.

This transfusion is unlike any other. You can't pay for it. The blood that gives eternal life is absolutely free. All you need do to receive this life giving blood is to trust Him now. For Christ doesn't convey Himself genetically. He isn't passed from one generation to the next. If He was then His offspring would be one-half Christ, one-fourth Christ, one-sixteenth Christ, and on and on until only faint evidence of his bloodline remained (cf. P. Brand. P. Yancey. *In His Image*).

Rather, through His Spirit, He chooses to convey Himself directly and incorruptibly, by offering each of us a transfusion of His blood. John 6:53-57 says, "I tell you the truth, unless you eat the flesh of the Son of Man and drink his blood, you have no life in you. Whoever eats my flesh and drinks my blood has eternal life, and I will raise him up at the last day. For my flesh is real food and my blood is real drink. Whoever eats my flesh and drinks my blood remains in me, and I in him. Just as the living Father sent me and I live because of the Father, so the one who feeds on me will live because of me."

So if you haven't done so, trust in Christ today. For "it is the blood that makes atonement for one's life" Leviticus 17:11.

> *There is a fountain filled with blood*
> *Drawn from Immanuel's veins;*
> *And sinners plunged beneath that flood,*
> *Lose all their guilty stains.*
> W. Cowper.

FINDING FORGIVENESS

Colossians 3:13 says, "Bear with each other and forgive whatever grievances you may have against one another. Forgive as the Lord forgave you." This is easier said than done. At some point most of us struggle to admit error, to shoulder blame, to be charitable, to apologize, to forgive and forget, and to begin over. Yet God wants us to find forgiveness, to be imitators of the forgiveness He extends to us. He wants us to decide to forgive and be the first to forgive. For we were never meant to harbour resentment.

Resentment is negative and poisonous. When we fail to forgive a grievance it diminishes and devours the very core of our being. It sets up a barrier between us and God. It destroys the bridge over which the one who cannot forgive must someday pass. Jesus put it this way, "For if you forgive men when they sin against you, your heavenly Father will also forgive you. But if you do not forgive men their sins, your Father will not forgive your sins" Matthew 6:14-15.

Like me you may have been deeply hurt by someone and believe they deserve to be punished. Even if a number of years have passed, the pain and memory of the offense is as sharp as ever. But that doesn't take away from the fact that Jesus wants you to forgive those who've sinned against you. And it doesn't take away from the fact that it's to your "glory to overlook an offense" Proverbs 19:11. So find forgiveness. Here are three essential steps:

Firstly, examine your heart. You can only be in right relationship with others when things are right in you. Finding forgiveness starts on the inside, starts with you - nowhere else. If there is bitterness, anger, or hatred in your heart it must be taken to the foot of the cross and left there. You'll not find forgiveness while you're carrying baggage. As long as you wallow in self-pity, yearn for revenge, or hope for some kind of retribution, you'll be handicapped and unable to live life to the full. David understood this principle. He knew that the words of his mouth and the meditation of his heart would only be pleasing in God's sight (cf. Psalm 19:14) if he asked God to forgive his hidden faults (cf. Psalm 19:12).

Secondly, "Submit to one another out of reverence for Christ" Ephesians 5:21. Having confessed the hidden faults of your heart you're ready for the next step. This is where you humble yourself for the sake of Christ by going to the person who's offended you and doing what needs to be done for reconciliation to take place. One hurdle in this process is realising that you need to relinquish the right to be right or the right to hurt back. Although this is hard to do don't forget that your motivation for doing this is because of your reverence for Christ. You forgive because He first forgave you (cf. Ephesians 4:32).

Finally, pray for those who've hurt you. Jesus says, "But I tell you: Love your enemies and pray for those who persecute you, that you may be sons of your Father in heaven" Matthew 5:44. Now you may think that God's asking a bit much in this text. If you've been wounded, it's not easy to pray for the offender and bless that person. But then God never expects you to do this in your own strength. He doesn't want you to take yourself by the scruff of the neck and just do it. He wants you to call on Him for help. Ask Him to fill you with His Spirit and give you His strength and love. For when you trust in Him, He's promised to never let you down.

NANA'S GREEN HAIR

It started out as a joke. One Sunday morning after church, while speaking to a few of the young people, Nana said to one of them, "Why don't you colour your hair green?" What possessed Nana to ask such a question is beyond me. One thing led to another and before long the tables had been turned and Nana had been counter challenged to colour her hair green. To which she said, "Okay. You're on."

We all wondered if she'd go through with it for it's not an everyday occurrence for a grandmother in her seventies to agree to colour her hair green. She later said, "I cannot believe I would be such an idiot! To do what I did was completely out of character for me. My pride and dignity were knocked right out from under me."

However, Nana had given her word and wasn't about to back down from the challenge. The following Sunday evening she arrived at church with bright green highlights. As you can imagine, it caused quite a stir. For it was the first, and hopefully the only time my mother-in-law has had a rush of colour to the head!

But there was method in Nana's "madness." It was payback time! Having taken on the challenge to dye her hair, she then counter challenged the young people of the church saying, "Can you take a challenge? . . . The Christian life is not for the wishy-washy wimp who stands for nothing and falls for anything. The Christian life is for those with guts. It's for those with strength of character, discipline in their Christian walk, courage to stand for what is right, and determination to carry on even when peers smirk and scoff. Remember they are the wimps, not you. If I make a mess of my hair, I can wash it out and no real damage is done. If you or I make a mess of our lives, it might not 'wash out' so easily . . ."

TUNE-UP

Believers are like cars, they're always on the go. In our journey through life we're covering a lot of ground, resulting in wear and tear on the "vehicle." That's why we need to have a tune-up at regular intervals. So drive on in for the Master Mechanic's fourteen point inspection.

EXTERNAL INSPECTION:

Lights - Are you living as children of light (cf. Ephesians 5:8). For "if we claim to have fellowship with him yet walk in the darkness, we lie and do not live by the truth. But if we walk in the light, as he is in the light, we have fellowship with one another, and the blood of Jesus, his Son, purifies us from all sin" 1 John 1:6-7.

Tyres - Do you have the necessary traction to stay on the narrow road that leads to life? (cf. Matthew 7:14). Are you pumped up for Him or feeling flat?

Mirrors - Are you reflecting Christ? Are you aware of "blind spots" in your life? James 1:22-25 says, "Do not merely listen to the word, and so deceive yourselves. Do what it says. Anyone who listens to the word but does not do what it says is like a man who looks at his face in a mirror and, after looking at himself, goes away and immediately forgets what he looks like. But the man who looks intently into the perfect law that gives freedom, and continues to do this, not forgetting what he has heard, but doing it - he will be blessed in what he does."

Wiper blades - When storms come can you keep going? How's your vision? "Where there's no vision the people perish" Proverbs 29:18 (KJV).

Exhaust system - Is your exhaust system working well? Is sin being confessed and thereby ejected from your life? Are you keeping short accounts with God? God's Word reminds us that we're not to harbour wicked thoughts, resentment, malice, anger, or bitter envy (cf. Deuteronomy 15:9; Job 36:13; Psalm 28:3; 103:9; James 3:14).

Shock absorbers - Are you rolling along smoothly for Him or are you bouncing all over the place? You'll have a rough ride if your suspension isn't set up properly but you'll handle the potholes and bumps of life when there's a balance of truth and Spirit (cf. John 4:24).

Body work - Are you keeping your "whole body in check" and learning to control it "in a way that is holy and honourable?" (cf. James 3:2; 1 Thessalonians 4:4). For your body "is a temple of the Holy Spirit" and you should "not offer the parts of your body to sin, as instruments of wickedness, but rather offer yourselves to God . . . as instruments of righteousness." (cf. 1 Corinthians 6:19; Romans 6:13).

INTERNAL INSPECTION:

Battery - Are you a starter? Are you passionate, enthusiastic, and charged up with the power of the Lord? Is every cell healthy and your level of commitment where it should be? (cf. Lamentations 3:40).

Air filter - Are you filtering out impurities, preventing the dirt of the world from entering your heart? (cf. Proverbs 4:23).

Spark plugs - Are you firing on all cylinders? Are you igniting the gift of God which is in you? (cf. 2 Timothy 1:6).

Oil - Oil is symbolic in God's Word for the Holy Spirit. Is your reservoir full of Him? (cf. Ephesians 5:18). Is your life lubricated by Him? Are you anointed with the oil of joy? (cf. Psalm 45:7).

Brakes - When it's time to stop do your brakes work? Do you know when to stop and consider God's wonders? (cf. Job 37:14). Do you know how to stop doing wrong? (cf. Isaiah 1:16; John 5:14). Do you know how to stop grumbling among yourselves? (cf. John 6:43). Do you know how to stop trusting in man? (cf. Isaiah 2:22). Do you know how to stop judging by mere appearances, stop passing judgment, and stop putting obstacles in your brother's way? (cf. John 7:24; Romans 14:13). And do you know how to stop thinking like children? (cf. 1 Corinthians 14:20).

Transmission - Are your gears working smoothly? Are you transmitting the love of God to others with actions and in truth? (cf. 1 John 3:18).

Motor - How are you running? Are you running in the power of the flesh or the power of the Spirit? Are you running aimlessly, just idling, or are you running at full revs, with His purpose and intent? (cf. 1 Corinthians 9:26).

ANGEL OF
THE LORD

"The angel of the Lord encamps around those who fear him, and he delivers them" Psalm 34:7.

Whenever anyone in our family reads this verse, they are reminded of my mother-in-law's deliverance. While travelling on a missionary safari in Africa, Mum was reading Psalm 34 when the driver of her vehicle lost control due to a blowout and rolled the van on a sharp curve in the road. This was before the days when seat belts were compulsory and as a result Mum was thrown clear of the vehicle and lay in the dirt with life threatening injuries. She remembers a peace coming over her as she anticipated meeting Jesus face to face. After Mum was rushed to the hospital, the doctors told Dad that Mum was more than likely going to die. But Dad prayed to the Lord for deliverance and despite the surgeon's negative prognosis Mum made a miraculous recovery.

Was it just good medical care that pulled Mum through? We don't believe it was. If I could show you the Bible she was reading at the time of the accident, you would see how verse seven of Psalm 34 is smeared with roadside dirt. It's as if God wanted to highlight the verse and make sure that Mum would never forget that "the angel of the Lord" is the One who delivered her from certain death.

But then, as we know from the Bible, God is the Deliverer. The "angel of the Lord," is none other than the Lord Jesus Christ. He is, in every sense of the word, our Saviour, the One who heals, the One who lifts us up when we are down.

Praise the Lord!

RUN TO
WIN

"Do you not know that in a race all the runners run, but only one gets the prize? Run in such a way as to get the prize. Everyone who competes in the games goes into strict training. They do it to get a crown that will not last; but we do it to get a crown that will last forever. Therefore I do not run like a man running aimlessly; I do not fight like a man beating the air. No, I beat my body and make it my slave so that after I have preached to others, I myself will not be disqualified for the prize" 1 Corinthians 9:24-27.

2 Timothy 4:7-8 says, "I have finished the race, I have kept the faith. Now there is in store for me the crown of righteousness, which the Lord, the righteous Judge, will award to me on that day - and not only to me, but also to all who have longed for his appearing."

Hebrews 12:1 says, "Therefore, since we are surrounded by such a great cloud of witnesses, let us throw off everything that hinders and the sin that so easily entangles, and let us run with perseverance the race marked out for us."

From a training perspective every runner needs to keep two basic things in mind if he wants to run to win: He must keep his weight down, and he must look after his feet.

It's the same for the Christian. You can't run the race of life if you're weighed down. You must "throw off everything that hinders" Hebrews 12:1. You must say, "No!" to excess spiritual fat or flab in your life. You must aim to be a lean, but not mean, running machine. You must divest yourself of any habits or actions that are sapping your energy or slowing you down in the pursuit of Christ. Even the good must be discarded for God's best. If your diet is all work with no time to pray, then it's time to deal with it. If you spend a couple of hours a day in leisure related activities but little to no time reading God's Word, then it's time to join a spiritual Weight Watchers group. And if the desires of your flesh are more important than the will of God, you need to be working out on the treadmill of repentance. Every handicap, every hindrance must be eliminated. For you can't run the race to win if you're weighed down.

You must also look after your feet. You must keep your "feet from every evil" Psalm 119:101. You must "throw off . . . the sin that so easily entangles" Hebrews 12:1. If you don't, if you ignore sin, you'll stumble and fall. That's what sin does. It trips you up. It gets tangled around your feet and before you know it you're flat on your face. And, as everyone knows, you can't run the race when you're flat on your face. You've got to be on your feet.

In the 1981 film *Chariots of Fire,* there's a scene in the early stages of the movie where Eric Liddell fell during a race. When a runner falls in a sprint he's as good as lost the race. But Liddell was a true competitor: He scrambled up and took off after the other runners for all he was worth. To the utter amazement of the spectators Liddell managed to catch up and actually win the race. That's what it's all about. Running "in such a way as to get the prize" 1 Corinthians 9:24. Even if you fall, you have to get up, remember the goal, run to win.

So keep your weight down and look after your feet, for when you do you're sure to win.

AN ETHIOPIAN CAN'T CHANGE HIS SKIN

An Ethiopian can't change his skin and a leopard can't change his spots (cf. Jeremiah 13:23). Which is another way of saying that you and I can never deal with the problem of temptation and sin. It's an impossibility. No amount of effort will ever help us overcome evil.

The story is told of a pastor who parked his car in a no parking zone in a large city because he was short of time and couldn't find a space with a meter. Having parked the car he hastily scribbled out a note and stuck it under the windshield wiper. It read, "I have circled the block ten times. If I don't park here, I'll miss my appointment. FORGIVE US OUR TRESPASSES." When he returned to his car he found a citation from a police officer along with this note: "I've circled this block for ten years. If I don't give you a ticket, I'll lose my job. LEAD US NOT INTO TEMPTATION."

That's funny, but it's also a reminder that temptation is something we all struggle with. But the good news is there's no struggle for God. He isn't limited like we are. He can overcome evil. He takes those who are dead in transgressions and sins, makes them alive in Christ (cf. Ephesians 2:1,5), and gives them a completely new nature. That's the only way sin can be dealt with. Because fallen man's problem is internal, the solution to his problem must be internal. Man must be given a new heart, a new nature, a new being. And that's what God does. He recreates us by changing us from our old nature of sin and death to a new nature of holiness and life. As God says in Ezekiel 36:26-27, "I will give you a new heart and put a new spirit in you; I will remove from you your heart of stone and give you a heart of flesh. And I will put my Spirit in you and move you to follow my decrees and be careful to keep my laws."

It doesn't get any plainer than that, does it? Not only theologically, but logically, this is the only way temptation and sin can be dealt with. For those who are dead in sin have no awareness or desire to turn from it, and no power or resources to change if they wanted to (cf. John 3:19-20). But "if anyone is in Christ, he is a new creation; the old has gone, the new has come!" 2 Corinthians 5:17.

There you have it. It's living in the reality of the new birth (cf. John 3:3-8) that helps us overcome temptation and sin. If we let the old nature tackle it, we will fail. But when we yield to the new nature, we will succeed; for the new nature comes from Christ and He is the Victor.

A Sunday School child explained the matter in simple terms: "Two men live in my heart: the old Adam and Jesus. When temptation knocks at the door, somebody has to answer. If I let Adam answer, I will sin; so I send Jesus to answer and He always wins!"

WHAT'S MISSING?

Shortly after I was saved, I began attending a popular local evangelical church in Johannesburg, South Africa. It was a shock to the system. I'd expected the people to be warm and loving like Jesus. And I'd expected to be welcomed in as one of the family. But it wasn't like that. The people were completely wrapped up with themselves and I was ignored for months.

Now I'm not stupid. I was obviously an object of suspicion. I didn't come from a Christian family. I wasn't connected with anyone in the church. And arriving in jeans, T-shirt, leather jacket and a motorcycle helmet didn't fit with the dignified suit and tie brigade of middle class suburbia.

It was a tough beginning for a new Christian but it taught me an invaluable lesson. I quickly learnt there can be beautiful church buildings, with steeples, crosses, stained glass windows and welcome signs on the manicured front lawns, and yet something could be missing.

You know what I'm talking about. There are churches where right liturgy is more important than real love. Where politics is more important than pursuing God. Where the sacred has become commonplace. Where the methodology is more important than His majesty. Where a person's wardrobe is more important than his or her worship. Where sensationalism takes precedence over sanctification. Where the service is so predictable it's little better than a bad rerun. Where religion is more important than righteousness. And where all the trappings of God exist but He's been marginalised or ignored for years.

So what should be done? How can there be renewal when God's people don't want to admit they possess less than everything? How can the emptiness be filled when Christians believe they're doing the right thing because they're performing every ritual to perfection, studying the Word inside out, and going through all the motions?

It begins with you and me. We must acknowledge that something is missing. We must come back to God. We must stop striving in the flesh. We must renew our respect for the holy things of God. And we must humbly call on God's people to bring God back into the center.

That's not easy. It's costly bringing God back into the center. There's a price to pay - something more than our sincerity, respectability, skill, or effort. For you and I can't, and never should attempt to handle the holy presence and glory of God with human hands. We can't take Him for granted. We can never assume we've got Him all figured out. The only way to see God in the center is when everything of the flesh is slain. We must be holy as He is holy. Purity must become dearer than life, sin must be confessed, we must consecrate ourselves according to His Word. There's no other way. The things that prevent God's presence from being in our midst must be released. We must separate ourselves from the things that soil us. We must stop doing things our way and start doing things His way. The only way to experience the presence of God is to kill the things of the flesh. We must come out from the world and be separate. As it says in 2 Corinthians 6:17, "Therefore come out from them and be separate, says the Lord. Touch no unclean thing, and I will receive you."

Well that's given us lots to think about, lots to pray about, and lots to pursue. So count the cost. Don't move on until you can trust God, by His Spirit, to make you holy as He is holy . . .

NAY-SAYERS

Numbers 13-14 tell about the twelve leaders of the Israelite tribes who were sent as spies to explore the land of Canaan in advance of a planned conquest. Two of the twelve spies, Caleb and Joshua, brought back a report in which they insisted that the Israelites could take possession of the land (cf. Numbers 13:30; 14:6-8). The other ten spies tried to kibosh the plan. If I'm to paraphrase, they essentially said, "Listen guys. Here's the facts. Let's be realistic. It can't be done" (cf. Numbers 13:31-33).

That's all it took - just ten pessimists. They became a greater obstacle to the Israelites than the giants and walled cities on the other side of the Jordan. Negative counsel has that effect. It can prevent God's children from experiencing His best for their lives. It can hinder or slow His plans. It can restrict access into a place flowing with milk and honey. It can obstruct a great work that God wants to accomplish. It can cause struggles and suffering in a wilderness of despair. It can delay the conquering of spiritual territory. It can limit the potential we have in God. It can freeze out revival. It can curb God's blessings. It can stir up discord. It can cause thousands to stop short of abundant life. And it can adversely affect the destiny of an individual, a family, a church, a community, or a country.

It doesn't take much. Numbers 13-14 indicate how the enemies of God weren't the Jebusites or Amorites. The Jordan wasn't the great barrier that kept the people out of the promised land. Jericho's walls didn't stop the Israelites. God's enemies weren't on the outside they were on the inside. They were ten men who, after seeing God's miracles in the Exodus from Egypt, should have known better. Ten men who said, "We can't do it. It's just not possible. We'll never be victorious." Ten negative men. Ten whiners who were out of touch with God. Ten losers who couldn't see the wood for the trees. Ten melancholiacs who had an influence and used it the wrong way. Ten men who spread "a bad report about the land they had explored" Numbers 13:32. Ten nay-sayers who said, "We can't attack those people; they are stronger than we are" Numbers 13:31.

So watch out for negative advice. Be on your guard against ungodly pessimists. Beware of carnal counsel. Don't listen to backsliders who have a narrow or minimal view of God. For it doesn't take a great multitude to limit the work of the Lord. One un-surrendered believer can set you on the wrong path and just a few unspiritual people can obstruct the good things God is wanting to accomplish in and through His people.

THE TRIP OF A LIFETIME

It's amazing what pops into one's mind when one sits down to write. As I looked into the grey backdrop of my computer screen I began to muse about the reaction someone would get from a Travel Agency if they were to walk in and say, "Good morning, I want to book the trip of a lifetime . . . I want to go to heaven!" Imagine the scene: "To where Sir?" "To heaven?" "Well, um, no one's offering any trips to heaven. Perhaps we could interest you in a trip to Bermuda . . . ?"

Now imagine another scene: This time when you ask for a trip to heaven the agent pulls out a glossy brochure and says; "We've just had a new brochure printed with all the latest information. Why don't you have a look?"

Opening it up you read the following:

Accommodation. Ample accommodation of the highest calibre has been prepared for you. There "are many rooms" John 14:2. The Master Builder, Jesus Christ, has spared no expense. The finest gold and "every kind of precious stone" has been used in its construction and "the kings of the earth will bring their splendour into it" Revelation 21:19,24.

Passports. Because you'll be going to a "new" country (Hebrews 11:16; Revelation 21:5) you will need a special passport. This passport is unlike any other. It's obtainable from Jesus Christ. He wants you to recognise Him as your Saviour, repent of your sin and receive Him by faith (cf. John 14:6; Acts 3:19; Romans 10:9). When you have believed, you will be "marked in him with a seal, the promised Holy Spirit, who is a deposit guaranteeing our inheritance . . ." Ephesians 1:13-14.

Tickets. Entitlement to travel rights and accommodation is obtained by "those whose names are written in the Lamb's book of life" Revelation 21:27.

Departure times. Only God knows the hour and the day you will leave so be prepared for an imminent departure (cf. Psalm 75:2; Acts 1:7; 1 Thessalonians. 5:1-6).

Time changes. You won't need your watches in heaven. There will be no sun and no moon, "for the glory of God gives it light" Revelation 21:23.

Luggage. Everything you need has been provided. You can't take anything with you "for we brought nothing into this world, and we can take nothing out of it" 1 Timothy 6:7.

Currency. There will be no need of money in heaven for God will be your provision. There will be no buying or selling as this is the old order of things and it will pass away (cf. Revelation 21:4).

Special events. You won't want to miss the spectacular coronation ceremony when Jesus places a crown on the head of everyone who loves Him (cf. 2 Timothy 4:8; James 1:12).

Don't delay. Make your reservation today. "I tell you, now is the time of God's favour, now is the day of salvation" 2 Corinthians 6:2.

THANK YOU JESUS . . .

When it comes to thanking Jesus for who He is and what He means to us we can never thank Him enough. Nonetheless, here's an attempt to say, "Thank you Jesus."

Thank you Jesus for always identifying yourself with the least, the last and the lost. In so doing You have stood as a rebuke to every form of pride and prejudice to which men and women are liable.

Thank you Jesus for being anything but tame. Your searing honesty cuts to the core. You defy categorization, refuse to be put in a box, and are radically unlike anyone else who has ever lived or will ever live.

Thank you Jesus for being our all in all. You alone are sufficient. You're our Prophet, our Priest, our Prince, our Pleasure, our Pardon, our Purpose, our Power, our Provision, and our Peace.

Thank you Jesus for never being soft on sin. You hold the highest standards of moral purity while simultaneously showing grace to those who fail to live up to those standards. In You alone there's a divine balance. For You embrace the sinner without encouraging the sin.

Thank you Jesus for being the God-Man. For being God's exact replica. You are "the image of the invisible God" Colossians 1:15. You gave us Yourself in the form of a person yet You are "Very God of Very God."

Thank you Jesus for being a man of joy; for being anointed by Your Father with the oil of gladness (cf. Hebrews 1:9). You never allowed Yourself to get wrapped up in religious smog but enjoyed life to the full and want the same thing for those who love You.

Thank you Jesus for making it harder, rather than easier, to accept You as Lord. You leave no room to manoeuver. We must decide; You are either the Son of God sent to save sinners, or a deluded imposter (cf. Lewis C. S. *Mere Christianity*).

Thank you Jesus for standing up to the scrutiny of the world. Thank you for standing up to my investigation. Without reservation, You are all I want my Lord to be.

Thank you Jesus for being the Author of life. The Cosmic Christ. The Word who was God. Through You all things were made; without You nothing was made that has been made (cf. John 1:3).

Thank you Jesus for being the focal point. In You we have clarity when life seems fuzzy.

Thank you Jesus for Your tenderness and sympathy. You never shout at us, never break us, and even though You could, and on many occasions probably should, You never snuff us out (cf. Isaiah 42:2-3).

Thank you Jesus for bringing God near. God isn't somewhere off in the distance. When You breathed Your final breath on the cross "the curtain of the temple was torn in two from top to bottom" Mark 15:38. Now God is no longer partitioned off in the Most Holy Place. Access to His presence is immediate. Your sacrifice has given us the intimacy with which we now know God as Abba, the loving Father.

Thank you Jesus for meaning more than the world to me. In You I've found the answer to my greatest needs, the satisfaction of my deepest longings, the dispelling of my darkest fears, and the fulfilment of my highest aspirations.

Thank you Jesus for speaking the truth. You are no mere prophet among prophets, teacher among teachers, or voice among many voices. You are the very Word of God (cf. John 1:1), the truth that sets us free (cf. John 8:32).

Thank you Jesus for being the sinless Friend of sinners. Your uncompromising blend of courtesy toward sinners and hostility toward sin is unsurpassed.

And thank you Jesus for giving us "a love that can never be fathomed; a life that can never die; a righteousness that can never be tarnished; a peace that can never be understood; a joy that can never be diminished; a hope that can never be disappointed; a glory that can never be clouded; a light that can never be darkened; a happiness that can never be enfeebled; a purity that can never be defiled; a beauty that can never be marred; a wisdom that can never be baffled; and resources that can never be exhausted" Anonymous.

DON'T GROWL

Trevor Warner has a fine sense of humour and is a valued teacher at the high school where he works. Apart from his teaching duties he serves as housemaster of a boarding establishment and remembers the time when he got fed up with a group of students who persisted with a terrible din late into the night. Determined to put a stop to their disruptive behaviour Trevor went through to the dormitory and told the young men off in no uncertain terms. But the boys were riled and decided to get back at Trevor. Thus, with their vacation imminent they prepared a poster that they planned to mount in the main corridor of the residence when they left for their homes. The day of their departure arrived and the students executed their plan.

Some days later Trevor was walking through the deserted hostel when he noticed the poster. The moment he read it he knew it had been made for his benefit. It said, "He who growls all day leads a dog's life!"

Trevor, of course, had a good chuckle at the poster and has left it on the wall to remind future generations of students that grumpy people lead a miserable existence. So don't growl. "Find satisfaction in (your) ... labour" and "banish anxiety from your heart" Ecclesiastes 5:18; 11:10. "Let your heart give you joy" and "accept (your) lot and be happy in (your) work - this is the gift of God" Ecclesiastes 11:9; 5:19. For "I know that there is nothing better for men than to be happy and do good while they live" Ecclesiastes 3:12. So be happy and show it. Greet everyone with a cheerful face (cf. Proverbs 15:13). And, in a nutshell, smile - don't scowl, be happy - don't growl.

RECEIVE THE WORD

The Word of God cannot work in our lives unless we receive it in the right way. James 1:19-21 says, "My dear brothers, take note of this: Everyone should be quick to listen, slow to speak and slow to become angry, for man's anger does not bring about the righteous life that God desires. Therefore, get rid of all moral filth and the evil that is so prevalent, and humbly accept the word planted in you, which can save you."

This text suggests four ways in which we should receive the Word:

Be swift to hear (v19a). Someone once said, "It's impossible for a worthwhile thought to enter your mind through an open mouth." The scriptures confirm the truth of this comment. Jesus, for example, had much to say about hearing and listening. In Matthew 13:9 He said, "He who has ears, let him hear." In Mark 4:24 He said, "Consider carefully what you hear." And in Luke 8:18 He said, "Consider carefully how you listen." Which indicates how the first step in receiving the Word is to pay attention to what God says. This is vital. For "faith comes from hearing the message, and the message is heard through the word of Christ" Romans 10:17. No wonder God gave us two ears and one mouth. It's probably because He wants us to spend twice as much time listening as talking. So be swift to hear God's Word. For, as it said on a sign on Lyndon B. Johnson's office wall when he was a Texas Senator, "You ain't learnin' nothin' when you're talkin'."

Be slow to speak (v19b). The story is told of a young man who asked a famous Roman orator to teach him the art of public speaking. From the moment they met, the young man babbled ceaselessly. Finally, when the famous orator managed to interject, he said, "Young man, to instruct you in oratory, I will have to charge you a double fee because I will have to teach you two skills: the first, how to hold your tongue, and the second, how to use it." The orator was right on target. For the second step in receiving God's Word is to know when it's appropriate to speak and when it's appropriate not to speak. Proverbs 10:19 and 17:27 says, "He who holds his tongue is wise" and "a man of knowledge uses words with restraint." Yes, we should be cautious, patient, and careful when we speak for the Lord. We should have the gravest concern that what we say both edifies those who hear, and honours the Lord on whose behalf we speak.

Be slow to anger (v19c-20). Some time ago I counselled some folk who claimed to be Christians and yet refused to act on God's Word. I pleaded with them to follow a clear, pertinent, and unambiguous biblical principle but they said, "No." They even went on to say that they didn't care what God's Word said, they would simply do what they felt like doing. These are the people James is speaking to when he indicates that the third step in receiving God's Word is being "slow to become angry, for man's anger does not bring about the righteous life that God desires." In saying this, James is speaking particularly about the kind of anger that comes about when the Word of God has confronted a person with their sin, upset their comfort zone, challenged their opinions or beliefs, or come into conflict with a particular standard of behaviour. Thus, the text is referring to any hostile disposition against scriptural truth. It's addressing those who hear God's Word and resent how it exposes their ungodly lifestyle or false ideas. And it identifies how God's righteousness can never grow from anger rooted in our likes and dislikes.

Be submissive in spirit (v21). Eugene Peterson in The Message, renders James 1:21 as follows; "In simple humility, let our gardener, God, landscape you with the Word, making a salvation-garden of your life." That's beautifully put. It indicates how the fourth step in receiving God's Word is a selfless, willing, teachable, and submissive spirit. J. A. Motyer commenting on the importance of a submissive spirit, says, "We might wonder why the ever-practical James does not proceed to outline schemes of daily Bible reading or the like, for surely these are the ways in which we offer a willing ear to the voice of God. But he does not help us in this way. Rather, he goes deeper, for there is little point in schemes and times if we have not got an attentive spirit. It is possible to be unfailingly regular in Bible reading, but to achieve no more than to have moved the bookmark forward: this is reading unrelated to an attentive spirit. The word is read but not heard. On the other hand, if we can develop an attentive spirit, this will spur us to create those conditions - a proper method in Bible reading, a discipline of time, and so on - by which the spirit will find itself satisfied in hearing the Word of God."

Now receive the Word as God intended. Be swift to hear, slow to speak, slow to anger, and be submissive in spirit. For when you do this, you will be blessed (cf. James 1:25).

DEATH

You may think that death isn't an ideal subject for the day's meditation, maybe even believe it's out of place in a book titled, Seize the Day. But before you dismiss the topic allow me to suggest that a person's conception of death determines his or her philosophy of life. With this in mind, here are some thoughts on death:

Death is certain. There's no escaping it. "One can survive everything nowadays except death" Oscar Wilde. It comes to the rich and the poor, the literate and the illiterate, the young and the old, the socially elite and the common folk. As someone once said, "The world is a very dangerous place - you never get out of it alive." Everyone has to look it in the eye. There are no family ties that death cannot loosen, no medicine to avert it, no power to stop it. Even paths of glory lead to the grave. We may be able to free ourselves from the womb but there's no scalpel sharp enough to cut the umbilical cord connecting us to the grave.

Yes, death is terminal. We all stand on the brink of another world. In an Indiana cemetery there's a tombstone which bears an epitaph which says, "Pause Stranger, when you pass me by. As you are now, so once was I. As I am now, so you will be. So prepare for death and follow me."

Don't ignore the obvious. Whether you're busy or asleep death will one day find you. For "death is the debt we must all pay" Euripedes. No exceptions are made. "Death takes no bribes" Benjamin Franklin. One out of one people die. You can't beat the odds. It's the last thing every one of us will do. As Joseph Bayly says, "The door of the hearse is never closed." Whether we're ready or not, at an hour known only to God, we will all face death and succumb to the grave. Hebrews 9:27 says it succinctly, "Man is destined to die once, and after that to face judgment."

One of the world's great tragedies is that so many people die for nothing. In a number of the funeral or memorial services I conduct there's very little to be said about the individual's life. It can be quite embarrassing at times. I remember one eulogy in which essentially two points were made - the individual concerned liked to have a beer with his pals and he enjoyed listening to the song, Puff the Magic Dragon. What a waste of a life. To have lived for oneself and no one else is a disaster.

So don't squander the time God has apportioned to you. "Life is too short to be little" Disraeli. Don't live as if you're oblivious to the fact that your life will cease. Rather, spend your energies on something that will last beyond your lifetime. Make provision for eternity. Take good care of your life. Live extravagantly, in such a way that your lamp will shine for Christ each and every day until your last day. For "life is not a cup to be drained, but a measure to be filled" Anonymous. The following poem, by a missionary to Egypt, sums it up:

When my life
is past, how
glad I shall
be that the
lamp of my
life has been shining for Thee.
I shall then not regret what I gave,
of labour, or money for sinners to
save. I shall not mind that the way
has been rough. That my Saviour
led me - that
will be enough.
When I am
dying how glad
I shall be, that
the lamp of my
life has been
shining for Thee.

I'M A "FAITHER"

John Audia is my Italian buddy. He's a roofer by trade and a Spirit-filled believer by night and day. He's a man of abundant joy, exceptional generosity, scrupulous integrity, and exercises an extraordinary gift of mercy. He's one of the biggest hearted men I know. He's also very quotable. On one occasion he said, "If God gives me the work He will also give me the weather, and if He gives me the weather, He will give me the strength and everything else I need." Another time, after asking me how my week was going, he said, "My happiest day as a non-Christian doesn't even compare to my lowest day as a Christian." And then there was the day he said, "Now I know you know this stuff but let's never forget that it behooves us Christians to show God off to an on-looking world in a real way. In your life and my life we have to do that . . ."

But I think the most memorable thing John has ever said was, "I'm a Faither." When he first said it I thought he had said, "I'm a Father." Which didn't make much sense seeing as he had that look in his eyes that clued me in to the realisation that he was about to proclaim his love for the Lord Jesus Christ (which he does at every conceivable opportunity). So I said, "What do you mean?" "Well it's like this. I'm a 'Faither' because I believe that faith is action based upon belief and sustained by confidence. As it says in Psalm 119:89, 'For ever, O Lord, thy word is settled in heaven.' So if it's settled in heaven it's good enough for me . . . Of course with faith, it does away with self righteousness and gets us stuck on Him . . . And here's a little something else: With faith God will send circumstances to stretch your faith. That's what the Christian life is all about . . ."

A REMARKABLE PLAN

Although the plan for our salvation was put in place before creation, it came into focus when it was birthed in the crib. There was no special treatment for the Son of God. He never paused to count the cost but came to earth to reach the lost. Not in a raging hurricane or a devouring fire. When God came to earth He humbled Himself. "The God who created matter took shape within it" Philip Yancey. He stepped forth from heaven, from the images and mental pictures we had of Him, and became one of us. "The God who roared, who could order armies and empires about like pawns on a chessboard, this God emerged in Palestine as a baby who could not speak or eat solid food or control his bladder, who depended on a teenager for shelter, food, and love" Philip Yancey.

It was a remarkable plan. The God of the universe, the great big God, the One who's beyond measure became little, He shrank down to become a single zygote. He became so small He was barely visible to the naked eye. The cells divided and the baby grew inside a peasant girl until the appointed time for His birth. Then, as with all births, the contractions began and He emerged with a cry on His lips. When Christ was born, it wasn't a sanitized fairy tale. Christ was born into the world like any other child. He was smeared in blood and helpless. The Father in heaven looked on as any human father would. The cord had to be cut, the baby cleaned and suckled, and the afterbirth removed.

What an inauguration. Hope was nurtured in a cradle. Our Saviour was born with His limbs wrapped tightly against His body. The Scriptures put it like this: In Philippians 2:7 it says, He "made himself nothing, taking the very nature of a servant, being made in human likeness." In John 1:14 it says, "The Word became flesh and lived for a while among us." An in 1 John 3:5 it says, "But you know that he appeared so that he might take away our sins."

C. S. Lewis grasps the essence of these texts when he says, "The Son of God became the Son of Man so that the sons of men may become sons of God." Isn't that marvellous? Christ came to save us. Through the birth of Jesus Christ, God created a way to relate to human beings so we wouldn't be afraid. He used the incarnation to disarm us. A crib de-emphasised the gulf that existed between God and humanity. For in the cradle we discover a God who chose to become flesh and live for a while among us (cf. John 1:14). Praise the Lord! "This is love: not that we loved God, but that he loved us and sent his Son as an atoning sacrifice for our sins" 1 John 4:10.

Yes, Christ was manifested to be the Saviour. He was born to reconcile estranged sinners to God. He was born to deal with the sum total of all the lawless thoughts, words, and deeds of the human race. He was born to take away your sin and mine. No sin is too much for Christ to take away, no sin too disgusting or too large for Him to evict. God's Word confirms it. "The reason the Son of God appeared was to destroy the devil's work" 1 John 3:8. He was sent as a helpless baby to wage war on the devil. Christ invaded human history to snatch the sceptre from the usurper. In a baby we have One who was strong enough to wreck the devil's transactions. He did this by turning hatred into love, casting darkness out by His light, and overcoming death by the gift of life. It was a remarkable plan. "He appeared so that he might take away our sins . . ." 1 John 3:5. He appeared to "save his people from their sins" Matthew 1:21.

PRIORITIES

Are you feeling swamped? Are 24 hours a day just not enough to get everything done that needs to be done? Are you drowning in information overload, over scheduled, struggling with too many opportunities?

You're not alone. It seems that part and parcel of being alive in the 21st century is being over-committed and overwhelmed. We ration our time between family, school, work, community involvement, church attendance, personal care, sport and recreation, home responsibilities, relationships, and a host of other things. On top of everything else we try to eat nutritionally balanced meals, read the latest book, squeeze in time for prayer and Bible study, and still get eight hours of sleep every night. It's exhausting just thinking about it!

God's Word addresses our dilemma. In Matthew 6:19-21 it says, "Do not store up for yourselves treasures on earth, where moth and rust destroy, and where thieves break in and steal. But store up for yourselves treasures in heaven, where moth and rust do not destroy, and where thieves do not break in and steal. For where your treasure is, there your heart will be also."

Grasp the essence of this text and live by what it teaches and I guarantee you'll never again feel over-committed or overwhelmed. That's right. If you take stock of your life and invest, not in earthly treasures, but in things that have eternal value, you'll be able to live a victorious Christian life.

But how do you do that? How do you make time count instead of counting time? How do you break out of the tyranny of the urgent? Jesus provides the answer. His life on earth had a purpose. He came to bring salvation to mankind through His death and resurrection. Similarly, you need to be very clear on God's purpose for your life. What has He called you to do? Whatever it is, make that your priority. Then, like Jesus, as you pursue God's purpose for your life, be sure to minister to needy people along the way. Ray Ortlund puts it in these words, "We must first be committed to Christ, then to one another in Christ, and finally to the work of Christ in the world." No matter who you are, if you are a Christian your ultimate purpose will always be to grow in your relationship with Jesus Christ and serve Him as He leads.

On a more down to earth level, put Christ first and then everything else will fall into place. Your priorities will be straightened out when it's all about Jesus and not about you. I begin each day prayerfully asking God to help me pursue His calling on my life. I ask Him to order my time, to schedule my appointments, and to help me keep Him in focus. Then, as I go through the day I look for the opportunity to encourage someone in need - the chance to extend a well-timed smile, a helping hand, a warm embrace, a word of prayer, a listening ear, a comment seasoned with love and grace. That's how Jesus seemed to do it. He kept it simple. He fixed His eyes steadfastly on His ultimate destination while reaching out to people along the way. That seemed to be His only plan. He never had a daily planner with scheduled healings, miraculous feedings, or appointed times for parables. He set out for Calvary using every opportunity to point others to the Father as each day brought Him closer to the final day. It should be no different for you and me. Our priority is to pursue the primary calling Christ has on our lives and reach out to others along the way.

FUDGING

Fudging is exaggeration in order to impress someone. It's a common form of lying. The Oxford Dictionary refers to it as "dishonesty or faking." The word "fudge" can be traced back 300 years to a Merchant Navy commander named Captain Fudge. He was famous for exaggerating his adventures on the high seas. As a result his crewmen began to call each other "Fudge" when they caught one of their number straying from the truth.

It's no different today. When the phrase "fudging the truth" is used, it's referring to someone who exaggerates to improve his or her standing, or to make a point. In Boardroom Reports, Peter Levine tells how the Port Authority of New York and New Jersey ran a help-wanted ad for electricians with expertise at using Sontag connectors. The Port Authority had 170 responses from electricians saying they knew how to use Sontag connectors. But there's no such thing as a Sontag connector. The Port Authority ran the ad simply to find out how many applicants falsified their resume.

I wonder if the Port Authority were surprised at their findings? It's common knowledge that many success oriented people exaggerate the truth. But stretching the truth is telling a lie. If you're exaggerating to build yourself up in the eyes of others, you're in conflict with the ninth commandment (cf. Exodus 20:16). "For exaggeration is a blood relation to falsehood" Hosea Ballou.

Don't be deceived, it's wrong to shade or exaggerate the facts. There's no middle ground. You're either telling the truth or telling a lie. There can be no grey areas. If you're in the habit of embellishing to impress others, you're lying. If you're in the habit of exaggerating for the sake of effect, you're lying.

Paul brings corrective counsel for the person who fudges. He says, "Do not think of yourself more highly than you ought, but rather think of yourself with sober judgment, in accordance with the measure of faith God has given you" Romans 12:3

FREEDOM

The famed escape artist, Harry Houdini, claimed he could be locked in any jail cell and free himself in no time at all. After a number of successful escapes from various jails he encountered a lock that he could not pick. He had been taken into the jail in his street clothes and the heavy metal doors had clanged shut behind him. Taking a concealed piece of metal from his belt he set to work but after thirty minutes he'd made no progress at all. There was something unusual about the lock. An hour passed and he'd still not managed to open the door. Finally, after struggling for two hours, Houdini collapsed in frustration and failure against the door he couldn't unlock. As he fell against it, it swung open! It had never been locked in the first place. But in his mind it had been locked and that was what had kept him from opening the door and walking out of the cell.

In searching for freedom you may be encountering frustration and failure. Like Houdini you're struggling to unlock the door in order to walk out of jail. Yet despite your efforts you're making no progress at all. The door remains shut and you're still locked in.

But that's because there's something unusual about the lock. It's already unlocked. When Christ died on the cross of Calvary as the sacrifice for sin He turned the key that unlocked the door once and for all. As it says unequivocally in Galatians 5:1, "Christ has set us free."

So, if you want freedom you need to respond to the truth of God's Word. For the way to freedom is through the truth, and until you come to the truth you are never free from your search. As long as your mind tells you the door is locked you will never be free. As long as you struggle in your own strength you'll stay incarcerated in the cell of your own limitations. But when you trust Christ for your salvation, the door swings open. There's no question about it. Salvation is the essence of freedom. Knowing Jesus releases you from bondage. "So I say to you: Ask and it will be given to you; seek and you will find; knock and the door will be opened to you. For everyone who asks receives; he who seeks finds; and to him who knocks, the door will be opened" Luke 11:9-10.

A SAFE PLACE

Jesus didn't come into this world for a change of scenery, for fresh air, for a vacation, or for any other trivial reason you might imagine. He came for a purpose. He came to save you. As He looked down from heaven His heart went out to you. He loved you and wanted you to know Him as Lord and Saviour. So He left heaven and came to dwell among us.

It wasn't a walk in the park. He endured all manner of opposition. It was a long, hard, humiliating road that led to death on a cross. And on the cross of Calvary He gave His life away so that you could have eternal life.

In the winter months on the Highveld in South Africa there's no rain. The long grass becomes tinder dry and often catches on fire. All it takes is a cigarette butt carelessly tossed aside and a roaring inferno quickly follows. The fires are so great and the winds so strong I've seen flames shooting up more than twenty metres in the air. Everything is destroyed. After a fire has swept across the veld, the charred remains of reptiles and other small animals are grim testimony to the fire's ferocity. It's not just small creatures that can be destroyed by a fire. Livestock and large game animals, even elephant, have died in veld fires. People have died too.

When I was twenty, I nearly died in a veld fire. I was helping fight a fire near Pelindaba, north of Johannesburg and was part of a skirmish line with a number of other men when we realised that the fire had somehow got in behind us and cut off our line of escape. It was a sticky wicket. We needed to act fast or face certain death. Fortunately we had an experienced fire fighter with us. He wasted no time in grouping us together and lighting the grass around us. The new fire burnt out and away from us and left us standing in the centre of a burned over section. As the flames from the rogue fire roared toward us, they encountered the flames from the fire that we'd set and in no time at all, with no fuel available, the one fire cancelled out the other.

Similarly, as the fires of hell and judgment burn toward us we'll only be safe if we find a place of safety. Christ has prepared the spot. There's one place where the fires have already burnt out. One spot where the danger has already passed. It's called Calvary. For at Calvary Christ paid the penalty for our sin. He bore our guilt and transgressions. As it says in 1 Peter 3:18, "Christ died for sins once for all, the righteous for the unrighteous, to bring you to God." And if we go to that spot, if we go to Calvary, we'll be safe from the fires of judgment and hell.

That's why Jesus came into the world. He came to take in His own body the fires of hell and judgment and to save us from them. For He doesn't want us to be fuel for the eternal fire. He doesn't want anyone to burn. He wants to save us from "the lake of fire" (Revelation 20:15) into which those whose names are not found written in the book of life will be thrown. But He can only save us if we come to Him. The only place that's safe is at the foot of the cross.

So if you haven't come, will you come? He's waiting to receive you. He's prepared a safe place. A place that will save you from being burnt alive. Will you come?

A VITAL QUESTION

What do you think of Christ?

This is what those who were against Him thought:

Judas betrayed Jesus to the chief priests and elders but before hanging himself said, "I have sinned . . . for I have betrayed innocent blood" Matthew 27:4.

Pilate's wife told her husband that Jesus was an "innocent man" Matthew 27:19.

The centurion and those guarding Jesus at His crucifixion exclaimed, "Surely he was the Son of God!" Matthew 27:54.

The demons gave a glowing testimony when they said that Jesus was the "Son of the Most High God" Luke 8:28.

The Pharisees and teachers of the law muttered, "This man welcomes sinners" Luke 15:2.

So Pilate asked Jesus, "'Are you the king of the Jews?' 'Yes, it is as you say,' Jesus replied. "Then Pilate announced to the chief priests and the crowd, 'I find no basis for a charge against this man'" Luke 23:3-4.

Both Herod and Pilate agreed that Jesus had "done nothing to deserve death" Luke 23:15.

The Pharisees exclaimed, "How can a sinner do such miraculous signs?" John 9:16.

This is what those who were for Him thought:

At Jesus' baptism God the Father, with a voice from heaven said, "This is my Son, whom I love; with him I am well pleased" Matthew 3:17.

When Jesus asked His disciples whom they thought He was Simon Peter said, "You are the Christ, the Son of the living God" Matthew 16:16.

The people of the Decapolis said, "He has done everything well" Mark 7:37.

When Jesus was on a high mountain God spoke from a cloud and said, "This is my Son, whom I love. Listen to him!" Mark 9:7.

John the Baptist said, "Look, the Lamb of God, who takes away the sin of the world! . . . I have seen and testify that this is the Son of God" John 1:29,34.

Thomas doubted that Jesus had been raised from the dead but when he saw Him he exclaimed, "My Lord and my God!" John 20:28.

The apostle Paul said, "I know whom I have believed" 2 Timothy 1:12.

The angels in heaven exclaimed, "Worthy is the Lamb, who was slain, to receive power and wealth and wisdom and strength and honour and glory and praise!" Revelation 5:12.

What do you think of Christ?

Have you thought enough of Him to confess your sin and by faith receive Him as your personal Saviour? Have you thought enough of Him to live for Him and for no other? Have you thought enough of Him to tell family, friends, and others about His love for them? And have you thought enough of Him to be like minded, having the same love, being one in spirit and purpose? (cf. Philippians 2:2).

EVERYDAY MAXIMS

Here are ten everyday maxims that will stand you in good stead:

1. Don't worry, it's the most unproductive of all human activities. Today's worries are like puddles, tomorrow they may have evaporated. "An anxious heart weighs a man down" Proverbs 12:25.

2. Don't be fearful, most of the things we fear never come to pass. "Have no fear of sudden disaster or of the ruin that overtakes the wicked, for the Lord will be your confidence and will keep your foot from being snared" Proverbs 3:25-26.

3. Never cross a bridge until you reach it. "Do not boast about tomorrow, for you do not know what a day may bring forth" Proverbs 27:1.

4. Don't run from trials or difficulties. "Our antagonist is our helper. He that wrestles with it strengthens our muscles and sharpens our skills" Edmund Burke. "Consider it pure joy, my brothers, whenever you face trials of many kinds, because you know that the testing of your faith develops perseverance" James 1:2-3.

5. Don't take problems to bed with you. They make poor bedfellows. "Lie down and sleep in peace, for (the Lord makes you) dwell in safety" Psalm 4:8.

6. Don't borrow other people's problems. "No one can hold two watermelons in one hand" Afghanistan proverb.

7. Don't try to re-live yesterday for good or bad. It's gone. Concentrate on what's happening in your life today. Counting time is not nearly as important as making time count. "This is the day the Lord has made; let us rejoice and be glad in it" Psalm 118:24.

8. Count your blessings. Never overlook the small ones. Many small blessings add up to a big one.

9. Be a good listener. The most important thing in communication is hearing what's being said. As long as you're talking, you'll learn nothing. "A man of understanding holds his tongue" Proverbs 11:12.

10. Be positive. See the cup as half full not half empty. See what can be done, not what can be undone. "Have I not commanded you? Be strong and courageous. Do not be terrified; do not be discouraged, for the Lord your God will be with you wherever you go" Joshua 1:9.

SHARE THE LOAD

Spring and Fall are always marked by the annual migration of birds. I know summer is on the way or winter is just around the corner when the Canada geese are seen in their almost perfect V formation knifing through the sky. The reason the Canada geese fly in the V formation is to decrease wind drag. This enables them to fly far further than if they flew alone. Some scientists have estimated that the updraft of air created by the lead bird enables a group of 25 birds to fly 70 percent further when flying in formation than flying alone. As I've watched them, I've noticed how they take turns being the lead bird. Obviously the one in the lead has to exert more effort. When the lead goose tires it drops back into the formation to rest a bit and another takes its place. It's a wonderful example of sharing the load.

Canada geese share the load in a number of other ways. Often while the flock is feeding, individuals will take turns acting as sentinels, warning the others of impending danger. They also mate for life and both parents raise the young. Once a male and female have come together, they stick with each other through thick and thin. They will only take a new partner if the mate dies. One captive pair was known to be together for 42 years and when the male was accidentally killed the female died a few months later.

A lesser known fact is that if a goose becomes ill, is wounded, or falls out of formation, at least one other will fall out with it and remain behind to nurse it until it recovers and is able to join another migratory flock.

We can learn from the Canada goose. As Christians we can go much further for the Lord if we work together instead of acting individually. "Carry each others burdens, and in this way you will fulfill the law of Christ" Galatians 6:2. So share the load. In so doing weariness will be prevented, we'll be more likely to be forewarned of impending danger, the sick and weak will be nursed back to wholeness, and leaders will be empowered to lead.

GRACE

Now what is grace? It's **G**od's **R**iches **A**t **C**hrist's **E**xpense. "Grace is God's love out loving itself" Anonymous. It's God doing something for us that we couldn't do for ourselves. It's "free sovereign favour to the ill deserving" Benjamin Warfield. It's "everything for nothing . . . going to those who cannot come in their own strength" Lehman Strauss. It's "the kindness of God toward undeserving people" Warren Wiersbe. Or as A. W. Tozer says, "Grace is the good pleasure of God that inclines Him to bestow benefits on the undeserving." Oh the grace of God. He shows kindness or favour, not because we merit help, but because He recognises our desperate need and is moved by love and compassion to exercise His power to meet us at our point of need. Praise the Lord!

Which is why I want to "see to it that no one misses the grace of God" Hebrews 12:15. Consider the realities of God's grace in the following selected scriptures:

God "gives grace to the humble" Proverbs 3:34.

"Grace and truth came through Jesus Christ" John 1:17.

"For all have sinned and fall short of the glory of God, and are justified freely by his grace through the redemption that came by Christ Jesus" Romans 3:23-24.

"For if, by the trespass of the one man, death reigned through that one man, how much more will those who receive God's abundant provision of grace and of the gift of righteousness reign in life through the one man, Jesus Christ" Romans 5:17.

"Sin shall not be your master, because you are not under law, but under grace" Romans 6:14.

"We have different gifts, according to the grace given us" Romans 12:6.

"And God is able to make all grace abound to you, so that in all things at all times, having all that you need, you will abound in every good work" 2 Corinthians 9:8.

"My grace is sufficient for you, for my power is made perfect in weakness" 2 Corinthians 12:9.

"In him we have redemption through his blood, the forgiveness of sins, in accordance with the riches of God's grace that he lavished on us with all wisdom and understanding" Ephesians 1:7-8.

"For it is by grace you have been saved, through faith - and this not from yourselves, it is the gift of God - not by works, so that no one can boast" Ephesians 2:8-9.

"But to each one of us grace has been given as Christ apportioned it" Ephesians 4:7.

"For the grace of God that brings salvation has appeared to all men" Titus 2:11.

"He saved us through the washing of rebirth and renewal by the Holy Spirit, whom he poured out on us generously through Jesus Christ our Saviour, so that, having been justified by his grace, we might become heirs having the hope of eternal life" Titus 3:5-7.

With God's grace in mind, be sure to "grow in the grace and knowledge of our Lord and Saviour Jesus Christ. To him be glory both now and forever! Amen" 2 Peter 3:18.

Grace Alone
"Every promise we can make, every prayer and step of faith,
Every difference we will make, is only by His grace.
Every mountain we will climb, every ray of hope we shine,
Every blessing left behind, is only by His grace.

Grace alone which God supplies, strength unknown He will provide,
Christ in us our Cornerstone; we will go forth in grace alone.

Every soul we long to reach, every heart we hope to teach,
Everywhere we share His peace, is only by His grace.
Every loving word we say, every tear we wipe away,
Every sorrow turned to praise, is only by His grace."

Scott Wesley Brown and Jeff Nelson.

IMMUNITY IN THE BLOOD

A medical author, Ronald J. Glasser says that "No matter how we may wish to view ourselves, despite all our fantasies of grandeur and dominion, all our fragile human successes, the real struggle . . . has always been against bacteria and viruses, against adversaries never more than seven microns wide."

That's a chilling reality. Viruses have killed more people than all the wars, fires, floods and earthquakes put together. For example, the First World War was responsible for the death of eight and a half million people but during the armistice that followed an influenza epidemic broke out and twenty-five million people around the world were dead within a year.

But tools have been developed to fight against the diseases that once wiped out entire populations. Jenner, Pasteur and others have given us a procedure called immunization. With immunization, a vaccination exposes the body to a virus in a safe form: either a weakened or "tired" virus, or a "killed" virus with its outer shell intact to stimulate antibody production. This gives the body an advantage. For when a virus attacks a previously immunized person it has a prepared assortment of antibodies in the blood that can quickly target, deploy, and fight off the invading disease.

Dr Paul Brand tells of how, as a child in a remote part of India, his parents were involved in the vaccination for smallpox. They had limited quantities of vaccine, and no facilities for cold storage, so runners would bring the vaccine up mountain paths and hand the precious lymph to his father. His father would waste no time in breaking open the tubes of lymph and vaccinating the waiting crowd. "Later, from one infected arm he would draw enough lymph to vaccinate ten other Indians. Those ten yielded enough to vaccinate a hundred more. The blood of each vaccinated person locked away the memory of the pox virus so that any contact with smallpox alerted an army of defenders capable of overcoming the threat."

This property of blood, which can be shared from person to person, helps explain how blood overcomes in the spiritual realm. For in the fight against the virus of sin a vaccination was needed. A vaccination which could be shared from Person to person. A vaccination that worked through the blood. So God became a man. In medical parlance, He entered our microbe world with the genetic material needed to correct it. And in so doing He overcame the virus of sin by taking it on Himself, and, finally, by forgiving it. "God made him who had no sin to be sin for us, so that in him we might become the righteousness of God" 2 Corinthians 5:21.

Which means that Christ overcame sin by taking on the shell of a victim cell of that repugnant virus in order to immunize humanity against death and destruction. This phenomenal achievement is summarized in Hebrews 2:14-18 when it says that Christ shared in our "humanity so that by his death he might destroy him who holds the power of death - that is, the devil - and free those who all their lives were held in slavery by their fear of death . . . For this reason he had to be made like his brothers in every way, in order that he might become a merciful and faithful high priest in service to God, and that he might make atonement for the sins of the people. Because he himself suffered when he was tempted, he is able to help those who are being tempted."

Yes, the blood of Jesus has overcome sin and the devil. Thus, when we are included in Christ we are inoculated with the "serum" that enables us to overcome sin and the devil, not by our own resilience or vitality, but as a result of the immunity in Christ's blood. Praise the Lord!

CHRISTIE

Thank you Christie for entering my world. When you were born, it was the most moving experience of my life. As Mum will tell you, I cried more than you did. I was the happiest dad in the world. And, as a result of whom you are today, I'm still the happiest dad in the world.

As I look back, I remember how you filled our home with boundless enthusiasm and bubbling joy. It hasn't changed. You continue to remind us that you didn't come into this world to be ignored and that life is to be lived to the full. Thank you. My life has been enriched because of whom you are. The melody in your voice, the sparkle in your eyes, the warmth of your hand, and the burst of your laughter floods my mind with special memories and brings happiness to my heart.

But I'm only scratching the surface. Call me a prejudiced father but I see a special anointing from God on your life. You're a spiritually sensitive woman. Wise, witty, and confident. Curious, imaginative and creative. A lover of peace but courageous enough to confront sin. Your lack of guile disarms us. Your integrity and transparency makes people sit up and pay attention. Your energy and persistence conquers all things.

As I think about you serving the Lord it's obvious you're blessed with many spiritual gifts. You have primary gifts of teaching, leadership, wisdom, knowledge, giving, helps, mercy, and service. I also see secondary gifts of hospitality, faith, and administration. With these strengths I know you can accomplish anything you set your mind to. So make sure you use these gifts to the full - never in your own strength, always for the glory of the Lord, and always remembering the One who gave them to you.

But back to our relationship. Thank you for all the fun times we've enjoyed as we've danced, sang, tobogganed, had breakfast out, shared devotions, prayed, chatted, watched movies, washed the car, shopped, canoed, shot hoops, shared our poetry, and so much more. Thank you too for feather-light kisses, for making me proud, for listening and learning, for your trust and love, and for giving me slack when I've made mistakes.

You're the best.

With all my love, Dad.

Now what about you? Have you ever written a letter to your son or daughter? Have you told your child of your love? After all, our heavenly Father never held back. The Bible is full of proclamations of His love. Here's one to get you going. In Jeremiah 31:3 He says, "I have loved you with an everlasting love; I have drawn you with loving-kindness."

That's the love of God. So why not follow His example and tell your children about your love for them.

SO HOW SHOULD I BEHAVE IN CHURCH?

"Everything should be done in a fitting and orderly way"
1 Corinthians 14:40.

Have you ever wondered how you should behave in church? Consider these guidelines from God's Word:

Put others first. In 1 Corinthians 9:19 Paul says, "Though I am free and belong to no man, I make myself a slave to everyone, to win as many as possible." First and foremost we should "submit to one another out of reverence for Christ" Ephesians 5:21. "Your attitude should be the same as that of Christ Jesus: Who, being in very nature God, did not consider equality with God something to be grasped, but made himself nothing, taking the very nature of a servant" Philippians 2:5-7. "Each of us should please his neighbour for his good, to build him up" Romans 15:2.

Act appropriately. What we do in church should be judged on the basis of a simple question, "Is my behaviour appropriate?" Let's not forget that one man's meat is another man's poison. You may think your behaviour is appropriate, yet it could be a stumbling block for someone else. Don't do anything that would cause a weaker brother or sister to fall. In 1 Corinthians 10:23-24 Paul says, "Everything is permissible' - but not everything is beneficial. 'Everything is permissible' - but not everything is constructive. Nobody should seek his own good, but the good of others."

Dress modestly. In 1 Timothy 2:9 one of the instructions on worship is for "women to dress modestly, with decency and propriety . . ." The clothes we wear shouldn't distract or divert others from worshipping God. It should go without saying that some fashions that are accepted as normal in the world are questionable for a Christian. So use your discretion and dress appropriately. In addition, consider 1 Peter 5:5 when it says, "Young men . . . clothe yourselves with humility towards one another."

Be polite. Love "is not rude" 1 Corinthians 13:5. Someone once said, "Manners are the happy ways of doing things." You can make your church a happy place by being polite. Unless it's an emergency you shouldn't go in and out of the auditorium once the service is in progress. Coffee, tea, and other drinks should be consumed before or after the service, not while the service is in progress. Don't distract others by talking during the time of worship or when the Pastor is proclaiming God's Word.

Remember the occasion. When God's people come together He is in the midst of them. No matter where we meet, when two or three are gathered together in His name, God is there by His Spirit. Coming to church isn't like going to the cinema or to a ball game. It's a special occasion - a time to meet with the King of kings. Reverence and holiness should be evident in all we say and do. When we're in the presence of royalty, our behaviour should be markedly different to how we regularly behave. "Exalt the Lord our God and worship at his holy mountain, for the Lord our God is holy" Psalm 99:9.

THE MAN OF NOBLE CHARACTER

Have you ever wondered what the husband of The Wife of Noble Character in Proverbs 31:10-31 would be like? Well here's a suggestion based on Proverbs 31 in a modern day setting:

The Man of Noble Character

Who can find a man of noble character?
He's worth far more than Bill Gates.

His wife has full confidence in him
and has everything she needs.

He brings her good, not harm,
all the days of his life.

He selects wood and screws
and builds with eager hands.

He's like Stuttaford Van Lines
bringing furniture from afar.

He gets up while it's still dark;
heading off to work so that his children and employees have all they need.

He considers a new store and purchases it;
out of his earnings he buys commodities.

He sets about his work vigorously;
weighing up his options.

He sees that his trading on the stock market is profitable,
and his office lamp is on late into the night.

He types away on the computer keyboard
and clicks the mouse with his index finger.

He reaches out to the poor
and washes dishes at the men's shelter.

When winter comes he has nothing to fear
for his house is insulated and heated by an electric furnace.

He washes and waxes the car;
he dresses up in a Pierre Cardin suit.

His wife is respected at the City Hall,
where she takes her seat among the councillors.

He runs a chain of hardware stores
supplying builders, roofers, and carpenters with a variety of products.

He's known as a man of principle and integrity;
with a sense of humour he takes each day in his stride.

He speaks with wisdom,
telling others how they can have fullness of life in Jesus Christ.

He keeps an eye on everything concerning his family,
there isn't an idle bone in his body.

His children say, "Dad's cool!"
His wife thinks he's fantastic and praises him saying:

"Many men do great things,
but you're the best of the best."

Ability to work hard diminishes, and strength ebbs away;
but the man who loves the Lord with all his heart, soul, and mind, should be praised.

Give him the reward he has earned,
and let his good works bring him praise in high places.

ONE ANOTHER

The focus for this devotion came to me during a time of interpersonal conflict in the church. It was a frustrating time, people were niggling over trivia and some decided to leave the church as a result. I was unsure about how to address the matter so I turned to God in prayer and asked Him to help me get the congregation tracking with Him as they should.

Even though the problem was among members of the congregation God began by speaking into my heart and getting me straightened up with Him. As I was reading through Romans in the Good News Bible a number of verses "jumped out" of the text and pierced my heart. I heard God saying: "Have the same concern for everyone. Do not be proud . . ." Romans 12:16. "Try to do what everyone considers to be good" Romans 12:17. "Do not let what you regard as good to get a bad name" Romans 14:16. "Accept one another, then, for the glory of God, as Christ has accepted you" Romans 15:7. "Always aim at those things that bring peace and that help strengthen one another" Romans 14:19.

God used these texts to turn on the light. The reason we have divisions and upset is because of selfishness (cf. James 4:1). Conflict occurs when our relationships become something that's all about us and no longer about Him. So in order to pull together when we're pulled apart our focus has to change. We've got to stop looking out for ourselves and start looking out for one another.

Here are some "one another" texts the Holy Spirit can use to restore or strengthen your relationships:

"As I have loved you, so you must love one another" John 13:34.

"Be devoted to one another in brotherly love" Romans 12:10.

"Honour one another above yourselves" Romans 12:10.

"Live in harmony with one another" Romans 12:16.

"Stop passing judgment on one another" Romans 14:13.

Always aim at those things that bring peace and that help strengthen one another" Romans 14:19 GNB.

"Accept one another, then, just as Christ accepted you . . ." Romans 15:7.

"Serve one another in love" Galatians 5:13.

"Carry each others burdens" Galatians 6:2.

"Be kind and compassionate to one another, forgiving each other, just as in Christ God forgave you" Ephesians 4:32.

"Submit to one another out of reverence for Christ" Ephesians 5:21.

"In humility consider others better than yourselves" Philippians 2:3.

"Do not lie to each other" Colossians 3:9.

"Teach and admonish one another with all wisdom" Colossians 3:16.

"Encourage one other and build each other up" 1 Thessalonians 5:11.

"Live in peace with each other" 1 Thessalonians 5:13.

"Spur one another on toward love and good deeds" Hebrews 10:24.

"Do not slander one another" James 4:11.

"Don't grumble against each other" James 5:9.

"Confess your sins to each other and pray for each other so that you may be healed" James 5:16.

TWO KINDS OF WISDOM

According to God's Word there are two kinds of wisdom: A wisdom from above and a wisdom from below. A heavenly wisdom from God and a worldly wisdom that's not from God. A supernatural wisdom and a natural wisdom. A selfless wisdom and a selfish wisdom. A wisdom which exists as a result of God-confidence and a wisdom which exists due to self-confidence. A divine wisdom and a demonic wisdom. A creative wisdom and a carnal wisdom. A wisdom that draws people together and a wisdom that drives them apart. A wisdom inclined to good deeds and a wisdom governed by opportunistic ambition. An ordered wisdom and a disordered wisdom. A spiritual wisdom and a sensual wisdom. A wisdom equated with loving God and living righteously, and a wisdom based on man's own understanding, standards, objectives and desires.

One kind of wisdom comes from the Holy Spirit (Ephesians 1:17), is given through the Word of God (Deuteronomy 4:5a, 6a), and found through believing prayer (James 1:5), while the other is "earthly, unspiritual, of the devil" James 3:15. One begins when a person is born again while the other begins when a person is born. One is a God thing while the other "is no more than an animal kind of thing" William Barclay. One serves the Master while the other serves man. One aims to satisfy God while the other is self-satisfied. One recognises that "every good and perfect gift is from above, coming down from the Father of the heavenly lights" (James 1:17), while the other rejects God's way, God's Word, and God's will.

These are vital distinctions. They indicate how earthly wisdom has its origin in man's nature totally apart from God whereas heavenly wisdom can never happen unless there's a relationship with God. As indicated in Proverbs 9:10, "The fear of the Lord is the beginning of wisdom, and knowledge of the Holy One is understanding." That's foundational. The source of true spiritual wisdom is in knowing God. It's only when we're in a vital relationship with Jesus Christ that we're able to access the wisdom that comes from above. It's in Jesus, and in Him alone, that all the treasures of wisdom and knowledge are hidden (cf. Colossians 2:3; 1 Corinthians 1:24, 30).

Finally a warning and a blessing: If you pursue worldly wisdom you'll encounter "disorder and every evil practice," but if you pursue heavenly wisdom you'll receive "a harvest of righteousness" James 3:16&18.

With this in mind, "be very careful, then, how you live - not as unwise but as wise, making the most of every opportunity, because the days are evil" Ephesians 5:15.

FOCUSSED ON HOME - FIXATED ON DAD

When Karen taught at St. Christopher's School, she worked with children struggling with neurological disorders. Nyal, a boy with cerebral palsy, was one of her students in the preschool department. At the beginning of his first school year he was dreadfully unhappy with the realisation that he was now separated from the cosseted and loving environment of his home. He would cry unremittingly, for two to three hours, and when he finally stopped crying he would constantly ask, "When is it home time? When is it home time?" To which Karen would reply, "After story time."

The fact that story time preceded home time eventually penetrated Nyal's consciousness. His continuous crying stopped and was replaced, from nine in the morning until twelve noon, with the incessant question, "When is it story time? When is it story time?"

Weeks later Nyal's questioning had abated and Karen was asking the children what they liked best about their school. She received all the usual responses from the children until she came to Nyal. When Nyal was asked the question, he responded, "When my Dad comes to get me!" Karen was not deterred. Following up with another question she asked, "Well, what is the second thing you like about our school?" To which Nyal responded in all seriousness, "When my mom comes to get me!"

Nyal was focussed on home and fixated on his Dad. Likewise we should be focussed on our heavenly home and fixated on our heavenly Father. For we "do not belong to the world," we have been "chosen . . . out of the world" and will one day "receive the promised eternal inheritance" that "can never perish, spoil or fade" John 15:19; Hebrews 9:15; 1 Peter 1:4.

Yes, this world is only a passing season, in much the same way as school will be for Nyal, and when the bell rings we'll get to go home and be with our Father. So live each day with eternity in mind. And feel free to think about your heavenly home and look forward to being with your heavenly Father.

THE CRADLE, THE CROSS, THE CAVE

The cradle, the cross, and the cave.
Each tell the story, each show the way.
Each bring salvation to a world gone astray.
For the cradle, the cross, and the cave telescope.
In these three you'll find that in Christ there is hope.

The cradle revealed, in a barn He was born.
Reaching out to the world, all sinners to warn.
That the link to restore a lost world was now here.
In strips of cloth bound, God's message was clear.

The cross resulted, at the place called The Skull.
The sinless One crucified, death to annul.
The penalty paid, for you and for me.
Stripped of His clothes, to set captives free.

The cave replied, hewn from the rock.
The Son of God laid, the door to unlock.
Wrapped in clean linen, the burial was done.
But the grave couldn't hold Him, resurrection had come!

The cradle, the cross, the cave, all three.
Good news now declared, but you must agree.
Hope is alive, His power conquers all.
And death is defeated when before Him we fall.

RIGHT OR WRONG

In a sinful world we're constantly having to decide between what's right and wrong. Conflicting demands for our obedience are encountered every day and somehow we have to find a course of action that's morally right, free from sin, and pleasing to God. That's not always easy. Our carnal nature, when left to its own devices, strives to go any way but God's way. As Paul says, "For what I want to do I do not do, but what I hate I do" Romans 7:15. Which is why I find it helpful to establish basic guidelines to determine what's right and wrong. Here are nine criteria that should help you discern and obey the will of God:

1. Scripturally - Is it expressly forbidden in God's Word?
2. Conscience - Is your conscience telling you it's wrong? When in doubt leave it out.
3. Personally - Will doing it make you a better or worse Christian?
4. WWJD - Ask yourself, "What would Jesus do?"
5. Practically - Will doing it bring desirable or undesirable results?
6. Universally - Suppose everyone did it?
7. Witness - Will this hinder or advance the progress of the kingdom of God?
8. Stewardship - Will doing it be a good usage of what God's entrusted to me or will it be a waste?
9. Socially - Will doing it influence others to be stronger or weaker believers?

"The Lord will guide you always; he will satisfy your needs in a sun-scorched land and will strengthen your frame. You will be like a well-watered garden, like a spring whose waters never fail" Isaiah 58:11.

THE GIFT
OF LOVE

The gift of love is one of the most important gifts we're given and one of the most important gifts we can give. In it we discover that joy is love's symphony. Peace is love's repose. Patience is love's waiting. Kindness is love's labour. Goodness is love's measure. Faithfulness is love's stick ability. Gentleness is love's conduct. And self-control is love's endurance. Each element is a vital piece of a beautiful whole (cf. Galatians 5:22-23).

The story is told of a grade two class who was asked to draw a picture of something that reminded them of a teacher in their school who had recently passed away. One youngster took a sheet of paper and a wax crayon and coloured the entire paper red. When asked why he'd done so, he explained, "I wanted to draw a picture of her heart but it was too big for the paper."

If we were to take all the paper in the world and all the red crayons and colour every page red we'd still not be able to draw a heart big enough to illustrate the unconditional love the Father has for us.

As F. M. Lehman so eloquently wrote:

> "Could we with ink the ocean fill,
> And were the skies of parchment made,
> Were every stalk on earth a quill,
> And every man a scribe by trade;
> To write the love of God above
> Would drain the ocean dry;
> Nor could the scroll contain the whole,
> Though stretched from sky to sky."

What a God! He's loved us completely and expressed it openly. His love is given regardless of any merit we may or may not have. And it's given in infinite measure so that we can enjoy an endless supply. Not that we should be sponges soaking it all up. As we've received from Him we should likewise pass it on. We should give love as generously as He's given it to us. The gift of love should be a part of who we are in such a way as to be a reflection of Whom we serve. So lavish it on others. Fill your words and define your actions by it. For God will always give you more than you can give away.

UNITY

In John 17:20-21 Jesus prays for unity. He prays that we might be one as He and the Father are one. It's one of the great prayers in the Bible.

It's also one of the things that believers live less than they preach. For unity doesn't just happen. It doesn't just drop out of the sky. It has to be developed. Divine and human causes have to bring it into being. With Christ as our model and means we have to learn how to be united (cf. Philippians 2:1-7).

It's not an easy thing to learn. Unity doesn't come without a fight. Satan doesn't want God's people to be united. His plan is to have believers at loggerheads with each other. He does everything in his power to upset the apple cart. The demons' standing orders are to sow seeds of discord and division. The powers of this dark world and the spiritual forces of evil are working hard to stir up conflict. For Satan knows that if he can divide us he will handicap both our message and our mission.

This was brought home to me recently when I checked on the internet to see how other pastors have preached on the subject of unity. To my surprise I discovered two web sites sponsored by the Satanic Church. Both sites had messages titled, Against Unity. Little wonder. After all, when Jesus knew the end was near his final prayer wasn't for his followers to have success, safety or happiness. He prayed for their unity. And ever since Jesus prayed for unity Satan has gone out of his way to oppose it.

That's why we need to know how to maintain and promote the unity we have in Christ. The following ten questions are designed to help you foster and foment unity. Don't rush through them. After considering each question, it may be a good idea to pause for prayer:

1. Am I single-mindedly focussed on Christ and His calling in my life?

2. Am I actively, with Christ's strength, promoting peace in my home, my church, and my community?

3. Am I making and maintaining meaningful long term friendships or do I push off to another church or community whenever I encounter a rough patch in my relationship with others?

4. Do I make it my practice not to speak evil of my brother and not to sow seeds of discord or dissent?

5. Do I abstain from prejudice and make every attempt to erase man-made lines of division in the Church?

6. Am I creating an atmosphere of unity by practising mutual submission and forgiveness?

7. Whose interests am I looking after, mine or others?

8. Am I praying for unity in Christ and asking God to protect us from any disunity?

9. Is it my goal to serve, rather than to be served?

10. Can we agree together to allow our differences to be our strength, to have unity in essentials, and liberty in nonessentials?

A GARDEN NEEDS A GARDENER

Deuteronomy 6:4-7 says, "The Lord our God, the Lord is one. Love the Lord your God with all your heart and with all your soul and with all your strength. These commandments that I give you today are to be upon your hearts. Impress them on your children. Talk about them when you sit at home and when you walk along the road, when you lie down and when you get up."

The responsibility for the spiritual, practical, intellectual and moral education of our children rests with Christian adults. As Christians we must "be careful, and watch (ourselves) closely so that (we) . . . teach . . . (our) children and . . . their children after them" Deuteronomy 4:9. There can be no other way.

Samuel Taylor Coleridge would agree. The great English poet was once talking with a man who told him that he did not believe in giving children any religious instruction whatsoever. His theory was that the child's mind should not be prejudiced in any direction, but when he came to years of discretion, he should be permitted to choose his religious opinions for himself. Coleridge said nothing, but after a while he asked his visitor if he would like to see his garden. The man said he would, and Coleridge took him out into the garden where only weeds were growing. The man looked at Coleridge in surprise, and said, "Why, this is not a garden! There are nothing but weeds here!" "Well, you see," answered Coleridge, "I did not wish to infringe upon the liberty of the garden in any way. I was just giving the garden a chance to express itself and to choose its own production."

Coleridge makes a good point. A garden needs a gardener. Likewise a child needs a parent who will take the time to plant the seed of the Word, keep the soil of life nourished by a good example, fertilize with prayer, and cultivate the crop in such a way that it will yield a harvest in the years ahead.

GREAT QUOTES

Here are some selected quotations as food for thought. They've helped me in my Christian pilgrimage. I don't know their sources (except for the last one) and can only thankfully acknowledge that others originated them.

You can give without loving but you can't love without giving.

Pray as if everything depended on God and work as if everything depended on you.

It is better to think without speaking than to speak without thinking.

When you're down to nothing, God is up to something!

You have to go outside the box to grow.

Some Christians give to the Lord's work weekly - others give weakly.

Never let yesterday use up too much of today.

I'm too blessed to be stressed.

The level of relationship you have with a person determines the level of correction you can bring to a person.

More often children need an example to follow than a hand to correct.

The task ahead of you is never as great as the power behind you.

The shortest distance between a problem and a solution is the distance between your knees and the floor.

Evangelism is loving men and women too much to allow them to go to hell.

Jesus is God spelt in a language that all men can understand.

If your Bible is falling apart, it's unlikely that your life will too.

Others will know what Christ can do for them when they see what He's done for you.

Prayer is taking hold of the willingness of God.

If you're not making a mistake every now and again you're not learning.

It's not so much our ability as our availability that God is looking for.

Anxiety is often the measure of a man's distance from his God.

Of what good is the pleasure of the cruise if the boat's heading for the falls?

There's a generation waiting on the other side of your obedience.

Generosity is giving away what you could use yourself.

When God kicks your feet from under you it's usually because He wants you on your knees.

It's better to talk to God about men before talking to men about God.

Humility is keeping your eyes off another's shortcomings and fixing them on your own.

Seven words with which to destroy a church: "We've always done it this way before!"

If there's disease and disharmony in the Body no new babes will be born.

You never get a second chance to make a good first impression.

"We who are strong ought to bear with the failings of the weak and not to please ourselves" Romans 15:1.

THE PSALM
OF PSALMS

Psalm 23 has been called the Psalm of psalms and the Creed of creeds. It's one of those intensely personal and sacred compositions which speaks of God's *provision* (23:1-3), *purpose* (23:3,6), and *protection* (23:4-5). It's therefore not surprising that countless people have received succour from the words of this psalm.

I'm one of those people. As I've encountered challenges and opposition I've turned to Psalm 23 and found the encouragement I've needed to press on. The psalm is therefore a trusted companion in my journey through life. Thus, in tribute to this great text, I hope you won't mind if I take some poetic licence, but not doctrinal licence, and rewrite it as a personal expression of my relationship with God.

> Yahweh is my Guide, everything I need I have.
> He makes me rest when I am weary,
> He leads me in search for truth,
> He helps me catch my breath.
> He guides me each step of the way for the glory of His name.
>
> Even if I go through the depths of despair and discouragement,
> I'll not be afraid, for you are right there at my side;
> Your protection and correction, are my comfort.
> You prepare the sustenance I need in the presence of my opposition.
> You lavish my head with the oil of refreshment; my life brims with blessing.
>
> Your goodness and love will chase me each day of my life,
> And Yahweh's house will be my home forever.

Now read the psalm again. Read it afresh. Read it as your psalm. For when this inspirational song is allowed to be the Holy Spirit's tool it has a beauty and power which will serve as a catalyst to *restore* your body, *renew* your mind, and *revive* your spirit.

UNDER CONTROL

Keil and Delitzsch translate Proverbs 20:3 saying, "It is an honour for a man to remain far from strife; but every fool shows his teeth." That's well said. The text reminds me of an irritable dog that growls and shows its teeth. Some parents are like that. They're easily irritated. It doesn't take much before they fly off the handle. They're quick to growl, quick to show their teeth, quick to snap.

In the Spring of 2002 I was in Couchiching Park, Orillia, with the Orillia Community Church Edge One Junior Youth group. Having completed our Bike and Blade event, we were sitting chatting when I noticed a father walking along with his daughter in hand. The girl was six or seven year's old. She was obviously tired and couldn't keep up with her father's lengthy stride. But the father could care less. He was no doubt in a hurry to get somewhere and was yanking her along in an effort to make her walk faster. Then, without warning, he barked his displeasure, let go of her hand, and gave her a hefty slap on the back of her head. She immediately burst into tears. It made no impression on the father. He grabbed her hand and increased his pace, virtually dragging her along for a few metres before grabbing her around the waist and bundling her into his pick up truck.

I was shocked. It was a graphic display of a parent's impatience and irritability.

God's Word has much to say on this subject. In Proverbs 16:32 it says, "Better a patient man than a warrior, a man who controls his temper than one who takes a city." In Proverbs 19:11 it says, "A man's wisdom gives him patience; it is to his glory to overlook an offense." And in Proverbs 29:11 it says, "A fool gives full vent to his anger, but a wise man keeps himself under control."

The texts are good reminders that children are more often in need of an example to follow, than a hand to correct. That's not to say that children don't occasionally need "the rod of correction" Proverbs 29:15. But a spanking should be the exception. Parents need to cultivate a pleasant, patient and positive disposition as they discipline their children. In practice that means parents should keep themselves under control. The Lord makes this possible. If you need an extra measure of patience for a difficult child, ask the Lord for it. He won't let you down. As it says in Matthew 7:7-8, "Ask and it will be given to you; seek and you will find; knock and the door will be opened to you. For everyone who asks receives; he who seeks finds; and to him who knocks, the door will be opened."

FRONT LINE CHRISTIANITY

I have a dream: I see countless believers on the march for Jesus. I see a dynamic and fresh movement of the Holy Spirit in which the bastions of sin and secularism are breached by the Gospel of salvation. I see an era of unprecedented spiritual activity in which the strongholds of darkness are stormed by the love of Christ. I see boldness - God's people fearlessly prevailing against anything the enemy throws at them. And I see a time when sinners fall down in the streets as they cry out for mercy - a season in which the primary concern of our youth will be, "What must I do to be saved?"

The time is coming when Christians will be "strong in the Lord and in his mighty power" Ephesians 6:10. There will be a time when God will raise up regiments of believers bringing healing and comfort to the sick, bringing help and hope to the poor, and bringing the love of Christ to more people than we've ever seen before.

D-day is coming. The Commander in Chief, the Lord of lords, is going to train us, arm us with confidence and strength, go before us, and lead us in a life changing movement in which every true believer will become a front line hero in the battle for the souls of this land. God has done it before and will do it again. Believers will move forward in His name, trusting in Him alone, and wielding "the sword of the Spirit, which is the word of God" Ephesians 6:17. There will be no more carnal cant and posturing. Spirit filled believers will raise up the spear to strike against godlessness and lukewarm religion.

This will be no minor skirmish. It will be all out combat. The safety of the trenches will be vacated. Believers will be head to head with the enemy and in hand to hand combat with the forces of darkness. It will be raw courage and gritty determination at its best. A struggle against overwhelming odds with a single-mindedness that won't allow Christians to stop until the victory is won. Once again there will be great exploits for the King.

So get ready. God is going to take ordinary people and help them do extraordinary things. Regular believers are going to take God at His Word and believe that with God fighting for them no one will be able to stand against them. The promises of God will become a reality. Christians will refuse to settle for mediocrity, refuse to be apathetic, and refuse to sit back and accept the status quo. God's men and women will be risk takers. They'll be prepared to face hostile cities, territories, and nations for the Lord. They will stand in the gap and fight valiantly in the power of the Spirit. And they'll take on impossible odds with no other hope but Him.

It doesn't stop there. There will be an overshadowing presence and power of God. The enemy will be driven back. Spiritual territory will be won in the name of Christ. The darkness will become light. The lost will be saved. The sick made well. Abortion clinics will wonder where their customers went. Crack houses will close. Incidents of alcoholism will plummet. Hollywood will acknowledge the shift in audience preferences. Casinos will become churches. School curriculums will be informed by a Christian world view. And local churches will become Holy Spirit centres of divine activity. For God isn't limited. He's stronger than anything the enemy can throw at us. He's superior to any bastions of sin. He's still the One with the resources of heaven for every warrior who fights the enemy in the name of Christ. And He still makes believers into front line heroes.

OVERCOMING YOUR FEAR

In Revelation 3:20 God says, "Here I am! I stand at the door and knock. If anyone hears my voice and opens the door, I will come in and eat with him, and he with me."

One of the obstacles to intimacy with Christ is fear. Maybe you've heard Christ knocking, but if the truth were known the reason why you haven't opened the door of your life to Christ is because you're afraid. Fear is the barrier between you and Christ.

Thomas Keating in his book Intimacy with God, addresses the problem saying: "Because trust is so important, our spiritual journey may be blocked if we carry negative attitudes toward God from early childhood. If we are afraid of God or see God as an angry father-figure, a suspicious policeman, or a harsh judge, it will be hard to develop enthusiasm, or even interest, in the journey."

You may identify with Keating's comment. You long for intimacy with Christ but you're scared because a mother, father, husband, wife, teacher, uncle, aunt, or someone else, wounded you in the past. Now you wonder if you can ever trust anyone again. That's why, even though you've heard Christ knocking, you fear the risk of opening the door. But let me assure you, on the authority of God's Word, Christ will never disappoint you, never let you down, never abuse you, never use you. Not now, not in the future, not ever. You have nothing to fear in Christ. He only wants what's good for you. There's no guile in Christ - no hidden agenda. He'll never manipulate you, never bully you, and never take advantage of you.

In 1 John 4:18 it says, "There is no fear in love. But perfect love drives out fear, because fear has to do with punishment. The man who fears is not made perfect in love." That's the truth. Christ only, always, treats people with love and respect. He's not the One to be feared because He's the One who drives out fear. And that's why there's not a single person who's opened the door to intimacy with Christ who's ever been disappointed.

So step out in faith. Reject the fear that's kept you from Christ. Be positive. It's not as difficult as you think. Take Ralph Emerson's suggestion, "Do the thing you fear and the death of fear is certain." Simply pray the prayer of the man mentioned in Mark 9:24 when he exclaimed, "I do believe; help me overcome my unbelief!" Then, once you've prayed the prayer, open up and welcome Christ in.

CHANGE AGENTS

"Christians are supposed not merely to endure change,
nor even to profit by it, but to cause it."
Harry Emerson Fosdick.

An important role of Christian leadership is to be change agents. Leaders need to exercise a transformational ministry. They need to affect others toward maturity in the Lord Jesus Christ. They need to be inventive and imaginative. They need to be catalysts that instigate metamorphosis. They need to be people who challenge the status quo. And they need to instill in others the motivation to develop into whom they ought to be.

That's a high calling. It takes a great deal of moral courage to step up to the plate when you know that an essential component of leadership is confrontation - challenging people to break out of their comfort zones.

Jesus is the prime example. He was confrontational in so much of what He said and did. The Gospels describe how He went head to head with the Scribes and Pharisees, how He chased the money changers out of the Temple, and how He challenged many of the accepted norms and traditions of His time. He was the greatest change agent the world had ever known. But He never confronted anyone the wrong way. There was no sin in Him, nothing negative, no selfish agenda. He was a change agent for one reason only - to point people to the Father.

Abraham is another good example. Even though he had no title and no one to command outside of his own household he was a good leader because he chose to be different, chose to be God's man. The choice was made when he separated himself from the sin and paganism of his day.

That's the key to being a change agent - being set apart to God's purposes. Abraham became the "father of many nations" (Genesis 17:5) because he walked before God and was blameless (cf. Genesis 17:1). He looked to God and only to Him. He took the road less travelled.

The results speak for themselves: Abraham established an inheritance that had a lasting impact - becoming a spiritual father to an extensive family of spiritual children.

Like Christ and Abraham, Christian leaders have to be change agents to fulfill the leadership mandate. They fall far short of God's ideal if they merely maintain, monitor, and mediate in accordance with the accepted norms and traditions of the church or organization in which they serve.

Maybe you're called to be a change agent. It's a high calling. You can't think about changing others until you've thought about changing yourself. Conviction, confession, courage, consecration, and commitment are needed. You must "throw off everything that hinders and the sin that so easily entangles . . . fix (your) eyes on Jesus, the author and perfecter of our faith, who for the joy set before him endured the cross . . . and . . . consider him who endured such opposition from sinful men, so that you will not grow weary and lose heart" Hebrews 12:1-3.

THANKFUL

One of my joys as a country pastor is the Fall Tour with the Galloping Grannies (and one or two obligatory men). It's much the same every year. After bundling into vehicles we take a slow drive through the countryside to admire the ruby red sumac, the russet maples, and the barren green fields which still serve as a reminder of warmer times. Along the way we'll stop to admire a pumpkin patch or take a photo of the group with arms wrapped around each other in anticipation of the cold to come. Then it's time for a cozy restaurant with good food and an opportunity to reminisce about bygone days.

Which reminds me of the many things for which I'm grateful. Here are a few:

Although I like turkey, and am somewhat partial to cranberry sauce, I'm thankful I don't have to eat it every day of the year.

I'm thankful for my mother-in-law (don't let her know!).

I'm thankful that I've never gone hungry, except when fasting.

I'm thankful for the storms that God has helped me weather.

I'm thankful for a wife who loves me through thick and thin.

I'm thankful for eyes to see, ears to hear, a mouth to speak, and a mind to learn.

I'm thankful that although things aren't always what I want them to be, they're never as bad as they could be.

I'm thankful for differences. Praise God everyone isn't like me!

I'm thankful that God's mercies are new every day.

I'm thankful for strength to meet the strain and stress along life's way.

I'm thankful for every smile and chuckle and grin.

I'm thankful for mountaintops but more thankful for valleys, because growth takes place down where the dirt is.

I'm thankful for indoor plumbing.

I'm thankful for comfort in times of despair.

I'm thankful for the tears that have been forgotten.

I'm thankful for Someone to thank - the Lord Jesus Christ.

I'm thankful for the memory to remember.

I'm thankful that I have more full years to count than lean.

I'm thankful that my hope isn't in the stuff of this earth - that I've got eternity to look forward to.

I'm thankful for the things that haven't happened, for the accidents I wasn't involved in, and for every untroubled day.

I'm thankful that "the Lord is good and his love endures forever" Psalm 100:5.

I'm thankful for the privilege of breathing His air and being alive in the midst of His beauty everywhere.

I'm thankful for three extraordinary children; Christie, Matthew and Jonathan - God's gifts to Karen and me.

And I'm thankful that I can count on God instead of myself.

What about you? Why not make your own list of thanksgiving. After all, in old Anglo-Saxon, to be "thankful" meant to be "thinkful."

ECCLESIASTICAL BIRDWATCHING

Welcome to the annual Ornithologists Conference. I hope you've come prepared with your binoculars and bird books because we're hoping to spot some of the rare and elusive Christians that have recently been spotted in the pews:

The Sickly Swallow. This bird is prevented from attending church by sniffles, sunburn, suspicious spots, sinus, stings, sprains, stress, and sties. Showers, sunshine, squalls and snow also seem to cause this bird to stay at home. Symptoms always appear on Sunday and are most acute early in the morning. However, the healing process is hastened by a Sunday afternoon drive or a trip in the boat and by Monday the Sickly Swallow is back to full health.

The Late Loon. Although it hasn't been scientifically established, it's believed that the Late Loon is allergic to greeters and ushers as she always arrives at church after the service has started. According to the church gossip the Late Loon will even be late for her own funeral!

The Great Speckled Sermon Snoozer. A large and variegated family, docile and easily domesticated. This breed takes readily to captivity and settles down contentedly in any suitable sanctuary. Once perched for the sermon instinct causes them to immediately fall asleep which they can do without putting their heads under their wings. They're faithful members of the flock and won't miss church for anything because they can't afford to miss out on their sleep.

The Cold Blooded Seat Shifter and Pew Penguin. These two birds attach themselves to a flock. The Cold Blooded Seat Shifter is often seen in full feather and wearing long sleeved plumage even in summer. No matter where she rests she shivers and quivers. The Pew Penguin is often seen plucking at his collar and wiping his brow. His nest is identified by a sweat stained pew and a hymn book with a broken binding from having been used as a fan. The Cold Blooded Seat Shifter and Pew Penguin have an affinity for Deacon Birds. After a service is over these two nervous bird's circle the church until they spot their unwary prey. Then, squawking loudly, both descend on the hapless Deacon Bird, one to complain that the church was too hot and the other to complain that it was too cold!

The Great White Bittern. This bird regards itself as the defender of both the purity of the flock and the faith. A very vocal bird, it squawks loudly as it tries to make the other birds conform to the tradition of the flock. In Bittern language, this is called "keeping them in their place."

The Migratory Mallard. It looks and quacks like the Common Duck but it has one distinguishing characteristic: It's constantly flitting from one church pond to another and never settles very long at any one. It will swim happily in a pond for a few months or years then something will trigger an urge to migrate and suddenly it's gone. Some leave the flock silently, but others leave the coop with much wing flapping and flutters of righteous indignation.

The Love Birds. These birds snuggle very close to each other despite the fact that there's plenty of room on the pew. Interested observers of this species report gentle cooing sounds and touching of wingtips during times of prayer. One avid birdwatcher also reported the rubbing of ankles during the sermon. [Source unknown].

Although these tongue in cheek illustrations of Christians aptly describe some of the funny birds that flutter about in the local flock they're not a biblical representation of the believer. According to God's Word a Christian is someone who is purified (cf. Acts 15:9; Titus 2:14), satisfied (cf. Psalm 34:8; 107:9), fortified (cf. Isaiah 41:10; 58:11; Colossians 1:11; Ephesians 3:16; 2 Thessalonians 3:3), occupied (cf. Luke 19:11-27; 1 Corinthians 15:58), and glorified (cf. 1 Corinthians 15:51-57).

Now don't fly off to do whatever you've got to do. Stay on your perch for a few more minutes. Open your Bible and look up the texts mentioned above and as you read each text ask yourself, "Does this describe me? Am I the Christian 'bird' God wants me to be?"

HE'S THERE FOR YOU

In 1989 Armenia was hit with an earthquake which killed more than 30 000 people in less that four minutes. After the earthquake hit a father rushed to the school where his son was supposed to be and discovered the building to be no more than a pancake of debris. He was shocked, and as the tears filled his eyes and the hopelessness of the situation became apparent he remembered how he had promised his son, "No matter what, I'll always be there for you!"

After the trauma of his initial shock the father determined to act on the commitment he had made his son and remembering that his son's classroom was in the back right corner of the building he began digging through the rubble with his bare hands.

As he dug other well meaning parents tried to pull him away from the task saying, "It's too late!" "They're dead!" "You can't help!" "Go home!" "You're just going to make things worse!" To each parent he simply responded, "Are you going to help me now?" Then the fire chief arrived and he tried to pull the man off the debris because of the fires that were breaking out. But the man persisted. Nothing could deter him. Soon the police appeared on the scene and said, "You're angry, distraught, and it's over. You're endangering others. Go home. We'll handle it!" To which he replied, "Are you going to help me now?" No one helped.

He dug for eight hours . . . twelve hours . . . twenty-four hours . . . and as he dug he kept wondering whether his son was dead or alive. He dug for thirty-six hours . . . then, in the thirty-eighth hour, he pulled back a boulder and heard his son's voice. He screamed his son's name, "Armand!" His son replied, "Dad!? It's me, Dad! I told the other kids not to worry. I told them that if you were alive, you'd save me and when you saved me, they'd be saved. You promised, 'No matter what, I'll always be there for you!' You did it Dad!"

There were fourteen out of thirty-three children in Armand's class who survived. The building had collapsed in such a way that it made a wedge and it was in this space that the scared, hungry, and thirsty children had lain waiting for help. Armand helped push all the other children out before he would get out because, as he said, "Dad, let the other kids out first because I know you'll get me! No matter what, I know you'll be there for me!"

Like Armand's father the heavenly Father is always there for you. That's a certainty. His Word confirms it and His character guarantees it. No matter what happens He will never leave you nor forsake you. So don't throw in the towel. No matter what it takes the Father will never give up, never tire, never stop doing His very best for you. As He says in Isaiah 43:1-3, "Fear not, for I have redeemed you; I have called you by name; you are mine. When you pass through the waters, I will be with you; and when you pass through the rivers, they will not sweep over you. When you walk through the fire, you will not be burned; the flames will not set you ablaze. For I am the Lord, your God, the Holy One of Israel, your Saviour."

DISCERNING THE DEVIL'S DEEDS

Satan uses a fivefold strategy to undermine the believer and damage the work of the Lord. This devotion uncovers the devil's repertoire of repression and reproach so that you're better able to avoid his snares and move forward in the victory you have in the Lord Jesus Christ.

Firstly, the devil *distracts*. He is the master of distraction, abstraction and inattention. He aims to divert you from clear thinking and focussed action. He does this by trying to entice your eyes, engage your ears, and entertain your senses. There's only one way to deal with the devil's distractions - give the Lord your full attention. James 4:7-8 says, "Submit yourselves, then, to God. Resist the devil, and he will flee from you. Come near to God and he will come near to you."

Secondly, the devil *deceives*. The work of deception is the work of pretense, trickery, swindling, lying, guile, falseness, and fraud. Jess C. Moody said, "The devil is the top hidden persuader - the master of subliminal motivation." His aim is to cause the wrong to seem right and the right to seem wrong. He attempts to tarnish the truth and cloud your judgement. So be on your guard for our enemy the devil has "no truth in him . . . he is a liar and the father of lies" John 8:44. You deal with deception by knowing God's Word, for when you know the truth the truth will set you free.

Thirdly, the devil *disgraces*. The devil tempts you through the lust of the flesh, the love of money, and the desire for popularity. He's constantly on the prowl for ways to discredit and disgrace you. As we read in Revelation 12:10, the devil is "the accuser of our brothers." He's the one pointing fingers at others. He's never idle. Day and night (cf. Revelation 12:10) he tries to bring disgrace with accusations of wrongdoing, sin, shortcoming, and false motives. The way to deal with these accusations is to "be self-controlled and alert" 1 Peter 5:8. You must "resist him" and stand "firm in the faith . . . and the God of all grace . . . will himself restore you and make you strong, firm and steadfast" 1 Peter 5:9-10.

Fourthly, the devil *depresses*. The devil works hard to bring believers down. He delights in discouraging God's children and takes every opportunity he can find to lower your spirits, sap your strength, and push you down. He afflicts believers with testing, trials, trouble, and torment. Like Job, the way to be victorious when the devil seeks to depress you is to be "blameless and upright; he feared God and shunned evil" Job 1:1.

Fifthly, the devil *destroys*. The devil is in the demolition business. His ultimate desire is to defeat and destroy God's people (cf. 1 Peter 5:8). As a Christian you are at war with the devil. He's your chief adversary. He's the one working to break down all that God is building up. But he's "neither omnipotent nor free to do everything he pleases. Prince of the world he may be, but the Prince of Peace has come and dealt him a death blow" Harold Lindsell.

That's the good news: The devil is a defeated foe. The Son of God, our Lord Jesus Christ has conquered Satan by overcoming sin and death. That means the devil can't harm you if you're in Christ (cf. Luke 10:19). "He can't handle the One to whom you're joined; he can't handle the One to whom you're united, and he can't handle the One whose nature dwells in your nature" A. W. Tozer. Yes, "Greater is he that is in you, than he that is in the world" 1 John 4:4 KJV. So even though the devil still seeks to distract, deceive, disgrace, depress and even attempts to destroy you, remember that he's already beaten. For "the reason the Son of God appeared was to destroy the devil's work" 1 John 3:8. Hallelujah!

RENEW YOUR LOVE

This is for all married couples. Renew your love with this application of 1 Corinthians 13.

I may be able to speak with human eloquence and angelic rhapsody, but if I don't love my spouse, I'm only a creaking rusty gate or an echo in the Grand Canyon. If I have a heart full of good intentions, share my life, and if I have faith to tackle every challenge we might encounter in our marriage, but don't love, I'm nothing. I may give everything I have to my spouse and even burn myself out for him/her, but if I don't love, my efforts are useless.

A spouse should love with a love that's constant. Love is patient. It doesn't demonstrate irritations or reflect anger. Love is respectful. It involves acceptance and is never intolerant or agitated. In marriage, love compliments the other, recognises the other's needs, and nurtures the other. Love is not possessive, neither smothering the other, nor begrudging the other. Love doesn't try to impress or create an image, or cherish inflated ideas of accomplishments. Love is honourable.

A spouse should love with a love that never fails. Love is for better or for worse. Love is faithful. Love has unlimited endurance and continues in the face of unreturned love. It tackles all obstacles with the confidence that comes from God. It conquers evil with good. It accepts humble duties. It submits to the other out of reverence for Christ. It always protects, always hopes, never looks back, and keeps going to the end.

Marriage should be a paradigm of good manners. Love is kind. It doesn't force itself on the other. It doesn't pursue selfish advantage, nor become touchy and hypersensitive, and certainly doesn't hold past mistakes against one's better half. For love does not criticize, fly off the handle, or take revenge. Rather, it acts creatively and constructively, recognising needs and contributing positively to the relationship.

A spouse should never delight in evil. Love does not gloat over the wickedness of another or compare self with others for self-justification. A spouse is unhappy when a loved one falls into sin but glad when truth prevails. When spouses have such love, trusting God implicitly, they will have unlimited endurance and confidence to bear all things and look for the best in each other and in every situation.

This God given love is eternal. It never dies. But inspired speech will become obsolete; family prayers and devotions will end; knowledge will be abandoned. For we only know a part of the truth and what we say about God is always incomplete, but when the Complete arrives, our shortcomings will pass away.

When we were children, we had the behaviour and immaturity of children. When we grew up, we turned our back on infantile ways. Now we seem to be peering through the fog at a silhouette; but the fog will eventually lift and we'll have clarity. Now we know partially; then we'll know completely - as totally as God's knowledge of us as husband and wife. But for now: in marriage we must have a steady faith, a consistent hope, and an extravagant love. But the greatest of these is love.

IS YOUR GOD TOO SAFE?

Is your god too safe? Stop, think about it. Is your god too safe? Is he predictable, easily tamed, part of the scenery, able to fit in your box? Is he comfortable, never one to take you by surprise, happy to stay in the background, yet always at your beck and call? If he is, then he's not much of a god at all. For any god who allows himself to be reduced to your restrictive view (and mine) doesn't deserve to be a god.

It's different with Almighty God. You can't constrain or constrict Him. He defies any and all attempts to rationalise or reduce Him. Try as you might, there's simply no way you'll mould Him, shape Him, or fashion Him. Even the breath the atheist uses to deny Him is sustained by Him. For God's not created in our image, nor birthed in our imagination. He stands distinct, unlike any other, over all and above all.

Don't be deceived. God will never be limited by our nearsightedness. He will do His thing as He's always done His thing. And when God does His thing, it's dramatic, out of the ordinary, beyond compare. He's the One who places the rainbow in the sky, divides the Red Sea, rains down manna in the desert, raises people from the dead, makes an axe head float on water, stills a storm, gives sight to the blind, makes the lame walk, enables a donkey to talk, opens the ears of the deaf, transforms a life from within, and so much more.

That's why we shouldn't parcel Him, patent Him, or paddock Him. God isn't conditioned or predetermined by anything or anyone other than Himself. Without compromise He authenticates Himself, is self-conscious, self-determined. All authority is His. His unlimited strength affects all His purposes in the way in which He ordained them.

Which is why I worship Him. For He's no ordinary god. He's extraordinary, bigger than any box, never safe . . .

WONDERFULLY MADE

What does iodine, velcro, the Dead Sea Scrolls, safety glass and X rays have in common? Now don't give up too quickly. Here's a clue. Penicillin, dynamite, the West Indies, vulcanization, and substitute sugar also have something in common with the items already mentioned. The answer - these diverse things were all discovered by accident.

The cure for malaria was also discovered by accident. An old legend tells of an Indian who, burning with fever and stumbling through the trees in the high jungle of the Andes, found a stagnant pool of bitter water which he drank deeply to quench his burning thirst. As he drank the water, he realized it was tainted with the bark of the cinchona tree (called quina-quina by the Indians). The tree was thought to be poisonous but the Indian was more concerned about getting some kind of relief for his fever than for the possible deadly after effects. To his surprise, he didn't die; in fact the fever dissipated and he made it back to his village with renewed strength. When friends and relatives heard his story, they began to use extracts from the bark of the quina-quina tree to cure further outbreaks of malaria.

By the early seventeenth century news of this discovery had reached Jesuit missionaries in Lima and they named the bark "Jesuit bark." In 1820 the active anti-malarial substance in the bark was isolated as quinine by the French chemists Pierre Pelletier and Joseph Caventou.

Archimedes accidentally discovered how to measure the volume of an irregular object in the public baths in Syracuse in the third century B. C. As he stepped into a bath of water and saw water running over the top of the bath he realized that the volume of the overflowing water was exactly equal to the bulk of his body placed in the water. He was so excited with his discovery he leapt out of the baths, forgot to put on his clothes, and dashed home naked shouting, "Eureka! Eureka!"

Jenner's accidental discovery of a vaccine for smallpox occurred after seeing cowpox scars on a milkmaid's hands. Luigi Galvani observed a frog leg hanging from an iron railing by a brass hook and how it contracted when it came in contact with another part of the railing. Galvani's accidental discovery later led to an understanding of electromagnetism.

I could tell you about hundreds of other things which have been discovered by accident. But here's today's clincher - you weren't one of them. You didn't happen along by chance. There's not a single living human being who was ever an accident, certainly not in God's economy. In Psalm 139:13-16 we read; "For you created my inmost being; you knit me together in my mother's womb. I praise you because I am fearfully and wonderfully made; your works are wonderful, I know that full well. My frame was not hidden from you when I was made in the secret place. When I was woven together in the depths of the earth, your eyes saw my unformed body. All the days ordained for me were written in your book before one of them came to be."

IS YOUR CHURCH HEALTHY?

There used to be a charismatic church in South Africa that had a number of homeless people build their shanties around the church. But the people of the church ignored the folk camping out on their property. Week in and week out when the believers arrived on Sunday morning they would step over the homeless people as they made their way into the sanctuary.

The irony of the situation is that this church believed they were experiencing a Holy Ghost revival. There was great singing, speaking in tongues, laughing, people slain in the Spirit, clapping of hands, healings, and dancing in the aisles. Yet no one in the church offered the homeless people any support or encouragement. Nothing was done to alleviate the distress of the poor.

The church is no longer in existence. I'm not surprised. Even though folk may have thought that the church looked healthy from the inside, it wasn't. For they had the potential for revival right around them, but they failed to recognise it.

Healthy looking churches can be sick and sick looking churches can be healthy. A church can have all the right signs; good numbers, quality music, a substantial bank balance, a multi-gifted pastor, creative use of technology, buildings in excellent condition, and numerous groups and programmes yet amount to little more than a once a week sacred concert. In contrast, a church may be deficient in all of the above and yet be right on track with what matters most to God.

So how can you tell if your church is healthy?

To begin, you should ask, "What are the things that matter most to God?" If the primary reason for gathering together is selfishness, then the church is unhealthy. If the church exists because the seniors want to keep the church going long enough for their funerals to take place in the building, then the priorities are all wrong. If the number one concern is flying the denominational flag, maintaining tradition, being a place of respite from the daily grind, or avoiding the shame of closing down, then church has become an end in itself - an idol that has displaced a genuine love for God.

Biblically speaking, a church is healthy when "each part does its work" Ephesians 4:16. You can take your church's pulse by simply analysing whether or not the members are 24/7 believers. If every member in your church is using their God given gift's twenty-four-hours a day, seven days a week, then your church is healthy. For the health of a church isn't primarily linked to what the pastor does or the programmes the church offers, the health of a church is determined by whether or not each part is playing its part.

By these criteria, many churches are actually in poor health. Outward signs can be misleading. If only 20% of a congregation are actively engaged in daily worship, witness and work for the extension of God's kingdom then the church is sick even if it looks healthy.

In case I haven't been clear, I'm not talking about believers being committed to worshipping, witnessing, and working in the many programmes run by the church. That's only part of it. The health of a church isn't entirely linked to its ability to staff the youth ministry, the Sunday school, the seniors group, and so on. A church can have all its programmes running smoothly and still be in maintenance mode, still be sick while appearing to be healthy. For God isn't primarily concerned with staffing programmes. He's concerned with seeing every believer worshipping, witnessing, and working in a ministry He has chosen for that person regardless of whether it corresponds with ministries already in place within the church.

In other words, a healthy church isn't a church in maintenance mode, it's a church in missionary mode. It's a church in which every believer is living out the reality of the Great Commission. A church in which each one is reaching one and teaching one. A church in which every believer is faithfully engaged as a "missionary" in his or her daily sphere of influence. A church in which every believer is putting their feet in gear and going and making disciples of all nations. A church in which every believer is using their mouth to teach someone else about faith in the Lord Jesus Christ. And it's a church in which every believer discovers and invests their lives in what God wants to do, in and through them, in a wide range of circumstances both inside and outside the church.

WE ARE
WHAT WE EAT

"Jesus declared, 'I am the bread of life. He who comes to me will never go hungry, and he who believes in me will never be thirsty'" John 6:35.

J esus is concerned about the whole person. He came that we might have life and have it to the full (cf. John 10:10). There are no half measures with Jesus. He is "the way and the truth and the life" John 14:6. He's concerned about the physical, mental, and spiritual aspects of our lives. Show me a religion or a way of life that fulfills these three areas completely and I'll change my beliefs!

Despite the fact that Jesus is "the bread of life" people continue to feed on junk food. I'm not talking about the natural realm. When folk physically survive on hamburgers, fizzy drinks, pastries, chips, ice cream, candy, cookies, and instant TV dinners, it's a crying shame, but when they spiritually feed on trashy literature, half-baked sitcoms, fleeting pleasures, the lusts of the flesh, and whatever else they sample from the world's menu, it's a tragedy. For we are what we eat.

As a youngster I used to keep silk worms. If I fed them mulberry leaves, they'd spin golden-yellow cocoons. If I fed them red cabbage leaves, they'd spin russet-red cocoons. The colours of the cocoons were directly related to what the silk worms ate.

I could cite other examples. There's a Brazilian parrot whose colour changes from green to yellow when it eats certain fish. And, if you made me eat black pudding, I'm sure my colour would change from pink to green!

Likewise, in the spiritual realm, we're gradually changed by what we continually take into our minds and bodies. "Those who live according to the sinful nature have their minds set on what that nature desires; but those who live in accordance with the Spirit have their minds set on what the Spirit desires" Romans 8:5.

So watch what you eat. "Like newborn babies, crave pure spiritual milk, so that by it you may grow up in your salvation, now that you have tasted that the Lord is good" 1 Peter 2:2-3.

During the Great Famine of China the people made bread from a kind of edible earth but this ingredient was devoid of any nutrients and those who ate the loaves starved to death. Don't miss the obvious. In the spiritual realm you can eat all manner of "bread" yet still starve to death. Only Jesus is "the bread of life" John 6:35. He's the only source of nourishment for a hungry heart, the only bread to satisfy and give fulness of life.

GIVE IT ALL YOU'VE GOT!

Jonathan is our youngest child, what South Africans refer to as a "laat lammetjie" (late lamb), being nine years younger than Christie and seven years younger than Matt. He was conceived in Canada, born in South Africa on 25 October 1994, and returned to Canada when he was two years old. Jono's a wonderful member of our family, a special blessing from the Lord, even though his older brother and sister jokingly tell him that he was adopted and they weren't, and that Mum and Dad love them more than they love him! (Both statements are false).

There are many gifts and character traits that make Jono the unique person he is. But one of the special things for which he's known is his ability to sing out. When he sings he opens his mouth, opens his lungs, and gives it all he's got. There's no holding back, no inhibitions. If it's a school or church production and the other children are a little timid, Jono comes through strong. In fact his Grade 2 teacher, Mary-Lou McPhedran, had a dream prior to the school Christmas play in which she dreamt that things hadn't worked out too well because Jono hadn't arrived. When she woke up, she was distressed enough to call us and make sure we'd be able to get Jono to school in time for him to sing!

Jono's singing is a wonderful testimony to those of us who know him. I'll sometimes walk into the kitchen and hear him singing a song about Jesus that he's composing on the spot, or hear him joining in with one of the other family members with a pleasant harmony or melody.

But more important than his special ability to sing is the obvious passion and delight with which he sings. As a youngster he knows more about the heart of a worshipper than many adults know. There's an abandonment to God in his singing, a lack of self-consciousness, an innocence, and a joy that bubbles from deep within his spirit.

Which is why, even though Jonathan doesn't realise it, he's been an example to me of how I should "worship the Father in spirit and truth" John 4:23. As he's stood next to me while we've sung in church I've begun to learn that unless I change my adult ways and become like a little child, I will "never enter the kingdom of heaven" Matthew 18:3.

I'm very thankful for Jonathan. Through his childlike faith and his "no holds barred" approach to worship, I'm discovering how God wants us to worship Him with all we've got. Nothing should get in the way of giving Him our very best. When we sing, we should let it rip, worship like we know we're His children, sing as if we're in the throne room of heaven, and praise Him as if there's no tomorrow.

SEIZE THE DAY

IS SOMETHING MISSING?

Davis Duggins wrote an article entitled, The Worship Gap - Is Something Missing in our Response to God? That's a good question. Is something missing in our worship? Randy Vader certainly thinks there is. Vader, a song writer and music publisher who's worked alongside Christian artists such as Bill and Gloria Gaither, says, "So much of what we do in church really is not worship . . . There's a lot of teaching that goes on, there's nurturing - so many things. That's not to say it's bad . . . but it's not worship."

Vader has a point. A church can have one of the finest orchestras in town, or one of the greatest choirs, and be clueless about worship. You can put some of the best preachers in the pulpit, have a technically outstanding praise band, and still not know how to worship the Lord.

Ronald Allen, a seminary professor and columnist for Worship Leader Magazine says, "There are a lot of times, frankly, when I've sat through a church service and haven't really been worshipping. I've been critical or apathetic or just there." You may relate to Allen's sentiments. You've experienced mindless or boring services. You've gone through the motions. You've desperately wanted to worship the Lord, yet it didn't happen. Which is why it's time for the "missing jewel" (A. W. Tozer) of worship to be restored.

Restoration should always be rooted in God's Word. The Bible describes worship as the reading of Scripture (cf. Colossians 4:16), teaching and preaching (cf. 1 Corinthians 14:26; 2 Timothy 4:2), singing (cf. Ephesians 5:19; Colossians 3:16), praying (cf. 1 Timothy 2:8), collecting money for the Lord's work (cf. Philippians 4:18), everyday words and deeds (cf. Colossians 3:17), taking communion (cf. 1 Corinthians 11:17-34), and confessing Christ's name (cf. Hebrews 13:15).

A study of the Hebrew and Greek words for worship is also helpful. The Hebrew word for worship is *shachah*, which means to "bow down" or to "prostrate oneself." Another common Hebrew word is *abad*, which means "to serve." In the Greek the most common word for worship is *proskuneo*, which literally means "to kiss (kuneo) toward (pros)." It's the same word that's used to describe the kissing of the hem or the feet of a superior. Another common Greek word for worship is *latreuo*, which means "to serve." Robert Webber says that if we put these Hebrew and Greek terms together we could say that worship is "an inner and outer homage to God as a token of awe and surrender."

Worship is therefore far more than Christians just singing or speaking about God's worth. It's also something more than an inner heartfelt response of thanksgiving. True worship isn't lip service - it's life service. It's a total response to divine truth. It's an all-encompassing attitude of 100 percent commitment. It's a life that's both inwardly and outwardly totally given over to serving God - a life of consecration and surrender. In the words of Romans 6:13, it's offering "the parts of your body to him as instruments of righteousness."

That's a far cry from what we see in today's church. As Paul Yerden, a music minister in the Midwest, says, "Church has become a spectator sport . . . We watch football games, we watch baseball games, we watch concerts, and we watch religion on TV. So we come to church, and we want to watch it happen there." Yerden exposes an insidious problem. It's common practice for churchgoers to shop around for pleasing worship experiences. If the "show" is good in one place they'll go there but if a better "show" starts up down the street they may go there. Instead of thinking of worship as something we give we've come to think of it as something we can get. The focus has become entertainment instead of involvement - about what we can see in worship instead of being about what we can make of worship.

Which is why we need to remind ourselves that worship involves the whole of the believer's body, mind and spirit. Nothing should be held back. Believers must engage in worship wholeheartedly. We must make it "a sacrifice of praise" Hebrews 13:15. For true worship is when you "quicken the conscience by the holiness of God, feed the mind with the truth of God, purge the imagination by the beauty of God, open the heart to the love of God, and devote the will to the purpose of God" William Temple.

It starts with you. You need to fill the worship gap (cf. Ezekiel 22:30). You need to do your part, in the power of the Holy Spirit, to restore whatever's missing in your response to God.

"A time is coming and has now come when the true worshippers will worship the Father in spirit and truth, for they are the kind of worshippers the Father seeks. God is spirit, and his worshippers must worship in spirit and in truth." John 4:23-24.

MORE . . .

There's one word that summarises the hopes and dreams of most North Americans - More. Hardly anyone's contented. Nearly everyone wants more. We live for more. We're obsessed with more. We never seem to have enough, and what we do have soon becomes commonplace. So we live for stuff that's bigger and better than before. For even though we know better, we've convinced ourselves that the grass is greener on the other side of the fence.

You know what I'm talking about. We're consumers by nature, passionate in our pursuit of the latest luxury, a better house, a faster computer. Every instinct, every impulse cries out, MORE! GIVE ME MORE! In actuality, even when we have every-thing we need, the voice of consumerism keeps telling us we need more.

But here's the rub. Discontentment, this business of wanting more, is an obstacle to knowing Christ.

Now you might say that's okay, but personally I think it's better to know Christ than to be discontented. Which raises a question. If discontentment is an obstacle to knowing Christ then how does one deal with discontentment? The answer: Learning to be content whatever the circumstances (cf. Philippians 4:11).

When I say that the answer to discontentment is learning to be content whatever the circumstances I'm not saying we should never want something or shouldn't enjoy a purchase here and there. I'm not promoting asceticism. The problem isn't how much stuff a person may have. The problem is whether or not a person is controlled by the passion to consume. For contentment is being satisfied in something beyond the material. More specifically, it's being satisfied in someone, in the Lord Jesus Christ. It's seeing Christ, and Christ alone, as our sufficiency. And it's the practical outworking of the reality that in having Him, we have it all.

God's Word brings it into focus. "But godliness with contentment is great gain. For we brought nothing into the world, and we can take nothing out of it. But if we have food and clothing, we will be content with that. People who want to get rich fall into temptation and a trap and into many foolish and harmful desires that plunge men into ruin and destruction. For the love of money is a root of all kinds of evil. Some people, eager for money, have wandered from the faith and pierced themselves with many griefs . . . Command those who are rich in this present world not to be arro-gant nor to put their hope in wealth, which is so uncertain, but to put their hope in God, who richly provides us with everything for our enjoyment" 1 Timothy 6:6-10,17.

SAVED THROUGH FAITH

Now what is faith? Augustine said, "Faith is to believe what we do not see." Bernard Ramm said, "Faith is a declaration of Dependence in opposition to sin which is man's Declaration of Independence." David Reed said, "Faith is not a leap in the dark; it is a leap out of darkness into the light." And someone else said, "Faith in God sees the invisible, believes the incredible, and receives the impossible." Martin Luther probably defines it best when he says, "Faith is a living, daring confidence in God's grace, so sure and certain that a man could stake his life on it a thousand times." And the Bible defines faith in Hebrews 11:1 saying, "Faith is being sure of what we hope for and certain of what we do not see."

In Ephesians 2:8 it says that "it is by grace you have been saved, through faith." Notice how grace and faith are involved in salvation. It's a case of God's grace and our faith which brings salvation. The two must go together. Grace is the remedy for our sin and faith is the means by which we appropriate the remedy. As W. Herschel Ford says, "Grace is like a reservoir of cold water on a hot day, and faith is the cup that we use to bring the cooling drink to our lips." Isn't that a wonderful analogy? Grace makes salvation possible and faith makes salvation actual. We cannot be saved without God's grace and we cannot be saved without our faith.

Now that's not to say that salvation comes from us. Far from it. We can't do anything on our own. There is no way we can save ourselves. Only God can save us. He is "the author and perfecter of our faith" Hebrews 12:2. He is the One, through His Spirit, who convicts men and women of sin. He is the One, through His Spirit, who causes us to repent. He is the One, through His Spirit, who enables us to have faith in His Son. God does it all. "Salvation belongs to our God, who sits on the throne, and to the Lamb" Revelation 7:10. Which means Jesus, and only Jesus, can save you.

A Christian who was out witnessing was very clear on this point. When an unsaved man became deeply convicted about his sin and asked the Christian what he could do to be saved, the Christian said, "Sorry, you're too late." "Too late!" exclaimed the man. "What do you mean? You mean I'm too late to be saved?" "No," said the Christian. "You're not too late to be saved. You're just too late to do anything yourself. Christ has done it all for you."

Yes, Christ has done it all. There's nothing you or I can do to earn salvation. We are "chosen by grace. And if by grace, then it is no longer by works; if it were, grace would no longer be grace" Romans 11:5-6.

This is the essence of the gospel: "For it is by grace you have been saved, through faith - and this not from yourselves, it is the gift of God - not by works, so that no one can boast" Ephesians 2:8

SEIZE THE DAY

DEAD OR DYNAMIC

I t's evident from James 2:14-26 that there are two kinds of faith, dead faith and dynamic faith.

Dead faith is when "a man claims to have faith but has no deeds" James 2:14. It's intellectual faith that never results in action. It's head knowledge that knows nothing about shoe leather. It's the pew warmer personified. It's the person that's full of talk but without the walk.

In contrast, dynamic faith is living faith. This is faith that has power. It's faith based on God's Word (cf. James 1:18). This is faith with an object - it's faith in the Lord Jesus Christ. It's faith that involves the whole person - it involves the mind, the emotions, and the will. It's faith that results in changed lives. And it's not an isolated event - it's faith which results in continual acts of obedience in response to God's will. For dynamic faith obeys God and proves itself in daily life and good works.

So what kind of faith do you have? Is it dead or dynamic? In 2 Corinthians 13:5 it says, "Examine yourselves to see whether you are in the faith; test yourselves."

Consider the following:

■ People with dead faith acknowledge the reality of sin. People with dynamic faith are grieved over the cause and root of sin and do everything in their power to admit responsibility, repent, and be reconciled with God.

■ People with dead faith say, "I believe in God." People with dynamic faith say, "Search me, O God . . . and know my anxious thoughts. See if there is any offensive way in me, and lead me in the way everlasting" Psalm 139:23-24.

■ People with dead faith agree with the teachings of God's Word. People with dynamic faith walk "according to the law of the Lord . . . keep His statutes, and seek him with all their heart" Psalm 119:1-2.

■ People with dead faith speak about caring for others. People with dynamic faith "look after orphans and widows in their distress" James 1:27.

■ People with dead faith know that Christ is going to one day return. People with dynamic faith live in a constant state of readiness for His return and have nothing to be ashamed of.

■ People with dead faith agree it's important to tell others about salvation in the Lord Jesus Christ. People with dynamic faith take every opportunity to reach out and share the good news with their neighbours. They'll step out of their comfort zones, and if need be, are prepared to be humiliated for the cause of Christ.

■ People with dead faith see the importance of financially supporting God's church. People with dynamic faith give tithes, offerings and alms. They make it their priority to give the first fruits of their labours to the Lord's work.

■ People with dead faith think that missionaries should be sent to every tribe and tongue and nation. People with dynamic faith say, "Here am I Lord, send me."

■ People with dead faith believe in the golden rule, "Love your neighbour as yourself." People with dynamic faith give the hungry something to eat, the thirsty something to drink, invite a stranger in, clothe those needing clothes, look after the sick, and visit those in prison (cf. Matthew 25:35-40).

■ People with dead faith have no problem with people praying - just as long as no-one asks them to pray. People with dynamic faith intercede for others, plead with God for revival, and "pray in the Spirit on all occasions with all kinds of prayers and requests" Ephesians 6:18.

I could go on. There are countless ways to test yourself and see if you have a dead faith or a dynamic faith. But at the end of the day it's evident in a changed life marked by consistent good works. For "what good is it, my brothers, if a man claims to have faith but has no deeds?" James 2:14.

HAS YOUR LOVE WANED?

Has your love waned? Have you walked away from your original devotion, affection, attraction, interest, warm attachment, adoration or gratitude for Christ? Is the glitter and sparkle of your relationship with Jesus no longer there? Has Christ been pushed out of the way, relegated to second place? Are you simply going through the motions of a faith that's essentially a side show? If you have, if you've "forsaken your first love" (Revelation 2:4), then read on to discover why your initial joy and satisfaction in Jesus has ebbed into passive indifference. There are three possible reasons:

Firstly, love wanes through lack of *devotion*. When your affection and loyalty for Christ doesn't surpass everything else, your love for Him grows cold. To prevent this happening you must identify whatever's competing with your love for Christ. This isn't an easy task. Your devotion can be diverted by any number of things. For example: Believers can get caught up with dogma at the expense of devotion. They can allow a system of beliefs to take the place of the One in whom they believe. If it's more important for you to guard your doctrine than it is to love Christ then you've forsaken your first love. Having identified what's competing with your love for Christ, you must deal with the problem. Two things are necessary: 1. Make sure your tongue doesn't get in the way of your trust, that the things you say about people don't come into conflict with your faith. In 1 John 4:20 it says, "If anyone says, 'I love God,' yet hates his brother, he is a liar. For anyone who does not love his brother, whom he has seen, cannot love God, whom he has not seen." 2. Make sure your head doesn't get in the way of your heart, that a religion of the mind doesn't exclude a passionate relationship with Jesus. For you can have right doctrine but fail to be in right relationship with Christ and you can have right practice but fail to be in intimate communion with Christ. In 1 John 3:18-19 it says, "Dear children, let us not love with words or tongue but with actions and in truth. This then is how we know that we belong to the truth, and how we set our hearts at rest in his presence."

Secondly, love wanes through lack of *desire*. When we desire something, we crave it more than anything else, nothing else will satisfy. Ask yourself the following questions: What do I crave more; prosperity or Christ, power or Christ, pleasure or Christ, pasta and pudding or Christ, prominence or Christ? "For where your treasure is, there your heart will be also" Luke 12:34.

Thirdly, love wanes through lack of *denial*. In Ephesians 4:22-24 Paul says, "You were taught, with regard to your former way of life, to put off your old self, which is being corrupted by its deceitful desires, to be made new in the attitudes of your minds, and to put on the new self, created to be like God in true righteousness and holiness." When you become a believer, you can't continue to be attracted to the things of the world. A relationship with Jesus is an all or nothing relationship. Christ wants first place. He refuses to be second best. He's a jealous God (cf. Exodus 34:14; Deuteronomy 5:9; Joshua 24:19; Nahum 1:2). He essentially says, "Everything with the old life has to go. It's rotten through and through. Get rid of it!" As Jesus said, "If anyone would come after me, he must deny himself and take up his cross daily and follow me" Luke 9:23.

So love wanes through a lack of devotion, a lack of desire, or a lack of denial. Now for some action. If your love has waned it's time to do something about it. Seize the day. Repent of your sin and return to your first love. "Put off your old self, which is being corrupted by its deceitful desires" (Ephesians 4:22), and "love the Lord your God with all your heart and with all your soul and with all your mind" Matthew 22:37.

SLAVE OR FREE

"It is for freedom that Christ has set us free. Stand firm, then, and do not let yourselves be burdened again by a yoke of slavery" Galatians 5:1.

Our spiritual identity in Christ is to be free. Yet it would seem from our practice that many Christians are anything but free. They're slaves to old habits, slaves to tradition, slaves to relationships, or slaves to the law. Instead of "onward Christian soldiers," they're "backward Christian soldiers." All because they don't really know what it means to be free.

So what does it mean to be free?

In one sentence: Allow Christ to take you captive.

When I was younger, a sparrow flew into my bedroom. After circling the room it landed on the windowsill, looked around, then spread its wings and once again took flight. A very brief flight. It crashed against the window pane and fell to the floor.

It was obviously a tough little bird because it quickly recovered and tried again. Another brief flight, another crash to the floor. It was a little slower in recovering the second time but still determined, for there was another brief flight and another crash to the floor.

With mounting concern I tried to direct the sparrow toward the open window through which it had flown; but with no success. My efforts only made matters worse. Every time I came close the sparrow flew frantically away and would flap around before taking another kamikaze dive at the window pane.

It was losing feathers fast and I was worried about it breaking its neck. So instead of trying to shoo it toward the open window I tried to catch it. After it fell to the floor for the umpteenth time, I managed to snag it. Folding my fingers gently around its wings and body I checked it over then took it outside and let it go. As I watched it fly away, I marvelled at the contrast. In my room, and without my help, the sparrow was trapped, powerless and vulnerable. But once it was released, it was empowered and free.

There's a spiritual parallel. You will only be free when you allow Christ to take you captive. If you keep flapping around, keep on trying to do it in your own strength, you'll never be free, you'll stay trapped in the constraints of your own efforts. But if you let Him take you captive. If you let Him pick you up and gently carry you along, then, and only then, can He set you free.

"So if the Son sets you free, you will be free indeed" John 8:36.

PERSISTENCE

"Suppose one of you has a friend, and he goes to him at midnight and says, 'Friend, lend me three loaves of bread, because a friend of mine on a journey has come to me, and I have nothing to set before him.' Then the one inside answers, 'Don't bother me. The door is already locked, and my children are with me in bed. I can't get up and give you anything.' I tell you, though he will not get up and give him the bread because he is his friend, yet because of the man's persistence he will get up and give him as much as he needs." Luke 11:5-8

One of the great examples of persistence is Abraham Lincoln. The word "quit" didn't seem to be in his dictionary. Born into poverty, Lincoln faced defeat all his life. But he learnt to do what he could with what he had. He never gave up. He believed, "A duty to strive is the duty of all of us." Here's a sketch of his road to the White House:

1816 His family was forced out of their home and he had to work to support them.

1818 His mother died.

1831 Failed in business.

1832 Ran for State Legislature - lost.

1832 Lost his job. Wanted to go to law school but couldn't get in.

1833 Borrowed money from a friend to start a business and was bankrupt by the end of the year. Spent the next seventeen years paying back the debt.

1834 Ran for State Legislature again - won.

1835 Engaged to be married. Fiancee died and his heart was broken.

1836 Had a nervous breakdown and was bed-bound for six months.

1838 Sought to become speaker of the State Legislature - defeated.

1840 Sought to become elector - defeated.

1843 Ran for Congress - lost.

1846 Ran for Congress - won. Went to Washington and did a good job.

1848 Ran for re-election to Congress - lost.

1849 Sought the job of land officer in his home state - rejected.

1854 Ran for Senate of the United States - lost.

1856 Sought the vice-presidential nomination at his party's national convention - got less than 100 votes.

1858 Ran for Senate of the United States - lost again.

1860 Elected President of the United States.

So if you've had a disappointment recently, don't give up, press on, pick yourself up, dust yourself off - give it another go. Remember, a slip is not a fall.

In *The Parable of the Persistent Widow,* Christ says, "Will not God bring about justice for his chosen ones, who cry out to him day and night? Will he keep putting them off? I tell you, he will see that they get justice, and quickly" Luke 18:7-8.

A CLEAR CONSCIENCE

Many years ago there was an Oprah Winfrey show in which a couple were interviewed about being riddled with guilt because they were gift recyclers. They had recently been married and with no time to go to the shops to buy a present for their best friend's wedding they wrapped up one of two water pitchers they had received at their wedding, and gave this to their friends. A week later they were out shopping and were mortified to discover that the pitcher they had given their best friend only cost $20. For several years they were niggled by a guilty conscience and when they received the opportunity to appear on the Oprah Winfrey show they used the occasion to confess their guilt, publicly apologise to their friend, and give the couple another present. With, I might add, the till slip proving they had bought the present themselves!

Some people will go to any lengths for a clear conscience. Paralysed by guilt they'll pay anything or do anything to be set free. Down through the centuries people have done all manner of things in an effort to cleanse their conscience. Some have entered a monastery or nunnery. Others have starved themselves, mutilated themselves, or debased themselves in some way. Still others have thrown themselves into a regimen of good works. In extreme cases some have even taken their own lives.

But there's nothing that anyone can do to clear the conscience. Adopting a religion won't clear the conscience. Obeying the law won't heal a guilty conscience. And even making a sacrifice to God won't be good enough.

However, there is One who can give a person a clear conscience. The Lord Jesus Christ can take a person's guilt and remove it as far as the east is from the west (cf. Psalm 103:12). Hebrews 9:14 tells how the blood of Christ cleanses a person's conscience. Jesus has done what no man could ever do, nor will ever be able to do; He died for our sins and thereby cleansed once for all, everyone who places his or her trust in Him.

That's the good news for today. You can bring your guilty conscience to the foot of the cross, ask for forgiveness, and Christ will set you free. There's no need for you to continue being eaten up on the inside, having sleepless nights, or continue carrying accusations of past failures. If you're struggling with a guilty conscience, you can turn to Jesus. Do that now - take it to Jesus and leave it with Him. For when you do, when you "draw near to God with a sincere heart in full assurance of faith" (cf Hebrews 10:22), He will cleanse your heart from a guilty conscience.

THE POWER
OF PRAYER

At 1:00 a.m. on 7 November, 1986, Erin Joy Jarvis was born at Park Lane Clinic in Johannesburg, South Africa. It was a fast delivery. Erin was a mottled blue colour and immediately whisked away by the medical staff because she didn't "pink up."

Being first time parents, Alan and Elaine didn't know that something was wrong. No one had given them any information to the contrary. But when the 5:00 a.m. feed time came and the other mothers were given their babies and Elaine wasn't, they realised there was a problem. It was nerve-racking. By 8:30 a.m. they still hadn't seen Erin. Finally, the doctor arrived and told Alan and Elaine he didn't know if Erin would live through the day. She had a pulmonary stenosis ventricular septal defect. Which, as best as I could understand, meant she had a hole in her heart.

The extended family and close friends were quickly informed. The moment we heard we started praying. They were SOS prayers. Everything was dropped as we focussed on Erin's plight and pleaded with the Father to intervene and perform a miracle.

At 10:00 a.m., still in a critical condition, Erin was transferred by ambulance to the Morningside Clinic where emergency preparations were being made for an angioplasty. The prognosis was bleak. But God answered prayer. During the ride in the ambulance Erin "pinked up."

We learnt the rest of the story from the Christian nurse in attendance. Erin was examined on arrival and the doctor said, "I can't understand it. I've never seen anything like this before!" The nurse, recognising that God had answered prayer, said to the doctor, "It's a miracle!" The angioplasty was cancelled. Erin was still kept under observation in the neonatal unit and finally, five days after her birth, Elaine was able to hold her newborn for the first time. Two weeks later Erin was discharged.

God had intervened to spare Erin's life. But Erin wasn't home free. When she was four years old, she had to have the angioplasty. The prognosis at this point was that Erin would only live to be 25 years old. But, as we well know, God numbers our days. Since then Erin has continued to grow in strength and the doctors now say she'll live a normal and full life. It certainly seems that way. In 2001 Erin played in the ODCVI girls' rugby team and along with her teammates won the district trophy as the best junior high side for the season.

So don't despair in times of crisis. God knows your plight. Elaine knew that God was with her in her time of need. On the morning of Erin's birth Elaine's reading in the Daily Light was from James 1:2-4; "Consider it pure joy, my brothers, whenever you face trials of many kinds, because you know that the testing of your faith develops perseverance. Perseverance must finish its work so that you may be mature and complete, not lacking anything."

THE WILL OF GOD

*"To know the will of God is the greatest knowledge.
To do the will of God is the greatest experience."
Dr. George W. Truett*

In 1 Peter 4:2 believers are told that they mustn't live their earthly lives "for evil human desires, but rather for the will of God." In a world of self-gratification God expects His children to be counter-cultural. He calls on Christians to deny the pleasures of the flesh and to give themselves totally into His service. The will of God is that every believer would be a 24/7 believer, i.e. living for Him twenty-four hours a day and seven days a week. He wants commitment in the morning, at noon, and in the night. In all your ways you must acknowledge Him (cf. Proverbs 3:6).

Paul was a 24/7 believer. In 1 Corinthians 15:31 he said, "I die every day." Like Paul you need to "die every day." This isn't a physical death. You must die to the desires of your flesh. It's death to everything outside of the will of God. Like David you must say, "To do your will, O my God, (is my) desire" Psalm 40:8. Can you say that with David? As you search your heart do you want nothing less than to do God's will?

Here are seven things to help you do the will of God:

1. Recognise that "it is God's will that you should be holy" 1 Thessalonians 4:3.

2. Identify and emulate Jesus' example of commitment, i.e. to do the will of the Father (cf. John 6:38).

3. Pray and ask God to teach you to do His will (cf. Psalm 143:10; 1 Thessalonians 5:18).

4. "Put no confidence in the flesh" (Philippians 3:3), but die to your human desires every day.

5. Stand firm. "Stand firm in all the will of God, mature and fully assured" Colossians 4:12.

6. Be courageous. "Do not throw away your confidence; it will be richly rewarded. You need to persevere so that when you have done the will of God, you will receive what he has promised" Hebrews 10:35-36.

7. See everything in the context of eternity. "The world and its desires pass away, but the man who does the will of God lives forever" 1 John 2:17.

"I ordered the Lord:
'Get right with me,
My will be done,
And instantly!'

And I don't know why,
But prayers fell numb,
Till I learned to pray
In Jesus' way:
'Thy kingdom come,
Thy will be done.'"

Henry Hubert Hutto

MINIMIZE
YOUR FEARS

In John 6:16-20 we read: "In the evening his disciples went down to the sea, got in the boat, and headed back across the water to Capernaum. It had grown quite dark and Jesus had not yet returned. A huge wind blew up, churning the sea. They were maybe three or four miles out when they saw Jesus walking on the sea, quite near the boat. They were scared senseless, but he reassured them, 'It's me. It's all right. Don't be afraid.' So they took him on board. In no time they reached land - the exact spot they were headed to." The Message.

At the heart of this story is the instruction from Jesus, "It is I; don't be afraid" John 6:20. What a wonderful word of encouragement. If you're terrified about a situation you're involved in, Jesus says, "Don't be afraid." If fear has disabled you in some way, Jesus says, "Don't be afraid." If there's something that's happened in your past that's left you feeling nervous or anxious, Jesus says, "Don't be afraid." And if fear has caused you to live a protective, rather than a progressive life, Jesus says, "Don't be afraid."

Now if I was to say to you, "Don't be afraid," it wouldn't amount to much. Compared to Jesus there's next to nothing that I can do to minimize or alleviate your fears. But God isn't limited in any way. In 2 Thessalonians 3:16 we discover the "Lord of peace himself" gives us "peace at all times and in every way." The text doesn't say that God gives you peace sometimes. There isn't a limited quota on the amount of peace God hands out. If you ask for peace God will give you "peace at all times and in every way."

Praise the Lord! Through the provision of peace God enables you to minimize your fears. So "Don't be afraid." Be reassured. "He will not let your foot slip - he who watches over you will not slumber; indeed, he . . . will neither slumber nor sleep . . . The Lord will keep you from all harm - he will watch over your life; the Lord will watch over your coming and going both now and forevermore" Psalm 121:3-4, 7-8.

AWOL

"Let us not give up meeting together, as some are in the habit of doing, but let us encourage one another - and all the more as you see the Day approaching" Hebrews 10:25.

Have you ever felt like quitting church? I'm not talking about giving up on God - just quitting church. If you have, you've probably got some good reasons to leave. Maybe you don't get to sing the songs you like to sing. Maybe the programmes aren't up to snuff. Maybe the time of the Sunday morning service isn't suitable. Maybe the deacons or elders have never paid you a visit. Maybe someone's been disrespectful to you. Maybe you're uncomfortable with some of the new ways of doing things. Or maybe, when you come to think of it, the main reason is because you can't remember a single one of the pastor's sermons.

This final complaint was certainly one person's excuse for quitting church. An AWOL (absent without leave) churchgoer wrote a letter to the editor of a newspaper and complained that it made no sense to go to church every Sunday. "I've gone for thirty years now," he wrote, "and in that time I have heard something like three-thousand sermons. But for the life of me, I can't remember a single one of them. So, I think I'm wasting my time and the pastors are wasting theirs by giving sermons at all!" It was signed, Missing the Message.

This started a real controversy in the Letters to the Editor column, much to the delight of the editor. It went on for weeks until someone wrote this reply: "I've been married for thirty years now. In that time my wife has cooked some thirty-two thousand meals for me. But for the life of me, I cannot recall the entire menu for a single one of those meals. But I do know this: They all nourished me and gave me the strength I needed to do my work. If my wife had not given me those meals, I would be physically dead today. Likewise, if I had not gone to church for nourishment, I would be spiritually dead today!" It was signed, Receiving the Message. [Source: Anonymous].

What a clincher. There will never be a valid reason for you to stop attending church. So don't go AWOL. Don't "give up meeting together, as some are in the habit of doing" Hebrews 10:25.

WDJD

You've probably heard of WWJD (What Would Jesus Do?) but it may be more appropriate to ask, WDJD (What Does Jesus Do?):

Universally speaking: Jesus is the Creator of all things (cf. Colossians 1:16), the Sustainer of all things (cf. Hebrews 1:3), the Lord over all (cf. John 1:1ff), the Giver of life (cf. John 1:4), a sure Foundation (cf. Isaiah 28:16), the Builder of everything (cf. Hebrews 3:4), the Word of God (cf. Revelation 19:13), the Commander of the Lord's army (cf. Joshua 5:14), and the Head over every power and authority (cf. Colossians 2:10).

On the global level: Jesus is King over all the earth (cf. Zechariah 14:9), the Head of every man (cf. 1 Corinthians 11:3), the Light of the world (cf. John 8:12), a Ransom for many (cf. Mark 10:45), and the Saviour of the world (cf. 1 John 4:14).

Concerning the Christian community: Jesus is the Head of the church (cf. Colossians 1:18), a Refuge for His people (cf. Joel 3:16), a Stronghold for His people (cf. Joel 3:16), a Witness to the people (cf. Isaiah 55:4), and the Leader and Commander of the people (cf. Isaiah 55:4).

In relationship to God the Father: Jesus is the Servant of the Father (cf. Matthew 12:18), the One who turns aside God's wrath (cf. Romans 3:25), the Image of the invisible God (cf. Colossians 1:15), the Mediator between God and man (cf. 1 Timothy 2:5), the faithful and true Witness to the Father (cf. Revelation 3:14), the One who speaks to the Father in our defence (cf. 1 John 2:1), the Door to the Father (cf. John 10:9), and the Arbitrator between God and man (cf. Job 9:33).

On the personal level: Jesus is the once for all Sacrifice for sins (cf. Hebrews 7:27), the Author of our salvation (cf. Hebrews 2:10), the Shepherd and Overseer of your soul (cf. 1 Peter 2:25), the Bread of Life (cf. John 6:35), the One who intercedes for us (cf. Hebrews 7:25), the One who goes before us (cf. Hebrews 6:20), the Counsellor (cf. Isaiah 9:6), the Physician (cf. Luke 4:23), the life-giving Spirit (cf. 1 Corinthians 15:45), the Teacher (cf. John 3:2), a Refuge from the storm (cf. Isaiah 25:4), the Deliverer (cf. Romans 11:26), and the One who gives strength to the poor (cf. Isaiah 25:4), the needy (cf. Isaiah 25:4), and those in distress (cf. Isaiah 25:4).

So what does Jesus do? . . . EVERYTHING! More specifically, everything that's good and right and true.

Praise the Lord!

BEWARE OF HYPOTHERMIA!

Patrick Laundy was lost. He was on a school excursion in the Drakensberg mountains, had wandered away from his classmates, and couldn't find his way to the campsite. As dusk came and went he was stumbling around in sub-zero temperatures with clothing that was inadequate against the biting cold. But he tottered on, and as he did he realised that he didn't feel quite as cold as he had before. In fact he felt strangely euphoric and there was now a tingly warmth to his body.

Later, one of Patrick's friends opened the door of their mountain hut and discovered Patrick sitting outside and blathering away. He was quickly brought inside and it was obvious he was suffering from severe hypothermia. Fortunately for Patrick he attended a school which offered outdoor pursuits as part of the curriculum. The young men in the hut were trained for such an eventuality.

Without wasting time they stripped off his damp clothes, pushed him into a thermal sleeping bag and established a regimen of treatment. Throughout the rest of the night they took turns undressing, climbing in with Patrick, and holding him tightly in order to facilitate the transfer of their body heat. They also kept him awake and urged him to stay focussed and hang in.

The next day qualified medical assistance arrived and the doctor confirmed that their efforts had saved Patrick's life.

It was special. Because of the efforts of his fellow students, Patrick's desk in the Geography class was once again filled as I attempted to coach him through his final year of high school.

Not many of us are likely to get hypothermia. But it is possible for believers to wander away from intimacy with the Lord and succumb to a spiritual hypothermia. The symptoms of this spiritual hypothermia are described in the final book of the New Testament where it records how the ailing person has "deeds . . . that are neither cold nor hot (but) lukewarm" Revelation 3:15-16. Furthermore, the person has a distorted euphoria for she or he does "not realise that (she or he is) wretched, pitiful, poor, blind and naked" Revelation 3:17.

But the good news is that no one need suffer with spiritual hypothermia. If you need treatment, turn to the Word. "Be earnest and repent" Revelation 3:19. That's the cure. No more, no less. Spiritual hypothermia is overcome when a person repents.

TELL THEM
BEFORE IT'S TOO LATE

One day a teacher asked her students to write down the names of their fellow students with enough space between each name for the students to write down the positive things they appreciated about one another. It took the whole period for the assignment to be completed and when the bell rang for the next class each student handed in their papers.

Then, on separate sheets of paper, the teacher compiled a list of everything that was said about an individual. The following day the students were given their lists. Before long the entire class was smiling. "Really?" she heard whispered. "I never knew that I meant anything to anyone!" "Do they like me that much?" The exercise had accomplished its purpose. For the remainder of the year the class was happy and harmonious.

Several years later one of the students was killed in the Vietnam War. The teacher attended Mark's funeral. The church was packed with many of the young man's former classmates. At the reception that followed Mark's parents came over to speak to the teacher. "We want to show you something," said the father as he took a wallet out of his pocket. "They found this on Mark when he was killed. We thought you might recognize it." Two worn pieces of paper that had obviously been folded and refolded repeatedly, were removed from the wallet. The teacher knew immediately what they were. The papers were the ones on which she'd listed all the good things Mark's classmates had said about him. Mark's teary eyed mother said, "Thank you so much for what you did. As you can see, it was a treasured possession."

As if on cue Mark's classmates had gathered around the teacher and parents. Charlie smiled sheepishly and said, "I still have my list. It's in the top drawer of my desk." Chuck's wife said, "Chuck asked me to put his in our wedding album." "I have mine too," Marilyn said. "It's in my diary." Then Vickie, another classmate, reached into her purse and took out her worn and frazzled list to show it to the group. "I carry this with me all the time." That's when the teacher sat down and cried. She cried for Mark and for all his friends who would never see him again.

Life comes to an end for all of us. We don't know when it's our time to go. A few days before my father-in-law died, he phoned Elaine (my sister-in-law) transcontinentally to say, "I love you my girl." Dad knew the importance of telling his family that they were treasured. Make sure you do the same. Tell the people you love and care for that they are special and important. Maybe you could take the time to tell them now. Whatever you do, tell them before it's too late.

ANGELS

In 1978, my sister-in-law, Elaine Jarvis, was turning at an intersection when another motorist ran a red traffic light and plowed into her car. In the months that followed Elaine developed migraines, coupled with pain down her left shoulder and arm, due to whiplash. Ten years later she was still suffering from headaches and pain and sent to a neurosurgeon for tests. He discovered a pinched nerve and several herniated discs in her neck but wasn't prepared to operate.

In May 1995, while Elaine was out walking with a friend, she stumbled and fell. The fall was minor but Elaine was in such agony she thought she was dying. A torrid time ensued. Painkillers gave little to no relief. She lost all strength in her left hand and arm and her two middle fingers were permanently numb. By October, the pain was so bad she didn't want to eat.

To top it all Elaine had an allergic reaction to the iodine-based dye that was used in a mylogram procedure and was hospitalized for a week. Once stabilized the surgeons operated on her neck.

You can imagine Elaine's situation. Six months of continuous pain and then, in addition to that, the sickness due to the iodine allergy. Elaine was tired and depressed.

That's when God intervened. In Elaine's words, "In hospital, while I was very low and obviously in pain, I felt as if angels surrounded me. It was as if I was really being hugged. I could see them all around my bed. There was one particular angel who held me right in my bed. To this day I can feel their loving touch. It was not my nurses nor my fellow patients. I could see those heavenly people and I knew that I was being taken care of that day and every day. I felt strong and also felt hope that I would get better. I was made aware that the Lord knows our weaknesses and cares for us. Nothing is too simple or small for Him."

The visit from the angels was a turning point. Elaine's health quickly improved and she was soon discharged.

But the story doesn't end here.

The day after Elaine arrived home from the hospital the family had gathered to celebrate when we received a telephone call from England and heard that Dad had died of a heart attack. We were numbed. The Lord had taken him suddenly, and in the way he had always wanted to go - in the pulpit preaching the Word.

That same day, although trivial in comparison to Dad's death, Elaine's favourite dog also died.

As you can well imagine, we were overwhelmed by the magnitude of events. Everything happened in quick succession, one incident piling on top of another. Life can be like that, you have to take it as it comes.

However, in retrospect we can see how fully and adequately God looks after His own. He doesn't promise to keep us from pain but He does promise to be with us through pain. The angels who ministered to Elaine in the hospital were sent to encourage her recovery and also to provide her with the needed strength to get through the week ahead. True to His Word, God commanded His angels concerning Elaine to guard her in all her ways (cf. Psalm 91:11). Elaine is thankful for God's grace and mercy. She's also grateful for having discovered that God "does not crush the weak or quench the smallest hope" Matthew 12:20 (Living Bible).

DEVOTE YOURSELVES . . .

"Devote yourselves to prayer, being watchful and thankful" Colossians 4:2.

Heavenly Father . . .

Forgive me for the things I've said and thought and done that displeased You.

Please help me to seize this day with a great attitude and tons of gratitude. By your Spirit, give me ears to hear You, eyes to see as You see, and lips to speak what You would have me say. Guard my heart, renew my mind, give me a thankful spirit, please help me walk in Your way.

Lord, help me not to sweat the small stuff. Please help me to honour you in my work and witness. Help me decrease so that You might increase. Help me not to get puffed up with any success You may send my way. Help me stay within the limits You set for me, to be patient, to know Your peace and joy, to follow Your leading without knowing where, to expect a miracle without knowing how, to persevere through the things that test my faith, to trust You more. Help me live by the Spirit and put the sinful nature to death. Help me to say, "Yes Lord," to whatever You ask of me. May Your passion be my passion, Your purpose my purpose, Your plans my plans. Help me surrender to Your grace, Your love, Your wisdom.

I can't do it without you Lord. Please enable me to be like-minded with Christ, having the same love, being one in spirit and purpose, looking not only to my own interests but also to the interests of others. For You know I don't want to do anything out of selfish ambition or vain conceit - You know I want to live for You and You alone.

And Lord, please help those who don't know the Way. Extend grace and mercy. You've said that You don't want "anyone to perish, but everyone to come to repentance" 2 Peter 3:9. So please save the lost, forgive their sin, revive the church, heal our land.

Thank you Lord.

In Jesus' name.

Amen.

TOTALLY JESUS

Christians must be all and only about Jesus. He must be first. He must be our focus. He must be the centre of everything. For the moment our view of Jesus is obstructed our faith is reduced to something less than what it's meant to be.

Satan is well aware of this. He does everything in his power to get our eyes off Jesus. One of the ways he does this is to get us sweating the small stuff, to get us focussed on less important issues, on the details, and on things God's Word calls "disputable matters" Romans 14:1.

There are countless subtle ways in which Satan crowds Jesus out of the picture. When people start complaining about the style of worship, the pastor's sermon, or the Sunday School programme, then Satan has managed to dupe them into doing his work for him. For the moment we get steamed up about people bringing a cup of coffee into the service, or the way people dress, or whether the sanctuary was too hot or too cold, or any other petty matter, then church quickly becomes all about "me" instead of all about Jesus.

So be on your guard. Get a grip. Train yourself to keep your eyes on Jesus. Refuse to be self-absorbed. Rise above the tyranny of the lesser. Repent of any lesser things that you've allowed to become preeminent. Choose to have attitudes that reflect His attitudes, to care about the things He cares about, and to love as He loves. For if you don't, if Jesus isn't your be all and end all, you'll quickly become divided and discouraged.

Reinforcing the point: Whatever was to your profit you must now consider a loss for the sake of Christ (cf. Philippians 3:7). He must be more important than your denomination, your theological persuasion, your Bible College education, your philosophical inclination, your political persuasion, your social interaction, or your family connection. This will only be possible if you come to the end of yourself. You must stop looking in and start looking up. His personality must become your personality, you must obey His Word even if it doesn't make any sense, and you must want His will and not your own.

That's a big step. It's easier to talk about making Christ your focus than putting it into practice. But don't let that stop you. Seize the day. Acknowledge the emptiness of your vanity. Appeal for forgiveness, especially for any selfishness and pride in your life. And ask the Holy Spirit to give you the inclination and strength to be totally centred on Christ, to seek His face always.

PRAY FOR YOUR CHURCH

In order for the work of the local church to advance, believers must pray regularly and specifically. Here are some suggestions to help guide you as you intercede.

For the worship time, pray:

■ For the power and presence of the Holy Spirit to be manifested and to fill the place of worship.

■ For God's anointing to be on the musicians, singers, sound engineers, and worship leaders.

■ For spiritual discernment to flow with the leading of the Holy Spirit.

■ For angels to come as ministering spirits "to serve those who will inherit salvation" Hebrews 1:14.

■ For a sacrificial and joyous spirit when the tithes and offerings are collected for the Lord's work.

■ For people to humble themselves before Almighty God, to worship in spirit and in truth, to seek His face, to be healed of their infirmities, to be strengthened in their faith, set free from demonic spirits, filled with the Holy Spirit, and revived again so that they might rejoice in Him.

For the teaching/preaching time, pray:

■ For the anointing of the Holy Spirit on the speaker.

■ For compassion, conviction and clarity in the preaching of God's Word.

■ For boldness to preach and teach the truth in love.

■ For the Holy Spirit to use the preaching of the Word to convict people of sin, to draw people to Christ, to minister salvation to non-Christians, to rebuke and correct those who have gone astray, to encourage the downhearted, to strengthen the weak, to heal the sick, to set the captives free, to train in righteousness, and to equip believers for every good work.

For the ministry time, pray:

■ For the Holy Spirit to powerfully refresh, renew, and revive believers.

■ For the gifts of the Holy Spirit to be manifested in a way that brings honour and glory to the Lord Jesus Christ.

■ For life changing transformations to take place that will be evidenced by increased holiness, reverence and devotion to God.

■ For a conviction of sin, righteousness and judgement to come so that the lost will be saved and the saved will not be lost.

"Ask and it will be given to you; seek and you will find; knock and the door will be opened to you. For everyone who asks receives; he who seeks finds; and to him who knocks, the door will be opened" Matthew 7:7-8.

WITH FREEDOM
AND CONFIDENCE

"In him and through faith in him we may approach God with freedom and confidence" Ephesians 3:12. What a wonderful inheritance. Even though we deserve the wrath of God due to our sin we have the liberty to enjoy a relationship with Him. Now I don't know about you but knowing that I can "approach God with freedom and confidence" is a reality that short circuits my little brain! It's incredible! Sinners can "approach the throne of grace with confidence" (Hebrews 4:16) because "the result of one act of righteousness was justification that brings life for all men" Romans 5:18.

The abolishment of slavery in Jamaica on August 1, 1838 is a fitting illustration. On July 31 a large number of slaves gathered on a beach to celebrate the eve of their emancipation. It was a solemn, yet joyous occasion and they had constructed a large mahogany coffin which they had placed on the sand next to a large hole that had been dug earlier that day. Through the evening they placed, with some ceremony, the symbols of their slavery into the coffin. There were chains, leg irons, shackles, whips, padlocks, and other items involved in their enslavement. Just before midnight the lid of the coffin was closed and the coffin was lowered into the hole. Sand was thrown over the coffin and then they joined together to sing, "Praise God from whom all blessings flow, praise Him all creatures here below, praise Him above ye heavenly host. Praise Father, Son, and Holy Ghost." They were finally and irrevocably free from slavery.

How much they were like Christians, who, through Christ's death are free from their slavery to sin. And how like them are Christians, who in heaven will be free from the very reminder and presence of sin. Yes, because of all that Christ accomplished on the cross of Calvary we are no longer slaves to sin and "in him and through faith in him we may approach God with freedom and confidence" Ephesians 3:12. Praise the Lord!

CODFISH AND CATFISH

It's reported that codfish are a big commercial enterprise in the Northeastern United States. However, the industry battled to transport the fish to the markets. When they froze the cod, they discovered the freezing took away much of the flavour. When they shipped the fish alive in great tanks of seawater they found the cod still lost their flavour, and, in addition, became soft and mushy. The problem was finally solved when some innovative person placed the codfish into the tank of seawater along with their natural enemy - the catfish. From the time the codfish left the East Coast until it arrived at its westernmost destination the catfish chased the codfish all around the tank. And, you guessed it, when the cod arrived at the market, they were as fresh as when they were first caught. There was no loss of flavour and no loss of texture, if anything they were better than before.

In a similar sense, each one of us is in a "tank" of particular and inescapable circumstances. It's painful staying in the tank. We don't like the fact that God has allowed certain "catfish" into the tank because they bring tension into our lives. But let's remember, the catfish are there to keep us alive, alert, and growing. The catfish of adversity are shaping our character, causing us to "swim" closer to Jesus. Then, as this happens we gain a greater flavour and a superior texture, becoming better than we were before, so that when the marketplace of the world encounters us they taste and see that the Lord is good.

So don't ask God to remove the catfish in your life. Keep "swimming" for Him. For "after you have suffered a little while . . . the God of all grace, who called you to his eternal glory in Christ . . . will himself restore you and make you strong, firm and steadfast. To him be the power for ever and ever. Amen" 1 Peter 5:10-11.

HOLINESS

"But just as he who called you is holy, so be holy in all you do; for it is written: 'Be holy, because I am holy.'"1 Peter 1:15-16.

Mary Bosanquet was a lady who dared to be different. Born in Essex County, England, in 1739, she grew up with a deep desire to be like Christ. Holy in all she did. Mary's desire to be holy wasn't something trivial. Her biographer reported that she was obsessed with being holy and was even prepared to die in the pursuit.

An extract from Anna McPherson's *She Walked in White* provides an insight into Mary's life: "'If I but think on the word holiness,' Mary told her father at one time, 'or of the adorable name of Jesus, my heart seems to take fire in an instant, and my desires are more intently fixed on God than ever before. As I cannot go with you to places of amusement anymore, so neither can I wear the expensive clothes you buy for me . . . I must be God's and His alone.' 'So - you - you - don't appreciate what I provide . . .' her father turned from her with wounded pride and walked away. But Mary followed desperately. 'Oh yes I do,' she protested. 'I do. But God forbids women professing godliness to let their adorning be in apparel. He says their ornaments should be those of a meek and quiet spirit. Besides, I must take the money I would spend on costly garments and help clothe the poor. I must take the time I would spend on adorning my person and use it for the advancement of God's kingdom.'"

That's exactly what Mary did. She spent her life in the advancement of God's kingdom. Even though her father threw her out of his home because of clashes over her desire to be holy she persevered with her single-minded pursuit. Despite severe setbacks in her life she led many folk to faith in the Lord Jesus Christ and ministered to the destitute orphans in Essex County. Out of her meagre resources she supported more than twenty orphans for twenty plus years. She never spent more than $25 a year on clothing for herself but spent more than $900 a year on clothing for the poor. She's reported to have said, "For what do I want with the rags of earth when His righteousness wearing and cleansed by His blood, bold shall I appear in the presence of God."

There's not too many Mary Bosanquet's to be found in today's church. Holiness isn't the "in thing" in Christian circles. As J. C. Ryle says in his book, Holiness; "I have had a deep conviction for many years that practical holiness and entire self consecration to God are not sufficiently attended by modern Christians . . . Politics, or controversy, or party spirit, or worldliness, have eaten out the heart of lively piety in too many of us. The subject of personal holiness has fallen sadly into the background . . ."

Ryle is right. Holiness, in large part, has been overlooked in Evangelical doctrine. A thorough revival of practical holiness is needed. If the church is going to make an impact for Jesus Christ then believers have to recover a true sense of biblical holiness. This will only happen when we choose to prepare our minds for action, reject self-indulgence, and live lives of self-discipline and self-control. "We must learn to look upon religion, upon a life like Christ's, having the very same mind that was in Him as the supreme object of daily life. It is only when a prayer such as that of M'Cheyne becomes ours, 'Lord, make me as holy as a pardoned sinner can be,' and begins to be offered by an increasing number of believers, that the promise of the New Covenant will become a matter of experience" Andrew Murray.

"So be holy in all you do" 1 Peter 1:15. Remember that holiness is the habit of being of one mind with Christ; hate what He hates, love what He loves, and gauge everything you say and do by the standard of His Word.

> More holiness give us,
> More sobriety within;
> More purpose in action,
> More sense of our sin;
> More strenuous minds,
> More hope in Christ's grace;
> More faith in our service,
> More love in this place.

STEPS TO INTIMACY WITH CHRIST

Roy L. Smith said, "No man is ever more than four steps from God: conviction, repentance, consecration and faith." Smith is spot on. Without these four steps there can be no intimacy with Christ. All four steps are necessary. If you take only two steps, you won't have a spiritual breakthrough. Even if you take steps one, two, and four; or steps one, two, and three; if you don't take all four steps you won't succeed.

Lets consider each step.

Step one. Conviction is the persuasion that you'd be doing the right thing if you pursued an intimate relationship with Christ. It's when you ask yourself, "Do I really want Christ to be my best friend?" Ask that question now. Say to yourself, "What do I really want? Is it self-sufficiency, or is it Christ?" Don't rush with the answer. Think it through, examine your heart. For it's only when you're fully convicted that you want an intimate relationship with Christ that you're ready to move onto the next step.

Step two. Acting on your conviction, you must repent. Repentance is turning around and facing God. It's saying, "Lord I'm sorry for having been self-sufficient," or, "Lord I'm sorry for having kept you at arm's length," or "Lord I'm sorry for my sin," or "Lord I'm sorry for all of the above." That's repentance. It's refusing to have any more to do with whatever's been an obstacle between you and God. It's saying, "I'm done with that! I'm sorry for what I've done. I'm not going to continue doing it any more."

Conviction and repentance. Only two steps remain.

Step three. The third step to intimacy with Christ is consecration. Consecration is when you declare your devotion to Christ. It's saying, "Lord, from here on out there's only one way, and that's going to be your way. I love you Lord. Nothing else matters. With your strength I'm going to live for you, and for you alone. Help me to imitate you. Help me to be holy."

Conviction, repentance, consecration. One step to go.

Step four. Faith. "Now faith is being sure of what we hope for and certain of what we do not see" Hebrews 11:1. It's complete trust and confidence in Christ. It's saying, "When it comes to Christ I'm dead to doubts, dumb to discouragements and blind to impossibilities" Anonymous.

That's all there is to it. If you honestly and earnestly take these four steps then the intimacy you want with Christ will be yours. Now you must continue to abide in that intimacy. And how do you do that? It takes four steps - conviction, repentance, consecration, and faith.

HYPOCRISY

According to the Collins Dictionary, hypocrisy is the practice of professing standards contrary to one's actual behaviour. Thus hypocrisy is more than lying with the lips, it's lying with one's life.

The church is full of hypocrites. By that I mean there are people who call themselves Christian but don't live a Christian life. If you profess Christ on Sunday but your actions through the week are inconsistent with your profession of faith, you're a hypocrite. If you put on a front with other Christians, hiding behind a mask of religiosity, you're a hypocrite. If you're saved, but you're a lover of yourself rather than a lover of God, you're a hypocrite (cf. 2 Timothy 3:2,4). If you have a form of godliness but deny its power, you're a hypocrite, you're lying to God (cf. 2 Timothy 3:5). If you promised to live for Jesus and be faithful to His church, but haven't done so, you're a hypocrite. If you promised Christ your life and have given Him nothing more than scraps, you're a hypocrite. If you're always learning but never able to acknowledge the truth, you're a hypocrite (cf. 2 Timothy 3:7). And if you promised to support the Great Commission but don't share your faith with others, you're a hypocrite.

Sometime ago I preached on remembering the Sabbath Day and keeping it holy. After the service a man came to me and said, "That was a great service pastor. From now on you'll see me in church every Sunday." I saw him only once after that. He lied to me and lied to God. Hypocrisy is like that, it's a double lie. It's a lie with horizontal and vertical dimensions.

Hypocrites won't get away with their lies. "You may be sure that your sin will find you out" Numbers 32:23. According to a story from Japan there was a man in the Imperial Orchestra who couldn't play a note. Because he was a man of considerable influence and wealth he managed to secure a place in the orchestra and fulfil his desire to "perform" before the emperor. The conductor agreed to let him sit in the second row with a flute. When the concert began the man raised the instrument to his lips and moved his fingers with the appropriate motions. But he never made a sound. After two years of this hypocrisy a new conductor arrived and insisted on auditioning each musician personally. The fake flautist was frantic with worry and pretended to be sick. But he couldn't avoid the inevitable. The conductor kept insisting that the man demonstrate his skill. Finally the man shamefacedly confessed he was a fake. It's from this incident that the expression, "face the music," is said to have originated. Yes, all hypocrites will one day have to "face the music."

So if you're a hypocrite, don't wait until it's too late. Rid yourself of deceit and hypocrisy of every kind (cf. 1 Peter 2:1). God's Word warns that there's a place assigned for hypocrites "where there will be weeping and gnashing of teeth" Matthew 24:51.

CLEANSED BY THE BLOOD

The cleansing power of blood is spoken of throughout the Bible. In Leviticus 14, for example, a priest sprinkled cleansing blood on a person with an infectious skin disease and on the mildewed walls of a house. In Revelation 7:14 we read that those who came out of the great tribulation "washed their robes and made them white in the blood of the Lamb."

The trouble is, when we read verses like these, we struggle to make sense of them. For nothing in our modern culture corresponds to blood as a cleansing agent. After all, we use soap, detergent, or stain removers if we want to get something clean. Not blood. Blood is something we try to scrub off, not scrub with! There's no advertising jingle saying, "Buy Rub a Dub-Dub and get cleansed by the blood." Obviously that's not the type of cleansing being referred to in the Bible.

Although the biblical writers didn't know the physiology behind the metaphor, modern science reveals how the theological symbol fits perfectly with the medical understanding of blood as a cleansing agent. For the blood in our bodies performs the most amazing of janitorial duties. Dr. Paul Brand says, "No cell lies more than a hair's breadth from a blood capillary, lest poisonous by-products pile up and cause ill effects. Through a basic chemical process of gas diffusion and transfer, individual red blood cells drifting along inside narrow capillaries simultaneously release their cargoes of fresh oxygen and absorb waste products (carbon dioxide, urea, and uric acid etc.) from these cells. The red cells then deliver the hazardous waste chemicals to organs that can dump them outside the body." In other words, on a physiological level, blood sustains life by carrying away harmful metabolites in our bodies.

It's the same on the spiritual level. Blood is needed to cleanse away the poison of sin. For sin is a paralysing toxin that destroys our health, clogs our spiritual arteries, and interferes with our relationship with God and other people. That's why, in the Old Testament, God established a covenant in which unblemished goats and bulls were ceremonially slaughtered and their blood shed for the forgiveness of sin. "For the life of a creature is in the blood, and I have given it to you to make atonement for yourselves on the altar; it is the blood that makes atonement for one's life" Leviticus 17:11.

But this covenant was only temporary - a foreshadowing of what was yet to come. A new covenant was instituted when God sent Jesus Christ as the perfect, once for all, sacrifice for sin. He died and shed His blood as a ransom to set us "free from the sins committed under the first covenant" Hebrews 9:15. And, as a result of this ultimate blood sacrifice we can have forgiveness of sin and "our consciences cleansed from acts that lead to death" Hebrews 9:14.

Thus, we no longer have to approach God through the blood sacrifice of animals. The blood of Jesus Christ has made us clean. As it says in 1 John 1:7, "The blood of Jesus Christ His Son cleanses us from all sin" NKJV.

FRIENDSHIP

A friend says nice things behind your back.

A friend doesn't walk ahead of you or behind you, he walks next to you.

A friend will double your joy and halve your grief.

A friend can be counted on to count on you.

A friend is like a shock absorber - he helps you over the bumps of life.

A friend knows you but still likes you anyway.

A friend understands your silence.

A friend helps you up (cf. Ecclesiastes 4:10).

A friend is someone who comes in when everyone else has gone out.

A friend is a very rare jewel.

A friend leaves footprints on your heart.

A friend sticks by you when you make a mistake.

A friend intercedes for you (cf. Job 16:20).

A friend in times of poverty is better than a friend in times of plenty.

A friend laughs with you, not at you.

A friend sticks closer than a brother.

A friend is one with whom you can be at peace.

A friend knows if it is well with your soul.

A friend will look you right in the eye.

A friend likes himself best when he's with you.

"A friend loves at all times" Proverbs 17:17.

A friend is more interested in you than he is in himself.

A friend is like old shoes - easily worn.

A friend bears your infirmities.

A friend helps you do what you can when you say that you can't.

"Greater love has no one than this, that one lay down his life for his friends" John 15:13.

DEMOLISHING WALLS

In 1945, after the Second World War, Germany was divided by the victors into two countries. East Germany was controlled by the communist regime of the Soviet Union and West Germany was a democracy supported by several Western nations. The former capital city of Berlin, although entirely within the borders of East Germany, was also partitioned into two segments. In 1961 the East Germans erected a one-hundred and sixty-six kilometre barrier to separate East from West Berlin. The Berlin Wall was a concrete and iron curtain that blocked free access in both directions for 28 years. At least 100 people were killed trying to cross the Berlin Wall.

In 1989, the Wall was opened. East and West German citizens could once again travel without restriction. Families were reunited after years of enforced separation. Official destruction of the Wall began on June 13, 1990. By November 30, 1991, the Wall, with the exception of six commemorative segments, was completely razed. This paved the way for the reunification of Germany.

Reflecting on the destruction of the Wall, German writer, Peter Schneider said, "Demolishing the Wall in the head will take longer than it will take for a demolition firm to do the same job." Schneider makes a good point. Most of us struggle in our heads to demolish the walls that divide us. But it's time to demolish the walls. The fences that keep us apart need to be torn down. Our walls of arrogance and ignorance must be destroyed. We must give up on the things that separate us. We must choose to live at peace with one another. Common ground must be found and misunderstandings dealt with and put away. This needs to happen individually, with families, with the community, and with the Church.

Concerning the Church: It's time for the "cold war" of denominationalism to come to an end. Religious pride must crumble with compassion for a world going to a lost eternity. We cannot allow ourselves to continue to be divided on nonessentials. There's strength in unity. We were never meant to be ostriches with our heads buried in the sands of separation due to matters of conscience or personal preference (cf. 1 Corinthians 1:10). Instead of breaking communion with one another it's time to make communion with each other. It's time for barriers to be immersed and cleansed in the blood of Christ. If the kingdom of God is going to advance then believers need to demolish the walls between them. We cannot allow the past to impede the future. Unity must be our heart cry, the cry of each Bible believing Spirit filled church, the cry for our cities, the cry for our nations.

Now that's not to say that churches should join together in an ecumenical brotherhood. Far from it. Unity is never achieved at the expense of sound doctrine. There can be no unity apart from the Fatherhood of God. The Bible is clear, God is Creator of all but only the Father of those who are born again, born from above, born of the Spirit. Thus the unity that is needed is for born again believers to serve each other in love. For by this all men will know that we are His disciples (cf. John 13:34-35; Colossians 2:2).

So as for me, by the grace of God, I volunteer to be a servant to any and all in order to reach a wide range of people: the religious and not yet believers, legalists, immoralists, the poor, the rich - whoever. I don't intend to take on their way of life. I'll always strive, in the power of the Spirit, to keep my bearings in Christ - but I'll endeavour to enter their world and try to experience things from their point of view. With God's help I'll become just about any sort of servant there is in attempts to lead those I meet into a vital relationship with Christ. I do all this for the Gospel of Jesus Christ. I don't just want to talk about it; I want to humbly and actively live it for His honour and glory (cf. 1 Corinthians 9:19-23).

Will you join me?

THE MYSTERY
OF CHRISTMAS

Christmas is once again around the corner. For many of us the coming and going of Christmas has become all too familiar. We've become used to the marketing hype of the retailers. We take the shopping frenzy for granted. We're au-fait with the jingles and carols. And we expect to enjoy family time and festive fare. But we should remind ourselves that even though we've visited the Christmas season many times before we can never exhaust the telling of the Christmas story. For the celebration of Christmas should always be one which demands our attention, draws us to the Saviour, and deepens our worship.

Why?

Because even though Christmas is a glorious reality there's an element of mystery in the Christmas story. There's something remarkable in the fact that God planned the incarnation of Christ before the foundations of the earth were laid (cf. John 1:1-18; Colossians 1:15-17). And there's a sense in which we will never fully comprehend why God chose to "walk down the stairs of heaven with a Baby in His arms" Paul Scherer.

Yes, the story of Christ's birth is certainly unusual. It was marked by prophecy, a unique conception, angelic announcements, adoring shepherds, an indifferent populace, persistent Magi, a supernatural star, and an odd birthplace. As if that wasn't enough, the story is especially exceptional because it's about God humbling Himself, "being made in human likeness. And being found in appearance as a man" Philippians 2:7-8.

SLOW
DOWN . . .

The story is told of a young man who joined a monastic order in a remote part of the country. Central to the ordered lifestyle of this group of monks was the discipline of silence. The brothers were only allowed to speak once a year, and then only two words.

After the first year the young man had a chance to address his superior. "Bed hard!" he said, and returned to his quarters and routines for another year. At the end of his second year, he once again took advantage of his privilege of addressing the superior.

"Tasteless food!" he announced with an appropriate facial gesture. At the end of the third year he approached his superior and his two allotted words were, "I quit!" "Well, I'm not surprised," the elder monk replied. "You've done nothing but complain ever since you arrived!"

I relate to the young man. There have been times in my life when I've felt like quitting. Those times are usually around Christmas. For I hate the commercialism, dislike shopping, and generally feel hassled and hurried at this time of the year. But I've learnt that when I feel like quitting on the Christmas season it's usually an indication that I need to slow down, take time to be quiet, and listen to the Lord. I suspect many of us need to learn this lesson and if you're one of those people let me suggest three ways in which you can slow down:

Firstly, *take time out*. Make a conscious decision that Christmas doesn't come and go without you experiencing the real meaning of the season - the birth of Jesus Christ. To make this possible you may want to read the Christmas narrative in one of the synoptic gospels, attend a Christmas carol service, or spend time in prayer and thanksgiving.

Secondly, *tarry with relatives*. Prior to Jesus' birth his mother, Mary, spent time with her relatives. So visit the extended family. One of the greatest gifts we can give others is to make room for them in our busy schedules. The Czechs do this. Their custom at Christmas is to visit their family, friends and foes, and forgive any misunderstandings that may have arisen during the year. Why not do the same?

Thirdly, *talk about Jesus*. In Luke 1:39-45 it's obvious that Mary, like any other mother, took a great deal of delight in talking about the child in her womb. In like manner, as we look forward to the celebration of Christ's birth, we should become more and more talkative about Him. We should tell others about the baby who came into this world with the mission of reconciling sinful humanity with a holy God. And we should tell others about the love of the Father who "gave his one and only Son, that whoever believes in him shall not perish but have eternal life" John 3:16.

So

take time

to slow down.

Stop spending your

days in hectic ways. Stop

hassling and striving and rushing

around. For Christmas time is here again.

And something's lost that should be found. So

won't you pause in simple faith. And stop and see what

God has done. He sent to earth Immanuel. Christ our Saviour,

His only Son.

REACH OUT

It's Christmas, and we want to reach our family members and friends who are not yet believers. But how do we go about that? How do we make the transition from gifts to glory? How do we effectively communicate the real reason for the season? Here are a few practical suggestions:

Begin with prayer. Every outreach should begin with up-reach. Pray specifically, by name, for those whom God has burdened on your heart. Ask Him to reveal Himself to them. Call on the Holy Spirit to make them receptive to His message. And when you pray, be prepared to be used by God - He may choose to send you.

Connect on a nonthreatening level. One way to communicate the essence of Christmas is to send E-cards or snail mail cards that focus on Jesus without being churchy. When you send cards add a personal note that let the recipients know that you care for them. You may also want to add a little something extra. Here's something we photocopied and sent as an enclosure in our cards a few years ago.

Christmas card list.
I have a list of folks I know, all written in a book,
And every year when Christmas comes, I go and take a look,
And that is when I realize that these names are just a part,
Not of the book they're written in, but of folk close to my heart,
For each one stands for someone who's crossed my path sometime,
And in that meeting they've become much more than just a name,
For while you may not be aware of any special "link,"
Just meeting you has changed my life a lot more than you think.
For once I've met somebody, the years cannot erase,
The memory of a pleasant word, or of a friendly face.
So never think my Christmas cards are just a mere routine,
Of names that are in a Christmas list, forgotten in between,
For when I send a Christmas card that is addressed to you,
It's because you're on the list of folks I'm indebted to,
And whether I have known you for many years or few,
In some way you have had a part, in shaping things I do,
So every year when Christmas comes, I realize anew,
The best gifts life can offer is meeting folk like you.

Give gifts that count. Solely giving a Christian book or CD to a not yet believer isn't always the best way to communicate the love of Christ. The gifts we give to others should be related to their interests. That's not to say that you shouldn't give gifts that proclaim the good news. It's simply suggesting that the best way to express your love may be to give a "regular" gift coupled with a "Christian" type gift.

Invite friends and family to church. After all, Christmas is a wonderful opportunity to do things together with others and most churches have a number of exciting events that you can confidently invite folk to. One way of making the occasion especially memorable is to combine it with a meal.

Whatever you do, remember that Christmas is an opportunity to make a difference for Jesus. If you are willing, God can uniquely use you to help someone meet Jesus this season. So be open to the prompting of the Holy Spirit. For Christmas is about following His lead, pursuing His agenda, and making it all count for eternity.

TWO BABES IN A MANGER

In 1994, two Americans answered an invitation from the Russian Department of Education to teach morals and ethics (based on biblical principles) in the public schools. They were invited to teach at prisons, businesses, the fire and police departments, and a large orphanage. About one hundred boys and girls who had been abandoned, abused, and left in the care of a government-run programme were in the orphanage. The Americans relate the following story in their own words:

It was nearing the holiday season, 1994, time for our orphans to hear, for the first time, the traditional story of Christmas. We told them about Mary and Joseph arriving in Bethlehem. Finding no room in the inn, the couple went to a stable, where the baby Jesus was born and placed in a manger.

Throughout the story, the children and orphanage staff sat in amazement as they listened. Some sat on the edges of their stools, trying to grasp every word. Completing the story, we gave the children three small pieces of cardboard to make a crude manger. Each child was given a small paper square, cut from yellow napkins I had brought with me. No coloured paper was available in the city.

Following instructions, the children tore the paper and carefully laid strips in the manger for straw. Small squares of flannel, cut from a worn-out nightgown an American lady was throwing away as she left Russia, were used for the baby's blanket. A doll-like baby was cut from tan felt we had brought from the United States. The orphans were busy assembling their manger as I walked among them to see if they needed any help.

All went well until I got to one table where little Misha sat. He looked to be about six years old and had finished his project. As I looked at the little boy's manger, I was startled to see not one, but two babies in the manger. Quickly, I called for the translator to ask the lad why there were two babies in the manger.

Crossing his arms in front of him and looking at this completed manger scene, the child began to repeat the story very seriously. For such a young boy, who had only heard the Christmas story once, he related the happenings accurately until he came to the part where Mary put the baby Jesus in the manger.

Then Misha started to ad-lib. He made up his own ending to the story as he said, "And when Maria laid the baby in the manger, Jesus looked at me and asked me if I had a place to stay. I told him I have no mamma and I have no papa, so I don't have any place to stay. Then Jesus told me I could stay with him. But I told him I couldn't, because I didn't have a gift to give him like everybody else did. But I wanted to stay with Jesus so much, so I thought about what I had that maybe I could use for a gift. I thought maybe if I kept him warm that would be a good gift. So I asked Jesus, 'If I keep you warm, will that be a good enough gift?' And Jesus told me, 'If you keep me warm, that will be the best gift anybody ever gave me.' So I got into the manger, and then Jesus looked at me and he told me I could stay with him - for always."

As little Misha finished his story, his eyes brimmed full of tears that splashed down his cheeks. Putting his hand over his face his head dropped to the table and his shoulders shook as he sobbed and sobbed. The little orphan had found someone who would never abandon nor abuse him, someone who would stay with him for always.

Which goes to show, it's not what you have in your life, but Whom you have in your life that counts.

IS THERE ROOM?

The story is told of a Sunday School Christmas production in which the children were encouraged to play their parts to the full. Finally the big day arrived. The church was packed to capacity with friends and relatives who had come to watch the children act out the story of the first Christmas. Everything was going along swimmingly until Joseph arrived at the innkeeper's door and asked for a room. "Sorry, I've got no room," said the innkeeper. "But I've got to have a room. My wife's pregnant," pleaded Joseph. "Well it's not my fault your wife is pregnant," said the innkeeper. To which Joseph replied, "And if you'd read your Bible you'd know it wasn't my fault either!"

On another occasion, with a different church and Sunday School Christmas production, Joseph was pleading with the innkeeper for a room and the boy playing the innkeeper, being a soft-hearted youngster, cracked under the pressure and said, "If it's that desperate you'd better come in and use my room!"

You can imagine the response. People were crying with laughter. It took several minutes before order was restored. In the second production the young innkeeper was so affronted by the response of the congregation he stomped off in a huff.

Maybe the boy was justified. After all, the original innkeeper didn't have to say no if his own room was available. However, he did, and in so doing missed out on one of the greatest moments in human history - the birth of God's Son, the Lord Jesus Christ.

Now the innkeeper may have been the first to say he had no room (cf. Luke 2:7) but he certainly wasn't the last. Since the first Christmas countless people have missed the reality of Christ's birth because they too have no room for Jesus. Not physical room. I'm talking about the room that needs to be made in hearts and lives. People can be so busy with parties, gift giving, decorating, visiting relatives, shopping sprees, and a dozen other things, they simply have no room left for Jesus. In reality their lives are like a hotel with the "No Vacancy" sign hung outside.

But it needn't be, and shouldn't be, that way. If your life is full of other priorities, you can choose to re-prioritize. You can make room for Jesus this Christmas. Let's not forget, you're the keeper of your inn. You have the final say. The right of admission is up to you. So if there's been no room in the past, why not make this the year you take down the "No Vacancy" sign and invite Him in. As the youngster in the play teaches us; it's never too late to say, "You can have my room."

IS THERE ROOM?

Arriving in Bethlehem one night, Joseph was dusty, tired, and worn;
Mary, his wife, was weary too, it was time for the child to be born.
At the door to the inn, Joseph said, "Is there room? We need some place to stay."
But the innkeeper shrugged, saying, "I've got no room. Try coming another day."
"Oh please," said Mary, "My time has come. Please don't turn us away."
"Well it isn't much," the innkeeper mumbled. "You can use the barn and the hay."

It was better than nothing and with nowhere to go, they settled down to wait.
While the stars did shine with brilliant hue, the darkness to penetrate.
Then a cry was heard and a son was born. A moment like never before.
In a manger laid, to take-away sin, the Saviour evermore.
And the shepherds nearby, by an angel sent, worshipped as they came.
Later some Magi, following His star, searching to do the same.

But what of the innkeeper with no room that night? And I wonder, how about you?
When Jesus asks you to let Him in, what will you decide to do?
Will you welcome Him in? Will you open your heart?
Will you say, "I want you to stay."
Or will you turn your back? Maybe look away? Then tell Him to go on His way?
Whatever you do, know the day will soon come, when you'll stand at heaven's door.
And you'll only get in, with a room in the inn, if Jesus as Lord you adore.

THREE TREES

"He grew up before him like a tender shoot, and like a root out of dry ground" Isaiah 53:2.

When I read this verse the words "grew," "shoot," "root," and "ground" captured my imagination and suggested a suitable starting point for a Christmas meditation. For in these words I conjured up a picture of a tree. More specifically - three trees. What we'll call the Genesis Tree, the Gospel Tree, and the German Tree. Two of the trees are described in the Word and the third points to the One who is the Word.

The Genesis Tree is mentioned in the second chapter of Genesis. Its full name is "the tree of the knowledge of good and evil" Genesis 2:9,17. It has a prominent part in the Christmas story. For, in one sense, the Christmas story begins with "a garden in the east, in Eden," where "the Lord God made all kinds of trees grow out of the ground - trees that were pleasing to the eye and good for food. In the middle of the garden were the tree of life and the tree of the knowledge of good and evil" and "the Lord God took the man" he had formed "and put him in the Garden of Eden to work it and take care of it. And the Lord commanded the man, 'You are free to eat from any tree in the garden; but you must not eat from the tree of the knowledge of good and evil, for when you eat of it you will surely die.'" Genesis 2:8,9,15-17. But the man disobeyed God. He sinned. He ate from the tree of the knowledge of good and evil. And because he ate from the tree "the Lord God banished him from the Garden of Eden . . . he drove the man out" Genesis 3:23-24.

Thus the Genesis Tree is the initial reason for Christmas. For if Satan had not used the tree to seduce man and thrust him into sin, there would be no need for the incarnation. No need for God to leave heaven. No need for the Son of Man to become the Son of God. No need to forgive our sin. No need for God to raise "up a horn of salvation for us" Luke 1:69. No need for God to prepare, in the sight of all the people, "a light for revelation to the Gentiles" and the Israelites (cf. Luke 2:30-32). And no need for the virgin to be with child, give birth to a son, and call Him Immanuel (cf. Matthew 1:23).

The Gospel Tree is mentioned in several places. It's the tree on which Christ was crucified (cf. Acts 5:30; 10:39; 13:29). The cross of Calvary. The means whereby "Christ redeemed us from the curse of the law by becoming a curse for us" Galatians 3:13.

But what has this tree got to do with Christmas? Everything. For the Gospel Tree is the culmination of the incarnation. It's the raison d'etre for Christ's birth, the justification for His coming, God's defining moment in salvation history.

Christ's birth and death go together. The advent reminds us that Jesus was born to reconcile man to God, born to break the enslaving chains of sin, born to bring peace to the human heart, strength to the weak, and give life to the spiritually dead. In essence, He was born to be the "all time one sacrifice for sins" Hebrews 10:12.

The Gospel Tree therefore does what no other tree can do. It points us to the One who offers forgiveness and hope. It symbolizes the removal of enmity between man and God. It illustrates how sin was rendered powerless (cf. Romans 6:6). And it draws us to the Saviour who was born to die for our sin. As C. S. Lewis said, "The Son of God became the Son of Man so that sons of men may become sons of God."

The German Tree is what we commonly refer to as the Christmas Tree. I've called it the German Tree because the earliest record of an evergreen tree being used and decorated for Christmas is 1521 in the German region of Alsace. However, the origins of this tree probably go back to the eleventh century and the religious plays called "mystery plays" which became quite popular in Europe. These plays were performed outdoors and in churches. The most popular was the "Paradise Play." This play opened with a portrayal of the creation of Adam and Eve, their sin, and their banishment from Eden, and ended with the promise of the coming Saviour and His incarnation (cf. Genesis 3:1-24). The Paradise Play was simple by today's standards. The only prop on stage was the "Paradise Tree," a fir tree adorned with apples. From this tree, at the appropriate time in the play, Eve would take the fruit, bite into it, and give it to Adam.

By the fifteenth century people had become so accustomed to the Paradise Play, they began decorating their homes with the Paradise Tree. The tree was put up on December 24 to commemorate the feast day of Adam and Eve in accordance with the custom of the Eastern Church. Because the tree symbolised both a tree of sin and a tree of life people decorated it with apples, to represent the fruit of sin, and with homemade wafers (like communion wafers), to represent the fruit of life. In the late Middle Ages candy and sweets were added and a large candle called the "Christmas light," symbolizing Christ who is the light of the world, was lit on Christmas Eve along with many smaller candles which were displayed on a wooden pyramid. In addition to the candles, other objects such as tinsel, glass balls, and the "star of Bethlehem" were placed on the tree. By the nineteenth century the Christmas tree had grown into the general custom it is today.

The German Tree therefore combines the message of the Genesis tree and the Gospel Tree. It's symbolic of the tree in Eden by which Adam and Eve were enticed into sin and it portrays the tree by which our sin was overcome, namely the tree called the cross of Calvary.

So when you look at a Christmas tree look beyond the ornaments. Don't rush past the tree and fail to recognise the One whom it announces. For in the branches of the tree is the symbol of a baby - the gift of life for sinners like you and me.

INVITE HIM TO STAY

On a wintry night,
A couple in distress.
No room in the Inn,
Only one place to rest.

In a barn with some hay,
Tired, weary and worn.
A mother with child,
About to be born.

The stars shining bright,
With shepherds nearby.
When all of a sudden,
An angel on high.

"Do not be afraid,
I bring you good news.
A Saviour in swaddling clothes,
The King of the Jews."

Then three wise men led,
The Christ child to seek.
In Bethlehem in Judea,
They found One so meek.

And His reason for coming?
To lead us to God.
Through death on a cross,
Spilt blood on earth's sod.

So turn to Him now,
No longer delay.
Make room in your heart,
Invite Him to stay.

THE SKEPTIC
WHO BELIEVED

Joseph was the skeptic who came to believe . . .

In reading Matthew 1:18-25, it's obvious that Joseph faced a variety of problems with Mary's unusual conception. Put yourself in his sandals and you'd probably be sceptical too. After all, if you were engaged to be married and your fiancee told you she was pregnant, and you knew you had nothing to do with it, there would only be one logical conclusion - she'd been unfaithful.

That's what Joseph must have thought. To make matters worse, in Joseph's day betrothal was unlike a modern day engagement; it was considered marriage. It lasted for one year and was already a binding contract terminable only by death or divorce. Betrothal became marriage when the husband took his wife home after a public ceremony. At this stage of the relationship, and only at this point, was sexual intercourse proper.

One of the purposes of betrothal, therefore, was to test the purity of the bride. So when Joseph discovered Mary's pregnancy and he hadn't yet taken her home to be his wife you can imagine his doubt. As C. S. Lewis says, "He knew enough biology for that!"

Not only did Joseph have the problem of Mary's pregnancy to fuel his scepticism, he also had his own righteousness. As a righteous man he didn't want to marry a seemingly impure and unfaithful woman. Within his moral framework it would have been impossible for him to join himself with someone who didn't share his standards. This was further complicated by the obvious desire, on Joseph's behalf, to avoid disgracing Mary publicly. For according to the Mishnah, an adulteress was to be taken to the Eastern Gate of Jerusalem where a priest would tear her garments, remove all her jewellery, and clothe her in black or ugly garments tied by a rope. The purpose of this ritual was "to disgrace her" so "that all women may be taught not to do after your lewdness" (Sotah 1:6).

So in order to avoid the Beth Din (rabbinical court), Joseph decided to seek a private divorce that would involve the notification of Mary's father and another two witnesses. In this way he could keep his conscience clear and his compassion intact.

Then God intervened.

Before Joseph could organise the divorce God sent an angel in a dream. The timing of this message was perfect and it dealt directly with Joseph's doubts. This is what the angel said, "Do not be afraid to take Mary home as your wife" Matthew 1:20. This was as good as saying, "Don't let your scepticism stand in the way of your marriage to Mary." Then an additional comment, "What is conceived in her is from the Holy Spirit" Matthew 1:20. Which was basically communicating to Joseph, "Mary has not committed adultery. I the Lord am responsible for the pregnancy." Furthermore, "She will give birth to a son, and you are to give him the name Jesus" Matthew 1:21. This final announcement may well have been the clincher in turning Joseph from scepticism to belief. For only five Old Testament people and one New Testament person, John the Baptist, had been given names directly from God. Now Joseph hears that Mary's baby should be called "Joshua" ("Yesua" - Yahweh saves. Yahweh is salvation. "Jesus" is the Greek form of "Joshua."). Thus at the very least Joseph would have understood that this was no ordinary child. He may even have recognised that Mary was carrying the promised Messiah.

Once convinced that Mary's son was due to a virgin conception from the Holy Spirit Joseph acts in accordance with what we'd expect of someone who'd totally accepted the explanation he'd been given. He "took Mary home as his wife" and respectfully "had no union with her until she gave birth to a son" Matthew 1:24-25. These subsequent acts demonstrate how Joseph sincerely believed in Mary's purity and the supernatural nature of her pregnancy. By his actions it's obvious that the skeptic had become a believer.

If Joseph then, the man with his honour and integrity, in fact his righteousness, at stake, could be convinced, then shouldn't we be too? For Joseph was no naive fool. He was never duped, and he certainly understood the ramifications of his actions. Yes, Joseph gives us one of the first testimonies that Jesus was and is the Messiah. By his response he leaps out of history and stands as a witness against all those who would reject the virgin birth. It should therefore come as no surprise that Joseph got the inestimable privilege of announcing to the world the name that is above all other names - Jesus (cf. Matthew 1:25).

HE BECAME FLESH

A man noticed a flock of hungry sparrows feasting on a sheaf of grain. Taking a step towards them, he noticed how they became uneasy. Taking another step towards them caused the birds' nervousness to increase and they flew away leaving their banquet unfinished. Reflecting on the event, the man realised that the sparrows had scattered because he was too big. How could he walk among the birds without frightening them by his size? His answer was plain to see: In order not to frighten the sparrows he would have to become like them and fly down among them.

The analogy is obvious. God was big and scary. Fearful of Him, people tried to stay out of reach, even running away. There was only one way for God to draw near. He would have to come down and be one of us. So "the Word became flesh and lived for a while among us" John 1:14.

Now don't rush on from this verse. Think about what you've just read. "The Word became flesh." That's profound. Let's not forget that the Word is the One through whom "all things were made" John 1:3. He was the preexistent One, i.e. He "was" John 1:1. And then He "became" John 1:14. He "became flesh." He stepped down from heaven to earth, from glory to humiliation, and from the worship of angels to the mocking of men.

Although there's no parallel or earthly illustration that could possibly capture the enormity of the Word becoming flesh the following story helps provide some insights.

At one time a wise and beloved Shah ruled Persia. One day he disguised himself as a poor man and went to visit the public baths. The water was heated by a furnace in the cellar, and the Shah made his way to that dark place to sit with the man who tended the fire. The Shah befriended him in his loneliness. Day after day the ruler went to visit the man and the worker became attached to this stranger because he "came where he was" Luke 10:33. By and by the fire tender learnt of the identity of the Shah, and when he did he looked with wonder into his leader's face and said, "You left your palace and your glory to sit with me in this dark place, to eat my coarse food and to breathe my filthy air. On others you may bestow rich gifts, but to me you have given yourself."

Similarly, Christ left His heavenly palace and His glory to sit with us in this dark place, to eat our food and to breathe our air. In so doing He gave us the greatest of all gifts, the gift of Himself - the gift of companionship. For when the Word became flesh loneliness was forever taken out of religion. As one little girl concluded, "Some people couldn't hear God's inside whisper so He sent Jesus to tell them out loud."

IN THE FULNESS
OF TIME

In the play Wingless Victory, by Maxwell Anderson, a young sea captain sails away from Salem, Massachusetts, in the year 1800. Seven years later he returned with a ship laden with riches from the Far East. He also returned with a beautiful young wife, a princess from Malay. Instead of the heart-warming reception he expected, the attitude of his friends and relatives was forbidding and cold. They raised a wall of racial prejudice, religious intolerance, and social cruelty because they believed the captain had affronted the traditional and exclusive environment of New England society. Although his wife had abandoned her former superstitions and tribal customs and embraced her husband's religion, the townsfolk refused to make her one of their own. Finally, breaking under the strain, she decided to end her life. As the bitter tragedy closes, she cries, "God of the children, God of the lesser children of the earth, the black, the unclean, the vengeful, you are mine now as when I was a child. 'He came too soon, this Christ of peace; men are not yet ready!'"

As we pause on the threshold of Christmas and think back to the story of Christ's birth, what should we think of this poor woman's remark? Was humanity ready and waiting for the coming of Christ? Did Christ come too soon? And is it true that men were not ready and may not be ready yet?

The answer is in the Word of God. Galatians 4:4 says "when the time had fully come, God sent his Son." The verdict of Scripture is that Christ came at exactly the right time. He came in "the fulness" of time, as the K.J.V says. He came at an hour when His coming couldn't have been more timely, opportune and useful. A study of history supports this verdict. When Jesus was born, it was at a time when people were heavily taxed and under the threat of world domination by a cruel, ungodly, power intoxicated band of men. Moral deterioration had corrupted the basic populace. Peace propaganda was heard everywhere in the midst of preparations for war. Intense nationalistic feeling was clashing openly with new and sinister forms of imperialism. Conformity was the spirit of the age. Interest rates were spiralling upward in the midst of an inflated economy. External religious observance was considered a political asset. Racial tension was at breaking point. And an abnormal emphasis was placed on sports, athletic contests, and banquets. (Extracts from Sherwood E. Wirt, Decision Magazine).

Yes, Jesus was born at just the right time. To say He came too soon or too late is nonsense. For He came "when the fulness of the time was come" Galatians 4:4 (K.J.V.). As James S. Stewart says, "There is a tide in the affairs of God; and it is when the tide reaches the flood, when all the preparatory work is done and world conditions are clamouring for it and human souls are open, it is then, at the flood-tide hour of history, that God launches His new adventure."

"GOOD NEWS OF GREAT JOY"

Imagine how exciting it would be to hear that you didn't have to pay tax for the next year. Picture your ebullition if you heard that you had inherited a million-dollar bequest from a distant relative! Envision the promotion you've always longed for actually becoming a reality! Or visualise the bank manager phoning you up and informing you that an anonymous person had paid off your mortgage!

If any of these scenarios became a reality, it would be good news.

Like most people, I like to celebrate good news with others. If something good has happened to me then I want to tell my friends and family all the details and let them share in my joy. When it's someone else's good news then I'm your man for a party!

That's why I enjoy Christmas so much. It's the celebration of the greatest news the world has ever heard - God is with us! "The Word became flesh and lived for a while among us" John 1:14. Without a doubt this is "good news of great joy" Luke 2:10.

Yes, Christians the world over are once again rejoicing because of the birth of the Messiah. They're giving thanks to God for His indescribable gift (cf. 2 Corinthians 9:15) and remembering how the angel of the Lord announced "good news of great joy that will be for all the people." Did you notice that? The "good news of great joy" is for "all the people." It's not just for Christians. Even though the Christians are busy celebrating the birth of Jesus, their celebration isn't exclusive. Everyone's welcome to share in the "good news of great joy." Every man, woman and child is invited to hear that "a Saviour has been born to you; he is Christ the Lord" Luke 2:11.

That's the kind of good news I like to hear. Good news for everyone. Good news for people of every tribe and tongue and nation. The trouble is, we're so conditioned to receiving bad news that we often miss the good news. Some folk miss the fact that the reason for the season is that "God so loved the world that he gave his one and only Son, that whoever believes in him shall not perish but have eternal life" John 3:16. "God did not send his Son into the world to condemn the world, but to save the world through him" John 3:17.

Isn't that awesome? I don't know why it hasn't been recorded in the Guinness Book of Records as the most newsworthy item of all time! After all, it's the only birth that's been ushered in with a great choir of angels praising God and saying, "Glory to God in the highest" Luke 2:14. And it's the only birthday that's been celebrated continuously for more than two thousand years!

THE CHRISTMAS NAIL

Years ago, in a Colorado town, snow began to fall on a young couple contemplating the approaching Christmas season. As their thoughts meandered from the stable manger to the shopping mall, they knew that their meagre wages would prevent them from purchasing costly Christmas gifts. Therefore, they set out to make their own that year.

A while later the young man was in a local hardware store when he spotted a very large nail. It was nearly ten inches long and very heavy. Seeing such a nail, his thoughts were drawn to the crucifixion of Christ. How large those nails must have been and how wicked their purpose. As he wondered around the store, he could not keep the sobering thoughts of that nail from his mind. He decided to buy one of the nails and show it to his wife. When she saw it, her response was exactly the same. Together they wondered if perhaps, this massive nail would cause other people to remember Christ's death at the time of His birth. "Wasn't He born to die?" they asked each other. What better time than at His birth, to recall His reason for coming and the gift He would give.

Those thoughts stayed with them for the rest of the evening. Without Christ's death and resurrection, there would be no celebration of Christmas as we know it today. No one would recall the intricate details accompanying the birth of just one more good person. No starry night in Bethlehem would mean anything today if it were not for the end of the story. And so, without plan or preparation, the young couple sat in their tiny attic apartment and began to scribble out a poem that would communicate the truth of Christmas. They considered the Christmas tree to be one of the most central symbols of the season and wondered whether their nail might become part of the time-honoured tradition of decorating one's Christmas tree. Then it struck them - without question or hesitation, this nail would be an ornament hung on the tree itself. It was weighty and would pull down any normal branch, therefore it had to be hung deep inside the tree near the trunk. They worried that such placement would not allow it to be seen as all ornaments are intended. Slowly, a powerful realization washed over both of them. This ornament, like the Saviour Himself, would not be like any other. It would be obscured just as Jesus has been obscured among the trappings of the stable and its animals. This ornament would become a private devotion for those who hung it. It would serve as a silent reminder each time they looked at their tree that it was a tree upon which Christ redeemed the world.

And so, with their poetry typed on an index card and fishing line attached to the nail, they wrapped their new gift in folds of white paper to present to their family. It was ungainly and ugly for an ornament but its message was simple and moving.

That Christmas Eve, as their family sat around the warm glow of the Christmas tree lights, the couple extended their odd ornament as an early gift to the family members gathered. The response was visibly moving. Then, reaching deep within the branches of their Christmas tree, they hung the very first Christmas Nail.

"This is the Christmas Nail,
It is to be hung on a sturdy branch,
a branch near
the trunk,
a branch that
will hold
such a spike
without
being noticed
by well-wishers
dropping by to
admire one's
tinselled tree.
The nail is
known only
to the home
that hangs it.
Understood
only by the
heart that
knows its
significance.
It is hung
with the
thought that
the Christmas
tree but
foreshadows
the Christ-tree,
which only
He could
decorate for us,
ornamented with
nails as this."
Source
unknown.

SON SHINE SKETCHES OF A LITTLE TOWN

As a recent immigrant from Africa I was somewhat surprised when I first drove into Orillia. In fact I wasn't just surprised, I was flabbergasted. Picture my dilemma. I had only been in Canada for a month and had never visited Orillia. In the midst of a winter snow storm I arrived to preach on Christmas Sunday as the guest speaker at Hillside Bible Chapel. As I turned off the highway, I saw an icy sign welcoming me to the sunshine city!

It was a paradox. And it had caught my attention. So, determined to unravel the enigma. I returned to Toronto and asked one or two guarded questions about the people up north. It wasn't long before someone told me I would only understand if I read Stephen Leacock's, *Sunshine Sketches of a Little Town.* The first sentence in the book had me hooked. "I don't know whether you know Mariposa . . ." As I read on it began to make sense. For Leacock is a master story teller with rare insights into what makes a little town warm and special.

Later that year I moved to Orillia and began collecting my own sketches of the town. They were somewhat different to Leacock's anecdotes for they were the perspectives of a pastor whose focus was no longer on the 'sunshine' but on the Son shine. Allow me to elaborate:

My first Son shine sketch of Orillia came while walking downtown along the board-walk in Couchiching Park. Pausing for a moment I gazed back over the city and was delighted to observe several church spires dominating the skyline. This gave me a measure of hope as well as a sense of gratitude that, at least in a physical sense, Christianity was at the heart of the town.

My second Son shine sketch was one of perception. As I met Christians from different denominations, I was encouraged to discover how we shared a deep-seated desire to see Christ as the raison d'etre of the town. We wanted Christ to be at the centre. We wanted Son shine love to reach into every nook and cranny of Orillian society.

But more importantly, it's not just the hope and prayer of Orillian Christians to see Son shine love reaching the people of their city, it's the essence of God's will for every hamlet, village, town, and city around the world. His Word declares "He is patient with (us), not wanting anyone to perish, but everyone to come to repentance" 2 Peter 3:9. For God wants each and every person to know that "while we were still sinners, Christ died for us" Romans 5:8.

So see your neighbourhood as a place for the Son to shine. Pray for the love of Christ to infiltrate every office and home. And work through the Christmas season to share the Son shine with everyone you meet.

THANK GOD
FOR HIS PRICELESS GIFT

Christmas is all about the Gift. A priceless Gift. An indescribable Gift. The greatest Gift of all.

Some two millennia ago the Father, out of His inestimable love for the world, sent His priceless Gift packaged in flesh and delivered in humble circumstances.

It was the right time. Roman roads had been built which would carry the news through the civilized world. The Greek language was universal in readiness for the proclamation of the event. In the heart of some people there was an expectancy that the Gift was on the way.

On top of this, the Father had arranged for a reception. A legion of angels heralded the occasion announcing, "Glory to God in the highest, and on earth peace to men on whom his favour rests" Luke 2:14. This was followed by wise men travelling from the east to come and welcome the Gift with presents of gold, frankincense and myrrh.

Apart from that the Gift was barely noticed. Work continued as usual. There was no tremendous upheaval in day-to-day activities. And the Advent wasn't spread throughout the world.

However, one ruler later heard about it and, feeling threatened, tried to eliminate the Gift by sending his soldiers on a murderous rampage through the vicinity in which it had arrived.

But the Father was prepared. He wasn't going to sit back and see the Gift destroyed. One of the angels was dispatched to deliver a message warning of the impending danger and the Gift was whisked off to safety during the course of the night.

Of course there's much more to the story. Suffice to say we continue to remember the Advent of the Gift by giving each other presents. For, after all, Christmas is the day of the Gift, the day we remember the greatest of gifts, the day we celebrate the birthday of the Gift, the day we rejoice because the Father sent His Son, Jesus Christ. The day we say, "Thanks be to God for his indescribable gift!" 2 Corinthians 9:15.

REFLECTING . . .

Reflecting on Christmas, it seems to me that a number of "insignificant" details are sometimes overlooked. Now that's not to say that the birth of Christ is insignificant in any way. Far from it. The incarnation is an essential and vital component in salvation history. When I say "insignificant" I'm referring to how the mundane elements in the Christmas narrative have so much to teach us about God. Consider the following:

At the time of Jesus' birth the happening place in the world was Rome. It was what London is to Europe or what New York is to North America. Rome was the hub. Politically, socially and economically Rome was all that mattered. No one cared much about Palestine. Even Nathanael asked, "Nazareth! Can anything good come from there?" John 1:46. But the size and importance of a place are of no account to God. He chose Bethlehem, a little town in an obscure region, to be the birthplace of the Saviour. God's like that, He choses insignificant places for significant events.

In Luke 2:1-2 some important people are mentioned. Caesar Augustus and Quirinius were the movers and shakers of their time. Like the President of the United States, Caesar was the most powerful man on the earth. When Caesar spoke people listened. But political clout is of little account with God. When God comes near it's the little person that matters. God uses the seemingly insignificant people as key players. He chose a poor young couple to be the parents of the Son of God. He sent shepherds to welcome the Saviour. And He used a very old woman to give thanks to God and tell others about the child who would be the redemption of Jerusalem (cf. Luke 2:36-38).

The big news of the time was the census. Everyone had to go to his own town to register (cf. Luke 2:3). This single event would have been the talk in every bazaar. I can imagine how, if newspapers had existed, the headlines of the Jerusalem Chronicle would have said something like, "Quirinius Counts." But in the Heavenly Times Quirinius wouldn't have counted at all. He wouldn't even have been mentioned. In the Heavenly Times the headline would have been, "It's a boy!" For the events that matter to God are sometimes as "insignificant" as the birth of a baby boy.

Yes, Christmas reminds us that what's significant with man may well be insignificant with God. He takes the seemingly mundane things of life and invests them with power for His honour and glory. But then we shouldn't be surprised. For as the Lord declares, "My thoughts are not your thoughts, neither are your ways my ways . . . As the heavens are higher than the earth, so are my ways higher than your ways and my thoughts than your thoughts" Isaiah 55:8-9.

JUST THE BEGINNING

The celebrations may be over but Christmas isn't. In Luke 2:20 it says, "The shepherds returned, glorifying and praising God for all the things they had heard and seen, which were just as they had been told." Christmas was just the beginning. Having seen Jesus the shepherds "let loose" as it says in The Message. There was no holding back. They returned to their jobs and their responsibilities with a radically different attitude. They may have gone back to being shepherds but they weren't the same men. The joy of the first Christmas had changed them.

It should be no different for us. Christmas is just the beginning. It should start in December and then continue through the whole year. When we return to work after the holidays, we should be unlike the people we were before December 25th. There should be no holding back. No matter what your vocation, go back to your job with a radically different attitude. You can't be the same man or woman you were before. If you've seen Jesus then you should return glorifying and praising God for all the things you've seen and heard.

Of course it's possible that you didn't see Jesus this Christmas. Don't despair. It's never too late for an encounter with the Saviour. You can visit with Him at any time. It was "after Jesus was born in Bethlehem in Judea" (Matthew 2:1) that Magi from the east came searching for the One who had been born king of the Jews. When they found Him "they bowed down and worshiped him" Matthew 2:11. You can do the same. It's never too late to complete the journey. So make a careful search. Continue the pursuit. Don't stop looking until you find Him. And when you come to Him be sure to bow down and worship Him

THE TEST

A first year university student made every effort to prepare for his ornithology exam. He studied his text books, reviewed the field trip notes, and evaluated previous test papers. He felt ready until he walked into the lecture room to discover the test consisted of thirty pictures on the wall. Pictures of birds' feet. Nothing else. There were no test booklets, no multiple choice questions and no photos of the birds - just their feet, and the expectation that the students would identify the birds. He was flabbergasted. Approaching the professor, the student complained. "This is ridiculous! You can't expect me to do this!" "But you have to," said the professor. "This is the final and it must be done." "Well I won't do it," replied the frustrated student. "I'm leaving!" "If you do, you'll fail the exam." "In that case, fail me," said the student as he headed for the door. "Okay, that's your choice. You've failed. What's your name?" demanded the professor. The student bent down, took off his shoes, removed his socks, and rolled up his pants to reveal his feet. Then, glaring at the professor he said, "You tell me!"

We laugh. But the truth of the matter is, life can sometimes be like that. We try to be prepared, plan for contingencies, do the things that prudent people do, and still end up striking out. Unfair? Maybe. Tough? Definitely. A reality? Certainly.

So is it possible to prepare for the test when life has a habit of throwing a curve ball? I believe it is. You need to do three things: First, realise you can never cope on your own. You need the Teacher. Second, have faith in the Teacher. "Trust in the Lord with all your heart" Proverbs 3:5. Third, listen to the Teacher. Do what God tells you to do. Persevere. Be obedient. Don't lean "on your own understanding" Proverbs 3:5. Then the Teacher will be with you through times of testing and you'll "receive the crown of life that God has promised to those who love him" James 1:12.

IN THE
YEAR AHEAD

Be like Enoch - Walk with God (cf. Genesis 5:22-24).

Be like Abraham - Trust implicitly in the Lord (cf. Genesis 15:6; Hebrews 11:8-12).

Be like Moses - Faithfully serve in God's house (cf. Hebrews 3:5).

Be like Aaron and Hur - Support and pray for the leaders (cf. Exodus 17:12).

Be like Caleb - Have a different spirit and follow the Lord wholeheartedly. Refuse to be discouraged by superior odds (cf. Numbers 14:9,24).

Be like Joshua - Don't let the Word of God "depart from your mouth; meditate on it day and night, so that you may be careful to do everything written in it" Joshua 1:8.

Be like Gideon - Do what the Lord tells you to do and advance even when you're outnumbered (cf. Judges 6:27; 7:1ff).

Be like Jehoshaphat - Pray and praise the Lord despite the circumstances
(cf. 2 Chronicles 20:3,22,27-28).

Be like Job - Be blameless and upright. Fear God and shun evil (cf. Job 1:8).

Be like David - Look up and recognise that your "help comes from the Lord, the Maker of heaven and earth" Psalm 121:2.

Be like Daniel - Continue with God through thick and thin (cf. Daniel 6:1ff).

Be like Andrew - Make it your priority to lead your family to Christ (cf. John 1:41).

Be like Stephen - Express a forgiving spirit toward those who hurt you (cf. Acts 7:60).

Be like Paul - Forget what is behind and strain toward what is ahead. Press on toward the goal to win the prize for which God has called you heavenward in Christ Jesus (cf. Philippians 3:13-14).

Then, above all, be like Jesus - Humble yourself, be like-minded, have the same love, do nothing out of selfish ambition, consider others better than yourself, and take the very nature of a servant (cf. John 13:1-17; Philippians 2:1-8).

Realizing you cannot hope to achieve any of these objectives in your own strength, be sure to rely on the power of God for you can only "do everything through him who gives (you) strength" Philippians 4:13.

POSTLUDE

"Lay any burden upon me, only sustain me;
Send me anywhere, only go with me;
Sever any tie but that which binds me to
Your service and to Your heart."

Anonymous.